D1171885

AMERICA'S
FORGOTTEN WARS

AMERICA'S
FORGOTTEN WARS

From Lord Dunmore to the Philippines

Ian Hernon

AMBERLEY

For Reuben, Freya and Theo

First published 2020

Amberley Publishing
The Hill, Stroud
Gloucestershire, GL5 4EP

www.amberley-books.com

British Library Cataloguing in Publication Data.
A catalogue record for this book is available from the British Library.

ISBN 978 1 4456 9530 3 (hardback)
ISBN 978 1 4456 9531 0 (ebook)

1 2 3 4 5 6 7 8 9 10

Typeset in 10.5pt on 12.5pt Sabon.
Typesetting by Aura Technology and Software Services, India.
Printed in the UK.

Contents

Acknowledgements

As with my previous book, *The Wild East: Gunfights, Massacres and Race War Far from the American Frontier*, this is not intended as an anti-American tract. My main intention has been to chronicle many astonishing conflicts which have, for many reasons, slipped from the forefront of the popular consciousness. I have always taken care to give a voice to the largely forgotten dead on all sides. In the process, however, it has proved impossible not to nail some of the cosy myths of American history ruthlessly exploited and twisted by populists, not least the current occupant of the White House.

The chapter on the Modoc War is an updated and re-jigged version of one in my first history book, *Massacre and Retribution*, published over twenty years ago. It was an anachronism then as every other chapter concerned British wars, and this book is its natural home.

I would like to thank the staff at libraries and local museums in Lakeland, Florida; Billings, Butte and Helena, Montana; Deadwood and Lead, South Dakota; and Cody, Ten Sleep, Buffalo and Sheridan, Wyoming, for access to dusty, eyewitness accounts of armed conflict. And for their insight into the American military mindset, my thanks go to the staff and customers in veterans' bars in all of the above, plus in Broadus, Hardin, Ybor City, West Yellowstone, Virginia City, Great Falls, Choteau, Missoula, Polson, Gardiner and Browning.

Closer to home, I must also thank Amberley commissioning editor Shaun Barrington, publicist Philip Dean and editor Cathy Stagg for their belief I still have stories to tell.

And, as always, my family.

Introduction

marching to a butcher's shop...

Shortly before his death, the movie and vaudeville actor W. C. Fields recorded a comedy track entitled 'The Temperance Lecture', which lampooned George Washington's role in putting down the Whiskey Rebellion. A neighbourhood and golf course in Columbus, Ohio, is named after the great Shawnee chief Little Turtle. US Route 202 through Pelham is called the Daniel Shays Highway after the protagonist in another uprising put down by military might. And the oldest military monument in the US honours the American heroes of the first war against Barbary pirates. Such a hotchpotch of commemoration underlines, rather than denies, the question: What is a 'forgotten' war? Academics may well disagree with my choices in the pages that follow. What criteria do I use? What is the motivation behind my choices? Above all, how is a British journalist qualified to answer the above?

My choice is admittedly arbitrary, but I make no apology for that. In my *Britain's Forgotten Wars* trilogy, spanning the nineteenth century, I took the view that most people were still taught about the Napoleonic and Boer wars that top-and-tailed that century, and the Zulu wars because the Cy Enfield movie was shown on TV most Christmases, but wrong-headedly believed that, with the exception of the Crimea mid-century, Queen Victoria's reign was a time of peace throughout the Empire. Pax Britannica, I explained, was a myth.

Equally, schools in America routinely teach, sometimes through rose-tinted spectacles, the Revolutionary War for Independence, the War of 1812 and the horrors of the Mexican War and the war between the states, and through TV, film and other media Americans have some idea of How the West Was Won, for good and ill. Growing up as part of the first TV-viewing generation during the 1950s and 60s I devoured Westerns at home and American war films at the cinema, but even as a youngster knew that they were, at the very least, part-fantasy; that scenarios with clearly defined 'goodies' and 'baddies' were far from the truth about battlefield or frontier violence.

America's overriding patriotic fervour manifests itself, as in Britain, with its war memorials and its public acknowledgement of past great deeds, from the veneration of the flag to the school recitations of the Declaration of Independence. In the US, as in the UK, almost every city and town has cenotaphs and other memorials to the fallen in the two World Wars, with names added from Korea, Vietnam, Afghanistan, Iraq and other conflicts. But where are the memorials to all the other conflicts, external and internal, that came after America's birth and during its violent adolescence and eventual adulthood? The Custer battlefield in Wyoming now celebrates both sides of that massacre, but elsewhere George Armstrong is venerated in art, film and Western literature. He was a glory-hunting butcher who led his men into disaster, yet remains far more celebrated, for example, than General Edward Canby, a far better man who gave his life in the search for an honourable peace during the Modoc War. For decades his memorial was a simple wooden cross, although a modest plaque now graces the Lava Beds National Monument.

In terms of the numbers participating, the Modoc War involved a greater attrition rate than any other. And in terms of actual casualties, St Clair's defeat in Little Turtle's War saw American casualties topping 1,000, including 832 deaths, compared to Custer's last stand and the wider Battle of the Little Bighorn in which just over 270 perished. Americans generally prefer either outright victory or 'glorious' failures to messy conflicts which don't quite gel with their own sense of history and national identity – a trait which Britons share, albeit to a lesser degree.

The burgeoning 'yellow press' influenced and affected military reputations, at least in the short term. Military history across the globe has had a high quota of boneheaded and bigoted buffoons who betray any received ideas of honour and heroism. One of the worst was the odious Brigadier General Jacob Hurd Smith, who ordered the killing of 10-year-olds suspected of insurgency and told his men to make the Philippines 'a howling wilderness'. He was dubbed 'Hell Roaring Jake' Smith, 'The Monster', and 'Howling Jake' by the press and whether such tags were considered endorsements or condemnations of his genocidal policy depended on the targeted readership. He was court-martialled and denied any involvement in the First World War, but after his death in March 1918 he was interred in Arlington National Cemetery, a place normally reserved for heroes.

America's recorded history is of course shorter than that of Europe and Asia, so its sense of urgency in military memorial to major wars is that much greater. The numerous small wars of conquest and colonialism in which America engaged across the globe tend to have been left behind. But there were exceptions. During the Presidency of Franklin D. Roosevelt, the US Post Office Department issued a series of stamps honouring the US Navy and various naval heroes. Stephen Decatur, hero of the Quasi War, the War of 1812 and the Barbary Wars, was one of the few chosen, appearing on the 2-cent issue.

The 'forgotten' tag is, of course, subjective and depends on geography. Many in Tex-Mex border communities are well aware of the Cortina disturbances; the Spanish descendants in Florida know of the short but decisive war across the water in Cuba; those with Filipino ancestors or relatives are well aware of the genocidal war in the Philippines. From 2011, the Whiskey Rebellion Festival has been held annually in Washington, Pennsylvania, with live music and historic re-enactments, including the 'tarring and feathering' of a tax collector. And every year the bloodless Pig War is commemorated by local people and re-enactors on the sites of the US and British Army camps in San Juan Island National Historical Park.

The forgotten wars can also, if you know the identities of the participants, be traced through place names on the map of America. At least forty-six communities in the United States have been named after Stephen Decatur, including towns and counties in Alabama, Georgia, Illinois, Texas, Iowa, Indiana, Kansas and Tennessee. Five US Navy warships were subsequently named after him.

The Spanish–American War was the first US conflict in which the motion picture camera played a role and some feature films were made about it. Teddy Roosevelt always recalled the Battle of San Juan as 'the great day of my life' and 'my crowded hour', and it played a part in his elevation to the White House. But it was not until 2001 that he was posthumously awarded the Medal of Honor for his actions; he had been nominated during the war, but army officials, annoyed at his grabbing the headlines, blocked it. Today the war's main memorial is the Guantanamo Bay detention camp, where suspected terrorists have been held without trial and brutalised. Established during the George W. Bush administration, Barack Obama promised to shut it, but didn't, and in January 2018, President Donald Trump signed an executive order to keep the prison camp open indefinitely.

Sometimes forgotten wars seep into parochial common memory and legend, adding to the myths. For example, a local legend claims that the renowned chief Cornstalk, murdered after Lord Dunmore's War, took his revenge in the 1960s by sending the mysterious Mothman to terrorise Point Pleasant, the scene of that war's greatest battle.

Few of those who took part in the German Coast slave uprising were ever memorialised. The plantations where the rebellion raged are under New Orleans' international airport, which, ironically, is named after the prominent African American Louis Armstrong. Nearby there is a small museum in a converted slave cabin.

But that is to be expected. American history follows the European model in being mainly written by the victors. 'Fake news' is no new thing.

* * *

From its troubled birth at the outbreak of the War of Independence in April 1775, America was suspicious of standing armies – understandable given previous British military rule. Before that each of the thirteen colonies had relied upon local and regional militia, made up of part-time civilian soldiers. But within days of the war's outbreak, the Massachusetts Provincial Congress authorised the raising of twenty-six company regiments, shortly followed by smaller forces raised by New Hampshire, Rhode Island and Connecticut. By the middle of June the Colonial Congress members agreed to raise a Continental Army under George Washington for common defence, incorporating 22,000 troops already in place outside Boston and 5,000 more outside New York. The first ten companies of riflemen from Pennsylvania, Maryland, Delaware and Virginia were put on a one-year enlistment as light infantry. Congress later authorised the creation of both field artillery and cavalry units.[1]

Washington was repeatedly outmanoeuvred by British generals with larger armies. He initially forced the British out of Boston in 1776 but was defeated and almost captured later that year when he lost New York City. After more reversals, revolutionary forces heavily backed by French troops and artillery captured two British armies at Saratoga (1777) and Yorktown (1781). Washington's genius was more administrative than military, managing to co-ordinate logistics and training within competing state governance and local militias.

After the war the Continental Army was quickly disbanded and irregular state militias became the new nation's ground army, save for a regiment to guard the western frontier and one battery of artillery guarding West Point's s arsenal. However, because of continuing conflict with Native American tribes, the need for a trained standing army became crystal clear. The Legion of the United States was established in 1792 at Fort Lafayette, Pennsylvania under Major General 'Mad' Anthony Wayne. The Legion proved critical in the Northwest Indian War (*see* chapter 2). After Wayne's death in 1796, the Legion was renamed the United States Army.

During the War of 1812, an invasion of Canada failed and US troops were unable to stop the British from burning the new capital of Washington DC. However, the Regular Army, under Generals Winfield Scott and Jacob Brown, in the Niagara campaign proved they were professional and capable of defeating a major invasion by the regular British Army. The Regular Army's great victory under Andrew Jackson at the Battle of New Orleans in January 1815 ended the war.

Glaring deficiencies which emerged during that war convinced Washington that major reform of the War Department was necessary. Secretary of War John C. Calhoun reorganised his department into a system of bureaus, whose chiefs held office for life, and a commanding general in the field. The bureau chiefs acted as advisers to the Secretary of War while commanding their own troops and field installations. The bureaus were often at each other's throats, competing for scarce resources and political influence.[2] Calhoun set up the Bureau of Indian Affairs in 1824, the main agency within the War Department for dealing with Native Americans until 1849, when Congress transferred it to the newly founded Department of the Interior.[3] For some years the main domestic military action involved warfare with the Seminole Indians in Florida, who refused to move west and effectively used the terrain as a defence. They were never wholly defeated.

Conditions of service in the Regular Army were easier than in those of Europe as Americans enlisted for only five years – and for just three years between 1833 and 1846 – and generally served within one's home country. Pay was set at $5 a month until 1833, $6 until 1854 and $10 thereafter – less than that of a labourer. But there were extra allowances for fatigues and construction work, plus full board.[4] Drunkenness was too often the outcome of brain-numbing boredom. Flogging was abolished in 1812, although later reinstated for a period, but other punishments were harsh, including branding with a hot iron on the head and body, suspension by the thumbs and the convict's ball and chain, although the ultimate sanction of execution was rarely used. As with all armies throughout history, food was a constant preoccupation. In some campaigns, troops suffered near-starvation. During the Revolutionary War, Americans fighting in Canada reported being forced to eat leather shot pouches, moose-skin britches, rawhide thongs, dog carcasses and squirrel heads in foul-tasting stews.[5]

Throughout the timespan of this book, chances of recovery for a wounded soldier were less than 50 per cent, dropping to almost zero for abdominal injuries. The most common surgical operations involved amputation. Such surgery, carried out in hastily erected hospital tents or on the battlefield itself, usually took place without anaesthetics or the sterilisation of cutting tools. After such operations surgeons would 'hurriedly remove the evidence of the visit in the hope that the body would permit the insult to pass unnoticed'.[6]

Transportation was key to all campaigns and the army was given full responsibility for navigation on the rivers. The steamboat, first used on the Ohio River in 1811, opened up the river systems, especially the Mississippi and Missouri rivers and their tributaries, vastly improving the speed with which forces could reach trouble spots. Between 1819 and 1825, Colonel Henry Atkinson developed keelboats with hand-powered paddle wheels.[7]

The Regular Army and many volunteer units were deployed in the 1846–48 Mexican War. The American strategy was to take control of New Mexico and California, invade Mexico from the north under general Zachary Taylor, then land troops and capture Mexico City with an army under General Winfield Scott. All the operations were successful; the Americans won all the major battles. The army expanded from 6,000 regulars to more than 115,000. Of these, approximately 1.5 per cent were killed in the fighting and nearly 10 per cent died of disease; another 12 per cent were wounded or discharged because of disease.

Widespread American antipathy to the concept of a standing army continued, with many statesmen advocating disbandment after every formal war had concluded. Samuel Adams wrote in 1768: 'It is a very improbable supposition, that any people can long remain free, with a strong military power in the heart of their country: unless that military power is under the direction of the people, and even then it is dangerous.'[8] There was a widespread view among Americans of all ranks that while they could be warlike when necessary, they were not of a military disposition. Budget constraints supported that view and by the outset of the Civil War the Regular Army had shrunk to just 16,400 men scattered around the frontier and along the coastline. As the Southern states seceded many experienced officers and men resigned or left to join the Confederate Army, further limiting the Regular Army's abilities. Both sides recruited large numbers of men into new volunteer armies raised by each state. Regiments were recruited locally, with company officers elected by the men.[9] Colonels – often local politicians with minimal or non-existent battle experience – were appointed by the governors, and generals were appointed by President Abraham Lincoln. The Union's Volunteer Army was so much larger than the Regular Army that entirely new units above the regimental level had to be formed. The grand plan involved geographical theatres, with armies named after rivers, comprising brigades, divisions and corps headquarters.[10]

Historian Marcus Cunliffe vividly described how patriotism merged with a lust for adventure to propel so many to the butcher's block:

> The American youths, on both sides, were caught up by emotions at once superficial and profound. They were escaping from ordinariness, seeking other selves, impelled by vanity and by nobility. So, enlisting, they cheered and sang and even perhaps wept a little. Once in uniform, they added to the effect of ferocity by sticking pistols and bowie knives into their belts and by cultivating moustaches. They crowded into photographers' parlours in their panoply, scowling at the camera as they tensed themselves in front of the incongruously genteel backcloth and the potted plants.[11]

The rapidly growing armies were poorly trained ahead of the first major battle at Bull Run in the middle of 1861. The embarrassing Union defeat and subsequent inability of the Confederacy to capitalise on their victory resulted in both sides spending more time organising and training their green armies. Much of the subsequent actions taken in 1861 were skirmishes between pro-Union and pro-Confederacy irregular forces in border states such as Missouri and Kentucky.

In 1862, the war became more extensive and bloody, with neither side able to gain a lasting strategic advantage over the other. However, the decisive 1863 battles at Gettysburg and Vicksburg shifted the momentum of the war in favour of the Union. Confederate forces were outmatched, outnumbered and outgunned by Union forces supported by an industrial war machine. An increasingly effective naval blockade further damaged the Southern war economy. It became a brutal war of attrition in which the fear of starvation at least matched that of bombardment. The Union supply system, even as it penetrated deeper into the South, maintained its efficiency. Quartermaster General Montgomery C. Meigs and his subordinates, responsible for most of the $3 billion spent for the war, operated out of sixteen major depots, which formed the basis of the system of procurement and supply throughout the war. The quartermasters supervised their own soldiers, and co-operated closely with state officials, manufacturers and wholesalers trying to sell directly to the army.

Lincoln's Emancipation Proclamation of 1 January 1863 enabled both free blacks and escaped slaves to join the Union Army, and about 190,000 volunteered. The Confederates dared not follow suit for fear of undermining the legitimacy of slavery. Black Union soldiers were mostly used in garrison duty, but they fought in several full-scale battles. When black soldiers and Confederates clashed head on, no quarter was given by either side. At Fort Pillow, on 12 April 1864, Confederate units under Major General Nathan Bedford Forrest massacred black soldiers attempting to surrender.

By 1864, the Confederacy was doomed but its death throes were on an epic scale. General Ulysses S. Grant fought a series of bloody battles with rebel commander Robert E. Lee in Virginia. Grant suffered higher casualties but could afford to; Lee could not replace his casualties and was forced to retreat into trenches around his capital at Richmond, Virginia. Meanwhile, William Tecumseh Sherman captured Atlanta in 1864. His March to the Sea destroyed a 100-mile-wide swath of Georgia. In all, 2.2 million men served in the Union ranks, 360,000 of whom died – two-thirds from disease. The Volunteer Army was demobilised in summer 1865.

Following the Civil War, the army engaged in long and messy wars with Native American tribes who resisted US expansion into the centre of the continent. Settler wagon trains were replaced by transcontinental railroads from 1869, and the military's mission was to clear the land of free-roaming

Indians and put them on reservations. The stiff resistance of battle-hardened, well-armed mounted Indian warriors should not have surprised anyone. Brutal wars against the Apache, Navajo and Comanche ensued, with successive army commanders pursuing scorched earth policies that verged on the genocidal. In June 1877, the Nez Perce under Chief Joseph, unwilling to give up their traditional lands and move to a reservation, undertook a 1,200-mile fighting retreat from Oregon to near the Canada–US border in Montana. Numbering only 200 warriors, the Nez Perce battled some 2,000 American regulars and volunteers in eighteen engagements.[12] Just 40 miles from Canada, they finally surrendered.

The Great Sioux War (1876–77) was sparked when the US broke treaty agreements after gold was discovered in the Black Hills. Sitting Bull and Crazy Horse defeated Custer's 7th Cavalry at Little Bighorn, but the scale of their victory led to their eventual demise as Washington, horrified by the unnecessary defeat, mobilised its overwhelming forces. The West was largely pacified by 1890, apart from small Indian raids along the Mexican border. Combat in the Indian wars resulted in the deaths of about 4,340 people, including soldiers, civilians and Native Americans. Over the course of the Indian Wars, from 1790 to 1910, regular cavalry units fought in about 1,000 engagements and suffered more than 2,000 killed and wounded.[13] Disease and accidents caused far more army casualties than combat; annually, 8 soldiers per 1,000 died from disease, and 5 per 1,000 died from battle wounds or accidents.

In the aftermath of the Indian Wars, the US Army again shrank dramatically. General Sherman wrote in January 1879: 'The People who were so grateful in 1865 for military service, now begrudge us every cent of pay and every ounce of bread we eat.'[14] By 1898 the army was down to 25,000 men, less than the number employed by the Pinkerton Detective Agency to break strikes in an era of industrial unrest. But that year's Spanish–American War, fought mainly in Cuba, and the subsequent suppression of the Philippines, saw a huge influx of volunteers (*see* chapters 15 and 16).

In 1910, the US Signal Corps acquired and flew the army's first aircraft, the Wright Type A biplane.[15] But the history of the US Air Force is not within the remit of this book.

The first formal step in the creation of a continental navy came from Rhode Island, a hotbed of smugglers severely harassed by British frigates. On 26 August 1775, Rhode Island passed a resolution that there be a single continental fleet funded by Congress. George Washington began to buy ships, starting with the schooner USS *Hannah*, paid for out of his own pocket.[16] However, the US Navy recognises 13 October 1775 as the date of its official establishment with the passage of a resolution of the Continental Congress. Two months later Congress authorised the building of thirteen frigates within the next three months: five ships of thirty-two guns, five with twenty-eight guns and three with twenty-four guns. By mid-1776, the resultant American ships were completely outmatched by the mighty Royal Navy, and nearly all were captured or sunk by 1781.[17] American privateers had more success, taking more than 2,200 British ships during periods of hostilities.

Two years after the Revolutionary War ended in 1783, the Continental Navy was disbanded and the remaining ships were sold to raise cash. The infant US desperately needed to boost income, however, and relied heavily on tariffs on imported goods. Rampant smuggling convinced Congress of the need for strong enforcement, and the Revenue-Marine, the forerunner of the US Coast Guard, was born.

Attacks on American shipping by Barbary pirates and the turmoil of the Napoleonic Wars led to the 1794 Naval Act which authorised the building of six frigates, four of forty-four guns and two of thirty-six guns. But after the Quasi War (*see* chapter 4) and successful operations on the Barbary Coast (*see* chapter 5), the navy was greatly reduced to again to save cash and, instead of regular ships, many gunboats were built, intended for coastal use only. This policy proved completely ineffective within a decade.[18] President Thomas Jefferson and his Republican Party opposed a strong navy, arguing that small gunboats in the major harbours were all the nation needed to defend itself. They proved useless in wartime.[19]

Much of the 1812 War with the British was fought at sea and the Americans were hopelessly outnumbered, allowing the landings that resulted in the burning of Washington. But American naval victories at Lakes Champlain and Erie halted the final British offensive in the north and helped to deny the British exclusive rights to the Great Lakes. In the final naval action of the war, on 30 June 1815, the sloop USS *Peacock* captured the East India Company brig *Nautilus*, the last enemy ship captured by the US Navy until the Second World War.

After the war, the navy's successes were rewarded with better funding which permitted a programme of shipbuilding. But the expense of manning and provisioning the larger ships resulted in many of them remaining in shipyards half-completed, in readiness for another war. The main force of the navy continued to be large sailing frigates together with a number of smaller sloops. By the 1840s, the navy began to adopt steam power and shell guns, but they lagged behind the French and British in adopting the new technologies.[20]

Enlisted sailors during this time included many foreign-born men, and native-born Americans were usually social outcasts escaping bankruptcy, social ostracism or punishment for crimes. In 1835 almost 3,000 men sailed with merchant ships out of Boston harbour, but only ninety men were recruited by the navy. It was unlawful for black men to serve in the navy, but the shortage of men was so acute this was frequently ignored.[21] Discipline followed the customs of the Royal Navy but punishment was much milder than typical in European navies. Sodomy was rarely prosecuted. The navy, unlike the army, kept flogging as a punishment until 1850.[22]

Between 1815 and 1822 an estimated 3,000 ships were captured by pirates in the Caribbean and Congress authorised President James Madison to deal with the threat. Since many of the culprits were Latin American privateers, he embarked on a strategy of gunboat diplomacy. An 1819 agreement with Venezuela failed to curb piracy and the US West India Squadron was deployed. Frigates escorted merchant ships while smaller craft searched the myriad coves and islands to chase and capture pirate vessels. During this campaign USS *Sea Gull* became the first steam-powered ship to see combat action.[23] By 1826 pirate attacks became rare and the region was declared free for commerce. Such operations gave the navy valuable experience as America began to compete on seas around the world.

The African Squadron was formed in 1820 to meet international obligations to end the slave trade. This was unpopular at home and led to charges of hypocrisy abroad given the scale of slave-holding across the US. The squadron was withdrawn in 1823 and did not return to the African coast until the passage of the Webster–Ashburton Treaty with Britain in 1842. After that the US used fewer ships than the treaty required, ordered the ships far from the coast of Africa, and deployed craft that were too large to operate close to shore. Between 1845 and 1850, the US Navy captured only ten slave vessels, while the British captured 423 carrying 27,000 captives.[24]

While Congress had authorised the establishment of the US Military Academy in 1802, it took almost fifty years to approve a similar school for naval officers. During that time midshipmen had few opportunities for promotion unless they had rich patrons. The poor quality of officer training was highlighted by a mutiny aboard the training ship USS *Somers* in 1842. Secretary of the Navy George Bancroft in 1845 decided to create a new academy for officers outside congressional approval. After six years, the new institution was finally designated as the US Naval Academy in 1851.

The navy played a crucial role in two major operations of the Mexican–American War (1845–1848). During the Battle of Veracruz, it landed 12,000 troops and their equipment in one day, eventually leading to the capture of Mexico City and the end of the war. Its Pacific Squadron facilitated the capture of California.[25]

Between the beginning of the war between the states and the end in 1861, 373 commissioned officers, warrant officers and midshipmen resigned or were dismissed from the United States Navy and went on to serve the Confederacy. On 20 April 1861, the Union burned its ships at the Norfolk Navy Yard to prevent their capture by the Confederates, but not all were completely destroyed. The screw frigate USS *Merrimack* was so hastily scuttled that her hull and steam engine remained intact and the South's Stephen Mallory raised her and then armoured her with iron plate. The salvaged ship was named USS *Virginia*.

Meanwhile, the North's John Ericsson had similar ideas, and received funding to build USS *Monitor*.[26] The age of the ironclads had arrived.

On 8 March 1862, *Virginia* successfully attacked the Union blockade ordered by President Lincoln. The next day, *Monitor* engaged *Virginia* in the Battle of Hampton Roads, the first clash of ironclads. Shells bounced off both ships and the battle ended in a draw. The Confederacy later lost *Virginia* when the ship was scuttled to prevent capture. *Monitor* was the prototype for the monitor warships, and many more were built by the Union Navy. The Confederacy lacked the ability to build or purchase ships that could effectively counter the monitors.[27]

Along with ironclad ships, the new technologies of naval mines, torpedoes and submarine warfare were introduced by the Confederacy. During the Battle of Mobile Bay, mines were used to protect the harbour and sank the Union monitor USS *Tecumseh*. The forerunner of the modern submarine, CSS *David*, attacked USS *New Ironsides* using a spar torpedo. The Union ship was barely damaged and the resultant water spout put out the fires in the submarine's boiler, rendering it immobile. Another submarine, CSS *H. L. Hunley*, was designed to dive and surface but ultimately sank five times during trials. In action against USS *Housatonic*, the submarine successfully sank its target but was lost in the same explosion.[28]

The naval blockade of the South caused the Confederate economy to collapse during the war, leading to shortages of food and supplies. The Union victory at the Second Battle of Fort Fisher in January 1865 closed the last useful Southern port, virtually ending blockade running and hastening the end of the conflict.

After the war, the navy went into another period of decline. In 1864, the navy had 51,500 men in uniform, almost 700 ships and about sixty monitor-type coastal ironclads, which made the US Navy the second largest in the world after the Royal Navy.[29] By 1880 the navy only had 48 ships in commission and 6,000 men, while the ships and shore facilities were decrepit due to Congressional penny-pinching.[30] The navy was unprepared to fight a major maritime war before 1897.

By the 1870s most of the ironclads from the Civil War were laid up in reserve. In 1873 a Spanish ironclad anchored in New York Harbour, forcing the US Navy to the uncomfortable realisation that it had no ship capable of taking on such a monster. The navy hastily issued contracts for the construction of five new ironclads and accelerated its existing repair programme for several more. But by the time the Garfield administration assumed office in 1881, the navy's condition had deteriorated still further. A review conducted on behalf of the new Secretary of the Navy, William H. Hunt, found that of 140 vessels on the navy's active list, only fifty-two were in an operational state, of which a mere seventeen were iron-hulled ships, including fourteen ageing Civil War era ironclads. Officers and sailors in foreign ports were all too aware that their old wooden ships would not survive long in a real shooting war. The limitations of the monitor type effectively prevented the US from projecting power overseas.[31] In 1882, Hunt requested funds to construct modern ships. The request was initially rejected, but in 1883 Congress authorised the construction of three protected cruisers and a dispatch vessel which together were popularly known as the White Squadron because of the colour of the hulls. These were used to train a generation of officers and men.[32]

With the pacification of the western frontier, some Americans began to look outwards, to the Caribbean, Hawaii and the Pacific. The doctrine of 'Manifest Destiny' provided a philosophical justification for empire building, and many saw the navy as an essential part of realising that doctrine beyond the limits of the American continent. That led to a programme of battleship building which brought the US Navy from twelfth place in 1870 to fifth place among the world's navies.[33]

* * *

Many were the casualties of America's wars. In an astonishing display of honesty, the colonel of the 3rd Ohio Infantry roused his men for a midnight attack on the Rappahannock in December 1862 with the words: 'The Third will lead the column. The secessionists have ten thousand men and forty rifled cannon. They are strongly fortified. They have more men and more cannon than we have. They will cut us to pieces. Marching to attack such an enemy, so entrenched and so armed, is marching to a butcher's shop rather than to a battle. There is bloody work ahead. Many of you boys will go out who will never come back again.'[34] He was proved right. Men were turned into memories too easily forgotten.

I

Lord Dunmore's War (1774) and Native Americans in the Revolutionary War (1775–1783)

... the Great Spirit has seen fit that we should die together

A long lifetime after the bloody events he described, the Reverend William Henry Foote wrote:

> There was a time when the name of Cornstalk thrilled every heart in West Virginia. Here and there among the mountains may be found an aged one, who remembers the terrors of Indian warfare as they raged on the rivers, and in the retired glens, west of the Blue Ridge, under that noted savage. Cornstalk was to the Indians of West Virginia, what Powhatan was to the tribes on the Sea Coast, the greatest and the last chief.[1]

In the last war of colonial America, and arguably in the first battles of the war for independence, the Shawnee warrior chief Cornstalk was pitted against an English aristocrat. When the gunshots faded, one would be murdered and the other in humiliating retreat. They were players in a conflict quickly overshadowed by events in Boston and the wider war that created the United States, which is now largely forgotten. So, too, is the active role that Native Americans played in the Revolutionary War – on both sides.

* * *

As revolutionary fervour swept through the American colonies, Native Americans were caught between competing European imperial powers and white colonists aiming to establish independence. Eventually they had to choose the loyalist or patriot cause – or somehow maintain a neutral stance – while trying to hold on to their homelands and maintain access to trade and supplies. Some allied themselves with the British, while others fought alongside the American colonists.[2]

The British had their own priorities. In 1763, George III proclaimed the regions west of the Allegheny mountains, territories once claimed by France, off limits to settlement by whites. Britain hoped to reduce conflict by separating the colonies from Indian territory. London was not prepared to finance security beyond the Alleghenies and endless war on the colonial American frontier. Speculators and veterans of the previous French and Indian Wars who expected to be rewarded with land beyond the mountains for their service were enraged. A subsequent series of treaties opening territory between the Ohio River and Alleghenies aimed to appease Virginia and Pennsylvania colonists, reducing risks of conflict with the Iroquois Confederacy to the north and the Cherokee Nation to the south. The Shawnee were stuck in the middle. The Iroquois, who claimed authority over the region, gave away traditional Shawnee hunting grounds.

The colonists poured into the region – first explorers and surveyors, then settlers – and came face to face with the tribes of the upper Ohio Valley. George Washington's diary entry for Saturday 17 November 1770 noted: 'The Indians who are very dexterous, even their women, in the Management of Canoes, have there (*sic*) Hunting Camps & Cabins all along the River for the convenience of Transporting their Skins by Water to Market.'

Eric Sterner wrote:

As whites flooded into the area, cultural interaction, conflicting notions of property, order, and justice made violence all but inevitable. Robbery became murder, followed by revenge raids, more murder, mutual racial animosity, and the destruction of small settlements along the Ohio. Animosity begat animosity and as violence between colonists and Indians living along the Ohio escalated in 1773 and 1774, war rumours, diplomatic attempts to secure allies, and efforts to mobilize martial resources intensified.[3]

General Thomas Gage reported in June 1773:

The Northern Nations ceded Tracts of Land at the Treaty of Fort Stanwix, inconvenient to the Indians of the Ohio, which exasperated them to a great Degree, but finding themselves too weak alone for the six Nations, they have been, and appear still to be endeavouring to form a general Union of all the Western & Southern Nations, and the Shawnese (*sic*) are supposed to be the Contrivers of the Scheme.

The six Nations in Return have strengthened their Alliance with the Canada and other Tribes. The six Nations have by Deputy's sent to Scioto threatened much, but Nothing has been undertaken openly on either Side … It has very often been reported, that the French and Spaniards have excited the Nations against the English, and been the Authors of many Mischiefs, tho' it has not been discovered that the Spanish Government has had any Concern therein. But it is probable the Traders at the Illinois as well British, as Spanish Subjects have been guilty of such iniquitous Practices to keep the trade to themselves…[4]

The Shawnee were at the forefront of resistance and soon organised a large confederacy opposed to the British and the Iroquois in order to enforce their claims.[5] British and Iroquois officials in turn worked to isolate the Shawnee diplomatically from other Indian nations. When full-blown hostilities broke out the Shawnee would find that they faced the Virginia militia with few allies.

In September 1773, Daniel Boone, then an obscure hunter and entrepreneur, led about fifty whites intent on establishing the first British settlement in Kentucky County, Virginia. On 9 October his eldest son, sixteen-year-old James, was one of a small group retrieving supplies who were attacked by a band of Shawnee, Delaware and Cherokee who had decided 'to send a message of their opposition to settlement'. James Boone and fellow teenager Henry Russell were captured and tortured to death. The brutality of the killings shocked the settlers along the frontier and was luridly reported by eastern seaboard newspapers. Boone's party abandoned their expedition.[6] Settlers were attacked all along the frontier. Those men captured were ritually mutilated and tortured to death, while surviving women and children were enslaved. Early the next year, field surveyor William Preston wrote to George Washington, then head engineer of frontier fort construction, to warn of trouble ahead. He reported that a survey party had disappeared around the Ohio. He wrote of other surveying outfits: 'I am really afraid the Indians will hinder them from doing any Business of Value this Season…'

Captain Michael Cresap, the owner of a trading post at Redstone Old Fort (now Brownsville, Pennsylvania) on the Monongahela River, was given authority by the colonial government to take control of extensive tracts below the mouth of Middle Island Creek. In early spring 1774 he led a heavily armed party to settle that land. At the same time Ebenezer Zane, later a famed frontier guide, led a similar enterprise near the mouth of Sandy Creek. And a third and larger group, which included future general George Rogers Clark, gathered at the mouth of the Little Kanawha River. Clark's group heard that hostile bands were attacking white travellers on the banks of the Ohio and decided to attack the village of Horsehead Bottom, near the mouth of the Scioto River on their intended route to Kentucky. They contacted Cresap, who with his men was camped 15 miles upriver, but the experienced fighter argued that such a raid would make war inevitable. The various parties agreed to join him upriver and, if the situation calmed, they could resume their journey to Kentucky. But when they arrived at 'Zaneburg' (now Wheeling), the area was in an uproar over lurid accounts of Indian attacks. Thrown into panic, British colonists had flocked into the tiny settlement for protection. They, and other volunteers, were spoiling for a fight.

Captain John Connolly, the commander of the garrison at Fort Pitt, asked them to delay action for a week until he could determine the intentions of the threatening tribes. Contradictory responses flooded in and a council of settlers in Cresap's encampment declared war. After spotting native canoes on the river, the settlers chased them 15 miles downriver to Pipe Creek. Shots were exchanged, resulting in only a handful of casualties, and in fear of retaliation the settlers moved with Cresap's men to his headquarters at Redstone Old Fort.[7]

The nearby Mingo chief Logan, who had previously been an advocate of peace, changed his mind after a brutal encounter with settlers. At the end of April a Mingo hunting party strayed across the river at Yellow Creek to trade with a local white rum trader 30 miles from Zaneburg. The party included Logan's younger brother, commonly known as John Petty, and two closely related women. The younger woman was pregnant and also carrying an infant girl. The father of both these children was John Gibson, a well-known trader. When the party entered the trading post, around thirty frontiersmen led by Daniel Greathouse crowded in and killed all the visitors except the baby.

When Logan heard of the massacre, he believed that Cresap, not Greathouse, was responsible. Cresap, truthfully, denied any involvement in the atrocity. Logan and small parties of Shawnee and Mingo soon began striking at frontier settlers in revenge for the murders at Yellow Creek. On 5 May 1774, the Shawnee delivered the message:

Brothers: We have received your Speeches by White Eyes... we look upon it all to be lies, and perhaps what you say may be lies also, but as it is the first time you have spoke to us we listen to you, and expect that what we may hear from you will be more confined to truth than what we usually hear from the white people. It is you who are frequently passing up and down the Ohio, and making settlements upon it, and as you have informed as that your wise people have met together to consult upon this matter, we desire you to be strong and consider it well. Brethren: We see you speak to us at the head of your warriors, who you have collected together at sundry places upon this river, where we understand they are building forts, and as you have requested us to listen to you, we will do it, but in the same manner that you appear to speak to us. Our people at the Lower Towns have no Chiefs among them, but are all warriors, and are also preparing themselves to be in readiness, that they may be better able to hear what you have to say ... You tell us not to take any notice of what your people have done to us; we desire you likewise not to take any notice of what our young men may now be doing, and as no doubt you can command your warriors when you desire them to listen to you, we have reason to expect that ours will take the same advice when we require it, that is, when we have heard from the Governour [sic] of Virginia.[8]

Virginia had by then politically and diplomatically beaten off Pennsylvania's claim to the region. If the Shawnee went to war to protect their dwindling territory, it would be against the might of Virginia, the strongest and most populous of the colonies. Shawnee raiding parties attacked isolated communities and farmsteads. The Virginia militia initially limited operations to defensive measures, while the British authorities strived to win a general peace, focusing their efforts on the Iroquois and Cherokee tribes. It became clear that the Iroquois were incapable of curbing the Shawnee; full-scale war became inevitable. The Shawnee had become largely isolated from the stronger neighbouring tribes, but by then they had a leader to be reckoned with.

Cornstalk was born around 1720 in a Shawnee village near the upper Susquehanna River. When a youngster, his family moved to Ohio River country on the Scioto River tributary in what is now southern Ohio. His Shawnee name was Hokoleskwa, which translates loosely into 'stalk of corn' in English. Cornstalk and the Shawnee sided with the French in the French and Indian War of the early 1760s, fearing the English would continue to advance into the Ohio country. When the Shawnee were defeated by Colonel Henry Bouquet, Cornstalk was briefly taken hostage and agreed to not fight the English again. By then he had become a principal leader of the tribe. In 1763 he led a raid up the Kanawha River to its Greenbrier reaches in a bid to halt expanding white settlement.[9] It has been claimed that Cornstalk and his band befriended the settlers and then murdered everyone at Muddy Creek and then some fifty more at Clendenin Settlement, but those claims are questionable. He also played a role in the 1766 peace negotiations which followed Pontiac's Rebellion. The constant arrival of more white settlers caused much tension. Cornstalk tried to peacefully ease the situation but he was in the minority by 1774. On 3 May 1774, English colonists murdered eleven Mingo Indians. Retribution was demanded by the Mingo and the Shawnee people. Cornstalk promised to protect the English fur traders because they were innocent of this crime. Cornstalk was described as a 'handsome man with a charismatic personality'. He was 'a great warrior, extremely proficient orator, brilliant organizer, and was admired by both his enemies and his tribe for his cunning strategy in warfare'.[10] Cornstalk's commanding presence also impressed American colonials.

A Virginia officer, Colonel Benjamin Wilson, wrote in 1774: 'I have heard the first orators in Virginia, but never have I heard one whose powers of delivery surpassed those of Cornstalk...'[11] The Reverend Foote wrote: 'Cornstalk possessed all the elements of savage greatness, oratory, statesmanship and heroism, with beauty of person and strength of frame. In appearance he was majestic, in manners easy and winning.'

The British Governor of Virginia was the imperious, overbearing John Murray, 4th Earl of Dunmore, a member of the Jacobite aristocracy distrusted at home but generally respected in the colony. Born in Taymouth, Scotland, aged just fifteen he and his father joined the ill-fated 1745 Rising against the British throne and was appointed as a page to 'Bonnie' Prince Charlie. After the rebellion was crushed, his father, William Murray, was imprisoned and his family was put under house arrest. William was eventually pardoned, and the twenty-year-old John joined the British Army and became an earl by succession in 1856. He was both a born rebel and a key figure in the Establishment; an experienced soldier of the 3rd Regiment of Foot Guards and an admirer of horse racing and dancing. He was appointed governor of the Province of New York in 1770 but within a year became Virginia's governor after the death of its incumbent. Murray and his attractive wife, Lady Charlotte, were initially well accepted by the socially conscious Virginians. The auburn-haired, brown-eyed Scotsman, who often wore a kilt, possessed the Stuart charm and settled into the Williamsburg social scene.

John Murray was intent on increasing his own personal fortune through landholdings. The vast acreages along the Ohio seemed available for possession and reapportionment under his patronage if freed from native control. Dunmore rapidly became a willing ally of the Virginia land speculators, who were scheming to obtain acquisitions of enormous scope.[12] The incendiary politics of the time led to claims that Dunmore colluded with the Shawnees to deplete the Virginia militia and help safeguard the Loyalist cause should there be a colonial rebellion, though he strenuously denied these claims.[13] But he was a canny operator and certainly saw advantage in British rule in the Shawnee raids.

Early in May 1774, Dunmore heard that fighting in Ohio had broken out and asked the legislature to authorise general militia forces and fund a volunteer expedition into the Ohio River valley 'to pacify the hostile Indian war bands'. Dunmore was acting from complex motives. He saw the crisis as an opportunity to open new western lands to occupation and settlement, an aim he had consistently pursued, and also as a means to distract Virginia's citizens from the escalating crisis taking shape in Boston and other northern ports. Instead of supporting the rebels, Dunmore hoped they would rally to his side. Later historians summed up his gamble: if it failed, he might be removed from office and disgraced for his unauthorised actions; if it succeeded, he might weather the storm and emerge a successful leader in a time of dramatic upheaval.[14]

Authorisation given, Dunmore opted for a punitive expedition deep into Shawnee territory in which a Northern Division under himself and Colonel Adam Stephen would descend the Ohio from Fort Dunmore, while a Southern Division, commanded by Colonel Andrew Lewis, would descend the Kanawha. Once united on the Ohio, the militia army would move against major Shawnee towns on the Scioto River. The attack would draw Shawnee raiding parties north of the Ohio to defend their territory and enable the Virginians to significantly damage the Shawnee ability to sustain raids.[15]

Historian James Swisher described the militia as

> ... composed of landholding farmers from the backcountry Shenandoah Valley counties of Augusta, Fincastle, and Botetourt. These spacious, thinly populated counties provided their citizens with freedom from the bonds of authority, encouraging the development of Mr. Jefferson's ideal 'republic of farmers'; the bedrock upon which the republic should be based. Provincially absorbed in local and personal affairs, these stout backwoodsmen were only a few generations removed from their Celtic or Germanic roots. Yet already they were expert hunters, skilled in the use of their long rifles, and accustomed to living on the disordered borderlands of civilization where violence was a way of life. Most developed a rural individualistic lifestyle supported by their belief in a strong, evangelical, protestant God and an equally intense distrust of any authority figure. They were almost impossible to discipline, as armies were wont to attempt, but could prove terrible, violent, and effective soldiers if properly motivated. Uninhibited, they replied to the war-whoop of the Shawnee with the long-drawn hallo of the hunter.'[16]

Cornstalk and his more sensible war chiefs recognised they too had to gamble in the face of such formidable foes. Ongoing raids might make the frontier uninhabitable for colonists but, more immediately, Dunmore's united forces would outnumber the Shawnee in any battle. Cornstalk opted to attack the Southern Division while Dunmore's army was divided. A quick victory might enable the Shawnee to negotiate favourable peace terms. Cornstalk's leadership had attracted warriors from other tribes, including small numbers of the Mingo, Delaware, Ottawa, Miami, and Wyandot nations. Their combined strength was up to 800 warriors against almost 3,000 of the enemy, but the British had divided their force.[17] Dunmore's North Division comprised about 1,700 men, while Lewis commanded 1,100. For Cornstalk, the immediate target was obvious.

On 6 September the vanguard of the army, the Augusta Regiment, marched out of Camp Union accompanied by 500 packhorses carrying 54,000 pounds of flour. Captain Matthew Arbuckle, an experienced woodsman, led the long file of men and horses. Fifers and drummers accompanied each regiment to relay commands, a reminder of Lewis's British military roots. The volunteers hacked through dense forest, climbed and descended steep defiles and forded fast-flowing streams. Upon reaching bottomland at Elk Creek, the column turned downstream to its junction with the Kanawha River, near where Charleston, West Virginia's state capital, now stands.

While Dunmore stopped to marshal his troops at Fincastle, Lewis reached the intended rendezvous at the headwaters of the Great Kanawha River on 6 October and established the camp known as Point Pleasant. Three days later Dunmore, via a messenger, ordered Lewis to cross the Ohio and meet him at the Shawnee towns. Cornstalk moved to intercept Lewis's army before the crossing could be achieved.

At Point Pleasant, canoes heavily laden with supplies and ammunition were unloaded and rude shelters of pine boughs were built. On 9 October, the Reverend Mr Terry presented a lengthy sermon attended by all. Resting in the afternoon, the soldiers were relaxed as the enemy was believed to be far away. The militia lounged in the shade of large trees and drank from springs of cold, pure water amid the calm beauty of an Appalachian upland autumn. Few wore uniforms, and discipline was lax. They mainly carried recently developed American long flintlocks, with a scattering of English muskets, plus tomahawks and scalping knives. So cocksure were these young militiamen that commissary officer William Ingles remarked later: 'We thought ourselves a terror to all the Indian tribes on the Ohio.'[18]

During the early hours of 10 October, Cornstalk and his men stealthily crossed the Ohio and grounded their canoes in Old Town Creek, less than 5 miles upriver. Camping within 2 miles of Lewis's force, the hostiles prepared to attack at dawn. Painted for war, the Indians slipped quietly through the forest toward the glow of campfires barely seen through an increasing ground fog. Armed with lightweight smoothbore flintlocks – formidable weapons at close range – obtained from French traders, the Indian warriors were prepared for face-to-face combat.

Before dawn, however, Virginians James Mooney and Joseph Hughey slipped out of camp to seek fresh game as they were tired of the stringy beef rations. Emerging from a pocket of dense fog, the duo confronted 'five acres of Indians'. Hughey fell under the initial volley, shot down by Tavender Ross, a white renegade. Mooney sprinted toward camp screaming a warning. The militia soldiers rolled out of their blankets and fell into company formations. Lewis, believing the enemy to be a scouting force, dispatched two detachments, each of 150 men, under Colonels Lewis and Fleming to confront the advancing hostiles. Fleming's men probed forward along the Ohio riverbank while Lewis's Augusta force advanced parallel, but farther inland abreast the Kanawha. After moving forward almost a half-mile the columns were abruptly checked by a hail of enemy gunfire.[19]

Colonel Charles Lewis ran to the front, conspicuous in his red officer's waistcoat, and was shot in the lower abdomen. Lewis exclaimed, 'I am wounded but go on and be brave' as he was carried rearward to his tent by his brother-in-law Captain Murray and William Bailey. His detachment began slowly to fall back. The pressure of the Indian fire then fell upon Fleming's unit. Fleming was shot in the chest and twice in the left arm but walked coolly to the rear. Colonel Field rallied forward with 200 colonial reinforcements, stabilising the line, but was killed by a shot to the head. A fellow officer stated that 'Field was shot at a great tree by two Indians on his right as he was endeavouring to get a shot at a hostile on his left.' Captain Evan Shelby took command of the hard-pressed line that stretched from the Ohio on the left flank to the Kanawha on the army's right, meaning it could not be flanked. Soldiers from the encampment stiffened the line. Each soldier found cover behind a rock, tree, or stump and fought his individual war. In the heavy fog and thick hanging gun smoke, the warriors pushed in close and hand-to-hand fighting erupted. Neither party could drive back the other, and neither would retreat. Rifles and muskets were used as clubs, along with tomahawks, knives, fists and feet. It was brutal work. No quarter was asked and none given.[20]

Cornstalk's voice could be heard above the ear-splitting din as he shouted, 'Be strong, be strong!' Taller than his followers and easily recognisable, Cornstalk appeared everywhere. Bullets whizzed all around him, but none struck. Both Shawnee and Virginians demonstrated the tactics and discipline of experienced and well-trained soldiers. William Foote wrote:

> Cornstalk was often seen with his warriors. Brave without being rash, he avoided exposure without shrinking; cautious without timidity in the hottest of the battle, he escaped without a wound. As one of the warriors near him showed some signs of timidity, the enraged chief, — with one blow of his tomahawk, cleft his skull. The faltering of the ranks encouraged the savages. As captain after captain, and files of men after files of men, fell, the yells of the Indians were more terrific and their assaults more furious.[21]

Historian Rembert Patrick described it as 'a typical Indian battle where every man found a tree, and military discipline in the English sense was unknown'. The struggle continued hour after hour with first one side rushing forward then the other. Warriors shouted, 'Why don't you whistle now?' as they derided the fifes that called the rifle companies to muster.

The Virginians had their backs to the rivers, and appeared to be trapped, but that precluded the Shawnee's favoured tactic of turning a flank and gaining their enemy's rear. The warriors came on frontally in brave rushes led by their chiefs, Red Hawk, Blue Jacket, Black Hoof, and Chiksikah, as well as Cornstalk and his son, Elinipisco. William Fleming wrote: 'Never did Indians stick closer to it, nor behave bolder.' The engagement lasted from an hour after sunrise to an hour before sunset. Captain James Ward fell, shot cleanly through the head, unaware that one of his sons, John, captured by the Shawnee at age three and renamed 'White Wolf', was firing his rifle with uncommon effect directly across the battle line.[22] The colonials gained a long ridge with logs and rocks that offered excellent cover. Slowly the Indians fell back to a second ridge that stretched from the Ohio to a swamp and firing gradually slackened. As the ground fog lifted, the superior rifle fire of the colonials became more effective

In the late afternoon, Lewis, while lighting his pipe, detailed Captains Isaac Shelby, George Matthews and John Stuart to form their companies and find a way to flank the enemy line. The three young officers led their men up the Kanawha, wading under cover of the riverbank. Turning up Crooked Creek, they emerged from the stream on a slight ridge in the enemy's left rear and opened a scalding fire. This sudden assault shocked the Indian warriors. Cornstalk was well aware from active scouts that Colonel William Christian was moving toward Point Pleasant with the remainder of the Fincastle Regiment; the flanking force was probably mistaken for that column, and Cornstalk began to withdraw his warriors. Cornstalk selected the best of his men to remain and continue the fight until all Indian wounded were carried across the Ohio. His brother, Silverheels, was badly wounded and carried back across the Ohio by their sister, Nonhelema, whose great strength had earned her the title 'Grenadier Squaw'. Cornstalk's forces melted into the forest.

When Christian's regiment from Fincastle arrived at about midnight, they found their compatriots in disarray, with the wounded suffering horribly; only minimal medical assistance was available. Fleming, a noted surgeon, was so injured his survival was doubtful. The colonial soldiers tried fortifying their camp by constructing log breastworks, but many were so tired they simply fell asleep. Captain George Mathews was credited with the flanking strike that turned the day, gaining him state-wide fame, which propelled him to the House of Burgesses.[23] Although the Southern Division suffered more casualties, it held the battlefield, and Cornstalk realised the war could not now be won. He said to his council: 'What shall we do now? The big knife is coming on us and we shall all be killed. Now we must fight or we are done? Then let us kill all our women and children and go fight until we die? I shall go and make peace!'[24] At nightfall, the Shawnees quietly withdrew back across the Ohio. The Virginians had held their ground.

The Virginians lost about seventy-five killed and 140 wounded, almost a fifth of those engaged. The dead included Colonel John Field, an ancestor of future Presidents George H. W. Bush and George W. Bush. John McKenney, who had two bullet holes and a tomahawk blow to his back, would be an invalid for life. So, too, would William Fleming, although his sharp mind would gain him political advancement. The Shawnees' losses could not be reliably determined, since they carried away their wounded and threw many of the dead into the river.[25] The morning after the battle Colonel Christian and his men found twenty-one dead braves in the open, and twelve more were discovered hastily covered with brush and old logs. Among those killed was Pucksinwah, the father of future hero and leader Tecumseh. There were no prisoners and the militia erected a pole on the Ohio riverbank adorned with eighteen Indian scalps. Besides scalps, the Virginians reportedly captured forty guns, many tomahawks and some plunder which was later sold at auction for £74 4s 6d.

Lewis buried his dead in long rows underneath the trees. Completion of the fortifications and care of the wounded occupied the army for several days. On 17 October Lewis crossed the Ohio, leaving a strong guard to protect the wounded. He advanced with his army, each man carrying 1½ pounds of lead and four days' rations, toward the Shawnee towns on the Scioto River, vengeance on the mind of each soldier. A messenger arrived as they neared the Scioto, informing Lewis that Dunmore was drawing up a treaty with the enemy and Lewis should advance no farther.

A participant in the Battle of Point Pleasant, Colonel John Stuart, wrote a memoir on the first pages of the Greenbrier County records when he was clerk of that county, in which he said in part:

> The battle of Point Pleasant was in fact the beginning of the Revolutionary War, that obtained for our county the liberty and independence enjoyed by the United States, for it is well known that the Indians were influenced by the British to commence the war to terrify and confound the people, before they commenced hostilities themselves the following year at Lexington. It was thought by British politicians that to incite an Indian war would prevent a combination of the colonies for opposing parliamentary measures to tax Americans. The blood therefore spilt upon this memorable battlefield will long be remembered by the good people of Virginia and the United States with gratitude.

The Southern Division continued the advance into Shawnee territory, joined forces with Dunmore's Northern Division, and quickly reached the upper Shawnee towns on the Scioto River, where they erected the temporary Camp Charlotte on Sippo Creek. There Cornstalk signed a treaty with Dunmore which reaffirmed the existing border and restored at least the illusion of peace along the Ohio. Colonel Benjamin Wilson reported that Cornstalk spoke 'in audible voice, without stammering, or repetition, and with peculiar emphasis. His looks while addressing Dunmore were truly grand, yet graceful and attractive.' The treaty also obliged the Shawnee to return all white captives and stop attacking barges of immigrants travelling on the Ohio River.[26]

The Mingo chief Logan, mourning his butchered family, agreed to stop fighting but refused to attend the peace conference. Consequently, Major William Crawford attacked his village of Seekunk (Salt Lick Town) with a force of 240 men. They destroyed the village, killing six and capturing fourteen, and rescued two white captives.[27]

Such operations closed what became known as Lord Dunmore's War, but there was no peace. In April 1775, before many of the Virginians had returned home, the Battles of Lexington and Concord had taken place and the Revolution had begun in earnest. Dunmore had a big problem – the same militiamen who had fought for him against the Shawnee were potential rebels. Tact and diplomacy were called for – but Dunmore possessed no such qualities. The Royal Governor's actions in the war which bore his name were soon questioned, with some claiming he had contrived to bring on the war for personal reasons. Many Virginians openly accused Lord Dunmore of duplicity in his dealings with the enemy. Colonel John Stuart, who marched with the force, avowed: 'Dunmore acted as a party to British politicians who wished to incite an Indian War which might prevent or distract the Virginia colony from the growing grievances with England.' For more than a year he governed autocratically without consulting either the Virginia House of Representatives or the colonial authorities. By the end of that year, the same men who had fought at Point Pleasant had driven him and his British troops out of Virginia.[28]

Dunmore gave the key to the Williamsburg magazine to Lieutenant Henry Colins, commander of HMS *Magdalen*, and ordered him to remove the powder to deprive the rebels of supplies. On the night of 20 April 1775, Royal Marines loaded fifteen half-barrels of powder into the governor's wagon, intent on transporting it to the James River and the British warship. Local militia rallied and word of the incident spread across the colony. The Hanover militia, led by Patrick Henry, arrived outside of Williamsburg on 3 May as Dunmore evacuated his family from the Governor's Palace to his hunting lodge, Porto Bello, in nearby York County. Henry was intent on forcing the return of the gunpowder to colony control. The matter was resolved without conflict when a payment of £330 was made to Henry. But three days later, Dunmore issued a proclamation against 'a certain Patrick Henry ... and a Number of deluded Followers' who had organised 'an Independent Company ... and put themselves in a Posture of War'. He threatened to impose martial law, but the militia attacked his country retreat. Wounded in the leg, Dunmore took sanctuary on the warship HMS *Fowey* on the York River on 8 June. British colonial governance of Virginia was over.

From a safe distance, Dunmore sent raiding parties to plunder rebel-owned plantations along the James, York and Potomac rivers and encourage slaves to rebel. In November 1775 Dunmore issued his Offer of Emancipation, which formally offered freedom to slaves who abandoned their Patriot masters to join the British. Dunmore had previously withheld his signature from a bill against the slave trade. By the end of the war, an estimated 800 to 2,000 escaped slaves sought refuge with the British.[29] George Washington commented: 'I do not think that forcing his lordship on shipboard is sufficient. Nothing less than depriving him of life or liberty will secure peace to Virginia, as motives of resentment actuate his conduct to a degree equal to the total destruction of that colony.' Dunmore organised the ex-slaves into an 'Ethiopian Regiment' which helped to win the Battle of Kemp's Landing. But his forces were decisively beaten in December at Great Bridge. Dunmore loaded his troops, and many Virginia Loyalists, on to British ships. Smallpox spread on board and about 500 of the 800 members of the Ethiopian Regiment died.

On New Year's Day in 1776, Dunmore ordered waterfront buildings in Norfolk burnt as Patriot troops were using them as a vantage point to fire on his ships. The fire spread and the whole city burned. Dunmore retreated to New York, realising that all hope of regaining control of Virginia had also gone up in flames. Dunmore returned to Britain in July 1776. He continued to draw his pay as the colony's governor until 1783, when Britain recognised American independence.

From 1787 to 1796, Dunmore served as governor of the Bahamas, issuing land grants to exiled American Loyalists, tripling the population within a few years. The Loyalists brought their slaves with them, and imported more from Africa for labour, as did the planters' descendants, but their cotton crops dwindled from soil exhaustion. Dunmore sat as a Scottish peer until 1790. He died on 25 February 1809 in Ramsgate, Kent.[30] Lake Dunmore, Vermont, was named after him in 1773, since he had claimed ownership of the area while he was Governor of New York.[31]

From the start of the Revolution, Cornstalk did his best to keep his people neutral, and represented the Shawnee at the Fort Pitt treaty councils in 1775 and 1776, the first Indian treaties ever negotiated by the United States. However, the tribe became split between Cornstalk's neutral faction and militant bands led by the warrior Blue Jacket, who believed that siding with the British would help them reclaim their lost lands. Cornstalk, a man of his word, abided by the peace treaty for the rest of his life. Cornstalk and one of his sons, Elinipisco, went to Point Pleasant to warn the Americans of the impending attack. They were detained by the fort commander, who had decided on his own initiative to take hostage any Shawnees who fell into his hands. When the settlers appeared suspicious of Cornstalk's motives, he said: 'When I was a young man and went to war, I thought that might be the last time, and I would return no more. Now I am here among you; you may kill me if you please; I can die but once; and it is all one to me, now or another time.'[32] Cornstalk was initially treated well and even began helping the Americans make maps and strategy for defeating the approaching enemies. A report came into the fort that an unknown Shawnee had killed an American soldier. Seeking revenge, the colonists mobbed Cornstalk. He told Elinipisc, 'My son, the Great Spirit has seen fit that we should die together; and has sent you here. It is his will. Let us submit. It is best...' Cornstalk was murdered on 10 November 1777 with his son and two other natives also held in custody.[33] One of the guards, Private Jacob McNeil, testified that he had tried to stop the killings but 'it was all in vain (because of) the American (soldiers) exasperated at the depredations of the Indians'. Breaking open the door of the jail, they fired a volley into the three imprisoned Indians. Seven musket balls struck Cornstalk, killing him instantly. Swisher wrote: 'It was an inglorious and tragic fate for such a brave, courageous, and noble chief who had been on a mission of peace.'

American political and military leaders were alarmed by Cornstalk's murder, believing that he was their only hope of securing Shawnee neutrality. At the insistence of Virginia Governor Patrick Henry, who described the killers as 'vile assassins', those responsible were eventually brought to trial, but, since their fellow soldiers would not testify against them, all were acquitted.

Cornstalk's murder did indeed drive many of the Shawnee to side with the British, although some remained neutral. Around 1,200 Shawnees led by Yellow Hawk and Black Stump had left Ohio and migrated west to Missouri. In May 1779, American Colonel John Bowan launched an attack on the Shawnee town of Chillicothe during which Chief Black Fish was mortally wounded. In summer 1780, when Virginia militia officer George Rogers Clark invaded the area, the Shawnee burned Chillicothe themselves to prevent it from falling to the Americans. Two years later, Clark returned to Shawnee territory and, according to Daniel Boone, who was involved in the expedition, burned five villages and entirely destroyed their crops.

Once the British lost the Revolutionary War, they tried to restrain the Shawnee warriors, urging them to make peace with the Americans. But the fighting continued long after the Treaty of Paris formally ended the war as more and more white settlers again encroached on the remaining Shawnee lands. The Shawnee were hit hard by the loss of British support but played a leading role in an emerging multi-tribal confederacy.[34]

* * *

The Shawnee experience is typical of a fact that is often conveniently forgotten about the Revolutionary War – that Native Americans played a key part in what was a messy, complicated conflict that was just as much America's first civil war as a struggle for independence from a colonial superpower. They fought on all sides, and sometimes against each other, as did the white colonists and the rebels.

Take the Iroquois Confederacy, or Six Nations, who spanned what is now New York State and Canada, made up of the Mohawks, Oneidas, Tuscaroras, Onondagas, Cayugas and Senecas. The Confederacy had been long-standing allies of the British, but when the Revolutionary War broke out they split in two when the Onondagas, Cayugas, Senecas and Mohawks sided with the British while the Tuscarora and the Oneida rallied to the embryonic American flag. Towns in the Mohawk and Susquehanna valleys were attacked by American troops for taking the wrong side.

In March 1779, Washington told Major General Horatio Gates 'to carry the war into the heart of the country of the six nations; to cut off their settlements, destroy their next year's crops, and do them every other mischief of which time and circumstances will permit'. American Colonel Goose Van Schaick raided the Onondaga settlements, destroying their crops and towns, slaughtering their livestock and capturing thirty-three prisoners. At the end of May, Washington wrote to Major General John Sullivan:

> The expedition you are appointed to command is to be directed against the hostile tribes of the six nations of Indians, with their associates and adherents. The immediate objects are the total destruction and devastation of their settlements and the capture of as many prisoners of every age and sex as possible. It will be essential to ruin their crops now in the ground and prevent their planting more.

Washington added that if the natives indicated they wanted peace, they must earn it:

> After you have very thoroughly completed the destruction of their settlements; if the Indians should show a disposition for peace, I would have you to encourage it, on condition that they will give some decisive evidence of their sincerity by delivering up some of the principal instigators of their past hostility into our hands—Butler, Brandt, the most mischievous of the Tories that have joined them or any other they may have in their power that we are interested to get into ours...

Sullivan took those instructions to heart and led an expedition that burnt forty towns and 160,000 bushels of corn and vegetables. Meanwhile, American General Daniel Brodhead and his 600 men attacked the western Iroquois towns, burning and plundering the Seneca and Munsee settlements on the Allegheny River. The tribes fled to Canada to subsist on British charity.

The Iroquois tribes that sided with the Americans, such as the Oneida and Tuscarora in western New York, did not fare much better because they suffered retaliation from the pro-British tribes. As the war raged on, opposing sides of the Iroquois Confederacy began to turn on each other, according to historian Colin Calloway: 'Pro-British warriors burned Oneida crops and houses in revenge; Oneidas retaliated by burning Mohawk homes. The Oneidas themselves split into factions; most supported by the Americas, whereas the Cayugas lent their weight to the crown. The Onondagas struggled to maintain neutrality until American troops burned their towns in 1779. For the Iroquois, the Revolution was a war in which, in some cases literally, brother killed brother.'[35] The Oneida fought in several key battles in the war, including those of Oriskany and Saratoga, and their support was considered a crucial factor in preventing an early American defeat in New York State.

In 1777, the British launched a major offensive from Canada, recruiting and arming Indian war parties to raid American settlements.[36] Large numbers of settlers were killed in present-day Kentucky, West Virginia and Pennsylvania.

The Virginians had attempted to defend their western border with militiamen garrisoned at three forts along the Ohio River, but the belligerent tribes simply bypassed them when raiding. In 1778, the Americans decided that offensive operations were needed. The first was a debacle. In February, General Edward Hand led 500 Pennsylvania militia from Fort Pitt on a surprise winter march towards Mingo towns on the Cuyahoga River where the British stored military supplies to distribute to Indian raiding parties. Appalling weather prevented the expedition from reaching its objective, and on the return march some of Hand's men attacked peaceful Delaware Indians, killing an unarmed man and several women and children, including relatives of the Delaware chief Captain Pipe. The expedition became derisively known as the 'squaw campaign'.[37] While under Hand's command, three men defected to the British and became valuable agents. Hand faced a congressional investigation for allowing them to defect and resigned in May 1778.[38]

Following the escalation of the war, two regiments of the Continental Army were diverted to the tribal side of the Ohio River where, it was hoped, the Americans could mount an expedition against Detroit. As the Americans needed the tacit support of the Delawares, in September 1778 they negotiated the Treaty of Fort Pitt. But Delaware leader White Eyes, having negotiated the treaty, was apparently murdered by American militiamen. His rival, Captain Pipe, who had seen his family slain by incomers, abandoned the American alliance and moved west, where he began receiving support from the British in Detroit.[39]

The Wabanaki Confederacy, an alliance of the Penobscot, Maliseet, Passamaquoddy, Abenaki and Micmac, were reluctant to join the war effort but were dragged in nonetheless. Some 500 were enlisted in the Continental Army after being falsely told that American victory would restore their lost hunting grounds, and they proved useful in spying out British intentions. Others were similarly conned by British promises; 100 principal men of the tribes took an oath of allegiance to King George.[40]

In December 1776, Washington asked the friendly tribes for warriors. The Penobscot and those Passamaquoddy who had not sworn allegiance to the British Crown duly sent 600 men. The following year the Passamaquoddy chief Francis Joseph Neptune fired one of the first shots of the Battle of Machias in Maine, hitting and killing a British officer standing on the deck of the British frigate *Mermaid*. The Massachusetts government continued to provide the Passamaquoddy with supplies and ammunition in recognition of their service. After the war ended in 1783, Neptune worked continuously to prevent white encroachment on Indian lands in Maine. In 1796, he and other tribal leaders secured a land treaty from the Massachusetts government that included a 23,000-acre reservation near Perry, Maine. Some Penobscot served as scouts for Washington's army and Penobscot warriors fought in the American campaign against Quebec in 1775 and the Penobscot Expedition in 1779. In recognition for their service, the Penobscot were later awarded a reservation at Indian Island, Old Town, Maine, around 1798.

The Abenaki in northern New England fought in small engagements for both the British and the Americans, but, according to Calloway,

> ... beneath the surface confusion and ambivalence, all Abenakis at all times shared the goal of preserving their community and keeping the war at arm's length. All they disagreed on was the means to that end. Neutrality was a perilous strategy, more likely to make the village a target than a haven when British and Americans alike adhered to the notion that if Indians were not fighting for you they would fight against you. Many Abenakis opted instead for limited and sometimes equivocal involvement in the conflict. The family band structure of Abenaki society meant that different people could espouse different allegiances without tearing the community apart. Individual participation on both sides, though limited and part of no master strategy, also allowed flexibility as the fortunes of war shifted. The Revolution would not leave the Abenakis alone, but they could divert it into less destructive channels.[41]

In 1777, the British recruited roughly 400 warriors for Burgoyne's campaign, a disaster which only strengthened the Abenaki's majority reluctance to support the British in the war. As a result, the Abenaki became even more divided.

In 1781, Colonel John Allen raised an Abenaki regiment at Machias which harassed British shipping along the Maine coast. Other Abenaki served with the British and raided Maine's Androscoggin valley. After the war ended, only about 1,000 Abenaki remained. With the American victory in the war, more and more white settlers began to encroach on Abenaki land. Eventually, most left the US and settled in Canada. Animosity between the Abenaki and the Americans continued into the nineteenth century, prompting many warriors to fight for the British in the war of 1812.

The 3,000-strong Micmac, who had sided with the French against the British, joined the American rebels after a direct appeal from Washington. Seven tribal leaders were ferried in some luxury to Watertown, Massachusetts, to sign a treaty of lasting friendship.

The Stockbridge Mohican tribe of Western Massachusetts switched from the British to the Americans. Bryan Rindfleisch wrote:

> While such a decision likely involved a multitude of factors, one cannot get past the fact that the Mohican were completely surrounded by a settler community, known for its rabid opposition to the Stamp Act as well as for being a hotbed of activity for the Sons of Liberty. It would take no leap of the imagination to believe that the Mohican felt enormous pressure, if not the threat of intimidation and violence, to join the revolutionary movement. Yet the Stockbridge-Mohican also saw the revolution undoubtedly as an opportunity. If they sided with the American rebels and proved their loyalty, the new nation might respect or honour their attempts to reclaim lost lands and to protect their sovereignty.[42]

Chief Solomon visited Boston and made a speech pledging the loyalty of his tribe.[43] The Stockbridge Mohicans lined up alongside American militiamen along Battle Road and fired upon British soldiers as they marched back to Boston and then joined the militiamen in Cambridge as they besieged the British Army. During the ten-month siege they helped build fortifications, patrolled the outer defences and ambushed British stragglers. They also fought in the Battle of Bunker Hill. A regiment of Stockbridge Mohicans participated in the campaign at Valcour Bay in October 1776 and in the Saratoga campaign in 1777, camped at Valley Forge in the winter of 1777/8 and took part in a campaign against pro-British Iroquois in 1779. But the warriors' families went hungry at home and their calls for aid were rebuffed by the Continental Congress despite pleas on their behalf from George Washington himself. White settlers continued to buy up native land in the Stockbridge area, and by 1783 the Stockbridge Mohicans had lost all of their land.[44] In the 1780s, they moved to New York to escape encroachment by white settlers in Massachusetts and lived alongside the Oneida tribe. When the US government started to buy up the Oneida land, the Mohicans migrated to present-day Wisconsin.

In 1782, 160 Pennsylvania militiamen under Lieutenant Colonel David Williamson rode into Ohio County, incorrectly believing that the Lenape Delaware were responsible for several recent raids. Although the Lenape strongly denied they had been involved, the militia held a council and voted to kill them, although several could not stomach that and left. One of those, Obadiah Holmes, Jr, wrote: 'One Nathan Rollins & brother

[who] had had a father & uncle killed took the lead in murdering the Indians, ... & Nathan Rollins had tomahawked nineteen of the poor Moravians, & after it was over he sat down & cried, & said it was no satisfaction for the loss of his father & uncle after all.'[45] After the Lenape were told of the American militia's vote, they requested time to prepare for death and spent the night praying and singing hymns. The next morning on 8 March, the militia brought the Lenape to two 'killing houses', one for men and the other for women and children. The American militia tied the Indians, stunned them with mallet blows to the head, and killed them with fatal scalping cuts. In all, the militia murdered and scalped twenty-eight men, twenty-nine women and thirty-nine children. Two Indian boys, one of whom had been scalped, survived to tell of what became known as the Gnadenhutten Massacre. The militia piled the bodies in the mission buildings and burned the village after looting it of plunder which needed eighty horses to carry. After the American victory in the Revolutionary War, the Delaware were forced to surrender most of their Ohio lands with the Treaty of Greenville in 1795.

The Wyandot (Huron), a tribe in the Great Lakes region, sided with the British during the war. In May 1782 Colonel William Crawford of the Continental Army came out of retirement to lead 480 Pennsylvania militia deep into Indian territory. Their opponents heard about the planned surprise attack and took about 440 men to the Sandusky River to halt the expedition. After a day of indecisive fighting, the Americans were surrounded and their retreat turned into a bloody rout. About seventy Americans were killed; Indian and British losses were minimal. Colonel Crawford and an unknown number of his men were captured. The Indians executed many of the captives in retaliation for the Gnadenhutten Massacre. Crawford was tortured for at least two hours before being burned at the stake.

The failure of the Crawford expedition caused alarm along the frontier, as many Americans feared that the Indians would be emboldened by their victory.[46] On 13 July 1782, the Mingo leader Guyasuta led about 100 Indians and several British volunteers into Pennsylvania, destroying Hannastown, killing nine settlers and capturing twelve. It was the hardest blow dealt by Indians in Western Pennsylvania during the war.[47] As a result, 1782 became known as the 'Bloody Year'.

In Kentucky, Colonel Benjamin Logan, commanding officer of the region, learned that the Wyandot warriors were on warpath. Aided by the British in Detroit, they had raided from Boonsborough past Estill's Station along the Kentucky River. Logan dispatched fifteen men to Estill's Station with orders to reconnoitre the country to the north and east. Estill reached the Kentucky River a few miles below the mouth of Station Camp Creek and camped that night at Sweet Lick. After they left, a war party attacked the Estill's Station fort at dawn, scalped and killed fourteen-year-old Jennie Glass and a Miss Innes; captured Monk, Captain Estill's slave; and killed all the cattle. Under interrogation, the courageous slave persuaded the Wyandots that the garrison was at full strength and impregnable. The warriors decided to retire. Two boys were sent from the fort to catch up to Estill with the news of the atrocity. Of the men with him, half had left families within the fort. They returned with the boys, while the remainder crossed the Kentucky River and found the Indian trail. Estill was forced to leave behind ten more men whose horses were too tired to continue. Finding fresh tracks, Estill and the twenty-five remaining men soon overtook the Wyandots at Little Mountain Creek.[48]

On the night of 22 March 1782, Estill and his militiamen fought a pitched battle for nearly two hours. The Wyandot leader, Sourhoowah, was reportedly shot by the first volley and urged his men to continue fighting as he lay dying. Firing at each other across the creek, both sides suffered heavy casualties. When the Wyandots began fording Little River Creek, Estill divided his forces into three groups. Estill took the right flank, the left being given to Lieutenant William Miller, while another officer held the centre. Miller was ordered to flank the rear of the Wyandots from the left. As he prepared to lead his men into battle, a musket ball apparently hit his rifle, knocking the flint from the jaws of the lock. Miller allegedly shouted that 'it was foolhardy to stay and be shot down', and he fled the scene with his men following him. With Estill's left flank now open and the creek defended by only four men, the Wyandots easily rushed in. Estill had already been wounded three times. As he attempted to escape with his remaining men, he was killed in hand-to-hand combat by a pursuing Wyandot warrior. Militiaman Joseph Proctor shot the warrior dead with his rifle.[49] Only a handful of men were left on each side, and the battle ended with the Kentuckians withdrawing from the field. The slave Monk, who had escaped during the battle, reported that seventeen Wyandots had been killed and two more wounded. William Miller became the scapegoat for both the Kentuckians' defeat and the death of Captain Estill. One of the survivors, David Cook, reportedly threatened his life twenty years after the battle. Monk won particular distinction for bravery during the battle and carried a wounded militiaman, James Berry, almost 25 miles back to Estill's Station. He was granted his freedom soon afterwards, the first slave to be freed in Kentucky.[50]

The 15,000-strong Choctaw, who inhabited about fifty villages in a key strategic position of the lower Mississippi, also sided with the British. In February 1778, Captain James Willing led an expedition down the river attacking British settlements. The British responded by organising a band of 155 Choctaw warriors to march to Natchez. The Americans had retreated by the time the Choctaw reached the settlement. After Spain declared war on Britain, hundreds of Choctaw warriors helped the British defend Mobile in 1780 and Pensacola in 1780–81.

The Cherokee, with a population of about 8,500, who lived in the interior hill country of the Carolinas and Georgia, also sided with the

British. In the spring of 1776, young warriors led by Chief Dragging Canoe launched attacks on the Carolinas and Georgia in retaliation for illegal encroachments on their lands; these warriors increasingly distrusted their elders' ability to prevent further land loss. In response, the colonial governments of Virginia, North Carolina, South Carolina and Georgia organised retaliatory expeditions. In August, American Colonel Andrew Williamson, with 1,800 troops and some Catawba scouts, marched to north-western South Carolina, burning Cherokee villages along the way. The following month, American General Griffith Rutherford attacked the Cherokee Middle settlements from North Carolina and destroyed thirty-six towns, along with livestock and cornfields, while Williamson attacked the Lower towns with his soldiers.

The two generals then joined forces and spent two weeks attacking and destroying the Cherokee Middle settlements while American Colonel William Christian and his 2,000 Virginia and North Carolina militiamen invaded the Cherokee Overhill towns, destroying their crops, apple trees, houses and food supplies.

The older Cherokee chiefs began pushing for peace, while Dragging Canoe and hundreds of like-minded followers moved south and west to establish new villages on Chickamauga Creek. Those settlements 'became the core of the Cherokee resistance, attracting warriors from other towns and supporting the war effort of the Shawnees and their northern allies. Other Cherokees suffered as a result of Chickamauga resistance, some helped the Americans, and the Revolution became a Cherokee civil war.'[51]

The American troops continued their attacks on Cherokee towns. In April 1779, American Colonel Ethan Shelby invaded Chickamauga Cherokee country. According to Thomas Jefferson, he inflicted catastrophic damage by 'killing about a half dozen men, burning 11 towns, 20,000 bushels of corn ... and taking as many goods as sold for twenty-five thousand pounds'. In the summer of 1779, British agent Alexander Cameron planned to raise a Cherokee force as soon as the crops were harvested but, in the meantime, American Brigadier General Andrew Williamson and 700 cavalrymen invaded, burned down their houses and cut down their corn. In December 1780, American Colonel Arthur Campbell, who as a fifteen-year-old Virginia militiaman had been captured and tortured by a war party, burned about 1,000 houses and 50,000 bushels of corn belonging to the Overhill Cherokee.

In 1781, Lieutenant Colonel John Sevier of the North Carolina militia, the son of a tavern keeper and future first governor of Tennessee, destroyed fifteen Middle Cherokee towns and, the following autumn and summer, destroyed new Lower Cherokee towns on the Coosa River. According to the mid-nineteenth-century historian J. G. M. Ramsey, Sevier led around 100 men who camped by Long Creek and sent out a scouting party:

On ascending a slight hill, they found themselves within forty yards of a large Indian force, before they discovered it. They fired from their horses and retreated to Sevier's camp. The Indians also fired, but without effect. Sevier prepared his command to receive a night attack. Before day, Captain Priuett reinforced him after a rapid march, with about seventy men. Thus reinforced, Sevier next morning pursued his march, expecting every minute to meet the enemy. When they came to the point at which the spies had met and fired upon the Indians, they found traces of a large body of them. They had, in their hasty retreat, left one warrior who had been killed the evening before by the spies. The pursuit was continued vigorously by the troops, who crossed French Broad at the Big Island and encamped on Boyd's Creek. The next day, early in the morning, the advance guard under the command of Captain Stinson continued the march, and at the distance of three miles found the encampment of the enemy and their fires still burning. A reinforcement was immediately ordered to the front, and the guard was directed if it came up with the Indians to fire upon them and retreat, and thus draw them on. Three-quarters of a mile from their camp, the enemy fired upon the advance from an ambuscade. It returned the fire and retreated, and, as had been anticipated, was pursued by the enemy till it joined the main body. This was formed into three divisions: the centre commanded by Col. John Sevier, the right wing by Major Jesse Walton, and the left by Major Jonathan Tipton. Orders were given that as soon as the enemy should approach the front, the right wing should wheel to the left, and the left wing to the right, and thus enclose them. In this order were the troops arranged when they met the Indians at Cedar Spring, who rushed forward after the guard with great rapidity, till checked by the opposition of the main body. Major Walton with the right wing wheeled briskly to the left, and performed the order which he was to execute with precise accuracy. But the left wing moved to the right with less celerity, and when the centre fired upon the Indians, doing immense execution, the latter retreated through the unoccupied space left open between the extremities of the right and left wings, and running into a swamp, escaped the destruction which otherwise seemed ready to involve them. The victory was decisive. The loss of the enemy amounted to twenty-eight killed on the ground and very many wounded, who got off without being taken. On the side of Sevier's troops not a man was even wounded. The victorious little army then returned to the Big Island—afterwards called Sevier's Island—and waited there the arrival of reinforcements that promised to follow. This prompt collection of troops, and rapid expedition of Sevier, saved the frontier from a bloody invasion. Had he been tardier, the Indians would have reached the settlements, scattered themselves along the extended border, driven them into stations, or perhaps massacred them in their cabins and fields. Their force was understood to be large and to be well armed.[52]

Another account of the battle said:

> The Indians had formed in a half-moon and lay concealed in the grass. Had their stratagem not been discovered, their position, and the shape of the ground, would have enabled them to enclose and overcome the horsemen. Lieutenant Lane and John Ward had dismounted for the fight, when Sevier, having noticed the semi-circular position of the Indians, ordered a halt, with the purpose of engaging the two extremes of the Indian line, and keeping up the action until the other part of his troops could come up. Lane and his comrade, Ward, remounted, and fell back upon Sevier without being hurt, though fired at by several warriors near them. A brisk fire was, for a short time, kept up by Sevier's party and the nearest Indians. The troops behind, hearing the first fire, had quickened their pace and were coming in sight. James Roddy, with about twenty men, quickly came up, and soon after the main body of the troops. The Indians noticed this reinforcement and closed their lines. Sevier immediately ordered the charge, which would have been still more fatal, but that the pursuit led through a swampy branch, which impeded the progress of the horsemen. In the charge, Sevier was in close pursuit of a warrior who, finding that he would be overtaken, turned and fired at him. The bullet cut the hair of his temple without doing further injury. Sevier then spurred his horse forward and attempted to kill the Indian with his sword, having emptied his pistols in the first moment of the charge. The warrior parried the licks from the sword with his empty gun. The conflict was becoming doubtful between the two combatants thus engaged, when one of the soldiers, rather ungallantly, came up, shot the warrior, and decided the combat in favour of his commander. The horse of Adam Sherrill threw his rider, and, in the fall, some of his ribs were broken. An Indian sprang upon him with his tomahawk drawn. When in the act of striking a ball from a comrade's rifle brought him to the ground, and Sherrill escaped. After a short pursuit, the Indians dispersed into the adjoining highlands and knolls, where the cavalry could not pursue them. Of the whites not one was killed, but three seriously wounded. This battle of Boyd's Creek has always been considered as one of the best fought battles in the border war of Tennessee.[53]

The Cherokee's price for taking the British side in the war was summed up by a headman: 'To the madmen of Virginia I have lost in different engagements six hundred warriors, my towns have been thrice destroyed and my corn fields laid waste by the enemy.'[54] It did not matter much what side the tribes took during the creation of the fledgling American nation. The drive west from the original colonies proved unstoppable. For the Native Americans there was worse to come.

2

Little Turtle's War (1785–1795)

We are involved in actual war!

The costliest rout of the US army by Native Americans up to 1791, in which 180 men were either killed or wounded, was called 'Harmar's Defeat' by the Americans. To the Indians it became known as the 'Battle of the Pumpkin Fields' because the steam from the scalped skulls reminded the Indians of squash steaming in the autumn air. It was followed by another engagement in which the US death rate, never surpassed, was more than three times higher than of the far more famous Battle of the Little Bighorn eighty-five years later.

Little Turtle's War, also known as the Ohio War and the Northwest Indian War, was an extension of the frontier wars detailed in the previous chapter and in many respects a brutal consequence of the American victory in the Revolutionary War.

As seen before, the Natives benefited from charismatic and brave leaders, the Americans from numbers and the irresistible tides of change.

* * *

The Miami, a tribe in the Great Lakes region, had sided with the British during the Revolutionary War. In late October 1780, French cavalry officer Augustin Mottin de LeBalme, who was aiding the Americans in the war, raided the Miami village of Kekionga. After LeBalme plundered the area for twelve days, on 5 November 1780, Chief Little Turtle attacked the force and killed LeBalme and thirty of his soldiers. The victory brought an end to the campaign and established Little Turtle's reputation as a war leader.[1]

Little Turtle, born with the name of Mihšihkinaahkwa around 1747, was one of the most famous Indian military leaders of his time. As an infant he lived in the Miami village of Pickawillany, Indiana.[2] Few details of his early life are certain, but he lived at Turtletown, along the Eel River, until 1780.[3] He was nearly 6 feet tall, treated drunkenness with contempt and had a serious demeanour despite a fondness for silver earrings and ornamentation.[4] Although he was war chief of the leading division of the tribe, Little Turtle was never the head chief of the Miami, which was a hereditary position.[5] Through the 1780s, Little Turtle continued to lead raids against colonial American settlements in Kentucky.

In the 1783 Treaty of Paris, which gave an uneasy close to the Revolutionary War, Britain ceded 'control' of the Northwest Territory but kept forts at strategic points and supported 45,000 Indian allies resisting settler encroachments. A Huron-led Western confederacy gathered at Fort Detroit in 1785 declared that lands north and west of the Ohio River were Indian territory. The confederacy was a loose association of primarily Algonquin-speaking tribes in the Great Lakes area. The Wyandot were the administrators while the Shawnee and Miami chiefly provided the fighters. Other tribes involved included the Delaware, Cherokee, Chippewa, Ottawa, Potawatomi, Kickapoo, Kaskaskia and Wabash Confederacy. Few tribes deployed as single units but allowed individual chiefs and warriors to act as they saw fit. Some Choctaw and Chickasaw tribes, traditional enemies of the confederacy, served as US scouts. The tribes were never wholly unified, and for that they would pay dearly.

British agents sold weapons and ammunition to the Indians and encouraged attacks on American settlers. Upper Canada Lieutenant Governor John Simcoe, a Revolutionary War veteran, aristocrat, legal reformer and opponent of slavery, aimed to use the tribes to create a neutral barrier between the US and his domain. Tensions increased when Chickasaw and Choctaw scouts for the US shot a number of Chippewa and Ottawa in the back at Fort Recovery and escaped without being identified, increasing distrust between the various nations within the confederacy.[6]

During the mid- and late 1780s, American settlers south of the Ohio River in Kentucky and travellers on and north of the Ohio River suffered badly, although reports of up to 1,500 casualties were a gross exaggeration by advocates of military intervention. Settlers retaliated with attacks on Indians deemed to be relatively defenceless. General Benjamin Logan led a force of Federal soldiers and mounted Kentucky militia against several Shawnee towns along the Mad River while the warriors were raiding forts elsewhere. Logan burned the settlements and food supplies, and killed or captured numerous natives, including their chief Moluntha, who was murdered by one of Logan's men. Logan's raid and the execution of the chief embittered the Shawnees, who retaliated by escalating their attacks on American settlers. Tit-for-tat atrocities were the norm.

In 1790, President George Washington and Secretary of War Henry Knox ordered General Josiah Harmar to launch a major western offensive into the Shawnee and Miami country. The Quaker-educated Harmar, a veteran of the American invasion of Canada and of Valley Forge, had thought his military days were over when the Revolutionary War concluded. But he ran up huge debts due to his lavish lifestyle while an envoy to the Versailles court of the doomed French king Louis XVI and his queen, Marie Antoinette, and was forced back into uniform. He may have fared better in other employment. Harmar was a martinet much influenced by Baron Friedrich von Steuben's *Regulations for the Order and Discipline of the Troops of the United States*, better known as the Blue Book, for the Prussian-style training of American troops.[7] The American historian William Guthman noted:

> Steuben's manual was aimed at combatting British and Hessian forces – not the backwoods guerrilla fighting of the highly skilled American Indian warriors the regiment would eventually fight. Shortsightedness on the part of the military was the reason that no preparatory training in guerrilla warfare was ever imposed on the Army ... no federal unit under Harmar or St Clair was ever instructed in the frontiersmen's method of war.

Harmar doggedly insisted on Prussian-style training designed for the clash of regular forces in Central Europe, not the frontier style of irregular warfare in the forests of the Old Northwest.

In October, Harmar's force was assembled near present-day Fort Wayne, Indiana. The primary objective of the campaign was the destruction of the main Miami village of Kekionga, where two streams join to form the Maumee River. The British at Fort Detroit were assured that the expedition was only against Indian tribes supposedly led by the famous warrior Little Turtle.[8] Harmar gathered 320 regulars of the First American Regiment and 1,133 militia from Kentucky and Pennsylvania with three horse-drawn 6-pounder cannon. From a distance it was impressive but it contained only a handful of experienced frontiersmen; the majority were recent untrained immigrants paid to take the place of established settlers. Lieutenant Ebenezer Denny wrote that the militia 'appear to be raw and unused to the gun or the woods'. There was no time for training because the campaign had to start before winter as the packhorses would starve when grass became scarce.

The punitive expedition was launched from Fort Washington on 7 October 1790 north along the Great Miami River, and a week later they had marched to within 25 miles of Kekionga. Kentuckian scouts captured a Shawnee, subjected him to 'intense' questioning, and were told that the Miami and Shawnee were gathering at Kekionga to meet Harmar's army. Before dawn on 15 October, Harmar dispatched 600 men under Colonel John Hardin north on a forced march to 'surprise' the Indians. Hardin, the son of a bar owner, was a seasoned veteran. He had been shot in the groin during action in Lord Dunmore's War – the musket ball remained lodged in his body for the rest of his life – and he had been a noted marksman during the Battle of Saratoga. When his detachment reached Kekionga, they found the village abandoned, burned it, and camped south of the smoking ruins. Meanwhile, Harmar reached other Miami villages and also found them abandoned – Little Turtle's scouts had reported pretty much every twist and turn of Harmar's approach, together with his inclination towards drunkenness.[9] British-affiliated traders among the Miami fled to Fort Detroit with their families and goods after first distributing arms and ammunition to the warriors.

On 19 October Harmar sent out a scouting party under Colonel Hardin consisting of 180 militia, a troop of cavalry under Major James Fontaine, and thirty regulars under Captain John Armstrong,[10] to estimate the strength of the Indians and attack the minor village of Chief Le Gris.[11] The party came within a few miles of Kekionga, where they spotted a warrior on horseback, who fled along a narrow trail. Hardin, who should have known better, ordered his force to pursue, but sent Major Fontaine's cavalry back to bring up a company that had been left behind. The warrior was a decoy and led Hardin into a swampy lowland by the Eel River. Little Turtle personally led the attack on Hardin's force, which came under fire from three sides. Most of the militia fled, warning Major Fontaine's cavalry to get out. The regulars stood their ground with some of the militia. Only eight of the thirty regulars survived; forty militia were killed,[12] and twelve Americans were wounded.[13] Captain Armstrong hid in the marsh and escaped. Sensitive to suspicions of his own cowardice, he blamed Hardin and the militia for the defeat, and claimed that only about 100 Indians had been involved, roughly the number of warriors available from Kekionga and Le Gris' village.[14]

The following day, General Harmar arrived at the camp outside Kekionga and sent 300 men under Ensign Phillip Hartshorn northward to scout for Indian movements. Some 8 miles above Kekionga, Hartshorn was ambushed by a large Indian force, which killed him and nineteen of his men. Harmar pulled back several miles south, failing even to send a burial detail to bury the dead. The experienced men were enraged at the cowardice of their commander, and morale plummeted. Hardin demanded that he be allowed to attack the Indians, or at the very least bury their fallen comrades.

On the night of 21 October, Hardin advanced with 300 militia and sixty regulars under regimental commander Major John P. Wyllys. At dawn they found an encampment of about 1,000 natives. Hardin immediately sent a runner requesting reinforcements. When the courier told Harmar, who was rumoured to have been drunk, about the strength of the enemy force, he became visibly shaken and possibly panicky. He ordered his 800–900 remaining men into a hollow defensive square and refused to go to Hardin's aid. Not fully aware of this, Hardin divided his command into four groups under Majors Wyllys, Hall, Fontaine and McMullen, planning to surround the enemy even though he was outnumbered at least two to one. Little Turtle attacked first, sending small parties to fire and retreat. The militia gave chase, leaving the regulars. Little Turtle then attacked Major Wyllys's detachment, with devastating results. Major Fontaine led a cavalry charge into a wooded area and was promptly ambushed. Little Turtle, emulating both Hardin's original, hoped-for tactics and those of military geniuses throughout history, attacked Hardin from three sides. Hardin's men put up a ferocious defence and held them back for over three hours before finally falling back to join the rest of the army

The army forces reported 129 men killed in action – fourteen officers, including Major Wyllys and Major Fontaine, and 115 enlisted men – and ninety-four wounded, including fifty of the regulars.[15] White estimates of Indian casualties ranged around 120 but that is likely to have been a gross exaggeration. Sober or not, after suffering such high casualties, Harmar decided that the approaching winter further threatened his command, as militia deserted and horses starved. He ordered a retreat and the force got back to Fort Washington on 3 November 1790.

It was the worst defeat of US forces by Indians up to that time,[16] but a court martial later cleared Harmar of any wrongdoing during the campaign. The battle established Little Turtle as a resistance hero and encouraged his compatriots across the Northwest Territory to fight back with even more vigour by attacking more white settlements. The results were mixed.[17]

The land-greedy Ohio Company of Associates, which had encouraged settlement of Marietta, in 1790 ignored the uproar on the frontier and sent thirty-six of its members to settle 'Big Bottom', a large area of level land on the east side of the Muskingum River. The settlers foolishly built no blockhouse or stockade and failed even to post sentries. On 2 January 1791, a war party of twenty-five Delaware and Wyandot men attacked, killing nine men, one woman and two children.[18] At least one captive, the son of an officer, later died.[19]

Exactly a week later, Dunlap's Station on the east bank of the Great Miami River was also attacked. Established in early 1790 to boost New Jersey-based land speculation, its settlers cleared the land, built three defensive blockhouses, and even shared a Christmas feast with neighbouring Shawnee. Ten settlers' cabins faced together, linked by 8-foot log pickets, and brush and trees had been cleared to provide a line of fire. But the confederated Indians believed that the militia were not up to defending the 1-acre site and authorised a raid under the 'white Indian' Simon Girty. Of Irish decent, Girty had been taken captive in Pennsylvania and became fully assimilated in Native American culture. He raided with his 'brothers', battled against white encroachment, and was an interpreter for the Six Nations.

Two days before the main onslaught, four civilian and military surveyors not from Dunlap's Station were surprised by Girty's scouts; one was killed and scalped, one captured and another wounded. The survivors made it to temporary safety.

Settlers and soldiers under the command of Lieutenant Jacob Kingsbury gathered in the blockhouses to prepare for the assault. Kingsbury was a career officer who had enlisted in the Continental Army, aged nineteen, at the siege of Boston. Although he had just twelve soldiers under his command, his experience would prove invaluable. Inside the blockhouses, women melted spoons to make musket balls. One participant later recalled: 'This night it rained, froze, and snow fell from four to five inches deep...' For the defenders the snow proved a life saver as Girty had planned an attack with blazing arrows and torches.

Girty's warriors openly approached the station and demanded surrender using their captive, Abner Hunt, as an interpreter. While the hour-long parlay was being conducted on the east side of the fort, gunfire was heard on the opposite side. That was kept up for two hours until the attackers pulled back to butcher their cattle and settle in for a siege.[20] The captive Hunt was killed under disputed circumstances. Kingsbury later reported to Harmar that he had been murdered in cold blood, and there were subsequent and probably accurate claims that he had died under torture. Fighting resumed the next day, 11 January, at the break of dawn but the Indians lacked siege weapons. They swiftly withdrew that morning, two hours before a relief force from Fort Washington arrived.

The 'siege of Dunlap's Station' was, at most, a small sideshow in the war, but the apparent torture of a surveyor by Indians led by a 'white traitor' was seized on by the press, helped by Kingsbury's glorification of his leadership. One newspaper reported: 'The lieutenant answered, that if they were three hundred devils, he would not surrender; and immediately fired on the Indians, twelve of whom were killed. The remainder, after having quartered Mr. Hunt, in the view of the fort, made a rapid retreat: none of the garrison were either killed or wounded.'[21] The station was later twice abandoned as being too vulnerable.

In August 1791, Little Turtle's daughter was among the women and children who were captured in a raid on a Miami village. It was led by the disreputable militia commander James Wilkinson, who, after his death, was exposed as being a well-paid Spanish spy. According to Theodore Roosevelt, 'In all our history, there is no more despicable character.'[22] Little Turtle made it a priority to rescue his daughter from Wilkinson's clutches.

President Washington had been furious at Harmar's defeat and lamented that 'my mind ... is prepared for the worst; that is, for expense without honor or profit'. He persuaded Congress to raise a second regiment of regular soldiers for six months, but due to pay cuts the First Regiment was soon reduced to 299 soldiers, while the new Second Regiment recruited only half of their authorised number. The militia would again be needed to boost the regulars, which would lead to an even bigger disaster than Harmar's expedition.[23]

In March 1791, Arthur St Clair succeeded Harmar as commander of the US Army and was commissioned as a major general. The scion of Scots merchants, St Clair served in the British Army during the French and Indian War and was with James Wolfe at the capture of Quebec. After that war he settled in Pennsylvania, where he made a fortune from land purchases and mill building. By the outbreak of the Revolutionary War he was too invested in his new land to take the side of his old compatriots. He accepted a commission in the 3rd Pennsylvania Regiment, saw much action as he rose through the upper echelons, and was with Washington when he crossed the Delaware. In April 1777, St Clair was sent to defend Fort Ticonderoga, which he relinquished to the British without much of a fight. A court martial exonerated him over the fort's loss, and he returned to duty as aide-de-camp to General Washington who, for unknown reasons, retained a high opinion of him. St Clair was at Yorktown when Lord Cornwallis surrendered his British troops. Post-war, he was appointed governor of the Northwest Territory where he aimed to clear the way for white settlement. His return to military command gave him the chance to do just that.

Washington urged St Clair to move north in the summer months, but the new military commander suffered many of the same handicaps as his predecessor, Harmar. Recruits were poorly trained, the food was substandard and the meagre supply of horses were of poor quality. As a result, the expedition failed to set out until October 1791. Again, its objective was Kekionga, the capital of the Miami. St Clair's army originally included 600 regulars, 800 six-month conscripts, and 600 militia.[24] This was its peak, but by the time the force finally got underway desertion had whittled down the total to about 1,480 men plus between 250 and 300 camp followers – wives, children, laundresses and prostitutes. Building supply posts along the way, progress was painfully slow. St Clair suffered agonies from gout and seemed incapable of maintaining discipline and order among the militia and new recruits. Indians constantly shadowed the column, stealing supplies and picking off a few stragglers.

By the start of November, through desertion and illness, St Clair's force had been further reduced to around 1,120, including the camp followers. He had fifty-two officers and 868 enlisted men and militia present for duty on 3 November. The force camped on an elevated meadow but did not construct any defensive works. While St Clair's army lost soldiers daily, the Western Confederacy grew stronger. An extra 480 warriors joined the 700 led by Little Turtle and the Shawnee war leader Blue Jacket.

On the evening of 3 November, St Clair's force established a camp on a high hill near the present-day location of Fort Recovery, close to the headwaters of the Wabash River, but did not construct any defensive works or send out reconnaissance patrols. Little Turtle and Blue Jacket, with their 1,000-plus men, waited in the nearby woods until dawn, when the whites in the camp stacked their weapons and paraded to their morning meals.[25] Little Turtle directed the first attack at the militia, who fled across a stream without their weapons. The regulars immediately formed battle lines and fired a volley into the warriors, forcing them back. Little Turtle responded by flanking them and closing in. Meanwhile, St Clair's artillery was stationed on a nearby bluff and was wheeling into position when the gun crews were killed by native sharpshooters, and the survivors were forced to spike their guns. Colonel William Darke ordered his battalion to fix bayonets and charge the main native position. Little Turtle's forces retreated to the woods, only to encircle Darke's battalion and destroy it. The Indians again charged the main line, which held with musketry and bayonets. St Clair himself led the regulars in a bayonet charge and had two horses shot out from under him. He received several bullet holes in his clothing and had a lock of hair shot away.[26] Major General Richard Butler, who was in command of the levy regiments, was shot twice and died in his tent. The battle raged on. Women camp followers fought desperately for their lives alongside the men. The US forces disintegrated – the barely trained recruits panicked and were slaughtered in what became known as St Clair's Defeat.

After three hours of fighting, St Clair called together the remaining officers and, faced with total annihilation, decided to attempt one last bayonet charge to get through the native line and escape. Supplies and wounded were left in camp as the terrified survivors broke through and ran for Fort Jefferson.[27] St Clair later admitted to the Secretary of War that it was not an orderly retreat, saying, 'It was, in fact, a flight.' They were pursued by Indians for about 3 miles before the latter broke off pursuit and returned to loot the camp. Exact numbers of wounded Americans and camp followers butchered in the camp are not known, but execution fires were said to be burning for several days afterwards.

The casualty rate was the highest percentage ever suffered by a US Army unit before or since – 97.4 per cent killed or wounded among the soldiers – and included St Clair's second in command. Of the fifty-two officers engaged, thirty-nine were killed and seven wounded; around 88 per cent of all officers became casualties. Overall, 632 out of 920 soldiers were killed and 264 wounded; only twenty-four came out unscathed. Nearly all of the 200 camp followers were slaughtered, making a total of 832 Americans killed. Around a quarter of the entire US Army had been wiped out in two hours. Native casualties were put at around sixty, with at least twenty-one killed.

Traditional accounts of the battle give most of the credit for the victory to Little Turtle, but Blue Jacket played at least an equal part in terms of bravery and leadership. The confederacy celebrated their triumph and brandished their bloody war trophies, but the majority of the force returned to their homes as that year's harvest had been poor and the warriors needed to hunt for winter provisions. A grand council was held on the banks of the Ottawa River to determine whether to continue the war against the US or negotiate a peace from a strong position, but a decision was deferred to the following year.[28]

Fort Jefferson did not have adequate supplies for the remnants of St Clair's force, so those who could travel continued their retreat. Many wounded were left behind with no medicine and little food. From Fort Washington, St Clair sent a supply convoy and 100 soldiers under Major David Zeigler back to Fort Jefferson; they found 116 survivors eating 'horse flesh and green hides'.[29] The self-serving Lieutenant Colonel James Wilkinson assumed command of the Second Regiment in January 1792 and led another convoy to Fort Jefferson, charged with burying the dead and collecting missing cannon. That task proved beyond Wilkinson, however, with 'upwards of six hundred bodies' at the battle site and at least seventy-eight bodies along the road.[30]

As with Harmar's Defeat, President Washington was outraged when he received news of the St Clair debacle. He wrote: 'We are involved in actual war!' Leaving Wilkinson in charge of Fort Washington, St Clair reached Philadelphia in January 1792 to report in person.[31] He blamed Quartermaster General Samuel Hodgdon and the War Department for the disaster and asked for a court martial in order to clear his name. Washington refused and insisted on St Clair's immediate resignation. St Clair obliged but with personal safeguards which remain shadowy.

The House of Representatives launched its own probe into the disaster, the very first Congressional Special Committee investigation, and for the first time the new United States brought together all Department heads. But the inquiry also established the principle of executive privilege in which the president could veto the release of any embarrassing papers that the public good required them to keep secret – a cover-up, in other words. The final committee report predictably took St Clair's side, finding that Hodgdon and other War Department officials had done a poor job of raising, equipping and supplying St Clair's expedition. The self-deluded St Clair expressed disappointment that his reputation was not officially cleared.

St Clair continued to serve as Governor of the Northwest Territory but fell out with Thomas Jefferson's administration over his ambitions to turn the territory into two federalist states. He was criticised for partisanship, high-handedness, and arrogance in office. He was blocked from any part in the creation of Ohio in 1803. St Clair's legacy was that the first Ohio Constitution ensured a weak governor and a strong legislature in reaction to his behaviour. He died in poverty in Greensburg in 1818, aged eighty-one.

Meanwhile, Washington urged Congress to raise an army capable of conducting a successful offensive against the American Indian Confederacy, which it did in March 1792 – establishing the Legion of the United States with three-year enlistments and increased pay. It was the beginning of a truly professional American army. Congress also passed two Militia Acts, which first empowered the president to call out the state militias at his own behest and ensure that every free able-bodied white male citizen between the ages of eighteen and forty-five enrolled in the militia of the state in which they resided. There was to be no repeat of the practice by which citizens could pay untrained new immigrants to take their place on a potential battlefield. Washington was determined to crush the Indian Confederacy, which had, so far, blocked US expansion. He was helped by the British decision to reach an agreement on disputed territories and withdraw support from their former Indian allies because of the threat posed by Revolutionary France.

James Wilkinson, America's most trusted traitor, got to work building Fort St Clair to improve communications between Fort Hamilton and Fort Jefferson and maintain supply lines.[32] The three forts were garrisoned with fewer than 150 men each, including sick and injured soldiers as well as servants.[33] On 11 June 1792, a force of about fifteen Shawnee and Delaware attacked the northernmost outpost, Fort Jefferson, while the detachment there was cutting hay – four soldiers were killed and fifteen were captured; eleven of the captives, including the sergeant in charge, were later killed, and the four remaining soldiers were sent to a Chippewa village.

That summer, two of Washington's emissaries were killed on peace missions in Shelby County and Ottawa, Ohio, after being mistaken for spies. In late September, several soldiers were killed while guarding cattle at Fort Jefferson.

The tribal Grand Council continued to insist that the Ohio River must remain the boundary of the United States and that the forts in the Ohio Country must be destroyed.[34] Their conditions were received with widespread indignation, but Henry Knox agreed to send treaty commissioners to the proposed peace council and suspend all offensive operations until that time. The council was delayed until late July, and by then Confederacy divisions were clear. The Shawnee and Delaware insisted that the US recognise the 1768 Fort Stanwix Treaty between the Six Nations and Britain, which had set the Ohio River as a boundary. A dissenting faction led by Joseph Brant countered that the Six Nations had nothing to gain from this demand. The US commissioners argued that it would be too expensive to move white settlers who had already established homesteads north of the Ohio River. In August, the Council, without the Six Nations, proposed that the US relocate white settlers using the money that would have been used to buy Ohio lands.[35] The council ended in disarray on all sides. And in September 1793, news arrived at Fort Jefferson that a force of over 1,500 warriors was ready to attack it.[36]

Early in November 1792, in line with the Grand Council decision, Little Turtle led a force of 200 Miami and Shawnee past Fort Jefferson and Fort St Clair and reached Fort Hamilton in time to attack nearby settlements on the anniversary of St Clair's Defeat. They captured two prisoners and learned that a large convoy of packhorses had left for Fort Jefferson. Little Turtle found the convoy, nearly 100 horses and 100 Kentucky militia camped just outside Fort St Clair.[37] The Indians attacked at dawn, just as outlying sentries were recalled. The militia conducted an organised retreat to the fort, losing six killed and four missing, while another five were wounded.[38] Little Turtle's force lost two warriors but captured the camp and all provisions. Wilkinson considered that the loss of the horses made the forts undefendable.[39]

After the previous year's disaster, Washington and Secretary of War Henry Knox examined several candidates to lead the new Legion of the United States. They rejected Wilkinson because of early suspicions of nefarious dealings, and it soon became clear there was only one obvious choice: 'Mad' Anthony Wayne. A former tanner and surveyor, Wayne had helped raise a Pennsylvania militia unit in 1775. During the Revolutionary War, his military exploits and fiery personality quickly earned him his nickname and promotion to brigadier general. He and his 4th Pennsylvania Regiment were part of the Continental Army's unsuccessful invasion of Canada, during which he commanded a successful rearguard action at the Battle of Ticonderoga. Washington put Wayne in charge of the Corps of Light Infantry, a temporary unit of four regiments of light infantry companies drawn from all the regiments in the main army. His successful attack on British positions in the Battle of Stony Point was the highlight of his Revolutionary War service.[40]

Unlike his predecessors, Wayne was given significant time to train the soldiers under his command and put his personal stamp on the army. For nearly two years, American delegates attempted to negotiate with the Indians, all to no avail. Originally, Wayne began training the Legion at Fort Fayette, near the frontier town of Pittsburgh. That town, however, thrived on vice – Wayne called it 'a frontier Gomorrah' – and he moved his troops 22 miles down the Ohio to a site he named Legionville. There he put in place a rigorous training programme for the Legion, instilling discipline in his inexperienced troops. Secretary Knox had stated that 'another conflict with raw recruits is to be avoided by all means'. Wayne needed little encouragement. He immediately provided all his officers down to company level with copies of Von Steuben's Blue Book drill manual and instructed them to use it until the Legion was familiar with close-order drill, which hopefully would prevent the troops from breaking and running on the battlefield. Their muskets and bayonets became extensions of themselves. He instructed the men on the art of field fortifications; the troops learned to build redoubts and abatis to protect their encampments. Wayne stressed the importance of individual marksmanship, something that the army had neglected because of the high cost of powder. To increase *esprit de corps*, Wayne gave each sub-legion distinctive colours for cap ornaments and uniform facings: white for the First Sub-legion, red for the Second, yellow for the Third and green for the Fourth. With the Legion trained, Wayne floated his forces down the Ohio to Cincinnati and Fort Washington and a camp he named Hobsons Choice because they had no other options.[41] There he received the disheartening news from Secretary Knox that recruitments lagged, forcing him to top up with Kentucky militia. On a personal note, he also received news that his wife had died.

With his force near full strength, Wayne marched north and established a new encampment, Fort Greene. On Christmas Day 1793, an advance party arrived at the St Clair's Defeat massacre site and found a horrifying scene as hundreds of skeletons lay scattered about. After burying the grisly remains across the site, the advance party established a new post, Fort Recovery, where some troops stayed for the winter while the rest remained encamped at Fort Greene.[42] The Legion recovered four copper cannons (two 6-pound and two 3-pound), two copper howitzers, and one iron carronade.[43] An Indian force with British officers arrived at Fort Recovery, intent on recovering the same cannons; the force destroyed an escort and captured or scattered several hundred packhorses used for supply convoys but failed to capture the fort, which was defended by artillery, dragoons and Chickasaw scouts.[44] The fort defenders suffered twenty-three killed, twenty-nine wounded, and three captured.[45] Contemporary estimates of the tribal casualties range from seventeen to fifty killed.[46]

By the spring of 1794, the Legion was ready to move. Reinforced by over 1,000 mounted Kentucky militia under the command of Brigadier General Charles Scott, Wayne advanced north, stopping to establish a string of forts along the way, including Fort Defiance, Fort Adams and Fort Deposit.

By August, Wayne and the Legion had reached north-western Ohio and the Maumee River, the stronghold of Indian forces and close to the British-held Fort Miamis. A tree fell on Wayne's tent while he camped at Fort Adams; he was knocked unconscious, but by the next day he had recovered sufficiently to resume the march.[47]

The Indians, now under the overall command of Chief Blue Jacket, were ready to inflict another devastating defeat on the incomers and intended to ambush Wayne's force. The proposed site was a clearing near present-day Toledo, known as Fallen Timbers as it was formed when a tornado had toppled hundreds of trees years before. Blue Jacket misjudged his enemy by assuming that the latest incursion would be by troops as callow as those slaughtered in the two earlier battles. Instead he was up against well-trained, well-armed and well-disciplined troops. Wayne also had the advantage of excellent Choctaw and Chickasaw scouts adept at sniffing out an ambush.

On the morning of 20 August, the Legion approached Fallen Timbers. Wayne divided his infantry into two wings, the right commanded by Wilkinson, the other by Colonel John Hamtramck. A brigade of mounted Kentuckians guarded the open left flank, while the Legion's cavalry secured the right along the Maumee. Scott's remaining forces formed a reserve. The vanguard of the Legion came under fire mid-morning. After some initial confusion, Wilkinson regained control of the situation. Wayne then rode forward, his eyes apparently flashing. He correctly determined the strength of the enemy and their positions, and quickly saw that mounted troops would be largely ineffective on the battlefield. Under fire and in intense pain from gout and his head injury, he immediately ordered a bayonet charge to flush out the enemy so they could be cut down by musket fire. The Indians, who had expected to be the ones charging, broke and ran pell-mell towards Fort Miamis. Dragoons from the Legion charged headlong at the log barriers, cutting down the Indian warriors with their sabres. The dragoons' charge completed the rout.[48] The battle had lasted less than an hour. At Fort Miamis they found the gate locked against them as the British commander had no wish to start another war with America – Britain and the US, unbeknown to the Indians, were close to reaching an accommodation to counter Jacobin France. At last, Wayne's army had won a decisive victory.

Wayne lost thirty-three men with around 100 wounded. His men claimed to have found thirty to forty dead warriors, although it was reported to the British Indian Department that the Indian Confederacy lost nineteen warriors killed, including Chief Turkey Foot of the Ottawa.[49] Six white men fighting on the Native American side were also killed, and Chiefs Egushaway and Little Otter of the Ottawa were wounded.[50] The soldiers spent several days destroying the nearby Native American villages and crops, then decamped. Wayne marched his army unopposed to the Miami capital of Kekionga and constructed Fort Wayne as a defiant symbol of US sovereignty in the heart of Indian Country.

By the Treaty of Greenville, signed by President Washington on 22 December 1795, the Northwest Native American tribes were forced to cede southern and eastern Ohio and various tracts of land around forts and settlements in Illinois County; to recognise the US rather than Britain as the ruling power in the Old Northwest; and to surrender ten chiefs as hostages until all American prisoners were returned. Blue Jacket was a reluctant signatory and faded into obscurity. Little Turtle travelled with his wife to Greenville and gave a speech encouraging his people 'to adopt American ways'. His wife died in camp the next day. Her funeral and burial included American soldiers as pallbearers, American music, and a three-gun salute. Two more peace treaties, Jay's and Pinckney's, defined post-colonial relations among the US, Britain and Spain.

Most of the western forts were abandoned in 1796; Fort Washington, the last, was moved across the Ohio River to Kentucky in 1803 and became the Newport Barracks. General Wayne supervised the surrender of British posts in the Northwest Territory but suffered a severe attack of gout and died in December 1796.[51] Large numbers of US settlers migrated to the Northwest Territory. Five years after the Treaty of Greenville, the territory was split into Ohio and Indiana Territory, and in February 1803 the State of Ohio was admitted to the Union.

Future Native American resistance movements were unable to form a union matching the size or capability seen during the Northwest Indian War. The region would remain largely peaceful until the 1811 Battle of Tippecanoe, fought by Tecumseh, a young Shawnee veteran of Fallen Timbers who refused to sign the Greenville Treaty and who would lead Indian resistance in the years ahead.

In 1797, Little Turtle met George Washington, who presented him with a ceremonial sword, as well as John Adams and Thomas Jefferson, with whom he discussed farming methods. On his way to meet Washington, Little Turtle met General Tadeusz Kosciuszko, who presented him with a matching pair of pistols and told him to use them on 'the first man who ever comes to subjugate you'.

For the remainder of his life, Little Turtle was a committed peacekeeper and refused an alliance with Tecumseh. Following his own advice, he began to adapt to the American way of life, buying his own land, but remained a vehement opponent of alcohol. Little Turtle made trips east to meet with three US presidents, and accepted annuity payments and African American slaves in exchange for his co-operation.[52]

In 1809, Little Turtle suffered a break with other Miami leaders when Governor William Henry Harrison forced through the Treaty of Fort Wayne, which secured 2.5 million acres of land for the federal government with the help of the chief and his son-in-law William Wells. As a result he was forcibly retired from Miami affairs. Little Turtle settled in a village 20 miles north-east of Fort Wayne. Following the War of 1812, Harrison ordered the destruction of all Miami villages within a two-day march of Fort Wayne. His forces burnt the village where Little Turtle lived, but spared his home, which the US government had built for his use.[53] Little Turtle died on 14 July 1812,[54] at the home of his son-in-law, not far from Kekionga, after suffering bouts of gout and rheumatism. He was honoured with a military-style funeral with full military honours at Fort Wayne. He was buried in his ancestral burial ground near Spy Run.

A small memorial stone placed at Little Turtle's gravesite reads: 'This site honors the great Chief of the Miamis, Meshekinoqua, "The Little Turtle," son of the great Chief Acquenacque. He is held in the hearts of his people, allies, and foes with the greatest of honor and respect for his courageous valor and peacemaking.'

3

Shays' Rebellion (1786–1787) and the Whiskey Rebellion (1791–1794)

The tree of liberty must be refreshed from time to time
with the blood of patriots and tyrants.

The commander of the Springfield armoury, confronted by grim-faced rebels, ordered that its cannon be loaded with grapeshot, which was detonated with deadly effect. But the Revolutionary War was over and the attackers were comrades he had fought alongside against the British. Shays' Rebellion highlighted that few wars, even those won, end without further bloodshed at home. Former Continental Army general Benjamin Lincoln wrote to George Washington: 'It is impossible for me to determine "when and how they will end" as I see little probability that they will be brought to a period, and the dignity of government supported without bloodshed. When a single drop is drawn, the most prophetic spirit will not, in my opinion, be able to determine when it will cease flowing.'

At issue, in a fledgling nation born out of ideals of liberty, were the civil liberties and prosperity of those who had fought for it. Although relatively small-scale, the birth pangs of America came close to sparking its first civil war.

* * *

Daniel Shays, a Continental Army veteran, was approaching forty and had a wife and six children when he threw himself into national prominence. The son of Irish immigrants, his youth was spent as a landless farm labourer who hired himself out to work. By the early 1770s, Shays was living on a farm in Brookfield, Massachusetts, where he was paid above the going rate for a labourer to reflect his performance as a 'smart, active' man. A neighbour recalled that as a youngster,

Shays 'had much taste for the military'. When young men assembled for militia training days, some armed only with wooden guns and swords, Shays enthusiastically drilled them.[1] In 1772, he married Abigail Gilbert and they settled on a small farm.[2] Both impoverished and patriotic, after the outbreak of the Revolutionary War he rose to captain in the 5th Massachusetts Regiment. He fought in the Boston Campaign, and the Battles of Bunker Hill, Lexington and Saratoga. His steady battlefield promotions were a testament to his courage and resourcefulness, but he suffered several wounds and resigned from the military in 1780 with no guaranteed pension and owed much back pay. When he returned home, he was summoned to court for unpaid local debts which he had no chance of settling.[3] General Lafayette had, on Shays' resignation, presented him with an ornamental sword in honour of his military service. He later sold it for a few dollars to help pay off some of his more pressing debts.[4] He was, however, far from alone in feeling justified resentment.

Shays swiftly discovered that many of his fellow veterans and farmers were in the same dire financial straits. At commoners' meetings they asserted that they too were owed back pay and were being squeezed by profiteering businessmen who regarded smallholders as mere prey to be fleeced. The rural economy was based on subsistence agriculture, with cash-strapped farmers holding few assets beyond their land and household property and who bartered with one another for goods and services. In lean times, they obtained goods on credit from suppliers in local market towns. When the war ended in 1783, the European business partners of Massachusetts merchants refused to extend lines of credit to them and insisted that they pay for goods with hard cash, despite the continent-wide shortage of such currency. Merchants began to demand the same from their local business partners, including those operating in the market towns.[5] Many of these merchants passed this demand on to their customers, although Governor John Hancock did not impose hard currency demands on poorer borrowers and refused to actively prosecute the collection of delinquent taxes.[6] Hard currency was scarce, but Congress had issued a requisition to the states in order to pay off their debt, roughly 30 per cent of which was to be paid in hard currency. The result was a shortage of money circulating within the states, leaving many farmers unable to pay. Commodities and property were confiscated in turn.[7] This led to strong resentments against tax collectors and the courts, where creditors obtained judgments against debtors authorising property seizures.[8]

Many Massachusetts rural communities initally tried to petition the legislature in Boston, but it was dominated by eastern seaboard merchants who largely ignored them because the petitions included a request to issue paper currency to speed up payments to those in immediate poverty. The merchants, including James Bowdoin, felt that would depreciate the currency, and as many of them were moneylenders they would lose out if high-value debts were paid with lower-valued paper.[9]

Veterans like Shays faced added difficulty collecting pay owed to them from the State or the Congress of the Confederation,[10] and some soldiers began to organise protests. A farmer identified as 'Plough Jogger' summarised the situation at a meeting convened by aggrieved commoners:

> I have been greatly abused, have been obliged to do more than my part in the war, been loaded with class rates, town rates, province rates, Continental rates and all rates ... been pulled and hauled by sheriffs, constables and collectors, and had my cattle sold for less than they were worth ... The great men are going to get all we have and I think it is time for us to rise and put a stop to it, and have no more courts, nor sheriffs, nor collectors nor lawyers.[11]

Shays began organising for debt relief.[12]

One early protest against the government was led by Job Shattuck of Groton, Massachusetts, who had served in the Continental Army alongside Shays. He urged residents to physically prevent tax collectors from doing their work. A second, larger-scale protest took place in Uxbridge on the Rhode Island border on 3 February 1783 when a mob seized property that had been confiscated by a constable and returned it to its owners. Anticipating more trouble ahead, Governor Hancock abruptly resigned in early 1785, citing dubious health issues, and his former rival Bowdoin replaced him. His elevation killed off lingering hopes of any compromise and Bowdoin stepped up civil actions to collect back taxes. With his connivance, the legislature raised the ante by levying an additional property tax for the State's portion of foreign debt payments. There was widespread outrage, even among conservatives: John Adams commented that the levies were 'heavier than the People could bear'.[13]

Protests across rural Massachusetts erupted in August 1786, after the state legislature adjourned without considering the many petitions.[14] On 29 August, Shays was among a well-organised force of protestors who marched on Northampton and successfully prevented the county court from sitting to penalise a debtor.[15] The leaders proclaimed that they were seeking relief from the burdensome judicial processes that were depriving the people of their land and possessions. They called themselves Regulators, a reference to a movement of North Carolina which had aimed to reform corrupt practices in the late 1760s.[16] On 2 September, Governor Bowdoin issued a proclamation denouncing mob action but was shocked when another court in Worcester was also shut down and the county militia refused to turn out, in sympathy with the protestors.

The Regulators in Rockingham County armed themselves and marched on Exeter to demand the New Hampshire general court immediately issue money. The courthouse was packed with townsfolk eager to hear if their reform petition would be heard. Much to their relief, New Hampshire President John Sullivan decided to skip any case where either party was not ready to proceed. He donned his Continental Army uniform, then proceeded to the courthouse. He listened to the crowd's demands; many of the rioters were former soldiers of his, which he used to his advantage. Feeling that they had achieved their goal, the rioters left the court to its business, and cheered General Sullivan for hearing their demands.[17] Sullivan had convinced the mob to disperse for the night with vague promises and appeals to their shared military experience during the war. He then raised the militia in surrounding towns and by the following morning around 2,000 men set out to ambush the rebels' camp. The rebels were caught completely off guard and scattered into the woods. Most of the leaders were captured.[18]

Following Sullivan's callous and cynical duplicity, neighbouring governors acted decisively, calling out the militia to hunt down protest ringleaders. Matters were resolved without violence in Rhode Island because the 'country party' gained control of the legislature and forced its merchants to trade debt instruments for devalued currency. Boston's merchants were incandescent over that compromise, especially Bowdoin, who held more than £3,000 in Massachusetts notes.[19]

Daniel Shays began to take a more active role in the uprising. The Supreme Judicial Court of Massachusetts indicted eleven leaders of the so-called paper money rebellion as 'disorderly, riotous, and seditious persons'. The court was scheduled to meet next in Springfield on 26 September, and Shays organised an attempt to shut down the Northampton court, while Luke Day, another veteran farmer, organised a similar attempt in Springfield. Local militia commander William Shepard, who knew both Shays and Day through military service, had meanwhile called up 300 militia to protect the Springfield courthouse. Both sides, former comrades-in-arms, knew exactly what the other was doing, and Shays and Day recruited a similar number but chose only to demonstrate, exercising their troops outside of Shepard's lines rather than attempting to seize the building. Shays cut an impressive figure in his Continental Army uniform. His dignified air of command and his confident knowledge of military protocols lent credence and respectability to the ranks marching on the courthouse. He rode forward to confer with General Shepard and successfully negotiated the peaceable abandonment of the courthouse by the judges and the militia. In return, Shays agreed that the Regulator troops would confine themselves to peaceably marching and demonstrating in front of the building rather than seeking to close it by force. Given the volatility of the situation, the judges sensibly postponed hearings and then adjourned on the

28th without hearing any cases. Shepard withdrew his force, which had grown to some 800 men, to around the Springfield Armory.[20]

Shays' appearance at the head of the Regulators at Springfield marked a turning point for him personally and for the Regulator movement in general. For the first time, the Regulators had closed not only the lower Court of Common Pleas but a session of the Supreme Judicial Court, and that was seen as a direct assault on the sovereignty of the state government. Almost overnight, Shays rose to the top of the government's most wanted list and was labelled the 'generalissimo' of the movement that the administration was now calling a rebellion.[21]

Other protests across Massachusetts also shut down courts in Concord, Great Barrington and Taunton. Former Paymaster General James Warren, a veteran of both the Little Turtle and Revolutionary Wars, wrote to John Adams on 22 October: 'We are now in a state of Anarchy and Confusion bordering on Civil War.'[22] Courts were able to meet in the larger towns and cities, but they required the protection of militia called out by Bowdoin, who told the legislature to 'vindicate the insulted dignity of government'. Bogus claims that 'British emissaries' were stirring up treason among the commoners led to the reading of a Riot Act and a resolution to permit suspects to be held in jail without trial. Adams proposed a new legal distinction that rebellion in a republic should be punished by execution, saying: 'Rebellion against a king may be pardoned, or lightly punished, but the man who dares to rebel against the laws of a republic ought to suffer death.' That proposal was put on hold, but the legislature went ahead with measures prohibiting speech critical of the government and offering pardons to turncoats. Such tyrannical legislative actions were unsuccessful in quelling the protests, and the suspension of *habeas corpus* alarmed many. The crisis had sparked a reaction which was seen as a travesty of the principle set out by the Founding Fathers and aspirations to create a 'land of the free' – that is, white property owners.

Warrants were issued for the arrest of several of the protest ringleaders, and a 300-strong posse rode to Groton on 28 November to arrest Job Shattuck and others in the area. Shattuck was chased down and during his arrest on the 30th was wounded by a sword slash. Such actions further inflamed the farming populace and rebel leaders spoke of smashing the 'tyrannical government of Massachusetts'. They began to organise an overthrow of the state government. A Shrewsbury resident wrote: 'The seeds of war are now sown.'

Bowdoin, however, was keenly aware that the federal government had no money to recruit and deploy regulars. On 4 January 1787, he proposed a privately funded militia army. General Benjamin Lincoln solicited funds and raised more than £6,000 from at least twenty-five merchants by the end of the month and recruited 3,000 militiamen from the eastern counties of Massachusetts who marched on Worcester.

Lincoln, a wealthy farmer described by Washington as 'a gentleman well worthy of notice in the Military Line', had overseen the largest American surrender of the war at the 1780 Siege of Charleston, but, as George Washington's second in command, had also formally accepted the British surrender at Yorktown. He had served from 1781 to 1783 as the Secretary of War and his appointment showed how seriously the administration was taking the situation.

Facing him, Shays, Day and others established regional regiments run by democratically elected committees. Their first major target was the federal armoury in Springfield where they could snatch arms and supplies for another revolution. Bowdoin, however, was ahead of them and authorised General Shepard to arm a militia force of 1,200, even though the armoury was federal property, not that of the state, and he did not have permission from Secretary of War Henry Knox.[23]

The insurgents were organised into three groups and intended to surround and attack the armoury simultaneously. Shays led one group east of Springfield, Luke Day led a second force across the Connecticut River in West Springfield, and Eli Parsons led the third to the north.[24] They planned their assault for 25 January, but Day changed this at the last minute and sent a message to Shays saying he would not be ready to attack until the following morning. Day's message was intercepted by Shepard's men, so Shays and Parsons approached the armoury on the 25th unaware that they would be on their own. They found Shepard's militia waiting for them. Shepard first ordered warning shots fired over their heads, but then told the crews of two cannons to fire grapeshot on the tentatively advancing force: four Shaysites were killed and twenty wounded.

Massachusetts militia officer Epaphras Hoyt, a twenty-one-year-old native of Deerfield, wrote to his brother Seth:

Yesterday being informed that the insurgents were upon the march toward our encampment ... with an intent to possess themselves of our barracks and our stores, the army immediately got under arms ... and put out patroles to scour the reach toward the enemy (I myself had the honour to command a patrole). ... Though the enemy were superior to us in number they were (as we afterwards found) very scantily provided with ammunition. ... Their commander had told them that we should not dare to fire on them, which they generally believed.

There was no more musket fire from either side and the rebel advance collapsed. Most of the rebel forces fled.

General Lincoln and his militia army immediately began marching west from Worcester, while the rebels moved north and east to avoid him, eventually establishing a camp at Petersham. They raided the shops of local merchants along the way and took some of them hostage. Lincoln led his militia on a forced march through a bitter snowstorm on the night of 3/4 February, arriving shortly before dawn. They surprised the rebel camp, which then scattered 'without time to call in their out parties or even their guards'.[25]

Lincoln reported to Washington:

Our troops were put in motion at 8 o Clock. The first part of the night was pleasant, and the weather clement; but between two and three o Clock in the morning, the wind shifting to the Westward, it became very cold and squally, with considerable snow. The wind immediately arose very high, and with the light snow which fell the day before and was falling, the paths were soon filled up, the men became fatigued, and they were in a part of the country where they could not be covered in the distance of eight miles, and the cold was so increased, that they could not halt in the road to refresh themselves. Under these circumstances they were obliged to continue their march. We reached Petersham about 9 o Clock in the morning exceedingly fatigued with a march of thirty miles, part of it in a deep snow and in a most violent storm; when this abated, the cold increased and a great proportion of our men were frozen in some part or other, but none dangerously. We approached nearly the centre of the Town where Shays had covered his men; and had we not been prevented from the steepness of a large hill at our entrance, and the depth of the snow from throwing our men rapidly into it we should have arrested very probably one half this force; for they were so surprised as it was that they had not time to call in their out-parties, or even their guards. About 150 fell into our hands, and none escaped but by the most precipitate flight in different directions. Thus that body of men who were a few days before offering the grossest insults to the best Citizens of this Commonwealth and were menacing even Government itself, were now nearly dispersed, without the shedding of blood but in an instance or two where the Insurgents rushed on their own destruction. That so little has been shed is owing in a measure to the patience and obedience, the zeal and the fortitude in our troops, which would have done honour to veterans. A different line of conduct which Shays flattered his troops would have been followed, would have given them support, and led them to acts of violence, whilst it must have buoyed up the hopes of their abettors, and stimulated them to greater exertions.

Lincoln's claim to have captured 150 men on the snow-covered, frozen ground (none of them officers) has since been questioned, as has his report more generally. Lincoln wrote to Shays and the other rebel leaders:

Your resources are few, your force is inconsiderable, and hourly decreasing from the disaffection of your men. You are in a post where you have neither cover nor supplies, and in a situation in which you can neither give aid to your friends, nor discomfort to the supporters of good order and government. Under these circumstances, you cannot hesitate a moment, to disband your deluded followers. If you should not, I must approach and apprehend the most influential characters among you. Should you attempt to fire upon the troops of government, the consequences might be fatal to many of your men the least guilty. To prevent bloodshed, you will communicate to your privates that if they will instantly lay down their arms, surrender themselves to government, and take and subscribe the oath of allegiance to this Commonwealth, they shall be recommended to the General Court for mercy. If you should either withhold this information from them, or suffer your people to fire upon our approach, you must be answerable for all the ills, which may exist in consequence thereof.

Most of the leadership escaped north into New Hampshire and Vermont, where they found shelter among likeminded communities.[26] Pockets of local resistance continued. About 120 rebels regrouped in New Lebanon, New York, and marched on the market town of Stockbridge, ransacking the shops and homes of merchants. Brigadier John Ashley mustered a force of some eighty men and caught up with the rebels in nearby Sheffield. It proved the bloodiest encounter of the rebellion: two rebels were killed and thirty wounded while the government forces lost at least one and an unspecified number wounded, some of whom are likely to have died later. Ashley, like Lincoln, claimed to have taken 150 prisoners, but that figure too has been disputed.[27] Lincoln reported the action:

Colo. Ashley having collected about Eighty Men, came to a resolution to march in pursuit of the rebels, & to attack them where he should find them; he very soon fell in with them. They were marching in files, had their prisoners in the centre. Their front division formed a line on one side of the road, that left our prisoners in the front of the rear. It is said they did not form; that the whole were routed before they had time to do it; two or three Men on a side were killed & a number wounded; among them one Hamlen, Commander of the party; his wounds are dangerous; as they retreated they fell into the hands of the Militia from Stockbridge & Lenox which were pursuing. About seventy of them have been taken: some are coming in and surrendering themselves. This Action has had very happy Effects upon the people of this County; it has given them great spirits, and they begin to discover that state of mind which they enjoyed before the Rebellion existed, by which the Friends of government in this part of the County have been exceedingly born down.[28]

Some rebels approached the British Quebec governor, Lord Dorchester, for help and he, it has been claimed, promised to deploy Mohawk

Indians on their behalf, but such fantasy last-gasp schemes came to nothing. The Massachusetts state legislature authorised full martial law, with payments to cover Lincoln and the merchants' personal costs, and poured in cash for more local troops. On 12 February, the legislature passed the Disqualification Act which forbade any acknowledged rebels from holding a variety of elected and appointed offices. The legislature echoed the crackdown that the British had imposed on the Jacobites earlier that century. Most of Lincoln's army melted away as enlistments expired.

In all, 4,000 people signed confessions admitting some role in the rebellion in exchange for amnesty. Several hundred more were indicted, but most of these were also pardoned. Only the supposed ringleaders were excluded from a general amnesty. Eighteen men were convicted and sentenced to death, but most of these were overturned on appeal, pardoned, or had the sentences commuted. Two rebels, John Bly and Charles Rose, were hanged on 6 December 1787 as they had been convicted of the common law crime of looting. Threats to property were, it turned out, treated more seriously than threats to life.

Founding Father Thomas Jefferson, in a letter to James Madison, wrote: 'I hold it that a little rebellion, now and then, is a good thing, and as necessary in the political world as storms in the physical. Unsuccessful rebellions, indeed, generally establish the encroachments on the rights of the people, which have produced them. An observation of this truth should render honest republican governors so mild in their punishment of rebellions, as not to discourage them too much. It is a medicine necessary for the sound health of government.' Later, he added: 'The tree of liberty must be refreshed from time to time with the blood of patriots and tyrants.'

Newspaper letters pages reflect both hostility to and support for the insurrection. Mary Pierce wrote:

I have been hearing around town and have been reading in the newspapers about these rebels that have been storming court houses and rallying against the so called outrageous prices and taxes that the Government has put forth. I was talking to my neighbor and we came to the conclusion that every new organization has its beginning problems. I decided we all have to bear with each other until it is all worked out. I think if word of this rebellion gets out to England they will just tell our representatives that we were wrong to separate from England. Instead our new country needs to manage problems together and peacefully. It may be time for our elected leaders to meet somewhere and write a new constitution because these Articles of Confederation fail to give our government the power to prevent such rebellions! I hope that leader of the rebellion, Daniel Shays, reads this and is informed of how I and my friends disapprove of forceful protest.

But, signing himself 'Revolutionary Veteran', I. B. Free wrote:

> I recently read about the rebellion in Springfield, led by the previous
> revolutionary war hero Daniel Shays. Back in the revolution days we
> were fighting for a free and independent country. Now our government
> is telling us what to do. And old Dan Shays did not like it. Neither do
> I and if I could I would have been helping Mr. Shays. He didn't violate
> any laws as far as I am concerned, just demonstrating for our rights.
> There's no question the taxes are too high, and we didn't even get to
> vote on them. I hope the skirmishing in Springfield helps this newborn
> Government see what they're doing.

The government's reaction, however, was forceful and undivided.

Through winter and spring of 1787, Shays would have heard news
of the men who had been run down, arrested and condemned to
death. Knowing he had been indicted on charges of high treason, he
moved from place to place, never staying longer than one or two days
in one location. From New Hampshire, he went to Vermont. His wife
Abigail joined him there, where she, too, lived a life on the run, afraid
to confide in anyone lest her husband be recognised and arrested.[29] But
the Massachusetts government and people alike seemed eager to put
the turmoil of the previous year behind them. Shays was pardoned in
1788 and he returned to Massachusetts from hiding in the Vermont
woods. He was hounded out of Boston by merchant-owned newspapers
who branded him an anarchist and a traitor, and he moved to New York.
He was a widower now, although it is not known when or where Abigail
Shays died. In 1815, Daniel Shays married Rhoda Havens, an innkeeper
and widow. Three years later, at age seventy-seven, Shays submitted
a petition to Congress under a Pension Act awarding assistance to
veterans who had served in the Continental Army during the American
Revolution. His petition documented his service record and declared that
'during the whole Time of his Service, he conducted with Fidelity, and
Reputation and attended to his Duty with the greatest Circumspection
and Diligence'. Citing a severe wound he received in 1775 that had made
him permanently 'unable to labour', and a 'large and Expensive Family
dependent on his Care and Support', he asked Congress for either the five
years' officer's pay he had never received, or to be placed on the pension
list. The government granted his petition for a pension, and Shays used
it to buy 12 acres of land where he built a house and barn. He died poor
and obscure in Sparta, New York, aged seventy-eight in 1825.

The crushing of the rebellion and the harsh terms of the Disqualification
Act did no longer-term political good for Governor Bowdoin. Receiving
next to no votes in the rural areas of the state, he was trounced by John
Hancock in the gubernatorial election of 1787. The legislature cut taxes,
placed a moratorium on debts and refocused state spending away from

interest payments, resulting in a 30 per cent decline in the value of Massachusetts securities.

Vermont, which had provided refuge to rebels, became an unexpected beneficiary of the outbreak. It had been seeking independent statehood against the powerful claims of New York merchants to the territory. Alexander Hamilton cited Vermont's *de facto* independence and its ability to cause trouble and introduced legislation to allow it to become a state. In return, Vermont quietly expelled refugees Eli Parsons and Luke Day.

The rebellion demonstrated the weaknesses of the federal government as constituted under the Articles of Confederation. Federalists argued for a stronger central government, and the seeds of a civil war were sown.[30] In early 1787, Founding Father and future Chief Justice John Jay wrote that the rural disturbances and the inability of the central government to fund troops in response made 'the inefficiency of the Federal government more and more manifest'. Henry Knox observed that the uprising in Massachusetts clearly influenced local leaders who had previously opposed a strong federal government. The timing of the rebellion 'convinced the elites of sovereign states that the proposed gathering at Philadelphia must take place'.[31] Some states delayed choosing delegates to a proposed convention, including Massachusetts, in part because it resembled the 'extra-legal' conventions organised by the protestors before the rebellion became violent.

The convention that met in Philadelphia was dominated by strong-government advocates who constantly used Shays' Rebellion in their arguments. Connecticut delegate Oliver Ellsworth argued that because the people could not be trusted, the members of the federal House of Representatives should be chosen by state legislatures, not by popular vote. While mindful of tyranny, delegates of the Constitutional Convention thought that the single executive would be more effective in responding to national disturbances.[32] The day was carried by a coalition of merchants, urban elites and market town leaders. A popular ballad, falsely purporting to be a *mea culpa* from Shays himself, concluded:

> America, let us rejoice
> In our new constitution.
> And never more pretend to think
> Of another revolution.

The shock of Shays' Rebellion drew retired General George Washington back into public life, leading to his two terms as the United States' first president. He was quick to put to use the military powers enshrined in the new constitution in the face of a new wave of discontent.

* * *

The alleged spark that led to the American Revolution was, famously and inaccurately, a tax protest known as the 'Boston tea party' so it seems particularly ironic that the next insurrection in the new post-war nation was over another tax, this time on whiskey. The main culprits were George Washington himself and Secretary of the Treasury Alexander Hamilton.

The new US federal government began operating in 1789 with the burden of $54 million in war debt, plus more in individual states' debt, but Hamilton aimed to create a financial system that would promote American prosperity and national unity. In the summer of 1790, Congress approved his proposal to consolidate the state and national debts into a single debt that would be funded by the federal government.[33] But more government revenue was needed to pay the bondholders to whom the debt was owed. By December 1790, Hamilton had successfully argued that import duties were as high as they could go without alienating the Revolution's fund-masters, so he introduced the first tax levied by the national government on a domestic product. Fatefully, it was on domestically produced distilled spirits.

Whiskey was by far the most popular distilled beverage, taxes were unpopular in any case, and farmers west of the Appalachian Mountains often supplemented their incomes by operating small stills for their excess grain. A whiskey tax would make western farmers less competitive with eastern grain producers. Additionally, cash was always in short supply on the frontier, so whiskey was used in barter. For poorer people who were so paid, the excise was essentially an income tax that wealthier easterners did not pay.[34] In addition, while social reformers argued that a 'sin tax' on alcohol was overdue, struggling farmers, many of them veterans, were incensed when Hamilton dubbed it a 'luxury' tax.[35] The Whiskey Act nevertheless became law in March 1791.[36] George Washington appointed the hapless inspectors who would have to collect it.

Small-scale farmers also protested that Hamilton's excise effectively gave unfair tax breaks to large distillers, most of whom were based in the east. There were two methods of paying the whiskey excise: a flat fee or by the gallon. Large distillers produced whiskey in volume and could easily afford the flat fee. The bigger they got, the less tax per gallon they would pay. Western farmers who owned small stills usually did not operate them year-round at full capacity, so they ended up paying a higher tax per gallon.[37] Whiskey also sold for considerably less on the cash-poor western frontier than in the wealthier and more populous east. Small-scale distillers believed that Hamilton deliberately designed the tax to ruin them and promote big business. The large distillers recognised the advantage that the excise gave them, and they supported it. In addition, westerners felt they were not adequately protected from Indian raids, and they were prohibited by Spain, which then owned Louisiana, from using the Mississippi River for commercial navigation. Westerners felt, not for the first or last time, that the government was ignoring their security and economic welfare; the whiskey excise could only increase tensions on the frontier.[38]

From the beginning, the Federal government had little success in collecting the whiskey tax along the frontier. Federal revenue officers and local residents who assisted them bore the brunt of the protesters' fury. Tax rebels harassed the tax collectors at every turn and threatened anyone who offered them aid or transient accommodation. Moderates appealed for calm, but the small farmers felt that legal avenues for redress had been exhausted. They picked up their guns. A tax collector named Robert Johnson was tarred and feathered by a gang in Washington County. An unfortunate man sent by officials to serve court warrants to Johnson's attackers was whipped, tarred and feathered.[39] By spring 1792 little tax had been collected as it was opposed in the western counties of every Appalachian state – Maryland, Virginia, North Carolina, South Carolina and Georgia. The tax went uncollected throughout the frontier state of Kentucky, where no one could be convinced to enforce the law or prosecute evaders. Hamilton advocated military action to suppress violent resistance in western North Carolina, but Attorney General Edmund Randolph argued that there was insufficient evidence to legally justify such a reaction.

In August 1792, a convention was held in Pittsburgh to discuss resistance to the whiskey tax. To the chagrin of the authorities, however, radicals took control. A militant group known as the Mingo Creek Association dominated the convention, raised liberty poles, cowed the local militia and physically discouraged lawsuits for debt collection and foreclosures. Hamilton was outraged and sent Pennsylvania tax official George Clymer to western Pennsylvania to investigate. Clymer only exacerbated the volatile situation with a clumsy attempt at traveling in disguise and compounded his own error by sending Washington a greatly exaggerated report on the degree of lawlessness. Washington and Hamilton viewed resistance to federal laws in Pennsylvania as particularly embarrassing, since the national capital was then located in that state. On his own initiative, Hamilton drafted a presidential proclamation denouncing resistance to the excise laws and submitted it to Attorney General Randolph, who toned down some of the language. Washington signed the proclamation on 15 September 1792.[40]

Federal tax inspector for western Pennsylvania General John Neville, a war veteran, slaveholder, land speculator and large-scale distiller, was determined to enforce the excise law. He had initially opposed the whiskey tax, but subsequently changed his mind due in part, it has to be assumed, to self-interest. In August 1792, Neville rented a room in Pittsburgh for his tax office, but the landlord turned him out after being threatened with violence by the Mingo Creek Association.

Resistance to the excise tax continued through 1793 in the frontier counties of Appalachia. Opposition remained especially strident in western Pennsylvania. In June, Neville was burned in effigy by a 100-strong mob in Washington County. Men broke into the home of tax collector Benjamin Wells in Fayette County and forced him to surrender his commission at gunpoint; President Washington offered a handsome reward for the arrest of the assailants. It was never collected, such was the strength of local feeling.

Resistance came to a climax in 1794. In May, Federal District Attorney William Rawle issued subpoenas for more than sixty small distillers in Pennsylvania who had not paid the excise tax. Under the law, those distillers would be obligated to travel to Philadelphia to appear in federal court. For farmers on the western frontier, such a journey was beyond their means. Congress modified this law on 5 June 1794, allowing excise trials to be held in local state courts.[41] But by that time, US Marshal David Lenox had already been sent to serve the writs summoning delinquent distillers to Philadelphia. He delivered most of the writs without incident. On 15 July, he was joined on his rounds by General Neville, who had offered to act as his guide in Allegheny County.[42] That evening, warning shots were fired at them at the Miller farm, about 10 miles south of Pittsburgh. Neville returned home while Lenox retreated to Pittsburgh.

On 16 July, at least thirty Mingo Creek militiamen surrounded Neville's fortified home of Bower Hill. They demanded the surrender of the federal marshal, whom they believed to be inside. Neville responded by firing a gunshot that mortally wounded Oliver Miller, one of the 'rebels'.[43] They opened fire but were unable to dislodge Neville, who had his slaves' help to defend the house. The rebels retreated to nearby Couch's Fort to gather reinforcements. The next day, they returned to Bower Hill. Their force had swelled to nearly 600 men, now commanded by war veteran Major James McFarlane. Neville had also received reinforcements: ten soldiers from Pittsburgh under Major Abraham Kirkpatrick, Neville's brother-in-law. Before the rebel force arrived, Kirkpatrick had Neville leave the house and hide in a nearby ravine. David Lenox and General Neville's son Presley also returned to the area, though they could not get into the house and were captured by the rebels. Following some fruitless negotiations, the women and children were allowed to leave the house, and then both sides began firing. After about an hour, McFarlane called a ceasefire; according to some, a white flag had been waved in the house. As McFarlane stepped into the open, a shot was fired from the house, and he fell mortally wounded. The enraged rebels then set fire to the house, including the slave quarters, and Kirkpatrick surrendered.[44] The number of casualties at Bower Hill is unclear; McFarlane and one or two other militiamen were killed; one soldier may have died from wounds received in the fight. The rebels sent the soldiers away. Kirkpatrick, Lenox and Presley Neville were kept as prisoners, but they later escaped.

McFarlane was given a hero's funeral on 18 July. His 'murder', as the rebels saw it, further radicalised the countryside. Moderates were hard-pressed to restrain the populace. Radical leader David Bradford led a gang which robbed the US mail as it left Pittsburgh, hoping to discover who in that town opposed them and finding several letters that condemned the rebels. Bradford and his band called for a military assembly to meet at Braddock's Field, about 8 miles east of Pittsburgh.[45] On 1 August, about 7,000 people gathered at the appointed rendezvous, mainly people who felt that property tycoons were riding roughshod over the poor. Some of the most radical protesters wanted to march on Pittsburgh (which they called 'Sodom'), loot the homes of the wealthy, and then burn the town to the ground. Others wanted to attack Fort Fayette. There was praise for the French Revolution and calls for bringing the guillotine to America. David Bradford, it was said, was comparing himself to Robespierre, architect of the Reign of Terror. There was excited talk of declaring independence from the United States and of joining with Spain or Britain. Radicals flew a specially designed flag that proclaimed their independence. Pittsburgh citizens helped to defuse the threat by banishing three men whose intercepted letters had given offense to the rebels, and by sending a delegation to Braddock's Field that expressed support for the gathering.

By now Washington was clearly confronted by an armed insurrection, and his cabinet recommended the full and immediate use of force.[46] Washington duly sent commissioners to meet with the rebels while raising a militia army. Hamilton railed against mob violence, blaming Democratic-Republican Societies which he claimed were launched in every state to foment civic unrest. On 4 August 1794, Justice James Wilson decreed that western Pennsylvania was in a state of rebellion.

Washington dispatched three peace commissioners who insisted on a popular referendum on the tax and on the legality of insurrection. Those who agreed to these terms would be given amnesty from further prosecution.[47] The ensuing referendum had wildly mixed results, and on 24 September 1794 Washington received a recommendation from the commissioners that in their judgment it was 'necessary that the civil authority should be aided by a military force in order to secure a due execution of the laws'. Washington swiftly issued a proclamation summoning the New Jersey, Pennsylvania, Maryland and Virginia militias into service and warned that anyone who aided the insurgents did so at their own peril. The proclamation included lines 'deploring that the American name should be sullied by the outrages of citizens on their own Government, commiserating such as remain obstinate from delusion, but resolved, in perfect reliance on that gracious Providence which so signally displays its goodness towards this country, to reduce the refractory to a due subordination to the law...'[48]

The federalised militia force of 12,950 men was of comparable size to Washington's armies during the Revolution, and a draft was needed to fill out the ranks. Draft evasion was widespread, and conscription efforts resulted in protests and riots, even in eastern areas. In Maryland, Governor Thomas Sim Lee sent 800 men to quash an anti-draft riot in Hagerston in which 150 were arrested. A liberty pole was raised in Carlisle,[49] and the federalised militia arrived in that town later that month and rounded up suspected pole raisers. An unarmed boy was shot by an officer whose pistol accidentally fired. Two days later, an 'Itinerant Person' was bayoneted to death by a soldier while resisting arrest. Washington ordered the arrest of the two soldiers and had them turned over to civilian authorities. A state judge determined that the deaths had been accidental, and the soldiers were released.

Washington left Philadelphia on 30 September to review the progress of the military expedition, leading to technically true claims that it was the first and only time a sitting American president led troops in the field. On the way he viewed the building of the Schuylkill Canal, on which the slain itinerant had been working. War veteran Colonel Jonathan Forman led the Third Infantry Regiment of New Jersey troops and wrote of his encounter with Washington: 'October 3d Marched early in the morning for Harrisburgh (*sic*), where we arrived about 12 O'clock. About 1 O'Clock recd. information of the Presidents approach on which, I had the regiment paraded, timely for his reception, & considerably to my satisfaction.'

Washington reviewed the southern wing of his army at Fort Cumberland, Maryland, and was there convinced that the federalised militia would meet little resistance. He placed Revolutionary war hero and Virginia Governor Major General Henry 'Lighthouse Harry' Lee in command of the army before returning to Philadelphia. Lee oversaw the southern wing, while another experienced and well-regarded veteran, Major General Daniel Morgan, took his men into Western Pennsylvania in October 1794. The overwhelming show of force brought an end to the protests without a shot being fired.[50] The insurrection collapsed.

Some of the most prominent leaders of the insurrection fled westward, and about 2,000 took refuge in the mountains, much to the chagrin of Hamilton, who wanted show trials in Philadelphia. The Federal militia, with some prisoners, arrived in Philadelphia on Christmas Day. Artillery was fired and church bells rang as 'a huge throng lined Broad Street to cheer the troops and mock the rebels … [Presley] Neville said he "could not help feeling sorry for them"'. The captured rebels were paraded down Broad Street, being 'humiliated, bedragged, [and] half-starved'. It took six months for those who were charged to be tried. Of the many suspects seized by the militia army, a mere twenty-four were selected to serve as examples. Most were acquitted due to mistaken identity, unreliable testimony and lack of witnesses. The only two convicted of treason and sentenced to hang were John Mitchell and Philip Wigle.[51] Wigle had beaten up a tax collector and burned his house; Mitchell was a 'simpleton' cajoled into robbing the US mail. They were later pardoned by Washington.[52] Pennsylvania state courts were more successful in prosecuting lawbreakers, securing numerous convictions for assault and rioting.

While violent opposition to the whiskey tax ended, political opposition continued. Opponents of internal taxes rallied around the candidacy of Thomas Jefferson and helped him defeat President John Adams in the 1800 election. By 1802, Congress repealed the distilled spirits excise tax and all other internal Federal taxes.

The Whiskey Rebellion demonstrated that the new national government had the willingness and ability to suppress violent resistance to its laws.[53] It also raised the question of what kinds of protests were permissible under the new Constitution. The events contributed to the formation of political parties, prompting anti-Federalist westerners to finally accept the Constitution and to seek change by voting for Republicans rather than resisting the government.

Two-party democracy – among whites, that is, and heavily weighted in favour of big business interests – was established and never relinquished.

4

The Quasi War (1798–1800)

The Yankee Racehorse

The new frigate USS *Constellation*, with its three masts and thirty-eight guns, was named by George Washington to reflect the far-reaching principles of the American Constitution. In February 1799 her guns opened devastating fire on an enemy warship, the French *L'Insurgente*. Ignoring appeals for a parley, the American captain ordered another broadside, which left the opposing crew dead, wounded or scrambling for safety. It was one of the first of many sea battles which established the reputation of the US Navy. There were two years of hostilities around the West Indies, and naval reputations were made and lost. But no war had been declared.

It is debateable whether George Washington's Continental Army could have won the Revolutionary War without French support. The French aristocracy and populace cheered the Declaration of Independence because it weakened their long-standing British enemies and strengthened their own ambitions for global domination. French support for the Americans, first covert and then fully open, proved invaluable in both sea and land campaigns, and it has been estimated that during the Saratoga campaign 90 per cent of American arms and ammunition was supplied by the French. They also contributed 5,500 men and heavy artillery to the front line, without which the British would not have been forced into surrender at Yorktown. After that capitulation, veteran British general Charles O'Hara, Cornwallis's second in command, wrote: 'Our Ministers will I hope be now persuaded that America is irretrievably lost … America is theirs.' In a supreme irony, however, all that changed with the French Revolution.

* * *

New US President John Adams had a long history of dealings with the French, and his views of them were mixed. Before the signing of the Declaration of Independence, Adams had urged negotiation of a commercial treaty with France. His 'Model Treaty' authorised a commercial agreement with France which adhered to the provision that 'free ships make free goods', allowing neutral nations to trade while exempting an agreed-upon list of contraband. During his tenure as the French-speaking American commissioner to France, he grew frustrated by what he regarded as their sluggish attitude to prior promises – an attitude that the new American nation emulated.

After the French Crown was overthrown, the cash-strapped US refused to continue repaying its large debt to France, claiming it was owed to a previous regime. The French Revolutionary leaders were also outraged by the 1794 Jay Treaty, which saw the US actively trading with Britain, with whom France was at war. The US claimed neutrality in the conflict. France authorised privateers to conduct attacks on American shipping engaged in trade with the British. The independent US, by its very birth, no longer had the protection of Britain, and was faced with the task of protecting its own ships and interests at sea, with few American ships capable of defending the coastline.

The French government severed diplomatic relations by refusing to receive the new US minister Charles Cotesworth Pinckney, an aristocratic planter, when he arrived in Paris in December 1796. In February 1797, Secretary of State Timothy Pickering told Congress that during the previous eleven months France had seized 316 US merchant ships. In President John Adams's annual message to Congress towards the end of 1797, he reported France's refusal to negotiate a settlement and stressed the need 'to place our country in a suitable posture of defense'. Adams offered George Washington a commission as lieutenant general and commander-in-chief.[1] As a condition for accepting, Washington insisted that Pinckney be offered a generalship, believing that Pinckney's military experience and political support in the South made him indispensable in defending against a possible invasion by the French.[2] In April 1798, President Adams exposed the 'XYZ' Affair in which agents of the French foreign minister Talleyrand demanded a large bribe before engaging in substantive negotiations with US diplomats. Talleyrand's strategy had been mainly one of delay. He intended to end attacks on US merchant shipping but first wanted to increase his personal wealth and strengthen his political position at home. Talleyrand's intermediaries were also interested in preserving peace with the US, as many of them had investments in US businesses.[3] Although such bribery was hardly uncommon in mainland European diplomacy of the time, the Americans were deeply offended and left France without ever engaging in formal negotiations. The slide towards all-out war seemed irresistible.

In a message to the Senate and the House of Representatives concerning one French privateer, on 5 February 1798 John Adams explained:

I have received a letter from His Excellency Charles Pinckney, esq., governor of the State of South Carolina, dated the 22d of October, 1797, inclosing a number of depositions of witnesses to several captures and outrages committed within and near the limits of the United States by a French privateer belonging to Cape Francois, or Monte Christo, called the *Vertitude* or *Fortitude*, and commanded by a person of the name of Jordan or Jourdain, and particularly upon an English merchant ship named the *Oracabissa*, which he first plundered and then burned, with the rest of her cargo, of great value, within the territory of the United States, in the harbor of Charleston, on the 17th day of October last, copies of which letter and depositions, and also of several other depositions relative to the same subject, received from the collector of Charleston, are herewith communicated.

Adams summed up his attitude towards the actions of Republican France in a message to Congress regarding the icy treatment of American representatives there:

The refusal on the part of France to receive our minister is, then, the denial of a right; but the refusal to receive him until we have acceded to their demands without discussion and without investigation is to treat us neither as allies nor as friends, nor as a sovereign state ... Such attempts ought to be repelled with a decision which shall convince France and the world that we are not a degraded people, humiliated under a colonial spirit of fear and sense of inferiority, fitted to be the miserable instruments of foreign influence, and regardless of national honor, character, and interest.

Talleyrand, realising his blunder, attempted to restore relations, and Congress approved a commission to negotiate an agreement with the French government. But meanwhile, French privateers had inflicted even more substantial losses on US shipping, cruising the length of the Atlantic seaboard virtually unopposed. The US government had nothing with which to combat them, as it had abolished the navy at the end of the Revolutionary War, selling its last warship in 1785. Only a flotilla of small Revenue cutters and a few neglected coastal forts formed a flimsy defence against the French privateers. In 1798 the government established the Department of Navy and the US Marine Corps. Benjamin Stoddert was appointed as Secretary of Navy. A former wartime cavalryman who had been severely injured at the Battle of Brandywine, Stoddert quickly realised that the infant navy possessed too few warships to protect a far-flung merchant marine by using convoys or by patrolling the North

American coast. He concluded that the best way to defeat the French was by offensive operations in the Caribbean, where most of the French cruisers were based. Simply put, his policy was to go to the source of the enemy's strength. Stoddert, a father of eight, was to prove himself a superb administrator of both daily operations and forward planning.

He had powerful supporters. George Washington stated: 'It follows then as certain as that night succeeds the day, that without a decisive naval force we can do nothing definitive, and with it, everything honorable and glorious.' President Adams agreed that 'naval power ... is the natural defense of the United States'.[4] Congress authorised the president to acquire, arm and man not more than twelve ships of up to twenty-two guns each. The first step was to build and equip three frigates, USS *Congress*, USS *Chesapeake* and USS *President*. Several merchantmen were immediately bought and refitted as ships of war.[5] Congress rescinded all treaties with France on 7 July 1798, and two days later Congress authorised the US to attack French warships in US waters. Open hostilities began, although no declaration of war was made by either side, hence its 'Quasi-War' title.

There were early American setbacks while new warships were being built and the French retained control of vast swathes of the sea. *Retaliation*, a captured privateer, and *La Croyable*, recently purchased by the navy, left Norfolk with USS *Montezuma* and USS *Norfolk* in October 1798 for the West Indies, and three weeks later the French frigates *L'Insurgente* and *Volontaire* overtook her while her consorts were elsewhere. On 20 November, commanding officer Lieutenant William Bainbridge surrendered the outgunned schooner having first mistaken the Frenchmen for British warships and foolishly approached them without identifying them. The two French frigates continued in their pursuit of other nearby American vessels. *Montezuma* and *Norfolk* escaped after Bainbridge convinced the senior French commander that those US warships were too powerful for his frigates and that he should abandon the chase. *Retaliation* was the first and last American warship to be captured.

Bainbridge was allowed to remain under guard on *Retaliation*, and after ten days was permitted to go ashore at Guadeloupe and negotiate terms of prisoner exchange with French governor General Desferneaux. The governor promised to free officers and crew if Bainbridge, acting as a US representative, would agree to declare Guadeloupe as neutral during the remainder of the war. Bainbridge instead protested the inhumane treatment of his prisoners. Eventually the governor, who wanted to foster his own trading cartel with the US, finally agreed to the release of prisoners and prepared a dispatch for Bainbridge to present to President Adams, assuring him of the neutrality of Guadeloupe. He released *Retaliation* into the command of Bainbridge with the stipulation that if their arrangement was not honoured Bainbridge and all released prisoners would be put to death if captured again. Bainbridge sailed home and presented the governor's offer, which was accepted. Bainbridge was ultimately promoted to Master and Commander and assigned to *Norfolk* for immediate service.[6]

By the following year the US Navy had a battle fleet of about twenty-five vessels. One was USS *Constellation*, a nominally rated wooden-hulled, three-masted frigate built on Harris Creek in Fell Point, Baltimore, by Joshua Humphreys, who made it and her sisters larger and more heavily armed than standard frigates of the period. An earlier visitor to the naval shipyard, the Duke de la Rochefoucauld-Liancourt, saw the *Constellation* under construction and noted in his journal: 'I thought her too much encumbered with wood-work within, but in other respects she is a fine vessel being built of those beautiful kinds of wood, the ever-green oak and cedar...'

Constellation encountered the French frigate *La Vengeance*, which was lighter but carried a heavier broadside.[7] *La Vengeance* attempted to run but an hour after sunset *Constellation* came into hailing range. When *La Vengeance* was ordered to stand to and surrender, she answered with a broadside. After an hour *Constellation*'s foresails failed and had to be repaired; she then overtook *La Vengeance* and the running battle continued, with both sides exchanging broadsides. Boarders were called for on both ships and US marines raked the enemy decks with small arms fire, leaving them covered in bodies. A young lieutenant standing next to French Captain Pitot saw his arm shot off. *Constellation* was victorious after a five-hour battle. *La Vengeance* was so holed in the hull and her rigging so cut up that she grounded outside the port of Curaçao rather than attempt to sail into port. Pitot accounted that his battleship had fired 742 rounds in the engagement while Captain Truxton of *Constellation* reported firing 1,229 rounds. *Constellation*'s rigging and spars were so damaged she dare not try to sail upwind and so went to port in Jamaica. Unable to complete a refit, she made it home on a jury rig.[8] The *Constellation*'s speed and power inspired the French to nickname her the 'Yankee Racehorse'.[9]

The first major clash of arms between broadly matched warships occurred on 9 February 1799 between the *Constellation* and the frigate *L'Insurgente*, the previous year's victor off Guadeloupe and reputed to be the fastest ship in the French Navy. Captain Thomas Truxton's insistence on high levels of training and repeated gunnery practice gave the Americans a huge confidence boost. In many ways, Truxton exemplified the mixed backgrounds of US Navy officers. The only son of an English country lawyer,[10] his father died when he was young and he spent his childhood with relatives in Jamaica.[11] With no chance of a formal education, he joined the crew of the British merchant ship *Pitt* at the age of twelve, against his dead father's previous wishes for him to pursue a career in politics.[12] By the time he was twenty, Truxton had won command of his own vessel, *Andrew Caldwell*. He was impressed into the Royal Navy and was offered a midshipman's warrant, which he turned down. Tellingly, given his later role, he was a US privateer during the Revolutionary War, commanding several ships. After the war he returned to the merchant marine, where he remained for twelve years. In 1786 he commanded *Canton*, operating from Philadelphia, one of the first American ships to engage in trade with China.

The battle started about 18 miles north-east of the island of Nevis about midday when *Constellation* spotted *L'Insurgente*, which again tried to flee. *Constellation* crowded on all sail despite a rising squall and swiftly narrowed the gap. *L'Insurgente's* rigging snapped, slowing her so much that Captain Barreaut raised the French Tricolor and asked for parley. Captain Truxton refused to answer as his orders were to attack any French warship or privateer. He ordered broadsides at the enemy's hull. *L'Insurgente* was devastated by the first broadside from double-shotted 24-pounders, which left many dead and others deserting the French guns. *L'Insurgente* tried to board and slowed to close but this allowed *Constellation* to shoot ahead and cross her bows for a bow rake with another broadside. *Constellation* crossed to windward and *L'Insurgente* turned to follow, with both crews now exchanging port broadsides instead of starboard. Heavy shot smashed through the hull of *L'Insurgente*, while its 12-pounders barely dented the *Constellation*'s hull and brought down rigging. Captain Barreaut, knowing that he was in a completely unequal contest, struck colours – the first major victory by an American-designed-and-built warship.[13] French losses were twenty-nine killed and forty-four wounded, while Truxton's crew only suffered one killed and two wounded.

By the beginning of July 1799, under the command of Stephen Decatur, USS *United States* had been refitted and repaired and embarked on its mission to patrol the South Atlantic coast and West Indies.[14] Decatur, the son of a naval commodore, had served as a midshipman on the warship the previous year. As *United States* was undergoing repairs, Decatur received orders to remain in Philadelphia to recruit and assemble a crew for the vessel. While there, the chief mate of an Indiaman used foul-mouthed epithets to describe Decatur and the US Navy as he had lost some of his crew to Decatur. Decatur initially ignored the insults, but his father insisted that he had to defend family honour. The result was a duel in which Decatur, a crack shot, deliberately inflicted a non-fatal would to his opponent's hip.[15]

After successfully completing its tour of the West Indies, *United States* was transporting two US envoys to Spain but encountered gale-force winds and instead deposited its passengers in England. *United States* suffered serious storm damage, and Decatur, not wanting to remain during the months of repairs and outfitting, obtained a transfer to the brig USS *Norfolk* and sailed to the West Indies. In the months that followed, twenty-four enemy craft were captured or destroyed. With orders to rendezvous with merchantmen bound for America, *Norfolk* continued to Cartagena (Colombia) with orders to escort the captured ships back to the US.[16] We will hear more of Decatur in a subsequent chapter.

USS *Enterprise*, whose first commander thought that she was too lightly built, also captured eight privateers and freed eleven US merchant ships from captivity. USS *Experiment* joined the squadron commanded by Captain Silas Talbot on the Santo Domingo station, and for seven months cruised against French privateers in the Caribbean, taking a number of valuable prizes including *Deux Amis* and *Diane*. On New Year's Day 1800, while becalmed in the Bight of Léogâne with a convoy of four merchantmen, *Experiment* was attacked by eleven armed pirate boats manned by over 400 buccaneers. In the seven hours of fighting that followed, the pirates boarded one merchantman, killing her captain, and towed off two other ships of the convoy after their crews had abandoned them. But *Experiment* sank two of the attacking craft, and killed and wounded many of the pirates, suffering only one man wounded. Arriving in the Delaware River early in July 1800, *Experiment* refitted and returned to the West Indies. Again successful in her patrols against the French, she captured several armed vessels, one of which was carrying a high-ranking army officer. She also recaptured a number of American merchantmen, and in January 1801 rescued sixty-five Spaniards from the ship *Eliza*, wrecked on a reef of the island of Saona.

USS *Boston* also cruised the West Indies from July 1799. Returning to Boston almost a year later, she sailed along the American coast until September when she went on to Guadeloupe Station. The next month she engaged and captured the French corvette *Berceau*, losing seven killed and eight wounded. She towed her prize to Boston and was greeted by cheering crowds.

In April 1800, Silas Talbot discovered that the French privateer *Sandwich* had taken refuge near Puerto Plata, Santo Domingo. On 8 May his squadron captured the sloop *Sally*, and Talbot devised a cunning ploy, using the familiarity of the *Sally* to allow the Americans access to the harbour.[17] First Lieutenant Isaac Hull led ninety sailors and marines into Puerto Plata without challenge on 11 May, capturing *Sandwich* and spiking the guns of the nearby Spanish fort.[18]

Revenue cutters serving in the predecessor to the US Coast Guard also engaged, often fighting well above their weight. USRC *Pickering*, commanded by Edward Preble, made two cruises to the West Indies and captured ten prizes. Preble turned command of *Pickering* over to Benjamin Hillar, who fought a notable engagement with the French privateer *L'Egypte Conquise* on 18 October 1799. The Frenchman carried fourteen 9-pounders, four 6-pounders and a crew of 250, while the American cutter had only fourteen 4-pounders and seventy men. After a nine-hour battle, however, the French ship was forced to surrender.

Pickering continued to cruise in the West Indies, and before her return home had captured four French privateers and recaptured the American merchant ship *Portland. Pickering* left Boston on 10 June 1800. Ordered to join Commodore Truxton's squadron on Guadeloupe Station, she sailed from Delaware on 20 August – and was never heard from again. She is presumed to have been lost with all hands in a gale in September, but this was never proven. That storm is also thought to have sunk USS *Insurgent*, which also vanished without a trace. Preble next commanded the frigate USS *Essex*, which he sailed around Cape Horn into the Pacific to protect US merchantmen in the East Indies. He recaptured several American ships that had been seized by French privateers.

During the course of the fighting, the new US Navy captured eighty-five French privateers, while losing approximately 2,000 merchant vessels.[19] The Americans had their own privateers. One such was the *Louisa* out of Philadelphia; its owners obtained a letter of marque that authorised her captain to act against French merchant shipping during the war. She was armed with twelve 6-pounder guns and manned by a crew of thirty officers and men.[20] In August 1800, several French privateers that sailed out of Algeciras, southern Spain, attacked her off Gibraltar.[21] Her captain, Thomas Haggard, was wounded and taken below to his cabin. However, *Louisa* fought off the attack, and Haggard was taken ashore at Gibraltar, where he subsequently died.[22]

Given their previous hostilities, the Royal Navy and the US Navy did not share operational plans, even though they were now battling the same French enemy. However, the British sold naval stores and munitions to the US government, and the two navies shared a signal system so they could recognise the other's warships at sea and allowed their merchantmen to join each other's convoys for safety.

By late 1800, both navies' fighting abilities had reduced the activity of the French privateers and warships. The growing weaknesses and final overthrow of the ruling French Directory led Talleyrand to reopen negotiations with the US. Napoleon had come to power and was seeking to re-obtain Louisiana from Spain. Consequently, Talleyrand wanted to prevent further hostility with the US, fearing that the Quasi War might escalate into a full-scale war; he let it be known that he would accept a new American diplomatic representative.

For his part, President Adams, feuding with Alexander Hamilton over control of his administration, also wanted to avoid a more widespread conflict. Adams took a sudden and unexpected turn, rejecting the anti-French hawks in his own party and offering peace to France. He sent William Vans Murray to France to negotiate, to the despair of the American Federalists. Hostilities ended with the signing of the Convention of 1800 on 30 September. It affirmed the rights of Americans as neutrals upon the sea and abrogated the alliance with France of 1778. However, it failed to provide compensation for the $20,000,000

'French Spoliation Claims' of the US. The agreement between the two nations implicitly ensured that the US would remain neutral toward France in the wars of Napoleon.[23] Despite a rocky beginning with the Quasi War and Napoleon's initial plans for a military occupation of the Louisiana Territory, France eventually negotiated the Louisiana Purchase with Thomas Jefferson's government, thus doubling the size of the ever-expanding United States.

The US Navy, threadbare and under-gunned at the start of this undeclared but costly war, had proven itself in battle, and its commanders had proved to be, by and large, effective and canny strategists. It was not long before they were needed again.

5

The Barbary Wars (1801–1805 and 1815)

every sailor held a dagger in each hand and a third in his mouth...

When they were not doing hard manual labour on land, the male captives manned the oars of galleys, in some cases for up to nineteen years. Rowers were shackled where they sat, and never allowed to leave. Sleeping, eating, defecation and urination took place at the seat. Overseers would crack the whip over the bare backs of any slaves considered to be slacking. The English-born Francis Knight recalled his enforced service, shackled to the oars for up to twenty hours a day: 'Not having so much room as to stretch legs. The stroke regular and punctual, their heads shaved unto the skull, their bodies all naked, only a short linen pair of breeches to cover their privities ... all their bodies pearled with a bloody sweat.'[1] But, to the outrage of the new United States, such slaves were not black, or brown, or mulatto – they were white Americans and Europeans captured in a centuries-old trade in human flesh, enthusiastically carried out by the maritime states of North Africa.

In March 1786, two future presidents – Thomas Jefferson, the US ambassador to France, and ambassador to Britain John Adams – met with the ambassador from Tripoli in London. They asked why American merchant ships were being attacked without provocation. The Barbary ambassador explained that Muslim pirates considered Americans to be infidels and they believed they simply had the right to plunder American ships.

With America entering a new century, early Washington spin doctors created what has been called the first 'war on terror'.

* * *

The Barbary pirates, sometimes called the Ottoman corsairs, were primarily based in the ports of Tunis, Tripoli and Algiers, known by

Europeans as the Barbary Coast. The slave trade had existed in North Africa since ancient times and the coastal towns were noted by the Romans for their thriving slave markets. Their hunting grounds extended throughout the Mediterranean, south along West Africa's seaboard, South America and as far north as Iceland. In addition to seizing ships, they engaged in regular raids on European coastal settlements in Spain, Italy, Portugal, France, England, Scotland, Wales, Ireland and the Netherlands. Their chief aim was to capture Christian slaves for the Islamic markets of North Africa and the Middle East. Their activities increased and became more cohesively and effectively organised when Algiers, Tunis and Tripoli came under the sovereignty of the Ottoman Empire, either as directly administered provinces or as autonomous dependencies known as the Barbary States. The pirates were an integral part of their society and of the economies of their countries, rather than go-it-alone buccaneers. Historian Linda Colley wrote: 'Need, greed and aggression linked all of these seafarers, but most North African "pirates" were not independent agents operating outside of their home communities' laws, so much as a vital and officially recognised part of their revenue-raising machinery.'[2] Approximately 8,500 new slaves had to be taken to the Barbary States each year simply to replenish numbers. In the 250 years since 1530 it is estimated that the total number of Europeans enslaved approached 1,250,000 – less than a tenth of the Africans taken as slaves to the Americas, but still an appalling tally of human misery.[3] The clergyman and traveller Samuel Purchas wrote of Algiers that it was 'the cage of unclean birds of prey; the habitation of sea-devils ... the whip of the Christian world, the wall of the barbarian; terror of Europe ... scourge of the islands, den of pirates'.

When the US was born, the Barbary corsairs saw American merchant shipping as a golden opportunity to extort ransom for the lives of captured sailors or, as an alternative, to claim blanket tribute from the new nation to avoid attack, as they already did with various European states.[4] For a while they were successful. Under British rule American shipping had been protected by the Royal Navy, and during the revolutionary years by France under the Treaty of Alliance. But when that treaty expired in 1783, the American ships were on their own. On 11 October 1784, Moroccan pirates seized the merchant brigantine *Betsey*.[5] The Spanish government negotiated the freedom of the captured ship and crew but strongly advised the US to pay tribute to prevent a repetition.

Congress had appointed Jefferson, John Adams and Benjamin Franklin as peace commissioners to negotiate treaties of amity and commerce with the principal states of Europe and the Mediterranean, including the Barbary States.[6] The commissioners reported the European view that tribute must be paid by Congress. The Barbary challenge to American merchant shipping sparked heated debate over how to cope with corsair aggression. Jefferson's early, hawkish view would remain solid in subsequent years. In November 1784, he doubted the American people would be willing to pay annual tribute: 'Would it not be better to offer them an equal treaty. If they refuse, why not go to war with them?' A month later he emphasized the hard line: 'Our trade to Portugal, Spain, and the Mediterranean is annihilated unless we do something decisive. Tribute or war is the usual alternative of these pirates. If we yield the former, it will require sums which our people will feel. Why not begin a navy then and decide on war? We cannot begin in a better cause nor against a weaker foe.' Jefferson was convinced this solution would be more honourable, more effective and less expensive than paying tribute.[7] In addition, he believed that America wanted to be a trading nation, and 'to carry as much as possible' in our own vessels. 'But,' he wrote to James Monroe, 'this will require a protecting force on the sea. Otherwise the smallest powers in Europe, every one which possesses a single ship of the line may dictate to us, and enforce their demands by captures on our commerce. Some naval force then is necessary if we mean to be commercial.' Adams, however, believed that paying tribute would be more economical and easier than convincing Americans to fund the building of a modern, expensive navy.[8]

In March 1786, Jefferson and Adams went to London to negotiate with Tripoli's envoy, ambassador Sidi Haji Abdrahaman. When they enquired 'concerning the ground of the pretensions to make war upon nations who had done them no injury', the ambassador replied: 'It was written in their Koran, that all nations which had not acknowledged the Prophet were sinners, whom it was the right and duty of the faithful to plunder and enslave; and that every Mussulman who was slain in this warfare was sure to go to paradise.' He added that the man 'who was the first to board a vessel had one slave over and above his share, and that when they sprang to the deck of an enemy's ship, every sailor held a dagger in each hand and a third in his mouth; which usually struck such terror into the foe that they cried out for quarter at once'.

Congress decided that peace should be bought and authorised $80,000 for negotiations. The Commissioners sent American consul Thomas Barclay to Morocco, and Connecticut sea captain John Lamb to Algiers. In Morocco the draft treaty Barclay carried with him was accepted with only minor changes. The Morocco treaty made American vessels safe from Moroccan corsairs and there was no call for future tribute.[9]

That did not work elsewhere in Barbary. Algiers was far more dependent than Morocco on the fruits of piracy — captured goods, slaves, the ransoms they brought, and tribute — and less amenable to a peace treaty with the US. While planning the Barbary missions the American Commissioners had learned that two American ships – *Maria* and *Dauphin* – had been captured by Algerian corsairs. Lamb was instructed to negotiate ransom for the captives in Algiers as well as a peace treaty to prevent further attacks on American vessels. This proved impossible with the limited budget Congress had approved.[10]

After the failure of the Lamb mission in 1786 Jefferson made further futile attempts to launch negotiations with the *Bey* (governor) of Algiers, both from Paris and later as Secretary of State under President Washington. During these years American vessels in the Mediterranean sailed in convoy with European ships, often with Portuguese naval protection, illegally flew European flags, or ventured out at considerable risk from Barbary corsairs. In the Atlantic, the Morocco Treaty provided protection from Moroccan corsairs and the Portuguese Navy kept away those from Algiers, Tunis and Tripoli in the Mediterranean. That was changed by an Algiers–Portugal treaty in 1793. In a few months Algerian corsairs seized eleven American merchant vessels — at least ten of them in the Atlantic — with over 100 crewmen and passengers.[11]

Captured sailors in letters home and in later testimonies described their captivity as slavery; most captives were pressed into hard labour in the galleys and quarries of Barbary, suffered extremely poor conditions and were exposed to vermin, putrid food and virulent disease. But their treatment was better than that imposed on Europeans and Africans for centuries as the *beys* understood their importance as bargaining chips. And Barbary imprisonment, unlike the gaols of America and Europe at the time, offered some degree of hope.[12] Barbary prisoners were able to obtain wealth and property, even freedom, particularly if they converted, albeit temporarily, to Islam. James Leander Cathcart, for example, for the first several years of his captivity, endured the same terrible living conditions as his fellow slaves. Cathcart was then set to work in the *bey*'s palace garden, caring for the lions, tigers and antelopes. Although his duties were relatively light, his masters provided scant food and administered several beatings to his feet, which meant he lost several of his toenails. Cathcart acquired additional skills that he used later as a diplomat, finding opportunities to demonstrate his concern for his fellow prisoners. During his slavery he learnt Arabic and Turkish, and when he became clerk of the prison, he was able to buy several taverns, a house with servants, and procure more food for his fellow crew members. Before his eventual release, he rose to the highest position a Christian slave could achieve in Algeria, becoming an adviser to the *bey*. Even so, and quite understandably, the stories of torture and cruel treatment suffered by white Americans filtered home, causing widespread public outrage.

America finally did make peace with Algiers in 1795, when Jefferson was no longer Secretary of State, agreeing partly in return for the release of 115 American sailors to pay annual tribute of over $1 million, about one-sixth of the entire US budget.[13] All four Barbary Coast states then demanded annual tribute of $660,000 each. However, the envoys were given only an allocated budget of $40,000 to achieve peace.

Diplomatic talks to reach a reasonable sum for tribute or for the ransom of the captured sailors struggled to make any headway. The crews of *Maria* and *Dauphin* remained enslaved for over a decade, and soon were joined by those of other captured ships. Treaties were also concluded with Tripoli in 1796 and Tunis in 1797. Soon after, American consuls were appointed in each Barbary state.

Jefferson continued to argue against payment of tribute, supported by George Washington. With the recommissioning of the American Navy in 1794 and the resulting increased firepower on the seas, it became viable for America to refuse payment, although by now the long-standing habit was hard to overturn. Humanitarian concerns were raised but, most importantly, the pirates were disrupting the commercial traffic which the new nation so desperately needed to generate taxes, personal wealth and public prosperity.

The government, having cut shipbuilding at the close of the Quasi War with France, had a change of heart and began building warships designed for conditions in the Mediterranean and eastern Atlantic seaboards. Just before Jefferson's inauguration as president in 1801, Congress passed naval legislation that provided for six frigates that 'shall be officered and manned as the President of the United States may direct'. In the event of a declaration of war on the United States by the Barbary powers, these ships were to 'protect our commerce and chastise their insolence—by sinking, burning or destroying their ships and vessels wherever you shall find them'. Ironically, until the crisis, President Jefferson's first concern with the US Navy was how best to disband it and best lay up its vessels. Secretary of the Treasury Albert Gallatin's primary concern was to reduce Federal spending, and the navy was a major expense. The actions in Tripoli changed all that. Work on the frigate *Philadelphia* was depicted in a painting titled *Preparation for WAR to Defend Commerce*. Tripoli and the other Barbary States were no longer major military powers, but their fast ships were capable of taking heavily laden and undefended merchant vessels. And their fearsome reputation still influenced strategic thinking.

The news from American consuls that awaited the new Jefferson administration in 1801 was distressing and tension was particularly great with Tripoli. Pasha Yusuf Qaramanli was threatening war, convinced the Americans treated him less well than they did the other Barbary rulers. He was right, but Tunis and Algiers had simply negotiated better treaties. In October 1800, five months before Jefferson took office, the American consul in Tripoli, James Cathcart, warned that the pasha's message was: 'If you don't give me a present I will forge a pretext to capture your defenceless merchantmen; he likewise says that he expects an answer as soon as possible, and that any delay on our side will only serve to injure our own interests...'

A week after that was written, a Tripolitan corsair took the American brig *Catharine* into Tripoli. The pasha immediately ordered the ship and her crew released and dismissed the corsair captain. Pasha Qaramanli's explanation was that he had told the president that 'before he would take any measures whatsoever against the United States' he would wait for the President's answer to his letter of five months earlier (25 May 1800). Later, however, in a meeting with Cathcart, Captain Carpenter of *Catharine* and local officials, the Pasha imposed a six-month deadline on an acceptable presidential cash settlement. Reporting on that public ultimatum, Cathcart explained to the Secretary of State why America owed nothing to the pasha and how he was regularly at war with some country or other from which he would demand beneficial negotiations. He was then at war with Sweden, which would soon agree to pay annual tribute and ransom for 131 captives; fourteen Swedish merchantmen had been seized by Tripolitan corsairs since the angered Pasha had broken an existing treaty and declared war a few months earlier.[14]

Historian Elizabeth Huff wrote:

> The demanding, threatening language Cathcart reported to the Secretary of State was more explicit than the Pasha's unanswered letter to president Adams of May 25 but no more so than the exchanges Cathcart had related then and previously. The consul had followed his report with a circular letter in November to American consuls and agents in the Mediterranean. He advised them to warn American ships of the possibility of hostile action by Tripolitan corsairs from the month of March, or possibly sooner, a warning he repeated in January after Tripoli made peace with Sweden. In February, efforts by the dey of Algiers and Cathcart to ease tensions with the pasha were fruitless, producing only more confirmation of the likelihood of war as the corsair fleet began fitting out.[15]

On 21 February 1801, in a new circular letter, Cathcart told the consuls and agents 'to detain all merchant vessels navigating under the flag of the United States, in port, and by no means to permit any of them to sail unless they are under convoy, as I am now convinced that the Bashaw of Tripoli will commence hostilities against the United States of America in less than sixty days'.[16]

Pasha Yusuf Qaramanli, on Jefferson's inauguration, made his final demand: a tribute of $225,000. In line with his long-held beliefs, Jefferson refused. Consequently, on 10 May 1801, the Pasha declared war on the US, not through any formal written documents but in the customary Barbary manner of cutting down the flagstaff in front of the US Consulate. Algiers and Tunis did not follow suit.

Before learning that Tripoli had declared war, Jefferson sent a small squadron of three frigates and one schooner under the command of Commodore Richard Dale with gifts and letters to attempt to maintain peace. As a proviso, in the event that war had been declared, Dale was instructed 'to protect American ships and citizens against potential aggression', but Jefferson insisted that he was 'unauthorized by the constitution, without the sanction of Congress, to go beyond the line of defense'. Although Congress never voted on a formal declaration of war, they did authorise the president to instruct the commanders of armed American vessels to seize all vessels and goods of the Pasha of Tripoli 'and also to cause to be done all such other acts of precaution or hostility as the state of war will justify'. The American squadron joined a Swedish flotilla under Rudolf Cederström in blockading Tripoli, the Swedes having been at war with them since the previous year. The American slogan became 'Millions for defense, but not one cent for tribute!'

On 31 May 1801, Commodore Edward Preble travelled to Messina, Sicily, to the court of Ferdinand IV of the Kingdom of Naples. The kingdom was at war with Napoleon, but Ferdinand supplied the Americans with manpower, craftsmen, supplies, gunboats and mortar boats, while the ports of Messina, Syracuse and Palermo were to be used as naval bases for launching operations against Tripoli. Such support was vital as the port of Tripoli was a walled fortress city protected by 150 pieces of heavy artillery and manned by 25,000 soldiers, assisted by a fleet of ten brigs of ten guns, two eight-gun schooners, two large galleys and nineteen gunboats.[17]

Commodore Dale sailed on USS *President* for the Strait of Gibraltar on 1 June 1801. He and the US Navy generally were not prepared for what they found – information about the reefs around Tripoli or the weather patterns of the region were, at best, sketchy. Blockading Tripoli thus proved difficult because of the weather, the size of the American frigates and the limited number of vessels. A rare action at sea was carried out by the schooner *Enterprise*, captained by Lieutenant Andrew Sterett, which engaged the fourteen-gun corsair galley *Tripoli* on 1 August. It was an unequal contest; the corsair was taken and about sixty killed. Sterett was unsure that he had the authority to seize ships as prizes, so he cut the masts and let the battered enemy vessel return to Tripoli. The Pasha was not pleased and, refusing to see the greater firepower of the American ship as any excuse for the humiliation, had Admiral Rais Mahomet Rous flogged and made to ride through the streets backwards on a donkey festooned with sheep entrails.[18]

Such naval encounters were rare, and Dale made no effort to attack Tripoli itself. President Jefferson was frustrated at both Dale's lack of action and the high cost of maintaining the American squadron in the Mediterranean, which was substantially greater than what Tripoli had demanded in payment. Jefferson pressed the issue the following year, with an increase in military force and deployment of many of the navy's best ships to the region throughout 1802. These included the largely untested *Philadelphia*, the Quasi-War veterans *Constellation*, *Constitution*, *Chesapeake* and *Enterprise*, plus *Argus*, *Intrepid* and *Syren*.

The next squadron was commanded by Richard Valentine Morris. He duly sailed for Gibraltar but showed little desire to engage the Barbary forces, preferring to stay in port enjoying some measure of domestic bliss as he had insisted on bringing his pregnant wife along. Morris kept *Chesapeake* in port and *Constellation*, commanded by Captain Alexander Murray, was used to blockade Tripoli. The smaller Tripolitan vessels could easily evade the deep-draft *Constellation*'s guns by keeping to shallow water and negotiating reefs which the larger American vessel dared not approach.

A frustrated Secretary Smith put the entire American force under Edward Preble, who proved a far more dynamic leader. Throughout 1803, Preble set up and maintained a blockade of the Barbary ports and executed a campaign of raids and attacks against the cities' fleets. Preble had begun his naval career as a midshipman, and when his ship was captured by the Royal Navy he was imprisoned on the notorious prison ship *Jersey*, but managed to survive, although his health was affected forever. As a US naval commander, he was a strict disciplinarian, but he earned his crew's respect as a fighter. He was prepared to aggressively press the attack on Tripoli. Preble, aboard his flagship *Constitution*, sailed for Gibraltar on 12 August and rendezvoused with *Philadelphia* the following month. *Philadelphia* had three ships under its control: the merchant brig *Celia* and the Moroccan ships *Miroka* and *Meshouda*.

Gibraltar and Malta had been used by the Americans, but there were problems in dealing with the Royal Navy, in part because a number of British deserters served on American vessels. To avoid potential clashes, Preble shifted his base of operations to Syracuse in Sicily. He ordered *Philadelphia* under Captain William Bainbridge to return to a station off Tripoli to enforce the blockade. Preble's strategy was sound, but the Americans then suffered an astonishing and largely accidental setback. Pursuing a Tripolitan vessel, *Philadelphia* ran aground on a reef outside the harbour approaches on 31 October. Her guns were thrown overboard in a bid to free the lightened vessel but all efforts failed. The ship was overrun by the Pasha's men. The ship, captain, and all officers and crew were taken ashore as hostages. *Philadelphia* was anchored in the harbour as a gun battery against her American commanders.

On the night of 16 February 1804, the then still virtually unknown Lieutenant Stephen Decatur led a detachment of marines aboard a captured corsair ketch rechristened USS *Intrepid*, to either recapture or destroy the *Philadelphia* to deny her use by the enemy. Under the dim light of a waxing crescent moon, *Intrepid* slowly sailed into Tripoli harbour. Decatur's vessel was made to look like a common merchant ship from Malta and was outfitted with British colours. To further avoid suspicion, on board were five Sicilian volunteers including the pilot Salvatore Catalano, who spoke Arabic. The boarding party remained hidden below in position, prepared to board *Philadelphia*. The men were given explicit instruction not to use of firearms unless absolutely necessary.[19] As Decatur's ship came closer to *Philadelphia*, Catalano called out to the harbour personnel in Arabic that their ship had lost its anchors during a recent storm and was seeking refuge at Tripoli for repairs.[20] By 9.30 p.m. Decatur's ship was within 200 yards of *Philadelphia*, whose lower yards were now resting on the deck with her foremast missing.[21]

When the two vessels were finally close enough, Catalano obtained permission for Decatur to tie *Intrepid* to the *Philadelphia*. Decatur completely surprised the Tripolitans when he shouted the order, 'Board!', signalling to the hidden crew below to storm the vessel.[22] Without losing a single man, Decatur and sixty of his men, dressed as Maltese sailors or Arab seamen and armed with swords and boarding pikes, reclaimed *Philadelphia* in less than ten minutes, killing at least twenty of the Tripolitan crew, capturing one wounded crewman, and forcing the rest to flee by jumping overboard. Only one of Decatur's men was slightly wounded by a sword blade. The boarding crew had hoped to launch the captured ship, but the vessel was in no condition to set sail for the open sea, and Decatur soon realised that the small *Intrepid* could not tow the larger and heavier warship out of the harbour. Decatur's crew placed combustibles about *Philadelphia* and set her ablaze. After making sure the fire was large enough to sustain itself, Decatur ordered his men to abandon the ship and was the last man to leave.[23] As the flames intensified, the Tripolitan guns aboard *Philadelphia*, all loaded and ready for battle, began discharging, some firing into the town and shore batteries, while the ropes securing the ship burned off, allowing the vessel to drift into the rocks at the western entrance of the harbour.[24]

When *Intrepid* came under fire from Tripolitans, the larger *Syren* provided covering fire at the shore batteries and gunboats. Under the cover of night *Intrepid* and *Syren* made their way back to Syracuse, arriving on 18 February.[25] After learning of Decatur's operation, British Vice Admiral Lord Horatio Nelson, at the time blockading the French port at Toulon, declared it 'the most bold and daring act of the Age'.[26] Decatur's success, albeit in destroying an American ship, made him an immediate national hero in the US, arguably the first of the post-Independence age.[27] In Naples, Decatur was dubbed 'Terror of the Foe' by the local newspapers. Pope Pius VII publicly declared that 'the United States, though in their infancy, had done more to humble and humiliate the anti-Christian barbarians on the African coast in one night than all the European states had done for a long period of time'.[28] Decatur resumed command of *Enterprise*.

Preble began his attack on the port itself on 14 July 1804, having secured gunboats from the Kingdom of Naples, which had suffered from Barbary attacks. Preble divided them into two divisions, putting Decatur in command of the second. It was an elaborately well-planned onslaught deploying brigs, schooners and bomb ketches. The Tripolitan pasha, Murad Reis, however, had been forewarned and had his own gunboats lined up in readiness within the harbour. The result was a stalemate. Throughout August Preble kept up the pressure, forcing the residents to flee into the countryside. During this time Decatur captured three Tripolitan gunboats and three others. The Tripolitans also inflicted considerable damage on some of the attacking vessels; Decatur's ship was struck with a 24-pound shot through her hull above the waterline. Before the battle ended, USS *John Adams*, commanded by Isaac Chauncey, arrived on the scene. On board the vessel were official documents promoting the twenty-five-year-old Decatur to captain, making him the youngest to have reached that rank before or since. *John Adams* also brought news that, upon the loss of the frigate *Philadelphia*, the government was sending four additional frigates – *President*, *Congress*, *Constellation* and *Essex* – to Tripoli with enough force to convince the pasha that peace was his only viable alternative. Because Preble's rank was not high enough for this command, *John Adams* also brought the news that he would have to surrender command to Commodore Barron.

However, Decatur's delight over his promotion was short-lived. During the fighting, his younger brother James, in command of a gunboat, was mortally wounded by a Tripolitan captain during the boarding of a vessel feigning surrender. Midshipman Brown, who was next in command after James, managed to break away from the ambushing vessel and immediately approached Decatur's gunboat with the tragic news. Decatur, who had just captured his first Tripolitan vessel, handed it over to Lieutenant Jonathan Thorn and immediately set out to avenge his brother's treacherous injury. After pulling alongside the Tripolitan ship, Decatur was the first to board the enemy vessel followed by Midshipman Macdonough and nine volunteer crew members. Decatur and his crew were outnumbered five to one but their discipline proved unstoppable as they fought ferociously in a wedge in which each man protected his neighbours. Decatur found the corsair captain and immediately engaged the large and formidable man, who was armed with a boarding pike. He thrust his weapon at Decatur's chest. Decatur deflected the lunge with his cutlass, breaking his own weapon at the hilt. Decatur was almost killed by another Tripolitan crew member, but his life was saved by the already wounded Daniel Frazier, a crewman who threw himself over Decatur just in time, receiving a blow intended for Decatur to his own head. The struggle continued, with the Tripolitan captain gaining the upper hand. He tried to stab Decatur in the heart, but while wrestling the arm of his adversary Decatur fired a pistol shot at point-blank range, immediately killing his foe. When the fighting was over, twenty-one Tripolitans were dead with only three taken alive. James Decatur was later taken aboard *Constitution*, where he was joined by his brother, who stayed with him until he died. The next day, after a funeral and military ceremony that was conducted by Preble, his remains were committed to the depths.

When days passed without the reinforcements of ships promised by President Jefferson, the attack on Tripoli was renewed by Preble on 24 August but the enemy showed no signs of surrender, prompting Preble to devise another plan. *Intrepid*, under Captain Richard Somers, was loaded with barrels of gunpowder and other ordnance and sent towards the enemy fleet at harbour, but it blew up prematurely, killing Somers and his entire crew. The American fleet relentlessly bombarded the town and the pasha's palace.

After such robust but ultimately inconclusive action, a fourth American squadron of four frigates was deployed under Samuel Barron who reached Gibraltar on 12 August 1804. The US Consul informed him that the Pasha of Morocco was considering taking advantage of the Tripoli war to attack American ships. He ordered Captain Rogers of *Congress* and his brother James Barron of *Essex* to make a show of force outside Tangier to deter the Moroccans. They would then join him sailing east to find Preble with the *President* and *Constellation*. After the successful rendezvous Preble returned home. Preble considered himself a failure but, thanks in part to the support of the president and Secretary Smith, he was surprised to find upon arrival that he was a national hero. Americans admired how he had taken the fight to the enemy. America needed heroes and by now they had two in Preble and the young Decatur. Moreover, Preble's battering of Tripoli had left the pasha wavering. Barron's arrival with additional ships – four new frigates – shocked Yusuf; he simply could not understand why the Americans were prepared to go to so much expense to avoid paying tribute.

Barron's command of the squadron was impaired by illness, but unexpectedly another front was opened by the Americans. William Eaton had been appointed consul to Tunis before the war and he and special diplomat James L. Cathcart had attempted to work out a settlement. They reached the conclusion that Yusuf would not make peace and came up with the idea of reinstalling his exiled brother, Hamet Karamanli. Congress agreed and Eaton returned to the Mediterranean with the new title of Navy Agent to the Barbary States. He organised a force in Alexandria to replace Yusuf. Eaton and 1st Lieutenant Presley O'Bannon led a ragtag army consisting of a small force of Hamat's supporters, seventy Greek mercenaries, 300 Arabs and Bedouins, eight marines and two midshipmen.

On 8 March 1805, Eaton, who claimed the title of general, and O'Bannon led the force out on a gruelling 500-mile trek westward across the Libyan North African desert from Egypt. Their first objective was the port city of Derna, capital of the Ottoman province of Cyrenaica in eastern modern Libya. The mercenary forces were promised supplies and money when they reached the city, but during the fifty-day trek relations became strained between the Christian Greeks and the Muslims. Supplies were rapidly consumed and Eaton reported: 'Our only provisions [are] a handful of rice and two biscuits a day.' A party of Arab mercenaries tried to raid the supply wagon but were beaten back by the marines and a few Greek artillerymen, who used the expedition's lone cannon. There was the constant threat of mutiny, and from 22 to 30 March several Arab mercenaries under the command of Sheik el Tahib did just that, but Eaton had suppressed the trouble by the time he crossed the province border. In late April, his army finally reached the port city of Bomba up the coast from Derna, where US warships *Argus*, *Nautilus* and *Hornet* with Commodore Barron and Captain Isaac Hull were waiting for him with fresh supplies.

On the morning of 26 April, Eaton sent a letter to Mustafa Bey, the governor of Derna, asking for safe passage through the city and additional supplies. Mustafa wrote back: 'My head or yours!' The following morning *Argus* sent a cannon ashore to use against an outlying fort. Captain Hull's ships then opened fire and bombarded Derna's heavily defended shore batteries for an hour. Meanwhile, Eaton divided his army into two separate attacking parties. Hamet personally led the Arab mercenaries south-west to cut the road to Tripoli before attacking the city's left flank and storming the weakly defended governor's palace. Eaton with the rest of the mercenaries and the squad of marines attacked the harbour fortress from landward, with O'Bannon and his marines leading the advance. Fifty Greek gunners trundled forwards the field piece from *Argus*, though the gun's effectiveness was lessened after the firing crew carelessly left the ramrod in the barrel. The harbour defences had been reinforced, and the attackers were temporarily halted. But this had weakened the defences elsewhere and allowed the Arab mercenaries to ride unopposed into the western section of the city.[29]

Eaton's mercenary army wavered under the enemy's musket fire, and a charge was the only way to regain the initiative. Leading it, Eaton was seriously wounded in the wrist by a musket ball. On *Argus*, Captain Hull saw the Americans and mercenaries were 'gaining ground very fast though a heavy fire of Musquetry [*sic*] was constantly kept upon them'. The ships ceased fire to allow the charge to continue. Eaton reported that O'Bannon with his marines and Greeks 'pass'd through a shower of Musketry from the Walls of houses, took possession of the Battery'. The defenders fled in haste, leaving their cannons loaded and ready to fire. O'Bannon raised the fifteen-star American flag – the Star-Spangled Banner – over the battery while Eaton turned the captured guns on the city. Hamet's force had by then seized the governor's palace and secured the western part of the city. Many of the defenders of the harbour fortress fled through the town and ran into Hamet's men and were cut down without compassion. By 4 p.m. the entire city had fallen, and for the first time in history, an American flag flew over foreign fortifications. American casualties were two killed and three wounded, while those among the Christian/Greek mercenaries were nine killed or wounded. Muslim Turkish/Arab mercenary casualties were unknown, as are those of the defenders.[30]

Yusuf in Tripoli had been told of the attack on Derna and had sent reinforcements to the city, but by the time they arrived it had fallen. His men dug in south of the city and prepared to recapture it. Eaton fortified his new position, while Hamet took up residence in the governor's palace and had his Arabs patrolling the outer areas of the city. On 13 May Yusuf's force attacked and drove Hamet's Arabs back, just failing to recapture the governor's palace. USS *Argus* and Eaton's captured batteries pounded the attackers, who finally fled under heavy fire. Nightfall found both sides back in their original positions. Skirmishes and several other minor attempts were made on the city in the following weeks, but with no concrete results.

From Derna, Eaton now planned to march across the desert and attack Tripoli from the land, but in transit he was informed of the treaty signed between American emissary Tobias Lear and Yusuf. He was ordered to return to Egypt with Hamet. The mercenaries were denied the promised plunder and were never fully paid for their services. The marines in Eaton's force were immortalised in the marines' battle hymn 'To the shores of Tripoli'. That is when the marines began wearing leather collars as they reduced the possibility of being beheaded while boarding enemy ships – the origin of the nickname Leathernecks.

Yusuf Karamanli had wearied of the blockade and raids, and knew he was under serious threat from an American-backed military effort to restore his older brother. The capture of Derna proved to be the last straw. He signed a new treaty with the Americans on 10 June. Article 2 of the treaty reads:

> The Bashaw of Tripoli shall deliver up to the American squadron now off Tripoli, all the Americans in his possession; and all the subjects of the Bashaw of Tripoli now in the power of the United States of America shall be delivered up to him; and as the number of Americans in possession of the Bashaw of Tripoli amounts to three hundred persons, more or less; and the number of Tripolino subjects in the power of the Americans to about one hundred more or less; The Bashaw of Tripoli shall receive from the United States of America, the sum of sixty thousand dollars, as a payment for the difference between the prisoners herein mentioned.

The returned prisoners included Commodore Bainbridge of *Philadelphia* and his surviving crew members, who had been held prisoner since October 1803.

In agreeing to pay a ransom of $60,000 for the American prisoners, the Jefferson administration drew a distinction between paying tribute and paying ransom. At the time, some argued that buying sailors out of slavery was a fair exchange to end the war. Others argued that the capture of Derna should have been used as a bargaining chip to obtain the release of American prisoners without having to pay ransom. The latter believed the honour of the US's reputation had been tarnished when it abandoned Hamet Karamanli after promising to restore him as leader of Tripoli. Such concerns were ignored because of strained international relations which would ultimately lead to the withdrawal of the US Navy from the area in 1807 and to the 1812 war with the British.[31]

The war with Tripoli and the resulting treaty is important not only because it ended the pasha's attacks on American shipping, but also because Tunis and Morocco, seeing the formidable American ships and the willingness of the Americans to aggressively use them, deemed it prudent not to follow Tripoli's example and target American ships. After the treaty was signed Commodore Barron went home and John Rogers, who had built a fighting reputation on the *John Adams*, was put in command of the remaining ships.

William Eaton returned a hero to his home in Massachusetts. He was elected to the state legislature, but only served one term. Having lost the Federalist vote because of his outspokenness, Eaton failed at his bid for re-election. His ill health, evident in North Africa, was exacerbated by gout and rheumatism. He drank heavily and amassed large gambling debts. He died on 1 June 1811, leaving a widow and seven children.

O'Bannon was awarded a sword of honour by his home state of Virginia. He resigned from the Marine Corps in 1807, moved to Kentucky and served several terms in the state legislature and the state senate. He married the daughter of Revolutionary War general Daniel Morgan and died, aged seventy-four, in 1850.

Preble helped establish many of the modern navy's rules and regulations and also dictated that his ships be kept in a state of readiness for any action while under sail. The officers serving under him during his career also went on to become influential in the Navy Department after his death, and together they proudly wore the unofficial title of 'Preble's Boys'. Preble's Mediterranean operations led directly to the US government's firm anti-negotiation stance. In September 1804, Preble requested relief due to long-term illness. He returned to the US in February 1805 and became engaged in the comparably light duty of shipbuilding activities at Portland. Congress presented him with a gold medal for the 'gallantry and good conduct' displayed by him and his squadron at Tripoli. President Jefferson offered him the Navy Department in 1806, but Preble declined the appointment due to his poor health. He died in Portland of a gastrointestinal illness in August 1807.[32]

The First Barbary War boosted the US Navy's and the marines' confidence and reputation and showed that America could execute a war far from home.[33] But the Barbary problem did not go away, and Decatur and Bainbridge would become heroes again.

* * *

By 1807, Algiers had gone back to taking American ships and seamen hostage. Distracted by the run-up to the 1812 War, and by the war itself, the US was unable to respond to the provocation until 1815. America's European allies had also been distracted by the wars against Napoleon. After the conclusion of the war against the British, on 3 March 1815, Congress authorised deployment of naval power against Algiers. Two squadrons were assembled, one at New York under the command of Stephen Decatur and one at Boston under the command of Commodore William Bainbridge.[34] Decatur's squadron of ten ships was ready first and set sail for Algiers on 20 May. At the time it was the largest US fleet ever assembled.

Decatur had enjoyed rapid promotion as in almost every theatre of operation his service was characterised by acts of heroism and exceptional performance. He was awarded the Congressional Gold Medal for distinguished service in the War of 1812. He evaded British blockades, supervised the building of gunboats, always led from the front and was for a while held captive in Bermuda by the British. He was renowned for his natural ability to lead and for his genuine concern for the seamen under his command. Now his flagship was USS *Guerriere*, and the squadron consisted of *Constellation*, *Macedonia*, *Epervier*, *Ontario*, *Firefly*, *Spark*, *Flambeau*, *Torch* and *Spitfire*.[35]

Aboard *Guerriere* was William Shaler, recently appointed by President Madison as the consul-general for the Barbary States, acting as joint commissioner with Commodores Decatur and Bainbridge.[36] Shaler carried a letter authorising them to negotiate terms of peace with the Algerian government, with the US demanding the release of Americans held captive, an end to annual tribute, and favourable prize agreements. Decatur was equally prepared to negotiate peace or resort to military measures.[37]

Before committing himself to the Mediterranean, Decatur learned from the American consuls[38] that a squadron under the command of the notorious Rais Hamidou had passed into the Mediterranean. Decatur's squadron arrived at Gibraltar on 15 June 1815 and Hamidou was swiftly informed. Decatur's visit lasted only for as long as it took meet the consul and send a short letter to the Secretary of the Navy informing him of earlier weather problems and that he was about to 'proceed in search of the enemy forthwith'.[39] He gave chase and cut off Hamidou's squadron before they could reach Algiers. With nine vessels, he spotted the forty-six-gun Algerian flagship *Mashouda* off Cape Gata. Hamidou, realising he was heavily outnumbered, made a run for it but was himself wounded by a broadside from the *Constellation*. He changed course for a neutral haven on the Spanish coast.[40] The *Constellation* and the sloop *Ontario* closed in to hammer the enemy frigate. The Algerians could only reply with close-range musket fire as the *Guerriere* pulled alongside and fired a devastating broadside, which crippled the ship and killed the admiral. The crew continued to fight bravely but hopelessly with muskets.

Decatur ordered a sloop to fire nine more broadsides. The few bloodied Algerians left on their feet surrendered.[41] They had thirty killed and 406 captured, most of them suffering wounds, many of which would eventually prove fatal. The American losses were only four dead and ten wounded, all on *Guerriere* and mainly due to the self-detonation of an on-board cannon. After sending the captured frigate to Cartagena, Decatur continued to cruise towards Algiers.

His squadron encountered twenty-two-gun Algerian brig *Estedio* off Cape Palos on 19 June. Decatur chased her into shoal waters near the Spanish coast. Fearing that his larger vessels might get beached, he sent the smaller vessels in his squadron to deal with the brig. They fought a thirty-minute engagement in which at least twenty-three of the enemy were killed and the ship shattered. As *Estedio*'s crew began to flee towards the cape in her boats, the American vessels began firing upon them, sinking one. The surviving eighty crew surrendered. A prize crew took *Estedio* to Cartagena, where Spanish authorities interned her.[42] They returned her to Algiers at the end of the war. Decatur's squadron regrouped and continued on its way to Algiers to force Dey Omar Agha to terms.

The loss of the *Mashouda* and, particularly, Admiral Hamidou greatly weakened Algerian morale as well as their naval capabilities. Once the American squadron reached Algiers they met no further opposition and by a mere show of force were able to bring the Dey to terms within forty-eight hours of Decatur's arrival, thus ending the war.[43] He signed a treaty aboard the *Guerriere* in the Bay of Algiers on 3 July 1815, in which Decatur agreed to return the captured *Meshuda* and *Estedio*. The Algerians returned ten or so American captives in exchange for about 500 subjects of the Dey. Algeria also paid $10,000 for seized shipping. The treaty guaranteed no further tributes by the US and granted America full shipping rights in the Mediterranean Sea. After bringing the government in Algiers to terms, Decatur's squadron set sail to Tunis and Tripoli to demand reimbursement for proceeds withheld by those governments during the War of 1812. With a similar show of force as exhibited at Algiers, Decatur received all of his demands. Victorious, he promptly sailed homewards.

Returning to the United States, Decatur reached New York on 12 November 1815 on the brig *Enterprise*, followed three days later by Bainbridge on *Guerriere*.[44] Decatur boasted to the Secretary of the Navy that the settlement had 'been dictated at the mouths of our cannon'. He became known as 'the Conqueror of the Barbary Pirates'. Secretary of War James Monroe wrote to him: 'I take much interest in informing you that the result of this expedition, so glorious to your country and honorable to yourself and the officers and men under your command, has been very satisfactory to the President.' Navy Secretary Benjamin Crowninshield offered him a place on the board of navy commissioners, which he gladly accepted.

Bey Omar Agha of Algeria repudiated the US treaty, refused to accept the terms of peace that had been ratified by the Congress of Vienna, and threatened the lives of all Christian inhabitants of Algiers. US commissioner in Algiers William Shaler had to flee aboard a British vessel and watch rockets and cannon shot fly over his house 'like hail'.[45]

It was Britain who finally ended Barbary piracy. In early 1816, Britain undertook a diplomatic mission, backed by a small squadron of ships of the line, to Tunis, Tripoli and Algiers to convince the Beys to stop their piracy and free enslaved European Christians. Tunis and Tripoli agreed without any resistance, but the Dey of Algiers was more recalcitrant, and the negotiations were stormy. The leader of the diplomatic mission, Edward Pellew, Viscount Exmouth, believed that he had negotiated a treaty to stop the slavery of Christians and returned to England. However, just after the treaty was signed, Algerian troops massacred 200 Corsican, Sicilian and Sardinian fishermen who had been classified as under British protection. This caused outrage in Britain and Europe, and Exmouth's negotiations were seen as a failure.[46]

Exmouth was ordered to sea again to complete the job and punish the Algerians. He gathered a squadron of five ships of the line, reinforced by a number of frigates, and later by a flotilla of six Dutch ships. On 27 August 1816, following a round of failed negotiations, the fleet delivered a punishing nine-hour bombardment of Algiers. The attack immobilised many of the Bey's corsairs and shore batteries, forcing him to accept a peace offer of the same terms as he had rejected the day before. Exmouth warned that if these terms were not accepted, he would continue the action. The Dey accepted the terms, but Exmouth had been bluffing; his fleet had already spent all its ammunition.[47] A treaty was signed on 24 September 1816. The British Consul and 1,083 other Christian slaves were freed, and the US ransom money repaid.

After the First Barbary War, the European nations had been engaged in warfare with one another during the Napoleonic Wars on the Continent, and the US with the British. But in the years immediately following the Second Barbary War there was no general European war, which allowed the Europeans to build up their resources and challenge Barbary power in the Mediterranean without distraction. The western nations built ever more sophisticated and expensive ships which the Barbary pirates could not match in numbers or technology.[48] No more tribute was paid. Over the following century, Algiers and Tunis were colonised by France in 1830 and 1881, respectively. In 1835, Tripoli returned to the control of the Ottoman Empire.

Over 120 years later, President Franklin D. Roosevelt wrote in his *Foreword to Naval Documents* related to the United States' wars with the Barbary Powers: 'Our exasperating experiences with the Barbary States of northern Africa, continuing for a generation after the United States had won its independence, constitute an interesting chapter of American history and one from which we may derive permanently valuable lessons.'

But the more immediate lesson of the war, in America, Britain and across the 'civilised' world, was clear and profound. The visceral terror of the Barbary pirates, which long outlasted their ability to do serious harm, saw the very institution of slavery marginalised and increasingly despised on both sides of the Atlantic. The transatlantic slave trade carried on but white slavers dealing in black flesh who argued that slavery was a natural order of race or religion lost much legitimacy, even in the contradictory moral and commercial climates of the time. Slaves in Barbary were black, brown and white, Catholic, Protestant, Orthodox, Jewish or of the Islamic faiths. Abolitionists used the example of Barbary to attack the universal degradation of slavery itself. Britain abolished the slave trade during the First Barbary War and slavery itself thirty years later. It took the 'land of the free' a lot longer.

* * *

Stephen Decatur served on the Board of Naval Commissioners from 1816 to 1820. One of his more notable decisions involved his strong objection to the reinstatement of James Barron upon his return to the US after being barred from command for five years for his 1807 surrender to the British of USS *Chesapeake* during an alleged search for British deserters on board.[49]

In October 1818, at the request of his close friend Oliver Hazard Perry, Decatur arrived in New York to act as his second in a duel between Perry and challenger Captain John Heath, commander of marines on USS *Java*. They had had a personal disagreement while aboard that ship. Perry had written to Decatur nearly a year previously, revealing that he had no intention of firing any shot at Heath. After the two duellists and their seconds assembled, one shot was fired; Heath missed his opponent while Perry, keeping his word, returned no fire. At this point Decatur approached Heath with Perry's letter and asked Heath if his honour had thus been satisfied. Heath admitted that it had. Decatur was relieved to finally see the matter resolved with no loss of life or limb to either of his friends.[50]

But in 1820, Commodore James Barron challenged Decatur to a duel over lingering resentments over the Chesapeake Affair. Barron had just returned to the US from military service in Copenhagen after being away for six years and was seeking reinstatement and Decatur was one of the most outspoken in strongly opposing that.[51] Barron's challenge to Decatur occurred during a period when duels between officers were so common that it was creating a shortage of experienced officers, forcing the War Department to threaten to discharge those who attempted to pursue the practice.

Barron's second was Captain Jesse Elliott, who hated Decatur for reasons now lost in time. Decatur had first asked his friend Thomas Macdonough to be his second, but Macdonough, who had always opposed duelling, refused.[52] Decatur then turned to his supposed friend Commodore William Bainbridge and he agreed. Decatur had made a poor choice: Bainbridge, who was five years his senior, had long been jealous of the younger and more famous Decatur.[53] The seconds met on 8 March to establish the time and place for the duel and the rules to be followed. The arrangements were exact. The duel was to take place at nine o'clock in the morning on 22 March, at Bladensburg Dueling Grounds, near Washington, at a distance of only eight paces. Decatur, an expert pistol shot, planned only to wound Barron in the hip.

Decatur did not tell his wife, Susan, about the forthcoming duel but instead wrote to her father asking that he come to Washington to stay with her.[54] On the morning of the 22nd the duelling party assembled. The conference between the two seconds lasted forty-five minutes. Just before the duel, Barron spoke to Decatur of conciliation; however, neither of the men's seconds attempted to halt the proceedings.[55] Both seconds, including Bainbridge, had arranged the rules in a way that made the wounding or death of both duellists very likely. The shooters would be standing close to each other, face to face; there would be no back-to-back pacing away and turning to fire, a procedure that often resulted in missing an opponent.

Each duellist raised his pistol, cocked the flintlock and while taking aim stood in silence. Bainbridge called out, 'One', Decatur and Barron both firing before the count of 'two'. Decatur's shot hit Barron in the lower abdomen and ricocheted into his thigh. Barron's shot hit Decatur in the pelvic area, severing arteries. Both fell almost at the same instant. Decatur, clutching his side, exclaimed, 'Oh, Lord, I am a dead man.' Barron, who would survive his wound, declared that the duel was carried out properly and honourably and told Decatur that he forgave him for all slights, real or imagined.[56]

Decatur's friend and mentor John Rodgers arrived after being belatedly informed of the duel. Decatur, in terrible pain, was carefully lifted by the accompanying surgeons, placed in Rodgers' carriage and carried back to his home on Lafayette Square. Before they departed Decatur called out to Barron that he should also be taken along, but Rodgers and the surgeons calmly disagreed. Barron cried: 'God bless you, Decatur' – and with a weak voice Decatur called back, 'Farewell, farewell, Barron.' At his home Decatur was taken to the front room while still conscious. He insisted that his wife and nieces be taken upstairs, sparing them the gory sight. A doctor and near neighbour, Thomas Simms, aided the naval physicians but for unclear reasons, Decatur refused to have the pistol ball extracted. Instead, he called for his last will and testament and signed it, leaving his wife all his worldly possessions.[57] Decatur died at approximately

10.30 that night. He is said to have cried out, 'I did not know that any man could suffer such pain!' He was forty-one and childless.

The nation mourned. Decatur's funeral was attended by Washington's elite, including President James Monroe and the justices of the Supreme Court, as well as most of Congress. Over 10,000 citizens of Washington and the surrounding area attended to pay their last respects to a national hero. The pallbearers were senior naval men. A grieving seaman unexpectedly came forward and proclaimed, 'He was the friend of the flag, the sailor's friend; the navy has lost its mainmast.'[58] His widow, Sarah, regarded the duel as an 'assassination' orchestrated by the seconds. She tried for seventeen years to receive a pension from the government, which was eventually granted by an Act of Congress. Although Decatur had left her $75,000, a fortune at the time, Sarah died virtually penniless in 1850.

Decatur helped determine the direction of the young nation, playing a significant role establishing its identity, and became an icon of American naval history. During his tenure as a Navy Commissioner, in April 1816, Decatur gave an after-dinner toast: 'Our country – in her intercourse with foreign nations, may she always be in the right, and always successful, right or wrong.'[59]

6

The German Coast Rebellion (1811)

a horde of brigands

No court decreed the fate of Charles Deslondes, a mulatto slave who had led a plantation uprising – it would have been considered a waste of time. A witness described the scene: 'Charles had his hands chopped off then shot in one thigh & then the other, until they were both broken — then shot in the body and before he had expired was put into a bundle of straw and roasted!' His dying cries sent a crystal-clear message to other escaped slaves.[1]

A detailed examination of the cruelties of slavery – often described as America's 'original sin' – is too well known to be included here. Many accounts have been published of how slave families were punished by whipping, shackling, hanging, beating, burning, mutilation, branding and imprisonment. The escaped slave William Wells Brown reported that on one plantation, slave men were required to pick 80 pounds per day of cotton, while women were required to pick 70 pounds. A whipping post stood next to the cotton scales and if any slave failed in his or her quota, they were subject to lashes for each pound they were short. A New York man who attended a slave auction reported that at least three-quarters of the male slaves he saw had scars on their backs from whipping. What is less understood, or conveniently forgotten, is how much prominent slaveholders influenced US politics and its economy. In the seventy-two years between the elections of George Washington and Abraham Lincoln, fifty had a slaveholder as president. Their prominence increased the power of Southern states in Congress for decades, affecting national policies and legislation. The planter elite dominated the Southern Congressional delegations.[2] That goes some way towards explaining the savagery by which the largest slave insurgency in US history was put down, and the efforts made to expunge it from the national consciousness.

***

In pre-Revolutionary America, Britain grew rich on the slave trade triangle to Africa, across the Atlantic and back again, boosting and enriching the ports of London, Bristol and Liverpool. The same applied to other European powers, particularly Spain, Portugal, France and the Netherlands, which owed all to sea power. Britain, however, became the world's leading slave-trading power – British ships were responsible for the forced transportation of at least 2 million Africans in that century. So dominant were British ships and merchants that they carried away African captives not only to British colonies in North America and the Caribbean but even to the colonies of their main economic rivals, the French and Spanish.

Under British rule, slave insurrections, despite the brutality that kept them in check, were not that rare. In 1712, for example, an uprising in New York City, then a British province, erupted when slaves were outraged to find that human rights guaranteed to them under former Dutch rule were torn up. Around a fifth of the population were black slaves, one of the largest slave populations of any of England's colonies, and resentments simmered for almost fifty years after the 1664 English takeover. The British government required slaves to carry a pass if traveling more than a mile, prohibited gatherings in groups of more than three persons, and required them to sit in separate galleries at church services.[3] A slave market was built near present-day Wall Street to accommodate the increase in slaves being imported by the Royal African Company. Slavery in the city differed from some of the other colonies because there were no large plantations. Slaves worked as domestic servants, artisans, dock workers and as skilled labourers. Enslaved Africans lived near each other, making communication easy. They also often worked among free blacks, a situation that did not exist on most plantations.

Twenty-three discontented slaves gathered on the night of 6 April 1712 and set fire to a building on Maiden Lane near Broadway. While the white colonists tried to put out the fire, enslaved blacks, armed with guns, hatchets and swords, attacked the whites, killing nine and injuring six. They ran away but colonial forces arrested seventy blacks and jailed them; six allegedly committed suicide in their cells, twenty-seven were put on trial of whom twenty-one were convicted and sentenced to death; twenty were publicly burned on pyres and one was executed on a breaking wheel in which limbs were hammered apart, a punishment by then outlawed for whites. The severity of punishment was an expression of white slave-owners' fear of slave insurrections.[4]

The colony required slave owners who wanted to free their slaves to pay a tax of £200 per person, which was much higher than the cost of a slave. In 1715, Governor Robert Hunter argued in London before the Lords of Trade that traditions which offered the chance for a slave to inherit part of a master's wealth was important to maintain in New York, and was a proper reward for a slave who had helped a master earn a lifetime's fortune. His appeal was rejected.

The Stono Rebellion, also called Cato's Conspiracy, began in early September 1739 in the colony of South Carolina. It saw twenty-five whites and up to fifty Africans killed. Their leader, known locally as Jemmy or Cato, was a literate slave owned by the Cater family who lived near the Ashley River north of the Stono River. He led twenty other enslaved Congolese, who may have been former soldiers and who had converted to Catholicism, in an armed march south for the less oppressive regime of Spanish Florida, where, to destabilise British rule, they were promised freedom and land at St Augustine. Jemmy recruited nearly sixty other slaves before being intercepted and defeated by South Carolina militia near the Edisto River. A group escaped the 'coon hunt' and travelled another 30 miles before the militia caught up with them. Most of the recaptured slaves were executed; the surviving few were sold to markets in the West Indies.[5]

The South Carolina legislature passed the Negro Act of 1740, which restricted slave assembly, education and movement. It also enacted a ten-year moratorium against importing African slaves because they were considered more rebellious, and established penalties against over-harsh treatment of slaves. Cruel treatment, however, grew across the colonies, particularly in the South, as lucrative field produce went some way to balancing Britain's massive costs in maintaining the thirteen colonies. Over subsequent decades, slave uprisings occurred independently in Georgia and South Carolina. Colonial officials claimed they were inspired by the Stono Rebellion, but the increasingly harsh conditions since the beginning of the eighteenth century on rice, sugar and cotton plantations were cause enough.

Harvard archivist Theresa McCulla wrote:

> Slavery is central to the history of colonial North America. For more than two centuries, European Americans treated enslaved men, women, and children as objects that could be bought and sold. The crude logic of enslaving human beings cast people as tools who required input (food and clothing) in order to produce the output of their labor. In the calculations of colonial-era businessmen, all of these components, including the body of the enslaved person, could be given a monetary value. For example, in February 1724, Harvard tutor Henry Flynt speculated as to the financial feasibility of operating a ferry with the assistance of a slave: 'If a man ... buys a negro at 60 pounds who lives 20 years his labour is (worth) but 3 pounds a year, and his Victuals 26 pounds per annum makes 29 pounds which with 6 pounds wear and tare and 50 pounds rent makes 85 pounds.' The man Flynt imagined was an aggregate of calculations: a business investment to manage. Flynt applied such arithmetic to personal matters as well. When Flynt's elderly mother passed away in the 1730s, he quibbled with his brother-in-law over Toney, the enslaved man who had worked for her. The men cared less for Toney's fate, though, than the cash he represented.

Toney became an element of Flynt's mother's estate to settle, alongside 'all the household stuff' that Flynt could tally, which included 'Brass Silver Iron bedding Linnenn.' Flynt sold Toney to another enslaver and balanced the price of the man's sale against the money he paid for his mother's final expenses: 'the Grave and bel ringing and pal etc.' Treated as an investment, Toney disappeared from Flynt's diary after his sale.[6]

Slavery, of course, is inherently evil even in the most domestic setting. And in the Southern colonies economic arguments were increasingly used to justify the most abhorrent acts. The lash, branding and mutilation became commonplace, inflicted on even the most valued commodities. Rape also became the norm, not just to satisfy the sexual demands of the powerful, but also to create new generations of chattels without the expense of importation.

* * *

By the turn of the century, Louisiana had a different slave-trade pattern and tradition than that of the former Thirteen Colonies. Most slaves originated from the French, and later Spanish, colonies of Senegal, the Bight of Benin and the Congo, rather than from British colonies.[7]

Louisiana's slave trade was initially governed by the French *Code Noir*, and later by its Spanish equivalent the *Código Negro*. The *Code Noir* gave unparalleled rights to slaves, including the right to marry, and although it authorised cruel corporal punishment against slaves, it outlawed outright torture. It also forbade separation of married couples, and the splitting of young children from their mothers, and required the owners to instruct slaves in the Catholic faith – this implied that Africans were human beings, endowed with a soul. The code acknowledged *gens de couleur libres* (free people of colour), often born to white fathers. Such factors meant that a far higher percentage of local African Americans were free – 13.2 per cent in Louisiana compared to 0.8 per cent in Mississippi. The free people of colour were exceptionally literate, with a significant number of them owning businesses, properties and even slaves themselves. The *Code Noir* also forbade interracial marriages, but interracial relationships were nevertheless common in New Orleans society. The mulattoes proved to be an intermediate social caste between the whites and the blacks, while in the English colonies the mulattoes and blacks were considered equal and discriminated against equally. Catholic social norms were deeply rooted in Louisiana; the contrast with predominantly Protestant parts of the young nation, where English norms prevailed, was evident.

The sugar boom on what was known as Louisiana's German Coast (named for immigrants in the 1720s) began after the Revolutionary War, while the area near New Orleans was still controlled by Spain. In the 1780s, Jean Saint Malo, an escaped slave, established a colony of Maroons (runaway enslaved Africans) in the swamps below New Orleans, which eventually led Spanish officials to send militia, who captured him. Saint Malo became a folk hero after his execution in New Orleans on 19 June 1784.

A decade later, during the height of the French Revolution, Spanish officials discovered a slave conspiracy at Pointe Coupee between Natchez and New Orleans. On 4 May 1795, the trial of fifty-seven slaves and three local white men was held in Point Coupee after a slave insurrection during which several planters' homes were burned down. In one slave cabin was discovered a copy of *Theorie de l'impôt*, a book which included the *Declaration of the Rights of Man* of 1789. The trial ended with twenty-three slaves being hanged, and their decapitated heads posted along the road, and thirty-one slaves sentenced to flogging and hard labour. All three white men were deported, with two sentenced to six years' forced labour in Havana.[8]

The demand for slaves increased in Louisiana and other parts of the Deep South after the 1803 Louisiana Purchase handed the territory to America. Following the Haitian Slave Revolution, planters attempted to establish similar hugely profitable sugarcane plantations on the Gulf Coast, resulting in a dense slave population. The planters converted from cotton and indigo plantations to sugarcane and seventy sugar plantations produced over 3,000 tons a year. They replicated the brutal conditions which had led to numerous revolts in Haiti – high profits were made by working slaves longer hours and punishing them more brutally, so that they lived shorter lives than any other slave society in North America.[9] Blacks outnumbered whites by nearly five to one by 1810, and about 90 per cent of whites in the area owned slaves. More than half of those enslaved may have been born outside Louisiana, many in Africa where various European nations established slave trading outposts.[10]

Both the Marquis de Lafayette and James Monroe declined to become the Territorial Governor. President Thomas Jefferson then turned to a fellow Virginian, William C. C. Claiborne, whom he appointed on an interim basis, and who arrived in New Orleans with 350 volunteers. Claiborne, a former clerk, had previously been Governor and Superintendent of Indian affairs in the Mississippi Territory from 1801 to 1803. Claiborne was generally sympathetic and conciliatory toward Native Americans, worked long and patiently to iron out differences that arose, and generally aimed to improve the material well-being of the Indians and his constituents. He was a strong proponent of law and order – he offered a $2,000 reward to wipe out an outlaw gang led by the notorious Samuel Mason.[11]

Despite his successes in Mississippi, and his brokerage of the Louisiana Purchase, Claiborne was still young and relatively inexperienced and he struggled to establish and maintain his authority in the face of the area's diverse population, particularly as he spoke neither French nor Spanish. The white elite were initially alarmed when Claiborne retained the services of free people of colour in the militia, who had served with considerable distinction during the preceding forty-year Spanish rule. Claiborne bestowed a ceremonial flag and 'colors' on the battalion, an act which would involve him in a duel three years later with his archenemy Daniel Clark. The governor was shot through one thigh, with the bullet lodging in the other leg.

Claiborne gradually gained the confidence of the French-born elite and oversaw the taking in of Francophone refugees from the Haitian Revolution. The mixed-race Creole and French-speaking population grew markedly. Claiborne was not used to a society with such a large number of free people of colour, nor the rapid spread of dangerous philosophies. Academic Nathan A. Buman wrote: 'Foreign goods, ideology, and knowledge flowed through the gateway of New Orleans into the rest of the territory. For Claiborne, New Orleans's status as a major port served as both a blessing and a curse. He benefited from the capital, labor, and innovative methods for agricultural production flowing into and out of the port while confronting the importation of radical, dangerous ideology.'

The Haitian Revolution, which ran from 1791 to 1804, was an ultimately successful insurrection by self-liberated slaves against French colonial rule. It involved blacks, mulattoes and French, Spanish and British participants, with the ex-slave Toussaint L'Ouverture emerging as the new independent nation's most charismatic hero. It was the only slave uprising that led to the founding of a state which was both free from slavery and ruled by non-whites and former captives.[12] Its effects on the institution of slavery were felt throughout the Americas as it challenged long-held European beliefs about alleged black inferiority and capacity to achieve and maintain their own freedom. The rebels' tenacity under pressure was to inspire other slave communities and shock and frighten slave owners. They were right to be scared.

Long-term French Creole residents complained to Washington, DC, about Claiborne's lack of understanding regarding local customs, railed against the influx of new US settlers in the territory, and wanted no part of President Jefferson's plan to pay 30,000 Americans to amalgamate with the long-established residents. In 1805 a delegation went to Washington to complain about the 'oppressive and degrading' form of the territorial government, but new President James Madison continued to support Claiborne, who had grave doubts about the planters' honesty and trustworthiness. Claiborne suspected that the Spanish in nearby West Florida might encourage an insurrection.

The US banned the importation of slaves in 1807–08. A brisk domestic slave trade developed; many thousands of black slaves were sold by slaveholders in the Upper South to buyers in the Deep South. In the overall Territory of Orleans, from 1803 to 1811, the free black population nearly tripled to 5,000, with 3,000 arriving as migrants from

Haiti via Cuba, in 1809–10. Furthermore, between 1790 and 1810, traders brought around 20,000 enslaved Africans to New Orleans.

The waterways and bayous around New Orleans, so convenient for the mobile slave trade, also offered easy escape routes and hiding places for runaway slaves. Some Maroon colonies continued to operate, if not flourish, for years within a few miles of New Orleans. With the spread of ideas of freedom from the French and Haitian revolutions, whites constantly fretted about slave uprising, and with good reason. When they found that a traveling Frenchman was preaching about liberty, equality and fraternity to the French-speaking slaves, he was swiftly arrested,[13] but to no wider effect. Wild talk of liberty was indeed infectious.

A group of slaves, during a rare work respite because the cane harvest had been collected, gathered on 6 January 1811 on the east bank of the Mississippi River in what is now St John the Baptist and St Charles parishes. As planter James Brown testified weeks later, 'The black Quamana [Kwamena, meaning 'born on Saturday'], owned by Mr. Brown, and the mulatto Harry, owned by Messrs. Kenner & Henderson, were at the home of Manuel Andry on the night of Saturday–Sunday of the current month in order to deliberate with the mulatto Charles Deslondes, chief of the brigands.' They spread word of a planned uprising among the slaves at plantations up and down the river.

The revolt began two days later on 8 January during a ferocious downpour on a cold, windy late Tuesday evening on the sugar plantation about 30 miles upriver from New Orleans that was owned by Manuel Andry, who possessed more than eighty slaves – more than any other slaveholder in the area. The slaves attacked the big house and assaulted Andry with an axe. Although severely wounded, he escaped. Andry later wrote: 'My poor son has been ferociously murdered by a horde of brigands who from my plantation to that of Mr. Fortier have committed every kind of mischief and excesses, which can be expected from a gang of atrocious bandittis of that nature.'[14] That was a lie, no doubt to stir up a desire for bloody vengeance among his white neighbours. The records of the archdiocese show that Gilbert had died of natural causes or accident on 2 January and had been buried on 3 January, five days before the uprising.

The rebellion quickly gained momentum. Approximately fifteen slaves at Andry's plantation joined another eight from the next-door plantation where Charles Deslondes, himself enslaved, was an overseer later described by one of the captured slaves as the 'principal chief of the brigands'. Charles Deslondes was born on the plantation of Jacques Deslondes in about 1789.[15] Plantation succession records described him as a 'Creole mulatto slave'. Reports that he was bought from Haiti or Saint-Domingue are probably incorrect. But he was a literate and charismatic leader of men. His position as a 'driver' of fellow slaves meant that more menial slaves were used to obeying his orders, a habit which perhaps kick-started the revolt.[16]

After looting Andry's estate, the insurgents rapidly moved southward along the east bank levee, following the contours of the Mississippi River through clusters of plantations containing the highest density of slaves in the territory. Small groups of slaves joined from every plantation the rebels passed. The rebels soon crossed into St Charles Parish and headed for New Orleans. They marched in military-style formation, beating drums, waving flags and carrying the tools of their enforced trade as weapons. The rebels recruited some slaves using force and intimidation to swell their ranks. The number of rebels fluctuated during the course of the insurrection; eyewitness estimates range from 150 to 500. They plundered several more estates, and in St Charles Parish the slave known as Kook axed to death the planter Jean François Trépagnier, who had attempted to defend the family manor house by standing on the veranda with a shotgun.[17] After the band passed the LaBranche plantation, they stopped at the home of the local doctor; finding him gone, Kook set his house on fire. As the slave party moved downriver, they passed larger plantations, from which many more slaves joined them. They laid waste to the Meuillion plantation, the largest and wealthiest estate on the German Coast. They tried to set the house alight, but a slave named Bazile fought the flames and saved the house.

After nightfall the rebels reached Cannes Brulees, about 15 miles northwest of New Orleans.[18] They were mostly young men between the ages of twenty and thirty who understood that, with a low life expectancy on the plantations, they had little to lose. Altogether during their march, the insurgents burned five plantation houses, three of them to the ground, plus several sugarhouses and numerous fields of crops.[19]

Panicked planters, their families and loyal staff scrambled for safety across the Mississippi or down the river road into New Orleans. Some planters later testified that they were warned by their slaves of the uprising. Many regularly stayed in New Orleans townhouses and trusted overseers to run their plantations. Governor Claiborne called out the militia, ordered a lockdown of shops and cabarets, and imposed a curfew. General Wade Hampton, commander of regular troops stationed in the area to guard the territorial frontier, had arrived in New Orleans two days before the revolt. He took command of a hastily mustered force of regular troops, militia and volunteers who headed northward, the first time in US history that federal troops were mobilised to suppress a slave insurrection. Hampton dispatched orders for Major Homer Virgil Milton in Baton Rouge to descend the river with another body of regulars, aiming to catch the rebels in a vicelike grip. Unknown to Milton and Hampton, Manuel Andry had – despite his wounds – rallied a sizeable militia force on the west bank of the river. By sunset, General Wade Hampton, Commodore John Shaw, and Governor Claiborne sent two companies of volunteer militia, thirty regular troops, and a detachment of forty seamen to fight the slaves.

A unit of Hampton's forces under Major John Darrington made first contact shortly after the rebels had crossed into Orleans Parish. By 4 a.m. on 10 January, the New Orleans forces had reached Jacques Fortier's plantation, about 18 miles from the city. The main body of rebels had spent the night on the plantation and Hampton planned to envelope them after dawn with a co-ordinated, multi-pronged attack. Once on the offensive, however, Hampton discovered to his astonishment that the reportedly drunk and disorderly rebels had abandoned Fortier's estate in the dead of night with a disciplined retreat northward.

The insurgents had started back upriver about two hours before, travelled about 15 miles and neared Bernard Bernoudy's plantation. There, planter Charles Perret, under the command of the badly injured Andry and in co-operation with Judge St Martin, had assembled a militia of about eighty men from the river's opposite side. At about 9 a.m., this local militia discovered slaves moving toward high ground on Bernoudy's plantation. Perret ordered them to attack the rebel slaves, which he later wrote numbered about 200 men. Lines of charging mounted militiamen, including free persons of colour, broke the rebels' ranks; the battle quickly turned into a rout. The slaves, on foot and with rudimentary weapons, were slashed, trampled and shot where they stood, and as they attempted to flee. Militiamen boasted it was like a 'turkey shoot'. Within half an hour, forty to forty-five slaves had been killed; the remainder slipped away into the woods and swamps clutching their wounds, some apparently driven mad by fear. Perret and Andry's militia tried to pursue them despite the difficult terrain. There were no reports of any militiamen being injured, let alone killed. Andry gleefully reported to Governor Claiborne that it was *'un grand carnage'* (a great slaughter).[20]

On 11 January, militia assisted by Native American trackers and hunting dogs captured Charles Deslondes and he was butchered in the manner previously described by witness Samuel Hambleton. The following day Pierre Griffee and Hans Wimprenn, who were thought to be the murderers of Francois Trépagnier, were captured and killed; their heads were hacked off for delivery to the Andry estate. Major Milton and the dragoons from Baton Rouge arrived and provided support for the militia.[21]

The presence in and around New Orleans of thousands of recently arrived white refugees from the Haitian Revolution intensified emotions. To deter future slave revolts, whites gathered the heads from multiple black corpses and placed them atop poles at regular intervals along the east-bank levee for more than 30 miles from Andry's plantation to the gates of New Orleans to intimidate other slaves. The Maryland-born naval officer Hambleton, witness to Deslondes' killing, recorded the 'characteristic barbarity' of the French oligarchy with disgust: 'Several [slaves] were wrested from the Guards & butchered on the spot.' Those captured later were interrogated and jailed before trials.

Slaveholding judges assembled in St John the Baptist Parish, St Charles Parish and New Orleans to try captured slaves. Sketchy records from two of the courts (St Charles Parish and New Orleans) survive. The busiest tribunal, comprising five elite slaveholders, convened on the Destrehan Plantation in St Charles Parish. Overseen by Judge Pierre Bauchet St Martin, that tribunal resulted in the execution of eighteen of twenty-one accused slaves by firing squad. Some slaves testified against others, but others refused to testify nor submit to the all-planter tribunal.[22] In New Orleans, Commodore Shaw presumed that 'but few of those who have been taken were acquitted'. The New Orleans trials resulted in the conviction and summary executions of eleven more slaves. Three were publicly hanged in the *Place d'Armes*, now Jackson Square. One of those spared was a thirteen-year-old who was ordered to witness another slave's death and then received thirty lashes. Another slave was treated with leniency because his uncle turned him in and begged for mercy. The sentence of a third slave was commuted because of the valuable information he had given.

US territorial law provided no appeal from a parish court's ruling, even in cases involving imposition of a death sentence on an enslaved individual. Governor Claiborne, recognising that fact, wrote to the judges of each court that he was willing to extend executive clemency 'in all cases where circumstances suggest the exercise of mercy a recommendation to that effect from the Court and Jury, will induce the Governor to extend to the convict a pardon'. In fact, Claiborne did commute two death sentences: those of Henry, and of Theodore, each referred by the Orleans Parish court.

Militias killed about ninety-five slaves in the battle, in summary arrests and executions, in 'accidental' killings during their march, as well as by execution after trials. No slave insurrection in US history left more black bodies in its aftermath. From the trial records, most of the leaders were mixed-race Creoles or mulattoes, although many of their followers were native-born Africans. Unlike the 1739 Stono rebellion in colonial South Carolina or the 1791 Pointe Coupee conspiracy in Spanish Louisiana, in which a single African ethnic group predominated, the 1811 insurrection combined African and Creole slaves, men and women, field hands and more privileged slaves, and mulattos and blacks. Fifty-six of the captured slaves involved in the revolt were returned to their masters, who may well have punished them cruelly or even fatally in some cases, although most wanted their valuable labourers back at work. Thirty more slaves were captured during the aftermath but returned to their masters after planters determined they had been forced under threat of murder to join the revolt.

Given the lack of surviving testimony from the slaves, no firm conclusion can be made regarding the aims of the insurgents. Wade Hampton accused Spanish agents of stirring up the slaves, but no evidence has surfaced to support his claim. Shifting troop movements related to the US annexation of West Florida in December 1810 may have helped kindle the revolt. The rapid movement of a disciplined force of slaves suggests not only a conscious assault on New Orleans, but also a mass slave breakout from the territory, possibly to Haiti. But the main cause must have been the brutality of life on the sugarcane plantations. During the revolt, one Congo slave, when asked why he was headed to New Orleans, replied succinctly, 'To kill whites.'

The planters and other elite had already been in a state of high alert, not against the slaves but against the abolitionist sentiment of the American Congress, which had restricted 'the African trade' and the importation of slaves into Louisiana. It is certain they panicked at rumours of a rebellion and rounded up 'likely' slaves to kill. It had happened before in Louisiana and other Southern states.

The heirs of the Meuillion plantation petitioned the legislature for permission to free the mulatto slave Bazile, who had worked to preserve his master's plantation. The Territory legislature approved compensation of $300 to planters for each slave killed or executed – a good illustration of planter influence.[23] The shock prompted an immediate tightening of security, and not only in Louisiana where militia conscription became enforced more rigorously. Both slaves and free blacks suffered new restrictions on their movements, and a larger federal military presence was deployed at Louisiana's own request. The legislatures of Kentucky, Tennessee and the Mississippi territory all likewise bolstered their militias in the wake of German Coast.

During the War of 1812, Louisiana's huge slave population made it a soft underbelly if the British were to land and arm the slaves. Planter Edward Livingston wrote to Andrew Jackson on behalf of the New Orleans Committee of Safety on 18 September 1814, urging federal aid in the face of such danger:

> This Country is strong by Nature, but extremely weak from the nature of its population, from the La Fourche downwards on both sides the River, that population consists (with inconsiderable exceptions) of Sugar Planters on whose large Estates there are on an average 25 slave to one White Inhabitant the maintenance of domestic tranquillity in this part of the state obviously forbids a call on any of the White Inhabitants to the defense of the frontier, and even requires a strong additional force, attempts have already it is said been detected, to excite insurrection, and the character of our Enemy leaves us no doubt that this flagitious mode of warfare will be resorted to, at any rate the evil is so great that no precautions against it can be deem'd superfluous.

Claiborne was the first elected governor after Louisiana gained statehood in 1812. In the war with the British, Claiborne raised militia companies and negotiated the aid of French privateer Jean Lafitte to defend New

Orleans from attack late in 1814. After his term as governor, Claiborne was elected to the Senate, serving until his death from liver disease on 23 November 1817. The slaves who survived faded into obscurity, with no markers or memorials to show they had ever existed.

Slavery continued to flourish, of course. In 1828, the nineteen-year-old Abraham Lincoln witnessed a New Orleans slave market. His friend Allen Gentry recalled that he 'doubled his fists tightly; his knuckles went white'. Men wearing black coats and white hats bought black field hands for $500 to $800. When the sale of 'fancy girls' began, Lincoln muttered to his friend: 'Allen that's a disgrace. If I ever get a lick at that thing I'll hit it hard.'[24] Slavery in Louisiana was officially abolished by the state constitution of 1864 during the American Civil War.

7

Aegean Sea Anti-piracy Operations (1825–1828)

the freedom of the seas for all

After decades of warfare against Britain, the French and the Barbary pirates, for a time American military action was mostly inward and inland, a continuation of the American Indian Wars: against the great chief Tecumseh in Indiana, effectively an add-on to the War of 1812; against Creek factions in a tribal civil war across Alabama and the Gulf Coast; against Seminoles in Florida; against Plains Indians starting in Texas in 1820; and against the Arikaras in South Dakota. At sea, America's merchant fleet, now apparently safe from enemy privateers, blossomed as lucrative new trade routes and opportunities opened up following the long carnage of the Napoleonic Wars. But a new threat emerged from an unexpected corner. And the battle zone was the turquoise waters of Homer's *Odyssey*.

* * *

An exception to the relative post-war calm were the anti-piracy operations between 1817 and 1825 in the Antilles in which the US West Indies Squadron pursued pirates on sea and land, primarily around Cuba and Puerto Rico. These operations came to a head in March 1825, when a flotilla led by USS *Gallinipper* under Lieutenant Isaac McKeever attacked a hostile schooner at the mouth of the Sagua la Grande, Cuba. American and British forces took the ship, killed eight and captured nineteen others with the loss of only one man wounded. In subsequent days another schooner was captured but the pirates escaped, and the vessel was taken without bloodshed. *El Mosquito*, the ship of famed pirate Roberto Cofresí, was disabled by USS *Grampus* along with two Spanish sloops off Boca del Inferno. With his crew scattered, the pirate captain fled inland, where a local by the name of Juan Garay recognised and ambushed him.

Cofresí was considered the last successful Caribbean pirate, and after his execution piracy declined in the region for good. However, the US Navy had gained more experience, which was immediately to become invaluable.

At the outbreak of the war for independence waged by Greek revolutionaries against the Ottoman Empire from 1821, American sympathies were naturally with the Greeks. The frigate *Hellas* – flagship of the Greek Navy fleet – was designed and built in America.[1] But following the 1823 Greek naval defeat at Bodrum, the Greek Navy turned to privateering to support the revolt and attacked merchantmen. That resulted in the breakdown of law and order and widespread pillaging across the Aegean Sea with its hundreds of islands, including those made famous by ancient sea battles such as Rhodes and Crete, where a particularly profitable trade had grown up between American ports and Smyrna.

Several American merchant ships had been plundered by 1825, when President James Monroe sent Commodore John Rodgers to protect American commerce. Seven American warships were put under his command in the Mediterranean Squadron – his mighty flagship USS *North Carolina*; the war-battered USS *Constitution*; the sloops *Fairfield*, *Lexington* and *Ontario*; and the schooners *Porpoise* and *Warren*. The sloops and schooners – the destroyers of their day – were mainly deployed against the pirates because the men-of-war were too large and too deep-hulled for the myriad shallow inlets and rock harbours of the region. They were pitted against the small, sleek and fast three-masted Greek *mistikos* armed with a bow gun, the primary vessel of the pirates.[2]

Conditions aboard an early nineteenth-century US Navy warship could be harsh, but no more so than in the Royal Navy on which regulations were based. Rations included salt beef and pork, butter and fish preserved in brine, which frequently became so bad they had to be thrown overboard. Fresh meat and vegetables were used in port by both officers and crew, and turtles, turtle eggs, coconuts, fruit and vegetables were secured whenever possible. A supply of bread or biscuit sufficient for several weeks was taken on board before sailing. This, too, often spoiled. Cornmeal and potatoes were also provided in quantities. Regulations of 1818 directed that wind sails and ventilators were to be kept in continual operation.

The men were encouraged to wash themselves two or three times a week depending on the climate and to change their linen at least twice weekly. The captain was directed to provide the sick and wounded with a comfortable place, with berths, cradles, cots, buckets with covers, and other conveniences. Rheumatism, consumption, syphilis, debility and scurvy were the most frequent causes of medical discharges. Yellow fever and smallpox were prevalent at certain seasons and in certain climates. Many officers continued service aboard ship during the last stages of consumption because of the lack of any sort of retirement benefits. Larger ships, such as frigates, had a surgeon and two or three inexperienced surgeon's mates on board, while the very small vessels had none. Many of the medics had never performed an operation before being called to operate in an emergency or during a battle.[3]

Rodgers was a veteran of the Quasi War, the Barbary Wars and the War of 1812. In the latter he personally fired the first shot of the war aboard his flagship, USS *President*, a shot which killed or wounded nine men.[4] He also played a leading role in the recapture of Washington after the capital was burned by the British, during which his own home was destroyed and his family displaced.[5] His tasks now were to protect American commerce and to negotiate a trade treaty that would increase American access to the Ottoman Empire. Accordingly, he escorted American merchantmen to Turkey, visited Greek ports, and spoke with Ottoman officials. His initial operations in the Aegean in 1825 did deter piracy, but he was unable to conclude the desired treaty.[6] The squadron did not fight any engagements and in 1826 it withdrew, but another was sent in 1827, again under Rodgers' command after a new escalation in piracy.

The newly built *Warren* sailed from Boston in February 1827 and would be the first to fight the brigands in a battle. In September, under the command of Lieutenant Lawrence Kearney, who was known for his tenacity in capturing slave traders off the West Indies, she captured her first 'piratical boat' and its crew of five. Later that same day, *Warren* captured a sixteen-gun brig flying the Greek flag. For the next three weeks, *Warren* cruised between Cape Matapan and Carabusa, a hotbed of privateering.[7]

Elsewhere, while sailing in convoy on 16 October, twenty-one-year-old Lieutenant Louis Goldsborough of *Porpoise* liberated the British brig *Comet* after watching its capture by 250 pirates in five vessels. In the ensuing battle, around ninety brigands were killed or wounded, while the Americans suffered no casualties. Three enemy brigs escaped but one was later captured off Chios and another was abandoned by her crew before it was taken. On 23 October, one American sailor from *Porpoise* was wounded in a skirmish near Andros.

Off Milos on 25 October, Kearny was told of recent pirate attacks on the American ships *Cherub* and *Rob Roy*. That same day, *Warren* chased a ten-gun pirate brig ashore at the island of Kimolos but the crew escaped into the nearby hills. The Americans cut away the masts of the pirate ship and stripped them of their sails, leaving the rigging submerged in the waters offshore. Three days later, *Warren* found *Cherub* and took possession of her. The brig *Lexington* assumed protective guard over the merchant ship while *Warren* returned to the pirate hunt. The next day, between Tinos and Mykonos, *Warren* found the recently plundered Austrian brig *Silence* and towed her back to Syros where she too was left in care of *Lexington*.

Warren captured a large Greek *tratta* equipped with forty oars before she put into Mykonos harbour on 1 November. The following day, after shelling the town, Kearny and his men recovered sails and some property taken from *Cherub* and two cases of opium taken from *Rob Roy*, as well as the sails and rigging from *Silence*.[8] The cowed local inhabitants turned over four men accused of being pirates while a landing party picked up a fifth from the mountains. Kearny also took an empty boat allegedly belonging to pirates and later burned it. Returning to Syros, Kearny restored the goods to *Cherub* and the sails and rigging from the Austrian ship. *Cherub*, escorted by *Lexington*, set sail for Smyrna. That evening, *Warren* put to sea, bound for the reputed pirate lair of Andros.

On 7 November, a boat expedition led by Lieutenant William Hudson left the ship to circle the island. A Greek brig with a convoy of up to 30 small boats loomed out of the darkness and opened fire with everything they had. Shot went through the Americans' sails, and even through men's clothing, but no one was hurt. Undaunted, Hudson landed his force near the south end of Andros town and burned a 'piratical craft'. At the head of a small bay, the American sailors blew up a house believed to have been owned by a pirate and raised and took possession of a boat which had been sunk by pirates to avoid detection by the Americans. *Rob Roy*'s master later identified the boat as the craft in which pirates had attacked his vessel.

Kearny, in *Warren*, remained in the vicinity until 14 November. The people of Andros again co-operated and produced a pirate boat which contained a 12-pounder carronade and some tools from *Cherub*. Four days later *Warren* made port at Milos, and on the 27th the American brigs *Sarah* and *Esther* and six other vessels arrived. Three days later, that convoy sailed for Smyrna under *Warren*'s protection. They arrived at their destination without incident.[9] *Warren* also landed men on Argentiere and Milos in December and convoyed eight American merchant vessels from Milos to Smyrna. In just over two months, *Warren* had captured or destroyed seven pirate vessels, rescued three merchant ships, recovered stolen property, escorted two convoys, and patrolled hundreds of miles in the Mediterranean. For the next two years, *Warren* remained in the western Mediterranean guarding American commerce.

Such tactical operations eased the Greek pirate threat to American commerce but did little to tackle its root causes: the desperation of the Greek rebels fighting for their nation's freedom from the Ottomans, and the reluctance of the European naval powers to intervene. As Lieutenant Kearny noted, 'piracy has ... the present seat of the Greek government, for its fountainhead'.[10]

That began to change in 1827. By the Treaty of London, the three great European naval powers – Britain, France and Russia – agreed to support Greek autonomy. Later that year, their combined fleets destroyed a Turkish-Egyptian Ottoman naval force at the Battle of Navarino. Initially that victory sparked a short-term increase in Greek pirate activity as they no longer had to fight the Turks at sea, so the Great Powers finally decided to take direct action themselves. In January 1828, an allied fleet descended on the main pirate base at Carabusa. The island's impressive fort had been taken by several hundred Cretans in 1825 and besieged by the Ottomans for more than two years. During that siege, they resorted to piracy to survive, building schools and a church from the proceeds.[11] The allies destroyed most of the pirate flotilla and then conducted similar operations farther north.

Pirate attacks tailed off, and by the end of 1828 US Navy Secretary Samuel Southard had declared that the threat of piracy was eliminated 'due to the restraints of the existing authorities in Greece; and the system of convoy'.[12] The show of force by Rodgers' squadron laid the groundwork for the 1830 commercial treaty with Turkey, opening ports of the Eastern Mediterranean and the Black Sea to American traders. As one of the largest naval forces, the US Navy's Mediterranean Squadron continued to protect American interests and commerce in the region for the rest of the century and beyond. At roughly the same time, on the other side of the world, American warships were embarking on a new campaign, this time against Malay pirates threatening American commerce in the Straits of Malacca.

John Rodgers, after several years of ill health, died in the arms of his butler in 1838. He had established a naval dynasty – his son John served in the Civil War and his great-grandson, also named John, served in the First World War. Several younger officers under his command had long and colourful naval careers. Laurence Kearney negotiated treaties which opened China to American trade; he died in 1868. William Hudson saw service in the Pacific, the Antarctic, the Southern Ocean and off North America before commanding the Boston Navy Yard. He died in 1862. Louis Goldsborough commanded the South Atlantic Blockading Squadron during the Civil War and returned to the reformed Mediterranean Squadron in 1865. He died a rear admiral in 1877.

The suppression of Greek piracy and the achievement of Greek independence in 1830 did not mean the end of Greek–American naval relations. While the frigate *Hellas* was blown up in 1831 during an internal Greek revolt, in 1914 the US sold to the Greek government the US Navy battleships *Mississippi* and *Idaho*, which became *Kilkis* and *Lemnos*. US Navy ships helped evacuate Greek refugees from Smyrna in 1922.

Naval historian Peter Swartz wrote:

The scourge of piracy continues to threaten the peaceful sea transport of goods throughout the world, so necessary for the continued expansion of the global economy and growth in world prosperity. After the Al Qaeda attacks of September 11, US Navy frigates, like the frigates of old, began once again to conduct antipiracy patrols in the Straits of Malacca, assisted this time by warships from the Indian Navy and other likeminded navies. The American merchant marine long ago ceased to be one of the leaders in the field, replaced by the merchantmen of other countries, like Greece. Nevertheless, the US Navy, as the world's leading naval force, continues to take seriously its mandate to maintain the freedom of the seas for all.[13]

8

Sumatra Expeditions (1832 and 1838)

suspicious as to the real motives of the Americans...

In the first half of the nineteenth century, the island of Sumatra became America and Europe's primary source of pepper, a hugely valuable commodity. The US merchant fleet sailed the Indonesian waters in search of the trade's massive profits, and small boats darted around the coast trading pepper with the merchant ships waiting offshore. In early 1831 the merchantman *Friendship*, under Captain Charles Endicott, arrived off the chiefdom of Kuala Batu. Endicott and four of his men went ashore, and while he was haggling over prices, three *proas* – flimsy but fast catamarans – attacked his ship, murdered the first officer and two others of her crew, and plundered its cargo.[1]

Endicott, his shore party and the other surviving members of his crew managed to escape to another port with the assistance of a friendly native chief, Po Adam. There they enlisted the help of three other merchant captains who agreed to help Endicott recover his vessel. With their help, Endicott retook the plundered ship and eventually sailed back to Salem, Massachusetts.

Allegedly fearful of widespread attacks on Western shipping, a Dutch expedition to the west coast of Sumatra was launched by the Royal Netherlands East Indies Army in direct response to the *Friendship* incident, which was used as an excuse to annex parts of the Aceh Sultanate for the Dutch. Given the distances involved and the time it took, the American response was slower. But when the news of the 'massacre' filtered home with the *Friendship* itself, there was a general public outcry. In response, President Andrew Jackson dispatched the frigate USS *Potomac* under Commodore John Downes to punish the natives while on a round-the-world trip.[2]

As a midshipman on the frigate *Congress*, Downes distinguished himself during the First Barbary War and again in a boat attack on Tripoli *feluccas*. His War of 1812 service was spent mainly in the Pacific, and he returned to the Mediterranean as a commander when, under Stephen Decatur, he took part in the capture of two Algerian warships. His record was somewhat tarnished during a three-year tour of South American waters when he made a personal fortune giving protection, passage and banking service to privateers and pirates. One of his midshipmen on that voyage, William Rodgers, became so sick of counting money on board that he resigned from the navy on his return, saying he had been unable to 'do what I joined this man's Navy to do. Not being able to serve my country but to simply be serving for the monetary good of Captain Downes.' However, by 1832 Downes was commander of the Pacific Squadron. His order from the president was that if there was a regular government that Downes could deal with, he was authorised to negotiate with it; otherwise he was to 'inflict chastisement' on any 'band of lawless pirates' responsible for the *Friendship* atrocity. He certainly had the tools necessary for such chastisement. *Potomac* was built to mount thirt-two carronades on her spar deck, thirty long guns on her gun deck, and two bow and three stern chasers on each of these decks, compared to the flimsy, mainly unarmed craft of the Malays.

Potomac reached Kuala Batu by way of the Cape of Good Hope and the Indian Ocean on 5 February 1832. There Downes met Po Adam who advised him that the local *uleëbalang* (rajah or chief) would not pay compensation for the attack on *Friendship,* adding that he was unlikely to negotiate 'except with a very sharp knife on his gullet'. That was good enough for Downes – there would not be any attempt at negotiation. In his mind the firmest action was justified, regardless of who the actual perpetrators had been. Downes disguised his ship as a Danish merchantman ready for his own onslaught. When a Malay party boarded *Potomac* attempting to sell a cargo of pepper they were detained so as not to alert Kuala Batu. The initial plan was to send a reconnaissance party to scout out the port defences, but as the longboat approached the beach, around 200 Acehnese, 'obviously suspicious as to the real motives of the Americans', rushed to the beach in force brandishing *krises* and blunderbusses. The longboat hovered in the waters beyond the breakers, its officers judging it imprudent to land, then returned to the frigate.[3]

The reconnaissance had, however, found that in addition to three *proas* in the harbour, five forts constructed of earth and wood were guarding the town.[4] Early on 7 February, Downes ordered a detachment of 282 marines and bluejackets into the ship's boats, some of which had been equipped with a few of the lighter cannon. They burnt the Malay vessels in Kuala Batu's harbour and assaulted the town's forts while support from the 30-pound guns of *Potomac* herself was used to suppress incoming fire. The American muskets were far superior to the outdated matchlocks of the Malays, and the fighting evolved into hand-to-hand combat in which the Americans held every advantage. The main *uleëbalang*, Mahomet, was killed as well as about 150 of his warriors. The four coastal forts were swiftly captured and burnt. Only two Americans died during the attack and another eleven sailors and marines suffered injuries.[5]

The remaining Malays fled toward a fifth fort to the rear of the town, but instead of laying siege, the Americans attacked the town itself. It suffered large-scale looting and a large number of civilians were killed. Downes later ordered his men to return to the ship and bombarded both the fifth fort and what remained of the town, killing another 300 natives in the process, until its surviving leaders agreed to surrender. It was a brutal, callous affair, an early version of 'shock and awe'. An *uleëbalang* who had survived both the fort attacks and the bombardment begged for mercy and Downes told him that if any American ships were attacked again the response would be even more draconian. Other *uleëbalang* from nearby states also sent delegations to the ship, pleading that Downes spare them from the same fate as Kuala Batu.

There was some talk of disciplinary action as Downes had not even tried to directly negotiate a settlement by peaceable means before embarking on general slaughter, but President Jackson supported him, saying the fighting would deter future aggression. The general public also approved of his warship 'diplomacy' and no action was taken against him.[6] *Potomac* then proceeded to circumnavigate the world, becoming only the second US naval vessel to do so.[7] The ship was also the first to host sitting royalty – the king and queen of Hawaii. It was Downes' last maritime posting. He commanded Charlestown Navy Yard in Boston Harbour before his death in 1856. The troubles with Kuala Batu were not over, however.

Six years later, in August 1838, the American trading vessel *Eclipse* was dealing with the Sumatran village of Trobongan when around two dozen Malays approached, apparently for trade. The ship's second mate allowed them to board after they gave up their weapons, but the weapons were then returned as a universal sign of friendship. The Malays promptly attacked the crew with knives. They killed the second mate first and then one by one the remaining men. Some of the American sailors jumped overboard but the Malays ruthlessly hunted them down. About $18,000 in gold was among the plunder, and the local rajah of Trabang distributed the loot to the rajahs in Kuala Batu and the village of Muckie.

News of the massacre reached Commodore George C. Read in December 1838 while he was sailing off Ceylon in command of the US East India Squadron. Irish-born Read had served on USS *Constitution* during the War of 1812. Early in his career, when his ship was under the command of his uncle, he was suspected of being an informant concerning a fight between two lieutenants. The ship's officers shunned

Read, who endured the treatment without complaint. When it was eventually learned that it was the captain's clerk and not Read who had informed, one of the lieutenants apologised to him and asked why he remained silent about the real informant. Read replied, 'That would have been doing the very thing for which you blamed me, Mr. Woolsey: turning informer.' The incident was seen as an example of Read's great self-restraint and self-respect. While on the USS *United States* under Stephen Decatur he took part in the capture of the British warship *Macedonian*. He served in the Barbary Wars, eventually captaining the *Constitution*.[8]

On hearing of the massacre, Read immediately set sail south-east for Sumatra in the frigate *Columbia* with the frigate *John Adams*, both of which were in the process of circumnavigating the globe in conjunction with, though not as part of, the US Exploring Expedition of 1838 to 1842. Coincidentally, the expedition to Sumatra required no detour. It was not the first or last time that American voyages of scientific exploration were used to punish supposed aggressors and extend the nation's global reach and reputation. *Columbia* held almost 500 men with fifty mounted guns. *John Adams* carried about 220 men and officers with thirty guns.[9]

They arrived off southern Sumatra on New Year's Day 1839 and headed for Kuala Batu, which they intended to destroy for breaking the earlier treaty. Although the town had not launched the attack, the Americans decided that accepting part of the loot was bad enough. On arrival, they formed a line of battle just in range of the five rebuilt forts and opened fire. Within an hour all five were smoking wrecks. The chief of the village surrendered and agreed never again to attack American ships.

Commodore Read set sail for Muckie, the next American target for reprisals, arriving the following day. The Americans landed a force of 360 officers, marines and sailors, all under the command of naval Commander T. W. Wyman. They attacked the town, while *Columbia* and *John Adams* provided covering cannon fire. Most of the inhabitants fled their village upon the outbreak of fighting, but some of the Malay men attempted to resist the attack and were overwhelmed as Muckie was engulfed in flames. The landing party then returned to their ships and sailed away.

The punitive expedition ended after the Muckie engagement, and Commodore Read continued his cruise around the world. Later he successively commanded the African and Mediterranean Squadrons, and after the outbreak of the Civil War was in charge of the Philadelphia Naval Asylum. He was promoted to Rear Admiral in July 1862 and died one month later after fifty-eight years of naval service.[10]

The second Sumatran expedition achieved what the first had not. Never again did Malays plunder an American merchant ship. Casualties are absent from records.[11]

9

The Pork and Beans War (1838–1839) and the Pig War (1859–1872)

... keep your potatoes out of my pig

It was a strange kind of war. American and British troops faced each other in readiness for a 'second Bunker Hill'. But as tensions eased, they celebrated the Fourth of July together, enjoyed picnics and sports tournaments together, and enjoyed drinking sessions together fuelled by the copious amounts of alcohol available. The only risk of violence, it turned out, was from overconsumption.

The so-called Pig War was the second of two armed confrontations over the disputed US–British Canada border. The first was equally bizarre, and part of America's labour pains regarding international diplomacy.

* * *

The 1783 Treaty of Paris may have ended the Revolutionary War but it had not clearly defined the nation's northern boundary, and the Commonwealth of Massachusetts issued land grants in Maine in areas to which the British had already laid claim. During the War of 1812, the British occupied most of eastern Maine for eight months and intended to annex the region into British North America. The 1814 Treaty of Ghent, which ended that conflict, saw a commission fail to resolve the dispute. When Maine broke away from Massachusetts as a separate state in 1820, the border emerged as a chief concern of the new administration. The British considered that Maine's territory protruding so deeply into their territory constituted a serious hindrance to communications between Canada and its colonial satellites on the Atlantic seaboard. As late as September 1825, Maine and Massachusetts land agents issued deeds, sold timber permits, took censuses and recorded births, deaths and marriages in the contested area of the Saint John River's valley and its tributaries. In the autumn of that year a forest fire destroyed thousands of acres of prime New Brunswick timber, killed hundreds of settlers, left thousands more homeless, and destroyed several thriving communities. It meant, according to the British, that the very survival of New Brunswick depended on the vast forests to the west in the area disputed with the United States.

Squabbles continued, increasing American–British tensions, and US commissioners asked King William of the Netherlands to adjudicate. He found it impossible to reconcile the often out-of-date maps being used with contradictory clauses in previous treaties, and simply drew a line between two options. Under the compromise the US received 7,908 square miles and Britain received 4,119 square miles. The British government accepted the deal, but Maine rejected it and the new treaty failed to pass the Senate. The American refusal to accept William's decision would ultimately cost the United States 900 square miles (2,300 km^2) of territory.[1]

Tit-for-tat actions, often motivated by short-term 'pork barrel' politics ensued. (Pork barrelling is the use of government funds for projects designed to please voters or legislators and win votes.) In 1835 the British rescinded their acceptance of the Dutch compromise and offered another boundary, which the Americans rejected. The US offered to ask Maine to accept the Saint John River as the boundary, which the British rejected. The following year US Representative Ebenezer Greeley began a census of the upper Aroostook River territory. New Brunswick Governor Sir John Harvey had Greeley arrested, accused his Maine counterpart of bribery and threatened military action if Maine continued to exercise jurisdiction in the basins of the Aroostook River and its tributaries. Maine Governor Robert Dunlap issued a general order announcing that a foreign power had invaded his state.[2] The state legislature authorised $800,000 for military defence, and Congress gave the president authority to raise the militia with a $10 million budget. Meanwhile across the ill-defined and disputed border, Nova Scotia voted $100,000 in funds to defend New Brunswick.[3]

Both American and Canadian lumberjacks cut timber in the disputed territory during the winter of 1838/39, resulting in the bloodless 'Battle of Caribou'. On 29 December, New Brunswick lumberjacks were seen felling trees on the estate that had formerly belonged to First Barbary War hero William Eaton. On New Year's Eve, the New Brunswick woodcutters returned, and were promptly ordered to leave by Eaton's hastily gathered force. Both sides drew firearms and prepared to fire. A short distance away, three Canadian lumberjacks were unexpectedly attacked by a black bear defending a small cub. The lumberjacks were able to shoot and kill the bear, but not before two of them suffered injuries. The Americans, assuming the shots were directed at them, fired several shots in retaliation. Though none of the Canadians were actually hit by fire, they withdrew carrying their bear-mauled comrades. News of the encounter quickly spread to both sides, fuelling rumour and outrageous exaggeration.

On 24 January 1839, the Maine Legislature authorised newly elected governor John Fairfield to send local land agent Rufus McIntire, the Penobscot County sheriff and a posse of volunteer militia to the upper Aroostook to pursue and arrest the 'unruly wood thieves'. The posse left Bangor two weeks later, established a camp at the junction of the Saint Croix and Aroostook Rivers and began confiscating New Brunswick lumbering equipment, and sending any lumbermen caught and arrested back to Maine for trial. The lumbermen, unable to retrieve their oxen and horses, broke into the Woodstock arsenal, armed themselves, formed their own posse and seized the Maine land agent and his assistants in the middle of the night. They were transported in chains to Woodstock and held for an 'interview'. Sir John Harvey regarded the Americans as 'political prisoners', and sent his military commander to order the Maine militia to leave the area. The Maine men promptly took the New Brunswick military commander himself into custody. It was a farce, but a potentially dangerous one.

The next month, the Maine Legislature authorised militia major general Isaac Hodsdon to lead 1,000 additional volunteers to augment the posse on the upper Aroostook River. The rush to actual war seemed unstoppable, with British troops arriving from the West Indies, reports of the Mohawk nation offering their services to Quebec, and further reports of New Brunswick forces gathering on the Saint John River. All that activity resulted in the issuance of General Order No. 7 on 19 February 1839, calling for a general draft of Maine militia. President Martin Van Buren assigned Brigadier General Winfield Scott to the conflict area and he arrived in Boston in early March 1839. After a lively debate Congress authorised a force of 50,000 men and appropriated $10 million, placed at the disposal of the president in the event foreign military troops crossing into US territory.

A bloodbath was averted by the mutual respect often displayed by military enemies. Sir John Harvey had supervised Winfield Scott during his time as a prisoner of war during the 1812 War and both men recognised the other's integrity. A truce was brokered, and the Maine militia was withdrawn in favour of a civil solution. The two nations agreed to refer the dispute to a boundary commission. Neither nation wanted a war that would have greatly interfered with the two nations' trade. Under another compromise treaty in 1842, the British retained the northern area of the disputed territory, including the Halifax Road with its year-round overland military communications between Quebec and Nova Scotia.[4] The US federal government agreed to pay the states of Maine and Massachusetts $150,000 each for the loss of their lands.[5]

The Pork and Beans War, also known as the Aroostook War, may not have resulted in any casualties – apart from the two lumberjacks mauled by a bear, but it had major consequences on the states' right to use military force on their own. In the aftermath of the crisis, the Federal government assumed complete control over military matters. But on the other side of the North American continent, similar disputes erupted over the physical integrity of the relatively new United States and their neighbour to the north.

The Oregon Treaty of 15 June 1846 appeared to resolve western boundary disputes with Canada but again it was flawed because of muddled lines in the maps of the time. It divided Oregon and Columbia between the US and Britain 'along the forty-ninth parallel of north latitude to the middle of the channel which separates the continent from Vancouver Island, and thence southerly through the middle of the said channel, and of the Strait of Juan de Fuca, to the Pacific Ocean'. The trouble was that there are two straits that could be called the middle of the channel: Haro Strait, along the west side of the San Juan Islands, named by the Spanish explorer Francisco de Eliza, who charted the islands in 1791; and Rosario, along the east. The most commonly available maps were those of George Vancouver (1798) and Charles Wilkes (1845), and neither were clear about which strait was which.[6]

In 1856, the US and Britain set up a Boundary Commission to resolve a number of boundary issues, including the water boundary from the Strait of Georgia to the Strait of Juan de Fuca. The commissioners from both sides met for the first time on board the British ship HMS *Satellite*, anchored in Esquimalt Harbour; the British insisted that the border ran through Rosario, while the Americans were equally adamant it ran through Haro. By December 1857 it was clear that neither side would convince the other. A compromise was rejected by the US and the commission adjourned, agreeing to report back to their respective governments.[7] San Juan Island was significant as a military strategic point – the British held Fort Victoria on Vancouver Island to the west, while the nation that held the San Juan Islands would be able to dominate all the straits connecting the Strait of Juan de Fuca with the Strait of Georgia.

The British leased the main island to the British Hudson's Bay Company for 7 shillings a year.[8] On 15 December 1853 the company transported 1,300 sheep and a few pigs to the island to start a ranch. The operation was put under the charge of Charles Griffin, aided by a few Hawaiian herdsmen, who built a tiny settlement he dubbed 'Belle Vue Farm'. In 1858 gold was struck in the region; thousands of excited American prospectors flooded the mainland. Although most of them returned home disappointed, some decided to settle; a few of these reached San Juan Island, built cabins and claimed land for their own use. Around twenty-five Americans set up residence, while the British population remained the same – one Irishman and a few Hawaiians. On 15 June 1859, exactly thirteen years after the adoption of the Oregon Treaty, the ambiguity led to direct conflict.

Griffin's new neighbour was Lyman Cutlar, an American farmer who had moved onto San Juan claiming rights to live there under the Donation Land Claim Act. They got on reasonably well until the newcomer dug up a third of an acre of one of Griffin's regular sheep runs to plant potatoes. One of Griffin's pigs managed slip into the potato field. Cutlar would later claim that the animal had 'been at several times a great annoyance'. This time he shot the pig. Griffin marched over to Cutlar's house and demanded compensation for his loss. Cutlar offered $10. Griffin claimed that the slain pig was a prize breeding boar and was worth at least $100. As tempers rose, Cutlar withdrew his initial offer ended the confrontation with the retort that he would 'as soon shoot [Griffin] as he would a hog if [Griffin] trespassed on his land'. According to local legend, Cutlar also said to Griffin, 'It was eating my potatoes,' to which Griffin replied, 'It is up to you to keep your potatoes out of my pig.'[9] That afternoon a Hudson's Bay Company vessel arrived carrying three company agents who promptly rode to Cutlar's house with Griffin. Cutlar insisted that the pig was 'worthless'. When warned that he risked arrest, Cutlar picked up his rifle and insisted that 'this is American soil, not English!' The unarmed British withdrew with a last retort: 'You will have to answer for this hereafter!'

The clash of stubbornness and pride on both sides quickly spiralled out of control. The American authorities were informed that Cutlar had 'offered to pay to the company twice the value of the pig'. It was deemed necessary that 'for the protection of our citizens' American soldiers be dispatched.[10] The British sent three warships under the command of Captain Geoffrey Hornby, who would later be promoted to Admiral of the Fleet and earn a reputation as a preeminent tactician and fleet commander. Brigadier General William S. Harney, military commander of the Department of Oregon, dispatched sixty-six American soldiers of the 9th Infantry under the command of Captain George Pickett – later of 'Pickett's Charge' fame – who was in charge of the initial American landing force to San Juan Island with orders to prevent the British from landing. Pickett was famously quoted as saying defiantly, 'We'll make a Bunker Hill of it,' although that bit of bravado was clearly aimed at his domestic audience to advance his military and political ambitions. The crisis continued to escalate. By 10 August 1859, 461 Americans with fourteen cannon under Colonel Silas Casey were opposed by five British warships mounting seventy guns and carrying 2,140 men. It was a dangerous stand-off, but a degree of common sense was deployed on both sides.

Vancouver Island governor James Douglas ordered British rear admiral Robert Baynes to land marines and engage Harney's forces, but Baynes refused, deciding that 'two great nations in a war over a squabble about a pig' was foolish. Local commanding officers on both sides had essentially been given the same orders: defend yourselves, but absolutely do not fire the first shot. For several days, the British and US soldiers exchanged insults, each side attempting to goad the other into firing that first shot, but discipline held on both sides. When news about the crisis reached Washington and London, officials from both nations were shocked and determined to calm the potentially explosive international incident.

Again General Winfield Scott was to dampen down the tinderbox. President James Buchanan sent him to negotiate with Governor Douglas, who was already being criticised at home for escalating tensions with his threat to deploy marines. President Buchanan, in turn, had much bigger crises on his hands, not least internal tensions which would lead to the Civil War. After arriving in the San Juan Islands in October, Scott began negotiations with Douglas.

They agreed to retain joint military occupation of the island until a final settlement could be reached, reducing their presence to a token force of no more than 100 men. The 'English Camp' was established on the north end of San Juan Island along the shoreline, for ease of supply and access; and the 'American Camp' was created on the south end on a high, windswept meadow, suitable for artillery barrages against shipping. Under Casey's command, the eminent engineer Henry Martyn Robert built the fortifications. Casey, who stayed for much of the occupation, went on in the Civil War to help build the defences of Washington, DC. Post-war he improved rivers in Oregon and Washington, and the harbours of New York, Philadelphia and Long Island Sound, and constructed locks and dams on the Cumberland and Tennessee Rivers.

Both sides intermingled amicably for the next twelve years, and the Americans stationed there were grateful that such a peaceful posting spared them the horrors of the Civil War. For the British, the occupation may have been peaceful but, as the National Historic Parks pointed out: 'The climate may have been healthful, and maladies few on San Juan Island, but nothing could help marines unable to contend with deep water.' The Royal Marine cemetery was established with the first marine death in 1863 halfway up the slopes of 650-foot Young Hill and seven were interred. Of those, four perished by drowning. Private Joseph Ellis, from Devon, and Private Thomas Kiddy, of Suffolk, drowned on 1 April 1863. Both were with the original camp contingent, having served in the 2nd battalion in China and transferred initially to police the Fraser River goldfields, then overwhelmed by thousands of American miners. As the Royal Marine Camp force (originally numbering eighty-four) was whittled down by deaths, discharges and transfers to the fleet, men were not replaced in-kind and by December 1866 the returns indicated one captain, two lieutenants, three sergeants, two corporals and thirty-nine privates.

Vancouver Island was merged with British Columbia in 1866, and in 1871 the enlarged colony joined the newly formed Dominion of Canada. That year, Britain and the US signed the Treaty of Washington which, among other territorial matters, agreed to resolve the San Juan dispute by international arbitration under the auspices of German Emperor Wilhelm I. His three-man commission met in Geneva for nearly a year, and on 21 October 1872 decided in favour of the US, choosing the marine boundary via Haro Strait.

On 25 November 1872, the British withdrew the Royal Marines from the British camp. The Americans followed by July 1874. San Juan Island is now mainly protected parkland, famed for its bears, orcas and other wildlife. Today the Union Jack still flies above the 'English Camp', being raised and lowered daily by park rangers, making it one of the few places without diplomatic status where US government employees regularly hoist the flag of another country.

* * *

The Canadian border featured in a largely forgotten coda to the run-up to the Second World War. America had belatedly joined Britain in defeating the Kaiser in the First World War, although US dominance of the treaty that ended that world war helped create the conditions that led to the next one. American isolation during the 1920s, powerful pro-German and Irish Nationalist lobbies, ambitions in and around the Pacific, recognition of the threat from Japan (a British ally at the time) and a juggernaut of industrial imperialism led to Joint Army and Navy Basic War Plan Red, also known as the Atlantic Strategic War Plan. A refinement envisaged a two-front war with both Japan and the British Empire, codenamed War Plan Red-Orange.

The trigger was the 1927 Geneva Naval Conference, which convinced some American top brass that a military confrontation was inevitable. They believed that Britain would initially have the upper hand by virtue of the strength of its navy and could use its dominion in Canada as a springboard from which to initiate a retaliatory invasion of the US. The assumption was that at first Britain would fight a defensive battle against invading American forces, but that the US would eventually defeat Britain by blockading the UK and economically isolating it, a scheme uncannily resonant of the German U-boat campaigns in both global wars.

War Plan Red initially set out a description of Canada's geography, military resources and transportation, and went on to evaluate a series of possible pre-emptive American campaigns to invade Canada in several areas and occupy key ports and railways before British troops could provide reinforcements. Based on extensive war games conducted at the Naval War College, the plan rejected attacking British shipping or attempting to destroy the British fleet. The main American fleet would instead stay in the western North Atlantic to block

British–Canadian traffic. The navy would wait for a good opportunity to engage the British fleet and, if successful, would then attack British trade and colonies in the Western Hemisphere. America planned to build three military airfields near the Canadian border and disguise them as civilian airports, but their existence was accidentally published by the Government Printing Office and reported on the front page of the *New York Times* on 1 May 1935. The same year the plans were shelved as the threat posed by Nazi Germany became clear; the documents were only declassified in 1974.[11]

10

More Pirates and 'Savages' (1838–1842)

Exploring Expedition (1838–1842)

land of no chiefs

The United States Exploring Expedition of 1838–1842, an ambitious move to survey the Pacific Ocean, aimed to fast-track the growth of American science, especially the infant discipline of oceanography, and to extend the nation's global spheres of influence. In most respects it succeeded in its lofty aims but there was a dark side to its supposed enlightenment. During the long cruise, armed conflict between Pacific islanders and the Americans was common and dozens of natives labelled as thieves, savages or even pirates were killed.

Commanded by Charles Wilkes, naturalists, botanists and other scientific personnel – derisively called 'clam diggers' and 'bug catchers' by navy crew members – were carried on the sloops-of-war USS *Vincenne*s and USS *Peacock*, the brig USS *Porpoise*, the store ship *Relief*, and the schooners *Sea Gull* and USS *Flying Fish*, which served as tenders. On the afternoon of 18 August 1838, the vessels weighed anchor in the Hampton Roads and set to sea under full sail. The squadron's epic voyage took in Madeira, Rio de Janeiro, Tierra del Fuego, Valparaiso, Samoa, Tahiti, New South Wales, the Antarctic Ocean, New Zealand and onwards to Fiji.

In July 1840, two members of the party, Lieutenant Underwood and Wilkes' nephew midshipman Wilkes Henry, were killed in a dispute, exacerbated by linguistic misunderstanding, while bartering for food on western Fiji's Malolo Island. The son of the local chief, who was being held as a hostage by the Americans to ensure 'good behaviour', escaped by jumping out of a boat and running through the shallow water for shore. The Americans fired over his head, and later claimed his escape was intended as a prearranged signal by the Fijians to attack, a theory ardently disputed by those on shore. The Americans landed a sixty-strong force and two villages were burned to the ground. Reports suggested that up to eighty Fijians were killed in the American reprisal,[1] but that is most likely overblown.

In August, *Vincennes* and *Peacock* sailed to the Sandwich Islands, with *Flying Fish* and *Porpoise* due to meet them in Oahu by October. The squadron departed Honolulu in early April 1841, *Porpoise* and *Vincennes* for the Pacific Northwest, *Peacock* and *Flying Fish* to resurvey Samoa before rejoining the squadron.[2] Both ships had briefly bombarded the island of Upolu, Samoa, following the death of an American merchant sailor on the island.[3] No casualties were reported by the Americans, and it remains a matter for conjecture how many, if any, natives were killed. The next incident, however, is better documented.

Peacock, under Lieutenant William L. Hudson, and *Flying Fish* surveyed Drummond's Island, named after an American expedition member, and heard from a member of his crew that a ship had wrecked off the island and her crew had been massacred by Gilbertese islanders. A 'white' woman and her child were said to be the only survivors. On 6 April, *Peacock* anchored off Utiroa on Drummond's Island, where the supposed massacre had allegedly taken place, and Hudson went ashore with a couple of navy officers, a marine detachment, and members of the Scientific Corps. The natives, described as calm and peaceful, led the Americans to their village, Tabiteuea. Its name was Gilbertese for 'land of no chiefs' – they believed in egalitarianism – which meant the Americans had no tribal chief to consult with.[4] While the scientists studied the flora and fauna of the island, Hudson inquired about the shipwreck and the whereabouts of the stranded woman and child. The natives said they knew nothing of the incident but wooden parts of a Western ship were found in several huts.

Hudson ordered in a small force of marines and sailors under William Walker to search the island for the supposed survivors. The reports were found to be bogus and, again, the natives were peaceful, although unsure of what they were being accused of. When the party was returning to their ship, Hudson noticed a member of his crew, John Anderson, was missing. Another search proved fruitless, but the American activity led to the Fijians to overtly arm themselves with swords, spears and wooden clubs. Hudson ordered Walker to return to shore and demand the return of the sailor. Walker shouted the demand and the natives charged for him, forcing the boats to turn back to the ships. The natives threw rocks and waved their weapons as the boats shoved off. No one was harmed. Frustrated, Hudson decided that on the next day, with the arrival of *Flying Fish*, they would bombard the native settlement and land again.

Hudson ordered Walker and around eighty marines back to shore. The marines divided into three sections, landing at dawn. *Peacock* took a firing position off the town and *Flying Fish* covered the landing of men in seven boats. Around 700 Gilbertese warriors were dancing near the beach as the boats pulled in and Lieutenant Walker again demanded that they release Seaman Anderson. He was ignored. Instead the islanders scrambled through the shallows, forcing the boats to pull back. Walker opened fire with a rocket at the mass of warriors, then ordered volley fire. The result was devastatingly predictable – the natives 'fled to the bush', according to the ship's logbook. The boats pulled into shore within pistol shot of the enemy.

Many islanders returned to defend their villages and unsuccessfully skirmished with Americans for hours. When all the buildings of Utiroa were burned, Walker and his men moved on to another nearby village and destroyed it too. There were no American combat casualties, while twelve islanders died and many more were presumed wounded. But there was still no sight of the missing American, so Walker led his men back to the boats.[5] Damage to the boats was repaired, and *Peacock* and *Flying Fish* rejoined the rest of the expedition. The fate of Anderson remains a mystery.[6]

Peacock went aground while attempting to enter the Columbia River and was lost with no casualties as the crew was able to lower six boats and get everyone ashore along with their journals, surveys, chronometers and scientific sketches. A one-eyed Indian named George then guided the *Flying Fish* into the same bay. Wilkes arrived with *Porpoise* and surveyed San Francisco and its tributaries before heading on its return trip via the Philippines, Borneo, Singapore, Polynesia and the Cape of Good Hope, reaching New York on 10 June 1842.

Wilkes and his officers had been at loggerheads throughout the voyage. Although commissioned only as a lieutenant, Wilkes had insisted on wearing of a captain's uniform and flying a commodore's pennants, and that rankled with his experienced and status-conscious subordinates. He was also seen as too keen on such punishments such as 'flogging round the fleet'. The disaffected officers, on their return America, effected a formal court martial. Wilkes was acquitted on all charges except that of illegally punishing men in his squadron.[7]

The Expedition played a major role in the development of nineteenth-century science and the growth of the American scientific establishment. In total, 280 islands, mostly in the Pacific, were explored, and more than 800 miles of Oregon was mapped. Over 60,000 plant and bird specimens were collected, along with the seeds of 648 species, which were later traded, planted and sent throughout the country. Many of the species and other items found by the expedition helped form the basis of collections at the new Smithsonian Institution. In addition, 254 live plants gathered on the home stretch of the journey went to the newly constructed greenhouse which later became the US Botanic Gardens.[8]

The expedition was a morale booster for the US, where it was regarded as the equal to the scientific exploration previously led by the British. Few gave a thought to the islanders who had perished during the search for natural history exhibits.

Ivory Coast (1842)

... gave three cheers and then applied the torch

On 24 April 1842, American captain Eben Farwell had docked his small schooner *Mary Carver* at the fortified port of Little Bereby on Africa's Ivory Coast to pick up a 600-pound load of camwood from local trader Young Crack-O. He discovered that his promised cargo was not ready for shipment and demanded a canoe as payment for late delivery. Crack-O reluctantly agreed and when the shipment was ready for transportation, it was taken to the *Mary Carver* by canoe. The ship's mate allowed some of the canoemen to board the schooner and help with stowing the cargo. Crack-O's men drew concealed weapons. The mate and the ship's cook were killed and one seaman was thrown overboard and drowned. A second seaman climbed the rigging to escape the massacre and when he finally came down he was 'butchered' by them. Farwell did not know his ship was under attack until the natives came for him. He asked for time to say one last prayer but was denied.[9] A Bereby women clubbed his face, smashing his eye socket. Farwell was tied up and thrown overboard; in the water he was able to free himself of the ropes and he made it to the surface only to be clubbed on the head again and killed.

The *Mary Carver* was plundered, and some pieces of the vessel were taken, with her American flag, which ended up in the home of the trader's father or uncle, tribal Chief Ben Crack-O, elsewhere in the town. The American response would be belated but brutal.

An Episcopalian missionary, E. L. Minor, was working 30 miles away in the town of Taboo but was quickly informed of the murders. He wrote to US Secretary of State Abel Upshur, strongly advising firm military retaliation to protect future American and European traders in the region. After another American ship, *Edward Barley*, was attacked Congress duly approved a punitive expedition under Commodore Matthew C. Perry.[10] Following the Sumatra expeditions, the Americans were in no mood to accept such attacks on the merchantmen who were making themselves and their country rich.

Perry claimed the Scottish resistance leader William Wallace and Mayflower passengers among his ancestors, but his own advocacy of modernising the US Navy earned him the epithet of 'Father of the Steam Navy'. He was a veteran of the War of 1812, the expeditions against both the Barbary and West Indies pirates, and had planted the American flag on Key West, previously part of Cuba. During a visit to Russia he was offered a commission in the Imperial Navy, which he declined. Once promoted to captain, he oversaw the construction of the navy's second steam frigate USS *Fulton*, which he commanded after its completion. He organised America's first corps of naval engineers and conducted the first US naval gunnery school while commanding *Fulton* from 1839 to 1841 off Sandy Hook.[11] Perry received the title of Commodore in June 1840 on his appointment as Commandant of New York Navy Yard.[12]

Commodore Perry hoisted sail at New York in the twenty-two-gun sloop-of-war *Saratoga* on 6 June. But in the Cape Verde Islands he transferred his flag to the thirty-eight-gun frigate *Macedonian*. His flotilla also included the sixteen-gun sloop *Decatur* and the ten-gun brigantine *Porpoise*, which had a contingent of marines on board. Firepower was not going to be a problem. Their chief task in the region was to support Liberia, an American colony for freed Afro-American slaves, in suppressing illicit slavers and pirates. That involved investigating both the *Mary Carver* and *Edward Barley* incidents.

Perry arrived off the West African coast near Sinoe in mid-November and his first objective was to gain proof regarding the piracy in that area. Perry disguised *Porpoise* as a merchantman, and as she approached the shore tribesmen in war canoes tried to take control of the ship. Its commander, Stellwagon, was able to get away without firing a shot. *Porpoise* left the expedition for duty elsewhere. Early in the morning of 29 November, seventy-five marines and sailors landed at Sinoe where Perry had a palaver with Liberia Governor Joseph Jenkins Roberts and his staff as well as the 'twenty kings' to discuss the earlier incident. The African leaders claimed that the American sailors were the 'aggressors' and that the Sinoes had attacked *Porpoise* in self-defence. Unimpressed by their rhetoric, Perry ordered that the nearby villages deemed responsible for sending out war canoes be burned. Three prisoners were also sent to Monrovia and the landing party then returned to their ships, taking Governor Roberts with them. By 1 December, the three navy vessels were off Blue Barra where another landing took place to escort Perry to another meeting with African authorities. The party returned later that night after dispersing gifts as a sign of friendship. A few days later there was another successful landing and meeting at Setra Koo. But the next one was not to be so trouble-free. Perry sailed for Cape Palmas and anchored off the town of Caval on 7 December where another palaver was held with Chief Ben Crack-O.[13] The landing and run-up to the meeting was tense, and Perry stationed sentries at the gates of the royal *kraal* (enclosure) to help with escape should it be necessary. Crack-O denied that his people had done anything wrong, touching his ears and his tongue with his sword as a gesture of truthfulness. Governor Roberts asked Crack-O if he would attend a 'Great Palaver' at Little Bereby and he accepted.

Perry sailed his squadron for Little Bereby on 11 December, arriving three days later, and landed his fifty marines and 150 sailors. The meeting was held in a house about 50 yards from the *kraal* gates, during which

Roberts began discussing with Crack-O the *Mary Carver* and *Edward Barley* affairs. Again the king insisted that he and his people were innocent of any piracy. The American officers and Governor Roberts felt the interpreter was an 'unskilful liar'. Perry stood up and said so before moving to confront King Crack-O. Crack-O allegedly tried to drag Perry to his spear, but the commodore fought him off. Crack-O tried to run out of the house, but before he could reach the door a marine sergeant fired his musket and hit the king while two others bayoneted him. The gathering broke down into a melee, with Crack-O's men running in all directions. His interpreter was shot dead while trying to run away. Perry ordered the town to be burned. The American sailors 'gave three cheers and then applied the torch' and in fifteen minutes the whole town was ablaze.[14]

After carrying out the objective of burning the town, the expedition's forces were returning to their ships when they were ambushed by native warriors in the woods. Another skirmish resulted and the marines and sailors charged towards the Africans and routed them. The three American warships also opened fire and helped silence the enemy. A few war canoes were captured. The Americans suffered no casualties, the Africans several dozen. The badly wounded Crack-O was taken prisoner and died from his wounds the next morning.

Perry then sailed down the coast, and the following morning he detected another Bereby settlement. The marines and sailors burned seven villages and inflicted serious losses upon the natives themselves, again without suffering any casualties themselves. Perry next decided – some thought belatedly – that the Bereby people had been punished enough. He ended the expedition and proceeded with other duties. Chief Crack-O's body was buried at sea and his spear was taken as a prize by Perry. Pieces of *Mary Carver* and her flag were also found at the *kraal*, evidence that the Bereby were responsible for the attack.

It had been a sordid and bloodily one-sided expedition, but Perry had done the job expected of him. In 1843, Perry took command of the African Squadron, charged with eradicating the slave trade on the high seas under the Webster-Ashburton Treaty, a job he continued through 1844. He commanded ships in the Mexican–American War of 1846–48 and played a leading role in the opening of Japan to the Western powers with the Convention of Kanagawa in 1854. After an assignment to the Naval Efficiency Board, he died awaiting further orders in New York in 1858 while suffering rheumatic fever, gout and alcoholism.[16]

Fiji Expeditions (1849 and 1859)

he moved silently and struck painfully

The Fijian citizens were perhaps overenthusiastic when they celebrated their own Independence Day in 1849. With no fireworks available, they fired cannon into the air. Unfortunately, several cannonballs fell on the house of American commercial agent and consul John Brown Williams. The property burned, setting off a chain of events that led to conflict in paradise.

Not that the locals would have necessarily regarded the islands as paradise, however, as the first half of the nineteenth century was rent by tribal warfare and raids from neighbouring Tonga. The increasing encroachment of Western powers and missionaries, the first of whom arrived from Tahiti in 1830, did not help, nor did a lucrative trade in weaponry carried out by the Swedish mercenary Charlie Savage. The result was a series of civil wars among the native Fijian confederacies. This saw the rise of a warlord/king called Seru Epenisa Cakobau.[17]

He was the son of a deposed *Vunivalu* (king) of Bau and took power in his early twenties by exploiting clan divisions. The traveller Mary Wallis, who met him in 1844, wrote: 'He is tall, rather good looking, appears fully aware of his consequence, and is not destitute of dignity. He wore an enormous quantity of hair on his head, and several yards of native cloth around his body.'[18] He was nicknamed Cikinovu or Centipede 'because he moved silently and struck painfully'. After he converted from cannibalism to Christianity thanks to the ministrations of missionary James Calvert, he took additional name of Epenisa (Ebenezer).[19] Cakobau insisted that his island, Bau, held suzerainty over the remainder of Fiji and claimed overall kingship. Chiefs on the other islands disagreed, and Cakobau consequently engaged in constant warfare for almost nineteen years to unify the islands under his authority.

The accidental destruction of Williams' house was followed just months later by a fire that destroyed his store, which strained relations with the trading Americans. USS *John Adams*, under Commander Edward Boutwell, was sent to monitor the unrest in October and her crew were landed several times to protect American interests. Boutwell demanded $5,000 in compensation for the loss of Williams' property from Cakobau, supplemented by further claims totalling $45,000. Cakobau was given a deadline to comply, otherwise US marines would be deployed to take him hostage. The king was between a rock and a hard place – if he acknowledged the debt, he did not have sufficient funds to pay it, but if he disclaimed it by saying that it fell under the jurisdiction of another chief, he would jeopardise his claim to the kingship. He decided to bide his time, hoping that the Americans were only bluffing.

They weren't, and a landing party was sent to the island's main town. Fijian warriors put up some resistance and one American serviceman was killed and two were wounded. The *John Adams* men routed a contingent of natives from Lautoka, but Cakobau and the survivors escaped. The immediate crisis passed. The Williams debt was never paid. Elsewhere on the islands, however, chiefs outside Cakobau's control kept up Fiji's bloodier customs.

In summer 1859, two American citizens on Waya were killed and eaten. When word reached the American consulate at Ovalau, the Pacific Squadron sent the sloop-of-war *Vandalia*. In early October it was decided that a vessel with a shallower draft was needed so the schooner *Mechanic* was chartered under the command of veteran lieutenant Charles Caldwell. A force of ten marines, forty sailors and a 12-pounder howitzer were mustered for the landing on Waya, along with a few Fijian guides and three American merchant sailors. The latter included Captain Josiah Knowles of the clipper *Wild Wave*, which had been wrecked off Oeno Island – he and forty crewmen had been rescued by *Vandalia* and taken to Fiji.[10]

The expedition left Ovalau on 6 October and sailed west around the northern end of the main island of Viti Levu to Waya. On the way a letter was received from the two Wayan chiefs responsible for the deaths of the American traders, saying: 'Do you suppose we have killed the two white men for nothing? No, we killed them and we have eaten them. We are great warriors, and we delight in war.' Caldwell later wrote, '[A]nd woe to the members of any strange tribe that falls into their hands ... to be clubbed to death and eaten is the only alternative for the captive. It is not a matter of surprise that the tribes along our route learned with feelings of satisfaction the nature of our expedition.'

At 3 a.m. on 9 October, the Americans landed unopposed and marched inland toward the village of Somatti over tropical and mountainous terrain. While being manhandled in the darkness, the 12-pounder fell 2,300 feet over a cliff and was abandoned. By daybreak the column reached Somatti, where over 300 native warriors lined up in defence. The Wayans wore white robes and were armed with clubs, rocks, spears, bows and some muskets. The battle began when Lieutenant Caldwell ordered a flanking manoeuver on the left side of the mass of warriors. This routed the natives and they fled into the jungle or took refuge in the settlement. Master's Mate John Bartlett led a group of sailors who sang 'Red, White and Blue' and let out three cheers before charging and capturing the village.

The crew of the 12-pounder, with no gun to fire, took charge of burning the village and more than 115 huts were destroyed. Marines under Lieutenant Alan Ramsey provided a rearguard for the sailors. Some Wayans regrouped and launched an attack from the jungle but were repulsed. After the fierce half-hour battle, fourteen warriors, including two chiefs, were counted as dead and at least thirty-six others were wounded. Of the Americans, two marines were wounded by musketry but survived, one marine was hit in the leg with an arrow, two sailors were badly hurt by rocks, and one from *Wild Wave* was also hurt.[21] After the battle, the Americans stopped at friendly Fijian fishing villages and spread the news of their victory, receiving much credit for leading one of the era's most impressive, albeit small-scale, US military campaigns in the South Pacific.

Meanwhile, Cakobau crushed the final rebellion against his rule at the Battle of Kaba. As a Christian convert, he pardoned all battlefield captives rather than follow pagan Fijian customs which would have seen them ceremonially humiliated, killed and eaten. Supported by foreign settlers, he finally succeeded in creating a united Fijian kingdom in 1871. He set up a constitutional monarchy and a legislative assembly dominated by foreigners. That proved unworkable and in 1874 he ceded authority to Britain's Queen Victoria. Ninety-six years of British rule followed. He lived quietly until his death on 1 February 1883.[22]

American sea power had proven that its reach, in terms of protecting trading enterprises and intimidating local inhabitants, extended to every sea, every ocean. It could not at this time be compared to the reach of the British Empire, which was then at the height of its power, but it was getting there.

II

Cortina Wars, Texas (1859–1861)

Flocks of vampires, in the guise of men.

Tejano Juan Nepomuceno Cortina was visiting the mainly white town of Brownsville when he saw town marshal Robert Shears, a notorious bully, verbally and physically abusing sixty-year-old Tomas Cabrero, who had previously worked for his family. He leapt onto his horse and charged the pair, shooting and wounding Shears. He pulled Cabrero on to his mount and fled the town before he could be arrested. It was the dramatic start to a series of conflicts that inspired legends, folk art and songs along the Tex-Mex border and provided a largely forgotten sideshow to the American Civil War.

Cortina was born on 16 May 1824 in Camargo, Tamaulipas. His mother had inherited a 260,000-acre land grant in the lower Rio Grande valley surrounding Brownsville and he spent his childhood in the area. From 1836 when Cortina was twelve, parts of the Cortina grant north of the Rio Grande River were in the disputed territory between the Rio Grande and the Nueces Rivers, claimed by both Mexico and the Republic of Texas. Cortina was firmly on the side of his Mexican family.

Cortina was twenty-two when the Mexican–American war began in 1846, and he formed a band of vaqueros (cowboys, cattle drivers) from his and neighbouring ranches into an irregular cavalry regiment called the Tamaulipas in an attempt to stop the advancing forces of American General Zachary Taylor. The regiment joined the forces of General Mariano Arista at Matamoros and subsequently fought at the Battles of Palo Alto, Resaca de la Palma and Palo Duro against General Taylor's troops. When the US triumphed in 1848, Mexico was forced to concede the disputed territory to Texas. Cortina opposed this concession, but he and his irregulars were easily defeated and forced to flee into Mexico. After the Treaty of Hidalgo, in which all rights were supposedly guaranteed for Mexicans who stayed behind, many saw their situation worsen.

In Texas, unlike California and Arizona, the state government entered the union with control over all its public land. A common problem for Mexicans was that the land was being appropriated through a high tax system that Mexicans couldn't afford. It was then resold to new Anglo settlers or wealthy Mexicans. Another problem was that Americans did not acknowledge or respect the original land claims granted during the Spanish colonial era.

Cortina's allegiance shifted from Mexican to American, however. After the war Cortina worked as a contractor in the US Quartermaster Corps for a brief period, paradoxically serving the army he fought against in the war. He was also involved in a few filibuster expeditions which sought to make their own 'Republic of the Sierra Madre', but these were failures. After the death of his father in 1855, he moved to the Espiritu Santo land grant in the southern Nueces strip. There he began cattle ranching and entered the political arena. He was popular among Mexicans, other vaqueros who nicknamed him 'Cheno', and with some Anglos including the Texan hero Sam Houston. Later, Houston counted on Cortina to prevent Texas from seceding in the run-up to the American Civil War, as they both opposed slavery.

Cortina saw first-hand the injustices practised against the Mexicans whose land was bit by bit being stolen by the post-war influx of American settlers. Taking the side of poorer Mexicans in disputes over land titles inevitably brought Cortina into conflict with a clique of judges and Brownsville attorneys whom he accused of using the unfamiliar American judicial system to cheat his fellow Tejanos. 'Flocks of vampires, in the guise of men,' he wrote, stripped Tejanos 'of their property, incarcerated, chased, murdered, and hunted them like wild beasts'. Meanwhile, Cortina also clashed with the law, twice being indicted on probably trumped-up charges of cattle theft, but he had become too popular and high-profile to arrest. Local Mexican-Americans, and some influential white Texans like Houston, saw the indictments as nothing more than the harassment of a patriot. Cortina assembled, trained, and armed his own private militia to resist the evictions of his fellow Tejanos. To many, Cortina became a 'Robin Hood' hero, the first 'socially motivated border bandit', establishing a tradition that later figures, such as Pancho Villa, would seek to exploit.[1]

The tension between Cortina and the Brownsville authorities broke into violence on 13 July 1859. Brownsville town marshal Robert Shears was brutalising Cortina's former ranch hand, who whites later claimed to have been drunk and 'causing a scene' in a coffee shop. Before the shooting began, Cortina asked Shears to let him handle the situation; Shears yelled at him: 'What is it to you, you damned Mexican?' Cortina fired a warning shot, then when Shears did not stop, he intervened and shot him in the shoulder. Cortina pulled the man up to his horse and rode out of town. A warrant was issued for attempted murder, which Cortina ignored. Instead he planned a fight back to sort out the long-running grievances.[2]

On 28 September he raided and occupied the town with a posse of between forty and eighty men. Most of his enemies, however, had fled, although five Texans were shot during the initial attack and occupation. No indiscriminate attacks on the rest of the Brownsville population or on their properties took place under Cortina's direct orders. Cortina issued a later-renowned proclamation to reveal his intentions to both communities:

> There is no need of fear. Orderly people and honest citizens are inviolable to us in their persons and interests. Our object, as you have seen, has been to chastise the villainy of our enemies, which heretofore has gone unpunished. These have connived with each other, and form, so to speak, a perfidious inquisitorial lodge to persecute and rob us, without any cause, and for no other crime on our part than that of being of Mexican origin, considering us, doubtless, destitute of those gifts which they themselves do not possess. (...) Mexicans! Peace be with you! Good inhabitants of the State of Texas, look on them as brothers, and keep in mind that which the Holy Spirit saith: 'Thou shalt not be the friend of the passionate man; nor join thyself to the madman, lest thou learn his mode of work and scandalize thy soul.'[3]

Cortina's occupation lasted two days, but he and his men were persuaded to leave by Mexican businessmen. The following day, the townsfolk formed the twenty-man 'Brownsville Tigers' vigilante posse, which promptly captured the hapless Tomas Cabrero. In November, the Brownsville Tigers learned that Cortina was at his mother's home, Rancho del Carman, 5 miles west of Brownsville. They immediately launched an attack, assisted by two cannon and a Matamoros militia company. Led by W. B. Thompson, the group moved so tentatively that when they finally encountered a few of Cortina's vaqueros near Santa Rita, and several shots were fired, the 'Tigers' abandoned their cannons and beat a hasty retreat back to Brownsville.[4]

Cortina threatened to burn Brownsville unless the authorities released Cabrera from jail. However, Governor Hardin Runnels had dispatched a company of Texas Rangers from San Antonio, under the command of Captain William G. Tobin, and they arrived before Cortina had an opportunity to carry out his threat. Unfortunately, Tobin's Rangers proved to be an undisciplined and drunken bunch whose first official act was to storm the jail and lynch Cabrera. Cortina quickly retaliated by killing three of Tobin's Rangers in an ambush.[5] Seeking revenge for the murder of his men, Tobin procured another cannon, reorganised the

Tigers and led them and his Rangers against Cortina's ranch. Again, the Brownsville men were easily routed and trundled the remaining cannon back to town.

The South Texas–North Tamaulipas region after 1850 was untypical of the border. Unlike Mexicans in California or further east in Texas, people of Mexican descent continued to enjoy a vast numerical superiority over Anglos and to varying degrees encroaching Anglo elites had to adapt themselves to continuing *tejano* political and economic power; many chose to marry into prominent *tejano* families. And when challenged by Cortina's uprising, Anglo officials could protect themselves only by calling in powerful outside forces, including the US Army.

Alarmed by the continued chaos on the border, Governor Runnels ordered John Salmon 'Rip' Ford to take control of the situation. The forty-four-year-old Tennessean had enjoyed a varied and colourful life as a medical doctor, lawyer and journalist. He had moved to Texas after an acrimonious divorce, practising medicine in San Augustine for eight years. He passed the Bar exam before winning election to the Texas legislature in 1844, advocating annexation by the US. The following year he moved to Austin, where he purchased the *Texas National Register* newspaper, renaming it the *Texas Democrat*. During the Mexican War he served as both adjutant and medical officer in the Texas Mounted Rifles and saw active service in Mexico as commander of a scouting company.[6] His nickname 'Rip' was bestowed on him for his peculiarity of including the words 'Rest in Peace' after each name when reading out his company's casualty lists. After exploring the country between San Antonio and El Paso in 1849 he was made captain in the Texas Rangers and was involved in various skirmishes along the Rio Grande, capturing a war chief in the process, until his unit was disbanded. In 1852 he was elected to the Texas Senate, returned to newspaper editorships and early in 1858 he accepted a commission as Senior Captain in the state troops, defeating hostile tribesmen in the Battle of Little Robe Creek on the Canadian River.[7]

Without waiting for the paperwork promoting him to the rank of major and authorising him to raise a large and organised company of Rangers, Ford crossed the Colorado on the ferry at the foot of Congress Avenue with only seven men and headed south. Because of appeals from Brownsville residents, the army sent troops from San Antonio to the nearby Fort Brown, which had been abandoned a few years before. The fort's new commander, Major Samuel Heintzelman, united and co-ordinated all armed groups to put an end to the Cortina threat.

The formal orders caught up with Ford on 17 November. He was to assume overall command of the Rangers on the border. According to Governor Runnels, 'The service required is to protect the western frontier against Cortina and his band and to arrest them if possible.' As Ford and his small band made their way south, word of the Rangers' mission spread quickly, and they were soon joined by dozens of well-armed volunteers. The citizens of Goliad, the scene of a notorious massacre of mainly white Texans after the Alamo, provided enough funds to equip and provision the entire company. While in Goliad, Ford learned that 165 regular army troops had been gathered by Heintzelman in the old Fort Brown.

When Ford's Rangers, now fifty-three men strong, reached the area in early December, a combined force of army regulars and Tobin's Rangers were already engaging Cortina's forces a few miles up the Rio Grande from Brownsville. Ford heard the echo of gunfire as the company approached town and brought his men to a gallop. A Brownsville lookout perched in a church steeple mistook them for Cortina's men and rang the alarm bell. Alarm turned to cheers when Ford's company were belatedly recognised for what they were. Ford led his men toward the sound of the guns, but they arrived at the tail end of the fighting in time to see Cortina's mounted men escape across the river. The Rangers spent the night camped with the army near the scene of the day's fighting, but a cold, steady rain kept them from getting much sleep. The following morning, Ford intended to mount and lead his men in pursuit of Cortina until he discovered that the rain had soaked his powder supply. Ford abandoned any idea of immediate pursuit and led his company to Fort Brown, where they replenished their powder while he met with Major Heintzelman and Captain Tobin. They agreed that Ford take command of all the Rangers on the border; they would scout Cortina's location ahead of the regular forces.[8]

Border historian Jeffrey Robenalt wrote:

> Cruel thorns tore at the flesh of both men and horses as the Rangers worked their way slowly upriver through the torturous mesquite and chaparral brush that grew thick along the Rio Grande. However, the tough going was made a little easier when they came across a campsite that was only a day or so old. Not long after, a string of burned out and smouldering ranches left a trail a blind man could follow; as if Cortina was determined to destroy everything in his path. The Rangers found the Neal ranch destroyed and the customs house and post office at Edinburg looted. A pall of smoke hung over the lower Rio Grande valley as Cortina and his men retreated.[9]

The Rangers spent a cold and miserable Christmas Day and Boxing Day before they heard that Cortina and his men had occupied the ramshackle Rio Grande City.[10] Most of the citizens fled while the insurgents plundered the town. Ford and Heintzelman agreed to move in during the early, pre-dawn hours. The army would advance straight up the road along the river, and Ford's Rangers would slip around the city, trapping Cortina in between. By late evening, the Rangers had advanced to an area not far from Ringgold Barracks, an old abandoned army post, where they bedded down for a few hours, sleeping on the ground with their horses' reins in their hands.

Well before dawn, Ford was awakened by the rumbling of Heintzelman's artillery caissons as they moved into position on the road to the town. Ford drove in Cortina's picket, forced back a reconnoitring party. Cortina's cavalry charged but Ford's troops left 'Cortina's bold riders ... on the ground'. Robenalt described the battle:

> A soupy, swirling fog had settled over the valley. Quickly mounting his ninety Rangers, Ford moved them out toward the town at a trot. Cortina's pickets greeted the advance with scattered gunfire as the column reached Ringgold Barracks, but a heavy volume of return fire from the Rangers' Colt revolvers easily drove the bandits back. Ford's advance scouts soon reported that Cortina had pulled his men back to a copse of ebony trees that stood on a small rise overlooking the town. Ford split his men into two columns, hoping to catch the bandits in a deadly crossfire, but as the Rangers neared the rise, the Mexicans opened fire with two cannons. Luckily, the grapeshot fired from the guns sailed high in the fog, shredding the tops of the trees above the Rangers' heads. Ford led a charge to within forty yards of the guns, before ordering the men to dismount and engage the bandits on foot. The firing was hot and heavy from both sides, but the swirling fog prevented either force from inflicting too many casualties. Suddenly a Mexican bugle sounded the charge and a line of mounted bandits swept out of the fog. The Rangers broke the fury of the charge with the firepower of their Colts and the bandits made a disorderly retreat. Seizing the moment, Ford ordered his men to remount and the Rangers began an immediate pursuit. The fight soon broke up into the kind of tangled, every-man-for-himself melee in which the Rangers marksmanship with their Colts made them so deadly. By the time the fighting ended, sixty Mexican bodies lay scattered between the rise where the bandits had made their initial stand and the Rio Grande. The Rangers suffered sixteen wounded. Cortina led the survivors across the river to the safety of Mexico.[11]

The Mexicans started to retreat as Heintzelman's troops arrived and helped Ford pursue the Mexicans to the river, killing many, and forcing them to abandon their cannon.[12]

Cortina's forces retreated into Mexico, taking refuge in the Burgos Mountains near Guerrero and Mier. Heintzelman moved up the Rio Grande to Roma while Ford marched to Brownsville forming a new company of 83 Texas Rangers. Fierce skirmishing continued on both sides of the border. In early February 1860, Ford and his Texas Rangers were placed under the command of Heintzelman and was responsible for clearing 'the country of robbing bands' and defending the steamer *Ranchero's* passage from Rio Grande City to Brownsville from Cortina. On the 4th, Ford and forty-eight Rangers crossed into Mexico, successfully defended their riverboat *Ranchero* at La Bolsa, and routed the Cortinistas. Ford stayed on the Mexican side of the Rio Grande until the 6th, when he received assurances the *Ranchero* would not be attacked. The *Ranchero* reached Brownsville safely two days later.[13]

The situation changed abruptly in April 1860. Texas elected a new governor, Cortina's old friend Sam Houston, who recognised the possibility of a looming civil war and ordered Ford to disband his Rangers and return to Austin. Ford had no choice but to reluctantly comply and he discharged his men, wrapped up his paperwork and began the long ride back to Austin. The first Cortina War had come to an end. Lieutenant Colonel Robert E. Lee relieved Major Heintzelman and the Mexican authorities offered to restrain their citizens 'from making predatory descents upon the territory and people of Texas'.[14] The first Cortina War was over but peace did not last long, thanks to the impact of a much larger conflict.

When the American Civil War began Cortina aligned himself with the US Federal government and invaded Zapata County, Texas. After he was defeated by Confederate captain and former Laredo judge Santos Benavides at the Battle of Carrizo, in which he lost eighteen men, Cortina retreated to Mexico. By the end of the Cortina troubles, at least 245 men had been killed, most of whom were Cortinistas. Cortina avoided any more large-scale military incursions within the US, although he was accused several times of promoting guerrilla actions against the richer Texan landowners in the following years. There is a strong suspicion that Cortina's fame meant he was blamed, with no evidence, for each and every ranch raid.

Cortina joined the liberal army that supported Benito Juarez, becoming his military commander, and in 1862 Cortina defended San Lorenzo, Puebla and Tamaulipas.[15] On 12 January 1864 fighting broke out in Matamoros between the French and the Juaristas, which would rage for two days. US Consul Leonard Pierce, Jnr, sent an urgent message for aid to the Union general Francis J. Herron, who commanded the garrison in Brownsville:

> General: A battle is now raging in the streets of this City between the forces of Governor Manuel Ruiz and Col. Juan N. Cortina. My person and family are in great danger as the road between here and the ferry is said to be infested with robbers. I have also about $1,000,000 in specie and a large amount of other valuable property under my charge in the consulate, and from the well-known character of Cortina and his followers, I fear the city will be plundered. I therefore earnestly request that you will send a sufficient force to

protect myself and property and to transport the money within the limits of the United States at the earliest possible moment.

Herron acted quickly, sending Colonel Henry Bertram with five companies of the 20th Wisconsin to protect the ferry and the consulate. The consulate was unmolested as the fighting raged from 12 to 14 January 1864. Cortina, leading the Juaristas, ultimately prevailed, proclaimed himself governor and the town was plundered as Pierce had predicted.

However, when the French eventually defeated the Mexican forces to establish Archduke Maximilian of Habsburg as sovereign of Mexico, Cortina switched sides, sensing an opportunity to consolidate his power in the Tamaulipas region. This alliance was short-lived, and Cortina then in turn rose against the French. Commanding a large army that he had personally gathered and equipped, he engaged the interventionist forces that had landed near Tampico and defeated them. He and his men fought across Central Mexico and he was present at the execution of Maximilian in June 1867. During this time, in the absence of a legal national authority, he appointed himself Governor of Tamaulipas twice – in 1864 and in 1865. He resigned from the office in 1866 in favour of Generals José María Carvajal and Santiago Tapia.

In Texas, his reputation was poles apart among different factions after the defeat of the Confederacy; he was seen as both villain and hero. He was dismissed as a bandit by land-grabbers and white business interests. Pro-Union factions in the Rio Grande valley admired both his support for the federal government and his defence, despite his predisposition to change sides when it suited him, of democracy in Mexico. After returning to his estates in Matamoros in 1870 he was formally invited on several occasions as guest of honour of the city of Brownsville. A former mayor endorsed a petition to the Texas legislature asking for a formal pardon for his alleged crimes during the border war. Although this motion and a subsequent one was eventually rejected due to the intervention of pro-Confederacy ranchers, Cortina was respected not just by Hispanics but also by white Texans sick of the stranglehold the rich had on the levers of power. The Mexican authorities appointed him brigadier general and the largest battalion of the state of Tamaulipas was renamed '*el Batallón Cortina*' (the 'Cortina Battalion').

But he became disillusioned with fellow republican leaders, and his political ambitions were shattered by internal disputes, revolutionary dogma and personality clashes. Cortina supported the military hero of the French intervention, General Porfirio Díaz, the political rival of Benito Juarez and his successor Sebastián Lerdo de Tejada. It was to prove a costly mistake. Cortina attempted to raise an army from the local population and sheltered Díaz following his failed rising. But Díaz, who eventually became president, callously disregarded Cortina's services when rich South Texas ranchers offered a bribe estimated at between $50,000 and $200,000 to remove Cortina under the pretext that he was rustling cattle across the border. Lerdo's administration saw those claims as public justification to detain him. In 1875, Cortina was arrested and taken to Mexico City. Cortina escaped prison but was caught on the border by Mexican authorities. He was court-martialled and sentenced to death, but intervention by Porfirio Díaz resulted in Cortina's survival under house arrest.

In November 1876, Díaz overthrew President Lerdo and Cortina was allowed to return to Tamaulipas, where he again tried to raise an armed force. But before he could put this new army to any use, Díaz ordered his arrest and confinement within Mexico City for the second time. Díaz was suspicious of Cortina's ambition to hold total power within Tamaulipas, a suspicion that may have been justified given his record of switching sides. The Texas bribe money was still on offer and quietly accepted. Most importantly, Díaz was ruthlessly determined to remain in absolute control of Mexico and would brook no potential rivals. He systematically removed all traces of opposition that could have challenged him; he ruled for thirty-three years. Under diplomatic pressure from the US, Díaz decreed the arrest and execution of his former ally.

General José Canales, a long-time enemy of Cortina, feared popular reprisals from the people of Tamaulipas if the death sentence was carried out. Cortina's old Texas Rangers adversary 'Rip' Ford also interceded on his behalf. He was kept at the military prison of Santiago Tlaltelolco, without being formally tried or sentenced. He remained there until 1890, when he was removed and placed under house arrest in a comfortable home in Azcapotzalco, north-west of Mexico City. Cortina remained there until his death on 30 October 1894.

'Rip' Ford saw active service for the Confederacy, and after raising 1,300 troops, known as 'The Cavalry of the West', and by now a full colonel, in May 1865 he led Confederate forces in the Battle of Palmito Ranch, judged by many to be the last battle of the Civil War. In the aftermath of that battle, Ford wrote:

> Some of the Sixty-Second Colored Regiment were taken. They had been led to believe that if captured they would either be shot or returned to slavery. They were agreeably surprised when they were paroled and permitted to depart with the white prisoners. Several of the prisoners were from Austin and vicinity. They were assured they would be treated as prisoners of war. There was no disposition to visit upon them a mean spirit of revenge.

When Colonel Ford surrendered his command he urged his men to honour their paroles. He insisted that 'the negro had a right to vote'.[16] Ford acted as a guide for the US military operating against 'cow-thieves and other disturbers of peace and quietude' and was a correspondent for the *Galveston News*. Later he established the *Brownsville Sentinel*.[17] He died in 1897.

Disputes along the Rio Grande border continued into the twentieth century and beyond. Popular mythology carved out a larger place for Juan Cortina than for Rip Ford. Anglo-Americans have generally treated him as a bandit and their legends have dissociated his actions from the larger context of US conquest and Anglo-American encroachment. Mexican-American folklore, on the other hand, stresses the connections between Cortina's exploits and this broader context. Juan Cortina was branded 'the Red Robber of the Rio Grande' by white Texans. To Mexican-Americans he is still known as the 'Robin Hood of the Rio Grande'.

12

The Shinmiyangyo Korean Expedition (1871)

I don't want to engage in any more sick business.

The human and commercial cost of the Civil War, in which the Union blockade of Confederate ports had played a major part, left the US desperate to extend its trading potential. America had already demonstrated its capacity to mount punitive operations against far-flung nations who interfered with its merchant shipping, and the mysterious disappearance of a merchantman and its crew in Korean waters offered another such excuse. In the resulting conflict, according to military historian Eric Niderost, 'the nineteenth century met the sixteenth century, and there was no question which epoch would prevail. Korean bravery simply could not compensate for an antiquated military system.'[1]

* * *

The US, with the European powers, was keen to open new trade in Asia and began making tentative inroads into China and its neighbours. Japan was opened after Commodore Matthew Perry sailed into harbour near modern-day Tokyo in July 1853 and, using the threat of modern firepower, forced a trade convention. As early as 1832, discussions on opening up Korea to trade were launched by USS *Peacock*'s Captain Edmund Roberts. But in 1844 a draft trade agreement tabled to the US Congress was shelved due to lack of interest.

The first actual contact was not hostile. Several Americans who were shipwrecked in Korea in 1855 and 1866 were treated well and sent to China for repatriation. However, the Joseon dynasty which ruled Korea was well aware of the damage done to the Chinese ruling class by the British-led Opium Wars and maintained a strict policy of isolationism. The 'Hermit Kingdom' had been under the domination of China for many centuries, refusing intercourse with the world. Her inhabitants were popularly believed in the West to be 'far superior to the Chinese in mental and physical resources'.²

That isolationist policy was threatened by the arrival of the iron-hulled trader *General Sherman*. First named *Princess Royal*, she was built in 1861 as a Confederate navy blockade runner. She weighed 619 tons, was 197 feet long, could make 11 knots and during her military life carried a crew of ninety and two 12-pound cannons. She was captured off Charleston in January 1863 and the Union Navy refitted her as a gunship. Later that year she helped to repulse the Confederate attack on Fort Butler, and in May 1865 she also helped destroy the Confederate warship *Denbigh* at Bird Key Spit, near Galveston. After the war she entered commercial service and was sent to 'survey' the waters of Korea.

The side-wheeled steamer carried a cargo of cotton, tin and glass goods purchased from the British trading firm Meadows & Co., based in Tientsin, China, and was heavily armed. On board were the ship's owner, American trader W. B. Preston; the ship's master, Captain Page; the Protestant missionary Robert Jermain Thomas, who acted as navigator and interpreter having learned some Korean words from the Korean Catholics at Chefoo; Englishman George Hogarth; and Chief Mate Wilson. The rest of the crew were fourteen Chinese and three Malay sailors. They departed China on 9 August 1866 and arrived on the coast of Korea a week later. *General Sherman*, assisted by Chinese junks, entered the Taedong River on Korea's west coast, sailing towards Pyongyang, and stopped at the Keupsa Gate. Yu Wautai, captain of one of the Chinese junks, had accompanied the Reverend Thomas on his previous trip to Korea's Hwanghae province. According to Thomas, Yu had twenty years' experience trading with Koreans. They jointly attempted to meet with Korean officials to begin negotiations for a trade treaty. The emissary informed them that Korea did not trade with foreigners and that only the king could change this law; further, that the governor had no authority to deal with the foreigners. He then offered to provide them with some provisions. They asked for flour and eggs.³

While the emissary left the ship to report to the governor, *General Sherman* weighed anchor and sailed up the river to Mangyungdae where the Crow Rapids stopped them from going any further. During the night, rain poured down on the mountains and the Tae-dong River rose rapidly. The day was the 15th of the lunar month, and there were also high tides. These two factors swelled the water to a level seldom seen before. The steamer was able to pass over the rapids; those on board apparently thought that the high-water level was normal and kept on sailing until they reached Yanggakdo Island. Regional governor Park Gyu-su sent Lee Hyon Ik, the deputy commander of the Pyongyang garrison, to the ship with four eggs and a message: 'You have reached the walls of our city when asked to stay put at Keupsa Gate. You insist on trading with us, which is forbidden. Your actions have created a grave situation so much so that I must inform my King and let him decide what to do with you people.' Korean Regent Dae Won Kun likewise believed that the foreign 'black ship' was a vanguard of invasion and commanded Park: 'Tell them to leave at once. If they do not obey, kill them.'[4] That was confirmed by the French priest Father Ridel in a report to Westerners in China.[5]

What happened next was not explained in any detail until an eyewitness account emerged in 1892:

The day before Dae's edict arrived, the river's water level dropped and the ship was hopelessly stranded. The governor ordered his troops to attack the foreigners. We had *wha-jun* (fire arrows) which could travel 800 feet and then explode. Our troops were dressed in dragon cloud armour and marched past a cheering crowd. We had several cannons rolled out to fight the invaders. The Americans saw our troops coming and took hostage of Deputy Commander Lee, who was on board the ship for a visit. Gov. Park told his troops to attack the ship notwithstanding Lee's safety.

The fighting continued for four days amidst a huge crowd of spectators. The foreigners fired large cannon balls that travelled more than 10 li. The cannons' thunders could be heard as far away as one day's walk. They aimed at the spectators and showers of deadly steel fragments rained down on them. Our troops retreated to a safe distance, from where their guns and bows could do little harm to the foreigners.

We then tried a Turtle boat, a boat covered with metal sheets and cow hides. The bow of this boat had a covered port for the cannon hidden inside. The Turtle boat approached the ship and fired many shots, but the shots bounced off the thick skin of the ship. The fight was not going too well for us. Then drill sergeant Park Choong-wun tied three boats together by the East Gate and loaded them up with firewood. He then poured sulfur and salt peter in the wood. Two long ropes were attached to both sides of the boats and the firewood were lit.

But the fire went out before the boats reached the ship. A second set of fire-boats was pushed away by the Americans. But the third set reached the enemy ship and success at last. The enemy ship caught on fire and began to burn. The crew faced suffocation by the stench and vapor of the burning sulfur and saltpeter. They tried in vain to put out the flames and as the smoke grew thicker and thicker they were forced one by one to jump into the water.

Our troops in boats surrounded the enemy ship and captured the enemy as they tried to escape. Drill-sergeant Park boarded the ship and rescued Lee. Some of the invaders waved white flags. Most of them were hacked to pieces before they reached the shore. Others were dragged ashore alive. These tried friendly smiles and soft words to win the goodwill of our people – in vain.[6]

Among those was the Reverend Thomas, the first Protestant missionary to come ashore on Korea. There are wildly conflicting accounts of his death. Some say he knelt down to say his last prayer and gave his Bible to his executioner before he was killed; others that he was screaming and pleading for mercy. A later account said:

> Choe Nam Hun (Thomas' Korean name) was bound in ropes at the time. He and Cho Nung Bong were handed over to the relatives of those Koreans killed by the crew. They were killed by sword. After this, the soldiers on the 24th killed the rest of the crew, moved their bodies to Moon Yi Jong and cremated them several days later. The ashes were buried on the Bong-rae-do.[7]

What is clear is that Thomas did not die for Christianity. He routinely carried a sword and pistol in accordance with the rugged brand of evangelicalism of the time. He may have distributed 500 Bibles during the voyage, but most reports suggest that he was in effective charge of the ship, not merely interpreting but making the key decisions on whether to advance or retreat. The scholar Han Gyu Mu wrote:

> Evangelism, trade and education were the main objectives of the *General Sherman*'s uninvited visit to Korea, but her primary mission was trade. It was clear that none of her crew with the sole exception of Thomas would have risked their life for Christianity. The Korean officials recognised that her main intention was trade. The crew intended to reach Pyongyang or Seoul for the purpose of trading in spite of Korea's wish for them to depart Korea immediately.

Han Gyu Mu continued: 'Thomas came to Korea aboard an armed merchant ship intent on reaching Pyongyang no matter what and in complete disregard of the laws of Korea. Thomas was involved in kidnapping, killing of civilians and open armed confrontation with the Korean officials. It may be argued that that was the norm in the days of Western imperialism.'[8] Garrison deputy commander Lee had been trying to capture a small boat carrying six of the crew when he was taken hostage. Later he was dismissed, along with a coastal watcher, for incompetence during the affair.

The account in Kojong government archives continued:

> The remains of the foreigners were trampled on and dragged around. Their body parts were cut off for medical use and what was left was burned. The enemy ship was totally burned down and there remained only her iron ribs that looked like posts driven into the ground. These irons were melted down and used in various ways. We captured two or three cannons, which are displayed in the armory of Pyongyang.

We also recovered her anchor chains, which hang from the East Gate Tower. (Other items salvaged from the *General Sherman* included two rifles, three cannon balls, and 162 shot.)

There was a big celebration over this victory of ours. Gov. Park provided food and wine. There was much joy and sadness over our losses. Gov. Park sent a special messenger to the King with the news: 'Drill sergeant Park rescued my deputy commander Lee from the burning enemy ship. He boarded the ship, took Lee under his arm and leaped with him a hundred yards across the Taedong river to safety.' When Dae Won Kun read this note, he laughed his heart out and made Park Chongwun his aide-de-camp in Ahn-ju. Park still lives in Kang-dong, Pyung-an Province. We lost one soldier and thirteen civilians.[9]

The Korean government's archives remain evasive about the burning of the *General Sherman*, due to the American demand for compensation for the ship and her crew. The royal administration claimed that the ship was burned by a civilian mob and that the government played no role. At the time, however, the US had no reliable intelligence as to what had happened to *General Sherman* beyond wild and partisan rumour. In January 1867 the USS *Wachusett* under Captain Robert W. Schufeldt went to investigate *General Sherman*'s demise, and offered a reward for information, but foul weather turned her back. The following spring the USS *Shenandoah* under Captain John C. Febiger reached the Taedong River's mouth and received an official letter acknowledging the death of all crewmen on *General Sherman*.

Some Koreans claimed that the real purpose of *General Sherman* was to seek treasures buried in the royal tombs near Pyongyang, citing the presence on board of a Chinese inspector of gold and silver and enquiries by Thomas, made to a Korean undercover officer, about the whereabouts of a 'white pagoda'. They also believed that the use of an armed metal-hulled gunboat was suspicious in a trade mission. Even among Westerners residing in China, there were concerns regarding *General Sherman* being heavily armed. It was well known that two months prior to the incident an armed vessel captained by the German Ernst Oppert had visited Korea and made the same demand for trade. It had been refused, but Oppert and his crewmen had been well treated and were returned to China safely by Governor Park Gyu-su.[10] The jury is out on such conspiracy theories. It seems highly unlikely that *General Sherman* was engaged in some sort of Indiana Jones-style graverobbing expedition. But relations on both sides were soured and the *General Sherman* incident was one factor in putting the two nations on course for war.

The disappearance of *General Sherman*, coupled closely with the expulsion of a French expedition, showed evidence of vigorous anti-foreign sentiment, manifested by tablets erected throughout the country which warned: 'The barbarians from beyond the seas have violated our borders and invaded our land. If we do not fight we must make treaties with them. Those who favor making a treaty sell their country.'[11]

By 1870 the American desire for trade with the Korean peninsula had grown because of the need to establish supply-and-demand links with China, Japan and South-East Asia as a whole. Given the distances and expense involved, it made commercial sense to develop triangular trade routes. The US expedition to Korea, known by the Koreans as the *Shinmiyangyo* (Western Disturbance in the Shinmi Year), was primarily to establish trade and political relations, to establish a treaty assuring aid for shipwrecked sailors, and, if feasible, to determine the fate of the *General Sherman*. It ended as a by now familiar punitive raid. A misunderstanding turned a diplomatic expedition into an armed conflict.

The American Minister to China, Frederick Ferdinand Low, was instructed to present the proposed treaty and, should the opportunity seem favourable, to obtain commercial advantages in Korea.[12] He sailed from Nagasaki for Boisée Island on the Salée River in May 1871 on board the USS *Colorado*, the flagship of Rear Admiral John Rodgers, then commanding the US Asiatic Squadron. The expedition consisted of about 650 men, over 500 sailors and 105 marines in five warships – *Colorado*, *Alaska*, *Palos*, *Monocacy* and *Benicia*, collectively mounting ninety-seven cannon – and several other supply and support vessels.[13]

A vivid account of the expedition revealing contemporary American attitudes was given by the expedition's marine commander, Captain McLane Tilton, in letters home to his wife Nannie. Off the coast of Japan he wrote:

> We are really on our way to Korea, the fleet sailing & steaming in double echelon ... the sky above being as blue as Italy's own, and the sea as smooth as a lake; the sun shining over all with a warmth that makes us as happy & comfortable as we could wish to be. I hope what you have read in the papers about the Expedition has not alarmed you as I do not think we are to have any trouble to speak of, our mission being a peaceful one, and for the purpose only of exacting a reasonable promise from the Korean Govt. that Christian seaman wrecked on their coast may be treated humanely. We have no knowledge of the country, and only very unreliable information in regard to the coast, as no surveys have yet been satisfactorily made; the only chart being one made of the vicinity of the Capitol, by the French Navy; The navigation will necessarily be somewhat dangerous but we all trust that by the exercise of great vigilance we will succeed in keeping off of rocks etc. My impression at this moment is, that the people will have no intercourse with us, and our journey will be so much love's labor lost.[14]

A few days later, Tilton wrote:

> We are all quite jolly, and every day the crews of our fleet are exercised
> in the Infantry drill & firing with small arms. Some months ago a
> Schooner came up here to trade, and the natives are said to have cut
> them up, and pickled them, took them in the interior and set them up
> as curiosities! The French came 3 years ago to avenge their priests, who
> had been murdered, when they skinned a French doctor, and crucified
> him on the beach under the eyes of the Frenchmen who had been
> driven off, and who were unable to help their friends. Whether this is
> positively true or not I can't say; but you may imagine it is with not a
> great pleasure I anticipate landing with the small force we have, against
> a populous country containing 10,000,000 of savages![15]

The Americans made contact with Korean officials, who refused to
discuss the *General Sherman*, probably from a reluctance to admit to
monetary liability for its destruction. Shortly after the flotilla's arrival,
three local officials – diplomats of the third and fifth ranks – visited
the *Colorado* to ascertain American intentions. Low deputised his
acting secretary Edward B. Drew to interview them. Drew informed the
Koreans that 'only officials of the first rank, who were empowered to
conduct negotiations, could be received and to such alone would a full
statement of the objects of the expedition be made'.[16] But he assured them
of the 'non-aggressive disposition' of the expedition and told them that
the squadron would take sounding of their waters and make surveys of
the shores, to which the Koreans made no apparent objection. However,
Rodgers' proxy message, couched in what the Americans regarded
as perfectly polite diplomatic language, was misinterpreted as a direct
challenge to Korean policy of prohibiting foreign ships from sailing on
the Han River as it led directly to the capital city of Hanyang, modern-
day Seoul. Given the expedition's aims of overturning the trade ban, the
Koreans' suspicions were understandable and perhaps well-founded.

The frostiness of the Koreans was evident, as Tilton wrote to his wife:

> The islands in our vicinity are inhabited by a few people only, living in
> thatched huts in the valleys, and all dress in white. They are seen every
> day clustering on the hill tops, where they squat and I suppose wonder
> what we are about to do. When our boats are sailing about & meet
> native boats, the latter always change their course, not appearing to
> desire any communication; and upon our boats landing on the beach,
> they get in theirs.[17]

Seemingly unaware of the danger, a survey party consisting of *Monocacy*,
Palos, steam launches from the whole fleet and a steam cutter from
Colorado was dispatched on 1 June. No indication of hostility was

evidenced until the party reached the lower end of Ganghwa Island, where a line of forts were connected by a wall and facing the river. A single shot initiated a heavy fire from masked batteries. The Americans, negotiating swift currents and jagged rocks, fired back. Damage to US vessels was light due to 'the bad gunnery of the Koreans, whose fire, although very hot for the 15 minutes in which they maintained it, was ill-directed, and consequently without effect'.[18] Tilton reported:

> The Koreans were not able to fire upon us on our returning, having been cleared out by our big shells. Their guns are very rude, seemed to be lashed to logs, and cannot be trained except on a point beforehand, which, when the vessel nears, they touch them off! The vessels were not struck at all, by large shot, and only by one or two rude balls from a small-arm called 'Jing-galls' which two men carry on their shoulders & touch off with a match! Only three of our men were touched, and only slightly wounded; you can judge then how unable they are to cope with us, armed as we are with the latest improvements. The slight damage to the *Monocacy* was repaired before midnight, by allowing her stern to rest on a soft mud bank, the tide receding lifting her out the water, and the little hole patched as good as new.[19]

But the initial Korean fusillade was considered an act of war. Immediately, on the expedition's return, Admiral Rodgers determined 'to equip the available landing force of all ships, and to return in the morning to attack and destroy the fortifications, but it was concluded to wait for the next neap tides',[20] when the currents would be less violent than the spring tides then running. While awaiting the fall of the tides, Admiral Rodgers and Low agreed it would be politic to set a reasonable time for the Korean government to apologise. It was decided that if an apology did not arrive within ten days an assault would be mounted against the forts.

Ashore, the local authorities dispatched a courier to the king with a report that:

> Two sailing vessels with two masts have suddenly forced their way into Sun-shih Passage. As this is a most important pass leading up into the river, ever since the (French) attack on our troops in 1866, we have increased the guard, and done everything to make it secure: even our own public and private vessels, if they gave no river pass, are not allowed to go through that way. How much less, then, can foreign armed men-of-war, which have not yet apprised us of their intentions, be allowed to go rushing about … The forces stationed in the Pass accordingly opened their guns to prevent them going by.

Ten days passed with no apology offered. On the eve of the expiry date, Commander H. C. Blake received orders from Admiral Rodgers 'to take and destroy the forts which have fired on our vessels, and to hold them long enough to demonstrate our ability to punish such offenses at pleasure'.[21]

The Korean forces on the island, known as 'Tiger Hunters', were led by General Eo Jae-yeon. Eric Niderost wrote:

> The Korean soldier of 1871 was an anachronism, a product of an inward-looking society that had been effectively isolated from the outside world for almost 300 years. The typical Choson soldier was of peasant stock, wearing traditional white garb as a uniform ... Weapons were virtually unchanged from the 15th or 16th centuries. The great Korean naval hero Yi Sun-Shin (1545–1598), who fought against the Japanese in the 1590s, would have been thoroughly familiar with the weapons employed in 1871. Soldiers were armed with spears (*ji chang*); a trident version called *sam-ji-chang* might also have been employed. Firearms were crude matchlocks, weapons that had been abandoned by the West some two centuries earlier. The *gingal* was also in use, a large and clumsy matchlock based on Chinese designs.

The Americans were not overly sure of their own military power. A 'penny-wise, pound-foolish' Congress had refused to sanction expensive upgrades within the Navy and Marine Corps and had come close to abolishing the latter in 1866. US Naval personnel were armed with the latest breech-loading Remington Rolling Block carbines, far more effective and reliable than the Civil War-era muzzle-loading Springfield rifle muskets. But the marines were still issued with the almost obsolete Springfields. Before the expedition left for Korea, Tilton, a firearms expert, had warned that 'one man with a breech loader is equal to twelve or fifteen armed as we are and in the event of any landing, or even chasing Coreans (*sic*) armed with an excellent repeater, what could Americans do with a blasted old muzzle fuzzel?'[22] As it turned out, he need not have worried so much. There were no 'Coreans with repeaters'.

On 10 June, the Americans landed. Admiral Rodgers recounted in his official report:

> The point chosen for the disembarkation, while seemingly as good as any in other respects, was, for military reasons, deemed the best, since it flanked the enemy's works, and left nothing to be feared in our rear. The character of the shore was unknown, and it proved to be most unfavourable for our purpose. Between the water and the firm land a broad belt of soft mud, traversed by deep gullies, had to be passed ... As soon as firm ground was attained, the infantry battalion was formed, and the marines deployed as skirmishers. The advance at once began...[23]

*Portrait of John Murray, 4th Earl of
Dunmore (1730–1809)*, by Sir Joshua
Reynolds; oil on canvas, 1765; Google Art
Project, courtesy of Wikimedia Commons.

LITTLE TURTLE.

Chief Little Turtle, date unknown,
author unknown. Source
http://www.army.mil/media/220061

Left: *Arthur St Clair* by Charles Willson Peale, watercolour on ivory. Courtesy of the Metropolitan Museum of Art.

Below: *St Clair's Defeat*, illustration of an article written by Theodore Roosevelt, for *Harper's New Monthly Magazine*, February 1896.

Shays' Rebels Repulsed from the Springfield Armory, by Edward Sylvester Ellis; illustration *c.* 1902.

Above: *Washington and his Troops*, painting attributed to Frederick Kemmelmeyer. It shows George Washington and his men near Fort Cumberland, Maryland, before their march on the whiskey rebels. Courtesy of Metropolitan Museum of Art.

Right: *Lieutenant William Bainbridge, US Navy (1774–1833)*. Photograph of a miniature portrait in the possession of Mrs Theodore Frothingham, Bainbridge's great-granddaughter, in 1936. It depicts Bainbridge in 1798, as a 24-year old Lieutenant. Courtesy Wiki Commons.

Left: *Commodore Stephen Decatur*, by John Wesley Jarvis. Courtesy of US Naval Academy Museum collection.

Below: *Stephen Decatur boarding a corsair gunboat during the bombardment of Tripoli*, painting by Dennis Malone Carter. (Naval Historical Center, Washington Navy Yard, NH 44647-KN)

USS Philadelphia *burning in Tripoli harbour*, by Edward Moran. Courtesy of US Naval Academy Museum collection (KN-10849)

Above: *Vincennes in Disappointment Bay,* engraving, 1844. Courtesy of Library of Congress.

Left: *Col John Salmon 'Rip' Ford,* Lorenzo de Zavala State Archives and Library Building, Austin, Texas. Courtesy of Wiki Commons.

Winema (Tobey) standing with her husband Frank Riddle and four Modoc women, photograph by Edward Muybridge, (US National Archives, no 533247), courtesy of Wiki Commons.

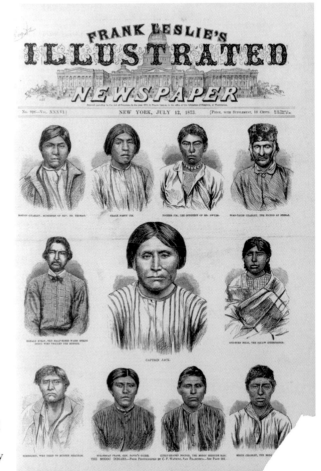

The Modoc Indians, wood engraving, from a photograph taken by Carleton. E. Watkins, San Francisco, published in 1873, on the front page of Frank Leslie's *Illustrated Newspaper* with portraits of eleven Modoc Indians, federal prisoners and alleged participants in a violent uprising. Courtesy of Library of Congress.

Left: *Portrait of Maj. Gen. Edward R. S. Canby, officer of the Federal Army*; negative: glass, wet collodion; photographed by Theo Lilienthal; published between 1860 and 1865. Courtesy of Library of Congress.

Below: *The Modoc war – Captain Jack's cave in the lava beds*, print from wood engraving. The illustration shows Modoc Indians in a cave; three Modoc men are carrying rifles while three Modoc women and a child sit near a fire. Courtesy of Library of Congress.

FRANK LESLIE'S
ILLUSTRATED
NEWSPAPER

No. 919—Vol. XXXVI.]   NEW YORK, MAY 10, 1873.   [Price, 10 Cents.

OREGON.—THE MODOC WAR—SCHONCHIN AND HIS ASSOCIATE "BUCKS" KILLED BY AN EXPLODING SHELL IN THE LAVA BEDS.—See Page 137.

Oregon. The Modoc war Schonchin and his associate 'Bucks' killed by an exploding shell in the lava beds, published in Frank Leslie's *Illustrated Newspaper*, 10 May 1873. Courtesy of Library of Congress.

Flag captured in attacks on the Salee rivers forts by Corporal Charles Brown and Private Hugh Purvis. This Korean flag was captured in the attack on the Salee River Forts, 10-11 June 1871. Pictured from left are Private Hugh Purvis of the USS *Alaska*, assisted by Corporal Charles Brown of the USS *Colorado*, and Captain McLane Tilton, Commanding Marines. Both Purvis and Brown were subsequently awarded Medals of Honor for this action. From the collection of Hugh Purvis, COLL/1171, United States Marine Corps Archives & Special Collections, courtesy of Wiki Commons.

Korean casualties after attack on Fort McKee, photograph by Felice Beato (NARA- 559259), courtesy of Wiki Commons.

The Hurricane at Somoa on the morning of March 16, wood engraving, 1889, after a sketch by Lt Monkton, of HMS *Calliope*, German barque, and wrecked schooner in heavy seas. Courtesy of Library of Congress.

After the Samoan Hurricane of 15/16 March 1889, wrecked ships are shown in Apia Harbour, Upolu, soon after the storm. The view looks north-westward, with the shattered bow of the German gunboat *Eber* on the beach in the foreground. The stern of USS *Trenton* is at right, with the sunken USS *Vandalia* alongside. The German gunboat *Adler* is on her side in the centre distance. *Trenton*'s starboard quarter gallery has been largely ripped away. Naval History and Heritage Command photograph, courtesy of Wiki Commons.

Left: *Wreck of the Maine, Havana, 1900*, photographic print on stereo card, which shows the badly damaged *Maine*, mostly underwater. Courtesy of Library of Congress.

Below: *Eighth US Infantry ready to embark for Cuba*, photographic print on stereo card, published New York, Underwood & Underwood c. 1898. Soldiers in formation are shown preparing to board ship. Courtesy of Library of Congress.

Charge of the Rough Riders at San Juan Hill, photographic print, reproduction of painting by Frederic Remington showing Theodore Roosevelt, on horseback, with his men running close behind him; some men are being shot while others lay dead in the grass. Courtesy of Library of Congress.

Colonel Roosevelt and his Rough Riders at the top of the hill they captured, Battle of San Juan Hill, photograph by William Dinwiddie, published 1898. Courtesy of Library of Congress.

Above: 'Till my regiment is mustered out,' Funston's reply when asked how long he could hold a captured trench, photographic print on stereo card, published in New York by Underwood & Underwood *c.* 1899. It shows US soldiers in a trench during the Philippine War. Courtesy of Library of Congress.

Below: Filipino prisoners of war, posed in a courtyard, 1899. Courtesy of Library of Congress.

Right: Hit him hard! President McKinley: 'Mosquitoes seem to be worse here in the Philippines than they were in Cuba'. A contemporary magazine cover illustrating the parallels drawn between the campaigns in Cuba and the Philippines. The mosquito McKinley is about to swat depicts revolutionary Emilio Aguinaldo. Courtesy of Library of Congress.

Below: Soldiers displaying skulls after a battle in the Philippines, photographic print, published between 1899 and 1901. Courtesy of Library of Congress.

The flag must 'stay put', print: chromolithograph, cartoon by John S. Pughe, published New York, J. Ottmann Lith. Co., Puck Bldg., 4 June 1902. It shows George F. Hoar, Carl Schurz, David B. Hill, and former Massachusetts Governor George S. Boutwell, anti-expansionists, placing their 'Anti-Expansion Speech' at the feet of a huge American soldier holding a rifle and the American flag, while opposite them Filipinos place guns and swords at the soldier's feet. Courtesy of Library of Congress.

They immediately attacked the lightly defended Choi Garrison along the Salée River and quickly overran it without serious resistance – in Rodgers' words, it was 'quietly occupied'. Tilton's report was less laconic:

All the boats cast off and pulled away for the shore, where we landed on a wide sloping beach, two hundred yards from high-water mark, with the mud over the knees of the tallest men, and crossed by deep sluices filled with softer and still deeper mud. After getting out of the boats a line of skirmishers was extended across the muddy beach, and parallel to a tongue of land jutting through it to the river, fortified on the point by a square redoubt in the right, and a crenulated wall extending a hundred yards to the left, along the river, with fields of grain and a small village immediately in its rear. The fortification had been silenced by the cannonade from the United States ship *Monocacy* and the steam launches, and the garrison fled though the brush and fields, firing a few shots as they retired at a distance. The marines, by order, then advanced on the place, sweeping through the grain fields and village, meeting no opposition, and remained in possession until the main body came up, when we were again ordered to push forward, which we did, scouring the fields as far as practicable from the left of the line of march, the river being on our right, and took commanding a fine view of the beautiful hills and inundated rice fields immediately around us, and distant about half a mile from the main body. A reconnaissance was then made toward the next fort – a square work of hewn granite foundation, with a split rock, mud, and mortar rampart, crenulated on each face, with a front of about 30 paces – and a messenger dispatched to headquarters with the information that the road was clear and passable for artillery. Pickets were posted on the flanks of our little position, five hundred yards to the right and left – a rice field inundated being in front – and a Dahlgren 12-pounder planted so as to command the junction of the only two approaches, which the commanding officer had ordered up to us as a support.[24]

The Americans waited before moving on to take their next objective, the Deokjin Garrison. The poorly armed Korean forces were kept from effective range by the 12-pounder. Tilton recorded:

An order having been sent to hold our position till morning, we bivouacked with our arms by our sides, dividing our force in three reliefs, one of which was continually on the alert. No incident occurred during the night except rapid firing of small-arms and howling from a hill inland from us, and about a third of a mile distant. Two or three shots from the artillery with the main body were fired across the left of our picket, in the direction of the noise, which presently ceased.

Sunday morning, the 11th of June, the main body came up, and we received orders to push forward, which we did, and after reaching the fields in the rear of the next line of fortifications, we threw a line of skirmishers across the peninsula of hills on which the fort stood, and after the main body came up we advanced toward the rear face, with two-thirds of our guards in reserve. We entered this second place, after reconnoitring it, without opposition, and dismantled the battlements by throwing over the fifty or sixty insignificant breech-loading brass cannon, all being loaded, and tore down the ramparts on the front and right face of the work to the level of the tread of the banquette.

The ramparts consisted of a pierced wall of chipped granite, with a filling of earth in the interstices and coated over with mortar, giving it the appearance of being more solid than it really was. The cannon were rolled over the cliff into the water by Bugler English, without much trouble, who climbed down for this purpose. I cannot give the weight, but the bore was not over two inches diameter. A photographer came on shore from the *Monocacy* and succeeded in taking a negative picture of the place. We were then ordered by the commanding officer to push forward and find the road leading to our objective point, and to cover the flanks of the main body, which we did with two-thirds of the marines deployed, the remainder in reserve.

We scoured the scrubby woods and fields of grain, stirring up two or three unarmed native refugees from the village we had just passed, who were not, however, molested; and, after progressing half a mile, down deep ravines and the steepest sort of hills, were fired upon from a high ridge a little to the left of us, up which our skirmish line cautiously wheeled, and upon reaching the summit saw the enemy on a parallel ridge opposite, who blazed away at us with their gingalls or matchlocks, their black heads popping up and down the while from the grass, but only one spent bullet struck us, without any injury. A piece of artillery was here brought up from the valley beneath us, by direction of Lieutenant Commander Cassel, by superhuman exertions on the part of his men, and several shells landed among the enemy grouped on a narrow range leading to the circular redoubt – our objective point, and known to us as the citadel, being the third work of the line of fortifications – the main body following in column of fours.[25]

The citadel housed the Gwangseong Garrison, where the badly shaken Korean forces, around 300 strong, had regrouped. Along the way, some Korean units tried to flank the US forces but were beaten off. The force moved on over a terrain of 'steep hills, with deep ravines between, with great fatigue', according to Rodgers.

Artillery fire from ground forces and *Monocacy* offshore pounded the citadel in preparation for an assault. A force of 546 sailors and soldiers, and 105 marines, grouped on the hills west of the fortress. Infantry troops were on one hill and artillery units on another, and both poured fire into the fortress while covering the Americans' flanks and rear.

Tilton wrote:

> Upon reaching a point a third of a mile from this work, a general halt was ordered to rest the men, who were greatly fatigued after their comparatively short, although extremely steep, march; the topography of the country being indescribable, resembling a sort of 'chopped sea,' of immense hills and deep ravines lying in every conceivable position. We then advanced cautiously, with our line of skirmishers parallel to the right face of the redoubt, which was our point of attack, concealed from view from the enemy, and took position along the crest of a hill one hundred and fifty yards from him, closing intervals to one pace on the right skirmisher; the line extending along the ridge, our right resting in a path leading to the redoubt, upon which planted about twenty-five banners in single file, a few feet apart, and at right angles to our line, the first banner being only four paces from our right skirmisher. Thirty paces in front of us was another ridge, parallel to the one we now occupy, but in order to reach it the whole line would be exposed to view. The main body came up and formed close behind us. The banners seemed to be a decoy, and several of us went from our right, took about fifteen of them, which drew a tremendous hail of bullets from the redoubt, which relaxed in half a minute, when away we pushed, availing ourselves of the opportunity to get to the next ridge, accomplishing the move with the loss of only one man, a marine from the United States ship *Alaska*, although for several seconds exposed to a galling fire, which recommenced immediately after the rush began.[26]

The vanguard of the charge on the citadel was led by twenty-seven-year-old Lieutenant Hugh McKee. Rodgers reported:

> Behind the crest of a hill which they occupied our men were formed for the assault upon the citadel, now distant about 150 yards ... When all was ready, the order to charge was given by Lieutenant Commander Casey, and our men rushed forward down the slope and up the opposite hill. The enemy maintained their fire with the utmost rapidity until our men got quite up the hill, then, having no time to load, they mounted the parapet and cast stones upon our men below, fighting with the greatest fury.

The slow reload time of the Korean matchlocks gave the Americans enough respite to clamber over the walls. McKee was the first to make it over the walls but was shot in the groin. He was replaced by Frederick Franklin, who shot the Korean soldier who had shot McKee.[27]

Tilton's account of the charge was:

Our lines were now only one hundred and twenty yards from the redoubt, but the abrupt slope of the hill and weeds covered us very well. The firing now commenced rapidly from both sides; ours increasing as the men got settled comfortably, and their fire was effective, as the forty or fifty killed and wounded inside the redoubts show. The firing continued for only a few minutes, say four, amidst the melancholy songs of the enemy, their bearing being courageous in the extreme, and they exposed themselves as far as the waist above the parapet fearlessly; and as little parties of our forces advanced closer and closed down the deep ravine between us, some of them mounted the parapet and threw stones, &c., at us, uttering the while exclamations seemingly of defiance.

Fifteen minutes of brutal hand-to-hand fighting showed the superiority of American weaponry. The Koreans, outnumbered two to one, fought back bravely with whatever they could grab – clubs, spears and rocks, as matchlocks were useless in close combat – but the outcome was certain from the moment the walls were scaled. It was a massacre. Private Hugh Purvis of the *Alaska* guard ran immediately to the flagstaff which bore the Korean colours and loosed the halyards. He was joined by Corporal Charles Brown and the pair tore down the 12-foot-square yellow cotton flag of the Korean commander, General Eo Jae-yŏn. General Eo himself was shot dead by Private James Dougherty of the *Benicia*.[28] *Colorado* carpenter Cyrus Hayden planted the US flag on the ramparts. Tilton reported: 'The Corean soldiers fought like tigers, having been told by the King if they lost the place the heads of everybody on Kang Hoa Island, on which the forts stood, should be cut off.'[29] Private Michael Owens, of the *Colorado*'s guard, was also shot through the groin as he was charging toward the redoubt, falling about forty paces from the parapet.

McKee died on board USS *Monocacy* later that afternoon and his body was sent to his ship *Colorado* the next day. His remains were later sent to Shanghai and from there to the US.[30] Two other Americans died in the battle – Seaman Seth Allen and Marine Corps Private Denis Hanrahan[31] – and ten were wounded. The Americans expended 1,600 cartridges in the action, around forty per man.

The Korean toll from the pounding of the forts by ships' cannon and the carnage inside the citadel was severe – 243 Koreans killed and most of the survivors wounded out of a force never put higher than around 300 men. Twenty Koreans were captured, several of them wounded, among them the Korean deputy commander.[32] In all, five Korean forts were taken, with forty artillery pieces and dozens of various small cannons.[33] But the carnage was sickening, as Tilton reported to his wife: 'The way the "gingal" or match-lock bullets whizzed was a caution to all those innocents engaged in war. My precious girl I am one of

those innocents, and I don't want to engage in any more sick business.'
He described some 'horrible' sights:

> Some of them were burnt coal black and dreadfully mangled by 9 inch
> shells bursting near them. There were forty heaped in a little place not
> bigger than our quarter deck, most all shot in the head as they looked
> over the parapet, and their clothes being white the blood was to be seen in
> more dreadful contrast than usual. They all bled like pigs & it is supposed
> in about one hour we killed 200 of them. I only saw about fifty killed but
> strange to say at the time it didn't affect me more than looking at so many
> dead hogs. One of our ship's Quarter-masters came to me with a pitiful
> expression and asked me if he should put some of the badly wounded
> out of their misery by shooting them in the head! I told him of course,
> such a thing would be murder, and he must let them remain as they were.
> This seemed to distress him as he thought it would be a kindness to put
> then out of their misery by shooting them in the head! I merely mention
> this little circumstance to show how different things seen from different
> standpoints. The Qr. Master's motive was kindness doubtless, but surely
> had he seen anyone injured in a peaceful way, it never would have seemed
> proper to him to put the sufferer out of his misery by shooting! I enclose
> a lock of the Corean hair, a large switch of which I got in a village all
> done up for wear, & perhaps it will be useful for ornamenting the pates
> of some of our black-haired girls at home. It is most too dark for you.[34]

Tilton added:

> The wounded were soon attended to by the surgeon's corps, who removed
> them to the *Monocacy*, lying in the stream. The place was occupied all
> Sunday night, the artillery being posted on the heights, and commanding
> the rear approaches, the men bivouacking with their companies on the
> hills. Early Monday morning the entire force re-embarked on board the
> *Monocacy*, the marines being the last to leave. The re-embarkation was
> accomplished in a masterly manner, in the space of an hour, no confusion
> whatever occurring, although the current was very strong, the rise of the
> tide being nearly 20 feet. The *Monocacy* then steamed to the fleet, some
> ten miles below, where we all rejoined our respective ships.[35]

The military operations of 10–12 June were a short-term victory, but
the overall expedition proved a dismal failure. The Americans hoped to
use their prisoners as a bargaining chip to meet with local officials, but
the Koreans refused, calling the captives cowards and saying that the
Americans were welcome to keep them. They said that they had been
around for 4,000 years without outside interference and saw no reason
for that to change. There would be no negotiations. The squadron stayed
at anchorage off Jakyak Island until 3 July, when they left for China.[36] The

regent, Daewongun, used the American incursion as a further reason to strengthen his policy of isolation. He issued a national proclamation against appeasing foreigners.[37]

Tilton wrote home:

> I am glad to say I am alive still and kicking, although at one time I never expected to see my Wife and baby any more, and if it hadn't been that the Coreans can't shoot true, I never should. It is all over now, and as I expected, we have failed to make any treaty with the Coreans. The local authorities near us return all our communications sent on shore to be forwarded to their King, and our Expedition so far as a treaty goes has turned out to be fruitless. We have not force enough to go to their Capital in the interior even if our government directed us to do so. The Country is beautiful; filled with lovely hills & valleys running in every direction and cultivated with grain of all kinds which even now is turning to the colors indicating ripening. Everything is pretty and green, and the little thatched villages are snugly built in little nooks, surrounded by pines & other evergreens.[38]

There were no further attacks on foreign ships. In 1876, Korea established a trade treaty with Japan after Japanese ships approached Ganghwa Island and threatened to fire on Seoul. Treaties with European countries and the US soon followed. From April to May 1882, Commodore Robert W. Schfeldt of the US Navy and Korea negotiated and approved a fourteen-article treaty which established mutual friendship and mutual assistance in case of attack and granted America 'most favoured nation' trading status. The treaty remained in effect until the annexation of Korea in 1910.

McLane Tilton stayed in the marines but his wish to never again see carnage like he witnessed in the Korean forts was largely granted – he commanded the marines stationed at the Navy Yard in Washington, DC, served as Fleet Marine Officer, European Station, from 1877 until 1880, saw duty at the Marine Barracks, Norfolk, Virginia, and retired a lieutenant colonel in February 1897.[39] This author could find no record of his retirement and death.

Corporal Brown, Privates Dougherty, Purvis, Coleman, McNamara and Owens of the marines, Carpenter Hayden, Quartermasters Grace, Troy, Franklin and Rogers, Ordinary Seaman Andrews and Landsmen Lukes and Merton were awarded the Medal of Honor, the first for actions in a foreign conflict.

Tilton recommended Brown for his 'coolness and courage' in jointly capturing the enemy standard and added: 'The command, to a man, acted in a very creditable manner, and all deserve equal mention. The officers of the marines were always to found in the front.' There is no record of Brown having received his medal for his 'inspiring and heroic' act as he deserted from the Marine Corps in October 1871.[40]

13

The Modoc War (1872–1873)

We mean peace but we are ready for war.

The Modoc War was a bloody shambles that has some claim as America's most inglorious conflict. The US government engaged more than 1,000 regular soldiers, 100 California and Oregon militiamen and about eighty Indian scouts yet still failed to humble a band of 'degenerate' Modoc tribesmen never numbering more than seventy-five warriors and their families. In skirmishes, raids and open battle, numerically inferior natives repeatedly thrashed well-trained soldiers, veterans of the Civil War, and enthusiastic volunteers. The casualties included the only full-blown Regular Army general to be killed in the Indian Wars (George Armstrong Custer held brevet rank only). Given the numbers involved, it was proportionately America's costliest war in terms of both blood and cash. In the end it was internal dissent and betrayal which beat the Modocs, not force of arms.

It is hardly the stuff of regimental honour to be toasted at military academies. But the ironies and the individual tragedies involved make this war rather more than a ferocious footnote in the development of the American West. It echoes the wider brutalities, misunderstandings and mutual suspicion which soured every stage of the settlers' dealings with the native population.

* * *

The Indian wars of the Pacific North West have never received the attention given to the more glamorous sweep of the Plains or the dust-dry ferocity of the Apache country, but they were every bit as savage. The native inhabitants of this, the last frontier, did not become aware of the white man's encroachments until relatively late. They enjoyed a bountiful land teeming with game. When the first settlers arrived, they were welcomed as there was more than enough for all. Then the miners came from California, bringing with them the soldiers. The newcomers were in no mood for compromise or accommodation. Their demands for land and access turned Northern California and Oregon into a place of bitter grudges, prejudice and violence, likened to a kettle constantly coming to the boil.[1] There was the 1848 Cayuse War, the Rogue River Wars of the 1850s, the Yakima War (1853–56) and the 1857 Coeur d'Alene War. Victory over the Paiutes in 1868 ended war in the rough lake lands until settlers began to complain about the 'apparently hostile dispositions' of a sizeable splinter of the Modoc tribe led by Kintpaush, known by the whites as Captain Jack.

The Modocs were a division of the once-powerful Lalacas who split from their brothers the Klamaths after a row over river fishing rights; the two remained bitter enemies. The Modoc lands straddled the present California–Oregon border around Tule Lake and the Lost River basin. When white settlers began to squeeze into their territory, the Modocs numbered approximately 600 under the head chief Old Schonchin. In March 1851 a mule train packer discovered gold near Yreka, extending the Gold Rush area into the border region, and by the following month some 2,000 miners had travelled along the old Emigrant Trail through Modoc territory.[2]

During the 1850s the Modocs regained the warlike reputation of their forefathers with a series of attacks on white and Indian interlopers but remained on good terms with some of the miners at Yreka, 50 miles to the west, with whom they traded. Old Schonchin had displayed great courage in early skirmishes with the whites but grew tired of conflict and remained neutral in the final war. A series of murders and small-scale massacres near the shore of Tule Lake, at a place thereafter called Bloody Point, did occur but a local tradition that sixty settlers died in a single attack was a myth.[3] After one raid, two white girls were taken captive and adopted the dress and traditions of the tribe until they were murdered by jealous Modoc women. The citizens of Yreka decided to launch a punitive expedition and Ben Wright was put in charge of a volunteer company. On reaching Modoc land, Wright claimed to have found the bodies of twenty-two whites. Wrongly assuming that the Modocs were responsible – in fact the attack was the work of the Pit River tribe – he invited the Indians to parley under a flag of truce and a feast was prepared. Wright had brought with him a stock of strychnine with which to poison his guests. Fearing treachery, the Modocs refused to eat until the whites had tucked in. Wright and his men then opened fire, killing around forty unarmed tribesmen. Only a handful escaped, among them the young Kintpaush. The treacherous act was not forgotten by the Modocs, and greatly influenced their behaviour twenty years later. Their own subsequent acts of treachery must be weighed against the white precedent.[4]

Kintpaush was the son of a Lost River chief who died in battle with Warm Springs Indians when Kintpaush was an infant, so he had royal blood. He was born on Lower Lost River around 1837. His Modoc name means 'He has water brash (pyrosis)'. Little is known of him until he was twenty-five, when he appeared as an advocate of peace, a cool-headed realist who believed that further warfare would destroy his people. He befriended some prominent citizens at Yreka and carried documents from them attesting to his good character. He became known as Captain Jack because of the brass-buttoned coat he wore, a gift from an army officer.

In 1864, North California's Acting Superintendent of Indian Affairs, Elisha Steele, concluded an informal treaty with the Modocs in which the tribe agreed to settle on an ill-defined reservation in Klamath territory within the boundaries of present-day Oregon. The two tribes agreed to keep the peace with each other, as well as with the whites.[5] Looking around for something to give emphasis to his pledge, Old Schonchin pointed to the distant butte and declared: 'That mountain shall fall, before Schonchin will again raise his hand against his white brother.'[6] Almost immediately Jack regretted the treaty. For a while he and his followers remained on the reservation, but their old enemies the Klamaths soon began demanding tribute and stealing lumber, and the promised supplies of food failed to materialise. Jack and his band of around forty warriors returned to their old home on Lost River, hemmed in on all sides. There they stayed for four years as pressure for their removal was put on the military and the Indian Bureau.

Contemporary reports differ greatly as to the band's behaviour. Considerable commerce was done with respectable white citizens, and a farmer called Miller voluntarily paid the Modocs grazing rent for his livestock. Jack's friendship with Yreka businessmen continued. But inevitably on both sides there was deep-seated suspicion and prejudice. One commentator wrote of Jack's encampment: 'They were a degenerate tribe, by common standards, whose men forfeited all claim to local esteem by profiting in the immoralities of their women, while affecting to be affronted by the proposal that they themselves be put to work.' Such is the language of bigotry, although doubtless there was a minority of dissolute and unruly Modocs. Among the whites, old fears and the memory of Bloody Point and other raids was vivid, while they were also determined to hold on to the Modoc land ceded to them by the US government.

In December 1869, Superintendent Alfred Meacham, who came from Oregon and knew the Modoc leaders, urged Jack to return to the Fort Klamath reservation. During the negotiations Jack dubbed all white men 'liars and swindlers' and refused to touch Meacham's proffered food for fear of poison. Nevertheless, the parley continued, aided by the white trapper Frank Riddle and his Modoc wife Winemah, who was Jack's cousin. At one point in the delicate negotiations Meacham feared that Jack was planning murder. He said: 'I am your friend but I am not afraid of you. Be careful what you do. We mean peace but we are ready for war. We will not begin, but if you do it will be the end of your people.' Among the Modocs, Schonchin John, the old chief's brother, urged the death of Meacham and his party. Jack insisted on peace with honour. Their wrangling was ended by the arrival of 200 soldiers, summoned by Meacham, who surrounded the camp. The Modocs, disarmed but granted face-saving gestures by Meacham, agreed to return to the despised reservation.

It was a short-lived solution. The Modocs met the Klamaths for another peace ceremony. Meacham told them: 'This country belongs to you all alike. Your interests are one. You can shake hands and be friends.' Within three months such hopes had been shattered. The Klamaths, by far the bigger band, taunted, insulted and exploited the outnumbered and dispirited Modocs. Jack called a council and led the majority of his followers, around seventy families, back to Lost River. He was convinced of the justice and common sense of his decision and won verbal support from some of his white friends.[7]

Meacham, by most accounts – particularly his own – a reasonable man, now believed that Jack's band should be forcibly returned to the reservation. The new Commander of the Department of the Columbia, General Edward Canby, disagreed. Canby would not commit his troops to such a dangerous and disruptive course of action while the government dithered over the site of a permanent home for the Modocs. Even the informal 1864 treaty remained unratified for two years and had to wait another six before it was formally proclaimed. Canby believed it would be 'impolitic if not cruel' to force the Modocs back. Canby, a humane man, authorised a limited issue of food to Jack's band.

Such an uneasy peace could not endure. Unusually, the flashpoint did not involve a clash with the white settlers. In June 1871 Jack was the arbiter in a matter of tribal justice. A shaman, paid in advance, failed to save the life of a sick child and thus forfeited his own. Jack authorised his execution. Friends of the dead shaman invoked the white man's law. An attempt to arrest Jack for murder failed, and Meacham knew that the territory was close to war. In a last bid to prevent the kettle exploding, Meacham suggested the creation of a small new reservation on Lost River for Jack's band. Canby agreed, and revoked the warrant for Jack's arrest. Two commissioners and two bodyguards met Jack on his home ground. Again, the militant faction within the band – led by Schonchin John, Hooker Jim and another shaman, Curly-Haired Doctor – urged assassination. They were overruled by Jack and his lieutenant Scarface Charley.

Tragically the plan came to nothing. Jack agreed to the proposed new reservation, as did the commissioners and Canby himself, and the proposal was sent to Washington where it was filed away in some dusty cubbyhole of the Department of Indian Affairs. The failure of faceless bureaucrats to grasp this sensible opportunity proved a major cause of the now inevitable war.

Jack authorised a raid on a cattle train under his half-brother Black Jack to underline the urgency of the situation. That raid apart, the Modocs held back, but every theft in the neighbourhood was blamed on them. Antagonistic whites agitated harder for the removal of the Modoc band. One petition from Jackson County, Oregon, called for the government's 'strong arm' to be used against this 'petty Indian chief with 20 desperadoes and a squallid [*sic*] band of miserable savages'.

In spring 1872 the sympathetic, if cynical, Meacham was replaced as Superintendent of Indian Affairs by Thomas Odenal, a stubborn and self-satisfied official who understood little of Modoc grievances and apparently could not care less.[8] He 'knew almost nothing of the background of the situation and had never met Jack or the Modocs' but was charged with 'getting the Modocs to leave Lost River'.[9] In turn, Odenal appointed a new US Indian agent, who was also unfamiliar with the parties and conditions. Odenal saw himself as a new broom, determined to sweep away such Modoc nonsense, and strongly recommended an enforced return to the Klamath reservation without further delay. In July the Indian Bureau agreed with him. Canby had his orders and forwarded them to Fort Klamath and the army at Camp Warner. The stage was set for conflict.

Canby, always a stickler for obeying both the spirit and the letter of his orders, told Lieutenant Colonel Frank Wheaton of the 21st Infantry and Major 'Uncle Johnny' Green of the 1st Cavalry that if troops had to be used 'the force employed should be so large as to secure the result at once and beyond peradventure'. Odenal waited until November before moving. Jack refused to talk to him, claiming the protection of natural justice and expecting the support of his influential white friends.[10] On 27 November, Odenal asked the army to carry out the July order 'at once'. Both Canby and Major Green, the officer closest to the scene, accepted Odenal's judgement uncritically. Green ordered Captain James Jackson and forty-three officers and men of B Troop, 1st Cavalry, to take charge of Jack's band. The detachment approached the west bank of Lost River, where Jack and fourteen Modoc families were camped, while a force of around twenty-five Linkville volunteers aimed for the east bank of the river where sub-chief Hooker Jim and Curly-Haired Doctor were camped. At dawn on 29 November the whites approached but surprise was lost by the shot of an early morning hunter. The two sides agreed to parley, the Modocs wiping the sleep from their eyes under the barrels of army guns. Jackson's demand for the surrender of weapons began to be obeyed and a messenger was sent to Linkville to report the success of the mission. On the far shore the militia had met with similar success, their charges sheepishly acquiescent.

All that changed when Scarface Charley, on Jack's side of the river, refused to give up his rifle, swearing and waving his weapon in Jack's face. Scarface Charley, who spoke good English, was foul tempered from

171

lack of sleep and because he'd been gambling all night and was possibly drunk – but since there was a warrant out for his arrest on a false murder charge, he wasn't going to go quietly. Lieutenant Frazier A. Boutelle of Company B went to arrest him while spewing profanities. They drew their revolvers and shot at each other, both missing. The rest of the Modocs scrambled for their weapons and set off a mutual fusillade. The ensuing sagebrush battle lasted three hours. Jackson claimed sixteen Indians slain but in fact only one, Watchman, died. The army lost two dead and six wounded. Jack directed his force, firing for the first time at an army messenger without effect. Jackson, who later admitted he had mishandled the affair, withdrew and burned the Indian camp as he went. On the far river bank the militiamen tried to stop the Modocs running to their canoes to go to the aid of their brothers. Several whites died in the following exchanges, and the Modocs lost a woman, her buckshot-riddled dead infant cradled in her arms.[11] The volunteers broke and ran.

The Modocs surveyed their short-term victory and hopeless prospects. Jack took the majority of the band direct to the natural fortress of the lava beds to the south of Tule Lake. Scarface Charley, whose shot had sparked the battle, insisted on staying behind to warn friendly white farmers, including the noted rancher John Fairchild, of the danger. But the Modoc militants, once again led by Hooker Jim and including Curly-Haired Doctor and Steamboat Frank, wanted a vengeance raid. Their war party took a longer route to the lava beds, around the east side of the lake, attacking every homestead along the way. They did not touch the women and children but dragged out the men, most of whom Odenal had neglected to warn of the impending action, and butchered them. Hooker Jim told a newly made widow: 'We are Modocs. We do not kill women and children.'[12] At least fourteen men died, including the farmer Miller who had been on such friendly terms with the band. His supposed friend Hooker Jim shot him dead, later claiming that he had not recognised him. The killers, laden with plunder, scalps and stolen ponies, reached Jack's lava bed stronghold with blood on their hands and a taint of dishonour that would remain a blemish on the tribe's reputation thereafter.

Jack bitterly denounced the murderers, perhaps sensing the scale of white vengeance about to be unleashed. Jack wanted to hand over Hooker Jim and the other culprits to the white authorities, but was overruled by a large majority vote after Curly-Haired Doctor vowed to 'take medicine' to protect them. Jack settled back to await the onslaught.[13] His band were joined by fourteen more families from Hot Creek, led by Shacknasty Jim, who had fled from the violence of outraged Linkville citizens. They had been warned by John Fairchild, the same rancher who had previously been warned by Scarface Charley.

Jack's refuge was a superb natural stronghold, a portion of the lava beds rippling from Tule Lake's southern shore, likened by army officers to 'an ocean surf frozen into black rock'. The Modocs called it their 'stone house', a place of refuge in times of trouble.[14] Formed of the roughest kind of lava, its ridges and escarpments, up to 50 feet high, were akin to battlements, while its pitted surfaces provided natural rifle pits and trenches. Countless caves and tunnels provided shelter and lines of escape. Crevices, gorges and sinuous canyons made it impossible to traverse in good military formation, the broken landscape perfectly designed for absorbing cannon blast. Circular soil mounds and grass patches provided pasture for the Modoc cattle. Sagebrush gave them fuel. Water could be obtained from winter ice in the darkest caverns, and more could be sneaked from the lake shallows. The rough terrain was ideal for the sort of hit-and-run fighting that the Modocs excelled at. They also knew every square yard of its 46,000 acres.

Major Green tracked the band to what became knowns as Jack's Stronghold. He was joined on 21 December by Colonel Wheaton from Camp Warner, who assumed overall command. They waited for more reinforcements, including troops and mountain howitzers from as far away as Fort Vancouver, and three companies of volunteers from both sides of the California–Oregon line. By mid-January 1873 Wheaton's force had grown to almost 400, with greatest concentration of troops at Van Brimmer's ranch, 12 miles west of the Stronghold.[15] Wheaton had seriously overestimated the number of warriors facing him, putting it at 150, more than double the actual number.

On the night of 16 January, the US force split into two, commanded respectively by Green and Captain Reuben Bernard, and approached the Stronghold from north and south. These officers and other seasoned regulars knew what to expect; the callow recruits and enthusiastic volunteers did not. Confident of an easy, exhilarating victory, most did not even bother to take blankets and bedrolls, expecting to be tucked up safely in camp the following night. One soldier said he planned to 'eat Modoc steak' while another said he intended to grab a Modoc woman to 'wash his dishes'.[16]

A dense fog fell around them, and at 4 p.m. on the 17th the bugler sounded the attack. Two 12-pound mountain howitzers dropped shells ahead of the skirmish lines. Cavalry dismounted and joined the infantry and volunteers, tramping over ground that grew increasingly hard and treacherous to the foot. Men crashed into each other in the murkiness, their positions pinpointed by their yells and clatter. From the fog ahead there was only silence; there was no sign of the Modocs, and it was assumed that they had fled. Then, without warning, the fog was sliced by yellow streaks of rifle fire. The first soldier to fall was hit in the neck. A second dropped and the soldiers responded with indiscriminate firing, fog and rocks their only targets. The army howitzer shells began to fall too close for comfort to the advancing bluecoats and the cannon were silenced. Major Green ordered a charge, but after several hundred yards, in which more men fell, the Modocs remained invisible. The accuracy and intensity of their sniping continued throughout the day as the two US columns ineffectually floundered about under fire from phantoms. When one officer was hit in the elbow his cries of pain were derided; a woman's voice came out of the fog: 'You come here to fight Indians and you make noise like that; you no man, you squaw.'[17]

Both columns came across chasms wide open to Indian fire which the officers thought suicidal to cross. An attempt to unite the two army groups almost succeeded but the fog lifted and the sunshine further exposed the vulnerable troops to enemy fire. Colonel Wheaton called a council of his senior officers as bullets whined overhead. Everywhere soldiers were in retreat or pinned down by murderous fire. The dead and wounded lay scattered among the rocks, lost to their comrades. Two troopers turned back for a wounded friend, but one was shot as they reached him. After further attempts to rescue them, both wounded men were left for the scalping knives. Trapped pockets of frightened men waited until nightfall before slipping away in the dark. Some of them did not stop running.

It was a humiliating rout. Many of the volunteers drifted home shamefaced. The men they left in the army camps were disheartened. They faced the prospect of cold, miserable winter billets and a long campaign with little glory. The confusion in the camp makes a true assessment of the US casualties difficult. Some reports put it at up to forty dead, but that figure includes some missing men who may have deserted. More reliable reports put it at between eleven and eighteen dead and twenty-six wounded. Not one Modoc was even hurt in the battle. Few troopers claimed to have even seen a single warrior.

That night the soldiers' bodies were stripped and scalped. The sound of the Modoc victory dances was carried on the night breezes to the ears of the chastened US forces. Jack did not dance. Curly-Haired Doctor, supported by Schonchin John, boasted of the protection of his medicine had given the tribe and Jack knew he would soon face a challenge to his authority.[18] Jack reminded his men that only the first battle was won and that the white man would come again in greater numbers. But he pledged he would fight on and would not make peace himself until 'the Modoc heart says peace'.

* * *

General Canby was neither an Indian-hating martinet nor a self-seeking careerist thirsty for personal glory, unlike so many of his officer-class contemporaries. The testaments of fellow officers and men who served with him throughout his career describe a compassionate, devout man, zealous in his sense of duty, brave but not foolhardy – unlike, for example, Custer. He was a born administrator although lacking in imagination and handicapped by an awe of greater authority.

The son of anti-slavery activists, Canby was born in 1817 and graduated from West Point in 1839. His promotion, though steady, was not meteoric. He did not enjoy the privilege of a wealthy or influential family but relied instead on a gruelling series of tough campaigns and thankless tasks in some of America's most inhospitable corners. As a lieutenant he waded through Florida's fever-ridden and deadly swamp to the Battle of Palaklakaha Hammock. As a captain in the Mexican War he was pinned down in the sand hills around Vera Cruz, witnessed the taking of Mexico City and fought in three major battles, being twice breveted for gallantry. In various frontier postings he hunted deserters heading for the California goldfields, and took part in the expedition sent to subdue rebellious Mormons. He advocated that troublesome Shawnee and Kickapoos should be treated 'with kindness and compassion'. During the Civil War, as colonel of the 19th Infantry in 1861, he opposed General Sibley's Confederate invasion of New Mexico. He fought and lost the Battle of Valverde and from then on avoided combat, drawing the rebel invaders deeper into the desert and letting heat, hunger and thirst whittle down the enemy. His tactics proved wholly successful: Sibley lost half his force and the survivors staggered back to Texas. In 1864, as major general commanding the Division of the Mississippi, he was shot by a Confederate sniper while sailing the White River on a gunboat. In Washington he was reported killed and his obituary was widely printed, but he recovered quickly enough to assemble his forces to attack Mobile. The city fell in April 1865, and the finest moment of his army career came when he took the surrender of the last Confederate armies in the field.

For five years Canby was shifted around the South, smoothing the path of Reconstruction, unblocking administrative bottlenecks. He fed freed slaves and protected them from assault while trying to stop unscrupulous Northern interests stealing Southern cattle markets. 'Wherever he went order, good feeling and tranquillity followed his footsteps,' enthused soldier-author General George Washington Callum. General Ulysses S. Grant believed that he lacked aggression but declared him irreplaceable for his knowledge of army regulations and constitutional law.[19] At fifty-two, Canby asked for and got command of the Department of the Columbia because he was tired and was looking for a 'quieter life'. General Sherman telegrammed his 'best wishes for a pleasant trip'.[20]

Nonetheless, Canby a 'soldier's soldier'. A Colorado volunteer in an earlier campaign described him:

Canby is usually seen near the head of the column, attended by his staff and a few mounted troopers as an escort. Tall and straight, coarsely dressed in citizen's clothes, his countenance hard and weather-beaten, his chin covered by a heavy grizzly beard of two week's growth, a cigar in his mouth which he never lights – using a pipe when he wishes to smoke – he certainly has an air of superiority, largely the gift of nature, though undoubtedly strengthened by long habits of command. His person is portly and commanding, his manner dignified and self-possessed, his whole appearance such as to inspire confidence and respect ... I think of him as a man of foresight and judgement – patient, prudent and cautious – of great courage, both moral and physical, and as true to the Government as any man in existence.

Some may well have viewed him as a prig and a cold fish, yet the variety and diligence of his career, which took him to the desolate lava beds of Modoc County, tends to belie such views and only highlights the tragedy that was to end it.

Captain Jack told the rancher John Fairchild, one of the few men trusted by both sides, that despite the words uttered at the post-battle scalp dance he wanted no more war. Former Superintendent Meacham agreed and told Washington that a peace commission had a better chance of bringing the Modocs to heel than further force. The Secretary of the Interior, Columbus Delano, concurred and also persuaded President Grant, whose own wider-ranging Indian peacekeeping policy was now largely discredited. Canby was told that the president 'seems disposed to let the peace men try their hands on Captain Jack'.[21] Meacham was appointed head of the peace commission, and in late March Canby was put in overall charge. The other commission members were Methodist minister Revd Ezekiel Thomas and the Indian agent of the Klamath Falls Agency, LeRoy Dyer. The interpreters were Frank and Winemah Riddle, the latter called 'Tobey' by the whites.

Canby set up his field headquarters at the Fairchild ranch and the commissioners negotiated with the Modocs through Fairchild and other go-betweens. As the weeks passed, such second-hand negotiations proved frustrating and inconclusive. An apparent willingness among Modocs to compromise would be offered and withdrawn within a day. The cause was not any deceit by Jack, as was then supposed, but increasingly damaging dissent within the tribe's ranks. Jack's leadership was under constant challenge from Curly-Haired Doctor and Hooker Jim, and he could not afford to bend too far towards peace and an honourable surrender. He demanded an amnesty for all his people and a reservation on Lost River. Canby and his civilian colleagues on the commission demanded that Jack hand over those responsible for the ranch massacres. In a bit of freelance negotiations, the sympathetic Judge Steele mistakenly believed that those terms had been agreed. He was lucky to escape with his life when he returned to the lava beds the next day and Hooker Jim and his cronies discovered that under his deal they would face the white man's justice. They need not have worried, as Jack had no intention of handing them in.[22]

Fairchild, one of the few men to emerge with any credit from the next sad chapter, explained to Jack the terms of an armistice while negotiations continued. Jack agreed, pledging that the commission members would be safe if they met him on neutral ground – scrubland at the foot of a bluff just outside the lava beds. He insisted that there should be no soldiers guarding the commission and promised that his warriors would keep their distance and 'we will not fire the first shot'.

Two Modocs, Boston Charley and Bogus Charley, returned with Fairchild to Canby's headquarters. The commissioners agreed to Jack's proposals for talks but sent the two Charleys back to Jack with the proviso that the delegations must be either both armed or both unarmed. The Charleys added their own first-hand observations: gossip in the army camp about a Grand Jury indictment against Hooker Jim and the others involved in the ranch massacres, about the lynch-mob mentality of Linkville citizens, about the white man's desire for revenge. Such talk fostered among the Modocs the belief that the commissioners were plotting treachery. That belief was strengthened by the very visible build-up of Canby's army, as reinforcements arrived almost daily. His troops at Jack's Stronghold moved to bivouacs ever closer to the lava beds and were now under the command of Major Alvin Gillem of the 1st Cavalry. The Modoc militants advocated the assassination of the commission, including Canby both as a pre-emptive strike and under the mistaken belief, common in the tribe, that killing a military leader would make the army go away.[23] Canby for his part wrote to his wife that the only possibility of permanent peace was to remove the tribe as far as possible away so they could never again come home to their Lost River lands.

Frank and Tobey Riddle, in constant touch with their Modoc friends and relatives, were keenly aware of the intentions of Hooker Jim and the warmongers. They repeatedly warned the commissioners to be on their guard. On 4 March the Modocs invited Meacham and several unarmed companions to a meeting inside the lava beds. Meacham believed the proposal 'undoubtedly means treachery' and refused. By April, however, hopes of a settlement had blossomed again. Modocs wandered freely about the army encampments. The commissioners' tent was erected on the spot Jack had suggested below the bluff, a mile from the Stronghold and roughly the same distance from the army lines. On 4 April it was used for the first time, in the middle of a fierce snowstorm. Jack talked for seven hours with Canby, Meacham, Fairchild and Judge Roseborough, who had been added to the commission. A further week of talking left all pretty much exhausted. Canby refused a new Modoc request that they should be allowed to set up a new reservation in the lava beds but expressed his desire that any new treaty should represent 'liberal and just treatment of the Indians'. Writing again to his wife, Canby described his adversaries: 'They are the strangest mixture of insolence and arrogance, ignorance and superstition ... They have no faith in themselves and have no confidence in anyone else. Treacherous themselves, they suspect treachery in everything.' He had clearly run out of patience, and much sympathy, after such a gruelling bout of talks.

At a tribal council on 10 April, the Riddles' worst fears were realised when the bloodlust of the militants overruled Jack's restraining authority. Despite their own misgivings about Canby's intentions, Jack and Scarface Charley bitterly opposed a scheme to murder the commissioners. Hooker Jim and others placed a bonnet on Jack's head, a shawl around his shoulders and called him a woman. They told him: 'The white man has stolen your soul. Your heart is no longer Modoc.' Shamed by the taunts, Jack threw the garments to the ground and declared: 'I am a Modoc. I am a chief. It shall be done if it costs every drop of blood in my heart. But hear me all my people – this day's work will cost the life of every Modoc brave. We will not live to see it ended.'[24]

Despite his own reluctance, the decision had been made and Jack began planning the crime with ruthless determination, as if to show his people he was worthy to lead them to destruction. As chief, he claimed the right to kill Canby himself. Schonchin John and Hooker Jim were to kill Meacham. Boston Charley and Bogus Charley were to kill Revd Thomas. Shacknasty Jim and a youth called Barncho were to kill Dyer. But Scarface Charley vowed that he would kill any Modoc who touched his friends Frank and Tobey Riddle. He warned Tobey of a plot during one of her many trips to the Modoc camp.[25]

The following morning, 11 April (Good Friday), Jack and his co-conspirators waited at the tent, guns hidden inside their clothing. More warriors with rifles were hidden among rocks a short distance away. Canby emerged from his tent in the army camp wearing full uniform but without his customary sidearms. Frank Riddle urged him and the other commissioners not to go. Most people seemed to share his suspicions. The scent of treachery was almost tangible, but Canby seemed impervious to it. Revd Thomas insisted that they should honour the terms of the peace conference and go unarmed. A weeping Tobey said: 'You no go, you no go, you get kill.' A small derringer was dropped in Meacham's pocket and he allowed it to remain there. Dyer permitted himself the same precaution. Canby meantime had ridden on ahead, unarmed, alongside Bogus Charley who carried his rifle in plain sight.

Shortly after 11 a.m. the commissioners, with the Riddles, who went along to interpret despite their strong fears, reached the council tent. Here the smell of treachery was even stronger. The council fire around which peace terms were to be discussed had been set out of sight of the troops, there were eight Modocs instead of the agreed six, and Jack himself was clearly troubled. Jack demanded the withdrawal of all US troops and again asked Canby to 'give us a home in our country'.[26] When this was refused, he fell into a moody silence. Schonchin John closed his speech with the words: 'I talk no more.'

There was a pause, then a war whoop which brought every man to his feet. Two youths, Barncho and Slolux, emerged from the rocks with rifles held ready. Jack took a revolver from the folds of his coat and shouted 'Ot we kau tux', the Modoc for 'All ready'. He pointed his gun at Canby's head but the first shot misfired. He turned the cylinder and fired again as the other Modocs opened up on their own targets. Jack's bullet entered Canby's head below the left eye, slicing downwards and breaking his jaw. He tried to stumble away but Jack held him down while the Modoc brave Ellen's Man cut his throat and shot him again in the head. They both stripped the body.[27]

Boston Charley shot Revd Thomas above the heart and Bogus Charley shot him in the head as he lay on the ground. The reverend's corpse was also stripped. Commissioner Dyer and Frank Riddle turned and ran. Hooker Jim fired repeatedly at Dyer, missing him every time. Dyer turned and faced him, drawing his own derringer. Hooker Jim dropped to the ground to avoid the shot, giving Dyer extra time to escape. Jack's half-brother Black Jim, who had been prominent at the peace talks, pursued Dyer further but turned back to help strip the bodies. Mindful of Scarface Charley's warning, no attempt was made to harm the Riddles.[28]

Meacham, who had known these Modocs personally for several years and who had done his utmost to both aid and curb them, refused to play the easy victim. At Jack's first signal he outdrew Schonchin John and pressed his derringer against the Indian's chest. Twice it misfired. Schonchin John fired point-blank at Meacham's face but missed. Meacham retreated backwards uncertainly. Schonchin John emptied his revolver, missing every time.[29] He took out another gun but twice his aim was spoiled by Tobey Riddle, who grappled with his arm despite suffering several blows to her head. Shacknasty Jim took aim but Tobey turned on him and knocked the gun from his hand. Schonchin John sat on a rock and took more careful aim. He scored a direct hit in Meacham's face but by some freak combination of ballistics and bone it merely gouged out a slice of eyebrow. Meacham fired back and struck Schonchin John, who fell off his rock, wounded. Other Modocs fired, hitting Meacham twice more and bringing him down. He lay twitching as Shacknasty Jim began to strip him, turning away a brave named Slolux who was about to shoot him in the head, saying: 'He is dead.' Tobey was left wailing beside the body, but Boston Charley returned to take his scalp. The knife had begun to do its work before Tobey chased Charley off, hurling rocks and telling him that soldiers were coming. Incredibly, Meacham was still alive although the troopers found him muttering in delirium: 'I am dead, I am dead.' Brandy was forced down his throat and Surgeon Cabanis operated and saved his life.[30]

On the far side of the Stronghold, Curly-Haired Doctor tried to lure Colonel Mason into a similar trap. Mason, an experienced Indian campaigner, refused to talk. The Modocs attacked two officers, wounding one in the thigh. Gillen, left in command, was dazed. His troops turned out in battle order, but by then the damage was done.

Newspaper reporters in the army camp despatched the story of Canby's murder to a shocked world. It sparked fury, shame and disgust. In Yreka and Jacksonville, Secretary Delano's effigy was hanged because of his efforts at conciliation with the Modocs. The *New York Times* reported: 'Seldom has an event created so deep a feeling of horror and indignation.' *The Times of London* labelled it 'an outrage'. Other newspapers demanded the immediate extermination of the renegade band. One of the few dissenting voices came from Athens' *Northeast Georgian*. Canby's Civil War successes were bitterly remembered in that part of the South and the newspaper's headline gloated: 'Capt Jack and Warriors Revenge the South by Murdering General Canby. Three Cheers for the Gallant Modocs.' The army was appalled and enraged by the only casualty of such rank. General Sherman telegraphed: 'Any measure of severity to the savages will be sustained.' In another message to officers he added: 'You will be fully justified in their utter extermination.'[31]

The murders did more grave damage to President Grant's peace policy, but the strategy was dying in any case. For five years, Grant, a hardened professional soldier, had counselled mercy, understanding and humanity in dealing with the Indians; that his policy had survived so long is in itself surprising. Now it was dead in the water. Canby's troopers in the field took the salute over his body in a simple ceremony. His remains were taken to Yreka and from there by special train to Portland where he lay in state. The tributes paid were almost equal to those that had been paid to Abraham Lincoln after his murder. After four services across the continent, Canby was at last buried in Crown Hill Cemetery, Indianapolis.

***

On 14 April the War Department named Canby's successor as the tough Jefferson C. Davis, colonel of the 23rd Infantry and a brevet major general. But the man on the spot was still Gillem. He was joined at his camp on the south shore of Tule Lake by Donald McKay and seventy-two Warm Springs Indian scouts, all clad in US Army uniforms. An escaped Modoc prisoner told Jack of their arrival, of Gillem's planned attack with 1,000 men, and of Meacham's survival. Jack sent the children and the elderly to well-protected caves and placed his men behind natural and artificial barricades. The women stayed to carry water and ammunition to their men.

Gillem's assault plan was very similar to Wheaton's. This time, however, there were enough men to give it a good chance of success despite the lava maze; there was no fog to add to the confusion, and there were fewer raw recruits and overconfident volunteers. On the other hand, the Modocs were now better armed, having stripped Wheaton's fallen men of their more modern rifles and ammunition. For three days Gillem's forces advanced slowly and methodically from two sides into the lava beds. At night howitzers and four mortars softened up the Indian positions.

On the first day the army lost five men dead and a large number wounded, the latter taken away by mule litters and by boats across the lake. The advance was temporarily halted, but Gillem and his men wore down their enemy with fatigue and force of numbers. The soldiers advanced, then rested while others overtook them. The Modocs in their rifle pits and entrenchments, their nerves stretched by the nightly bombardments, enjoyed no such relief. To the immediate west of Jack's Stronghold, Lieutenant Egan tried to cross an exposed wasteland. He soon fell wounded, but he and his men dug in to a crucial position within range of the Indian defenders. The young officer was tended at his post by the tireless surgeon Cabanis. Even now the onslaught might have failed to dislodge the Modocs save for the desperate shortage of water. The band's supply, never great, had dwindled to nothing. Jack sent warriors crawling through the sagebrush to bring back water from the lake. Clashing with army pickets, they failed to break through, but neither were they beaten back and a temporary stalemate ensued. The army let several old Modoc women cross their lines to the shore. Among them was discovered a young warrior in disguise. He was killed and scalped by soldiers, who managed to take five scalps from his head as trophies of their daring. Hooker Jim led a raid on the army teamsters, killing one. The raiders tried to encircle the baggage camp but withdrew after a few shots. That was the last action of a gruelling three-day battle that had consisted mainly of sniping and occasional bursts of individual initiative. Modoc casualties were two boys who tried to open a cannon shell that exploded, one warrior and several Modoc women reported to have died from sickness. Crucially, US soldiers had crossed magic lines set by Curly-Haired Doctor and Modocs had died; the shaman's protection was broken.[32]

On the morning of the fourth day the soldiers found the Indian positions eerily deserted.[33] Jack and his band had slipped away, leaving the bodies of two warriors and a woman, and a sick old man who was too infirm to move. The soldiers decided, incorrectly, that he was Schonchin John and shot him to pieces. Once again a single Indian scalp was divided into many ugly trophies. The fusillade that killed the unknown geriatric was faintly heard by Jack's band, hiding a few miles to the south. Far from being defeated, they had merely retreated deeper into the lava beds where there was a little more precious water. They concealed themselves so well that the army had no idea of their whereabouts. For several days there was an uneasy lull as the Modocs rested, creeping out from time to time to pick off the odd sentry.

Fourteen Modocs under Scarface Charley were spotted returning to the lake for more water. They beat off a company of troopers who returned to camp with three dead. The Modocs fired into the lines of army tents. Artillery was swung around to bear on them. As each round curved through the air the Indians merely sheltered behind rocks, emerging after each shell burst to taunt the gunners. They fired bunched volleys into the camp while several hundred soldiers stood by and made no effort to stop them. All fourteen braves returned unscathed to the Modoc hideout.

By 26 April the Warm Springs scouts had found the Modoc camp, but Gillem was determined to proceed cautiously as he did not want another debacle. That is exactly what he got. Captain Evan Thomas and at least sixty-four officers and men were sent ahead to reconnoitre the Modoc positions. Their chief task was to discover whether artillery could be placed to bombard the camp. Gillem expressly ordered Thomas to avoid engaging the enemy. The detachment stopped for lunch under a butte and Thomas called in his skirmishers to eat. Lieutenant Arthur Cranston and five men volunteered to explore the rugged ground and were soon out of sight of the main party. They were ambushed by twenty-four Modocs hidden in rocks. Every man died in a brief slaughter. Thomas, hearing the gunshots, sent two more lieutenants, Wright and Harris, with men to dig in at the side of the butte. When they reached it, the Modocs, firing from above, simply continued the massacre. Thomas's command was thrown into fatal confusion as the twenty-four soldiers panicked and ran. The rest stayed for what they were sure would be a doomed last stand.[34] Donald McKay and fourteen of his scouts arrived on the scene to prevent their total annihilation, but not in time to save Thomas himself. All five field officers were dead, alongside twenty enlisted men; sixteen were wounded, including the only officer to survive the engagement, Assistant Surgeon Senig. Not one Modoc was reported hurt. It was later claimed that Scarface Charley had allowed some soldiers out of the trap, calling on his fellows to stop shooting and crying out: 'My heart is sick seeing so much blood and so many men lying dead.'[35]

Army morale plunged while its shame soared. For three hours the battle had raged within sight and sound of an army signal station. More than twenty survivors limped back to base camp before any reinforcements were sent. A superior force had been routed and half wiped out by a small band of Modocs. The shock waves that this new fiasco sent through the War Department were heightened by the family connections of the dead officers: Thomas was the son of Lorenzo Thomas, a former Adjutant General; Thomas Wright was the son of a famous Indian fighter and general who had died at sea eight years earlier; Lieutenant Albion Howe was the son of Major General Albion P. Howe of the 4th Artillery.

Jefferson Davis arrived on 2 May to take command of a force of which he was deeply contemptuous. In his eyes the Thomas massacre proved that many of the soldiers were 'only cowardly beefeaters'. His first move was to send out McKay's scouts to locate the enemy and protect local settlers. He waited for further reinforcements and, with the force of his personality, raised camp morale. On 6 May the bodies of Cranston and his men were found. The following day a score of Modocs attacked a supply train escort of equal numbers, sending the white men fleeing with three wounded.

Davis sent two companies, under Captain Henry Hasbrouck, to sweep the region outside the lava beds. They were issued with five days' rations. On 10 May, at Dry Lake, they were attacked at dawn. Perhaps determined to atone for the shame of the previous engagements, the soldiers stood their ground and coolly returned fire. A cavalry sergeant yelled: 'Goddamn it, let's charge!' and sprinted towards the Modocs with a handful of troopers.[36] Ellen's Man, who with Jack had butchered Canby, was killed in the skirmish. Jack was seen amid the fighting, wearing Canby's plundered jacket. Yet again the Warm Springs scouts proved invaluable. They helped push the Modocs 3 miles back towards the lava beds. It was the army's first, if modest, victory of the campaign.[37]

The Modocs returned to their encampment with just a few casualties. But the death of Ellen's Man caused Jack more trouble. He was accused of keeping his own relatives out of danger while better men risked their lives in the forefront of battle. The lack of water remained a desperate problem. Hooker Jim, Curly-Haired Doctor and others who had been the first to urge the killing of the peace commission were losing heart. The setback at Dry Lake had exposed as a fraud the medicine man's supposed protection. The band broke into two groups, both of which left the lava beds for the last time.[38]

* * *

Fourteen families under Hooker Jim went west. On 18 May they blundered into a mounted squadron commanded by Hasbrouck and scattered south of Lower Klamath Lake after a running fight. Four days later most had surrendered. Hooker Jim and his fellows offered Davis their help in tracking down Jack, with or without the promise of an amnesty. It was a remarkable act of double treachery as all had earlier voted for war and several were involved in the killing of Canby and Thomas and the earlier ranch massacres. Davis regarded Hooker Jim as 'an unmitigated cut-throat'. He accepted the offer.

Hooker Jim, Bogus Charley, Shacknasty Jim and Steamboat Frank were set free and pursued their task with diligence. They guessed correctly that Jack and their former comrades would head for Willow Creek, an offshoot of Lost River. They found them after three days. The four urged Jack's followers – thirty-seven warriors and their families – to surrender, saying they could not fight and run forever. Jack's men were war-weary, tired, cold and hungry, and many were wounded. Yet they called the renegades squaws and Jack told Hooker Jim: 'You intend to buy your liberty and freedom by running me to earth ... You realise life is sweet but you did not think so when you forced me to promise that I would kill that man Canby.' He added: 'Oh, you bird-hearted men, you turned against me...'[39] Jack sent them away to 'live like white men'.

The four reported to Davis on 28 May that Jack intended to attack a nearby ranch. A cavalry detachment under Major John Green was the first to reach the ranch while two squadrons under Hasbrouck and Jackson followed. The next afternoon the troopers surprised Jack's band on Willow Creek, just across the Oregon state boundary. The Modocs fled to Langell Valley. The various US units now in the field vied with each other to be the ones to kill or capture Captain Jack. The Modoc War ended as 'a chase after wild beasts'.[40] The Indians scattered as warriors sought to save their women and children. In ones, pairs or family groups, they surrendered to the soldiers.

On 3 June, Jack and his family were cornered in a cave by cavalrymen under Captain David Perry. The chief was utterly dejected and only two or three braves remained with him. He agreed to give up without a struggle, explaining simply: 'My legs have given out.'[41] He was taken in manacles to join the rest of his dispirited band at the Tule Lake Army Camp. General Sherman was not best pleased with the sordid, inglorious round-up which had closed the war. He wrote: 'Davis should have killed every Modoc before taking him if possible. Then there would have been no complications.' The tribe, he said, should be dispersed throughout the Indian reservations 'so that the name of Modoc should cease'. But Davis, not a noted humanitarian, had good reason to show restraint. He was well aware of the acrimony heaped upon officers involved in the massacre of Indians elsewhere and Grant's peace policy was not quite dead and buried. Davis had decided that instead of taking general vengeance on the band, Jack and eight other supposed ringleaders should face a drumhead trial followed by swift execution. A scaffold was built before proceedings began.[42] Ironically, given the general's previous pronouncements, new orders from Sherman stopped it being used. He had decided that Jack and the others involved in Canby's murder should be tried by military court while Hooker Jim and the other Lost River murderers should be handed over to civil courts. Six men were charged by Davis's military court; none of the four renegades joined them in the dock.

After the round-up of the last scattered Modocs, Fairchild's brother James took charge of fifteen men, women and children to take them by mule wagon to the army camp. They met a group of Oregon volunteers who threatened the families, but Fairchild persuaded them that his prisoners were unimportant Indians. A few miles on he was stopped by two horsemen who held a pistol to his head. They killed four unarmed braves in the wagon and wounded a woman before fleeing as an army patrol approached. The murderers, though well known locally, were never pursued or charged, never mind brought to trial.

Meanwhile there was still the matter of the Lost River killers and Sherman's order that they be handed over to civilian justice. Davis invited the families of the dead settlers to the camp to pick out the murderers. Two widows identified Hooker Jim and Steamboat Frank. The two women pulled out a pistol and a knife but were disarmed by soldiers. Neither man ever faced trial. The Modoc renegades had helped the army restore its pride and so were rewarded. Curly-Haired Doctor, perhaps the greatest villain of the whole affair, conveniently shot himself dead.

At Fort Klamath on 5 July the military trial opened in a bare hall dominated by a rough wooden table. Beside Jack in the dock stood his half-brother Black Jack, Schonchin John and Boston Charley. On the floor sat Barncho and Slolux, the two youths who had supplied the rifles for the *coup de grace* on Canby and the attempt on Meacham. The judge advocate was Major H. P. Curtis and the panel included Captain Hasbrouck. The Riddles were present throughout, acting as both witnesses and interpreters. An army unit with fixed bayonets stood to one side. Among the unruly crowd of spectators, widows and reporters stood Hooker Jim, Bogus Charley, Shacknasty Jim and Steamboat Frank, who watched the proceedings with interest, occasional amusement and not the slightest sign of guilt. The defendants were charged with the murders of Canby and Thomas 'in violation of the laws of war' and the attempted slayings of Meacham and Dyer.

On the third day the Modoc renegades gave their damning evidence. That afternoon Meacham, still suffering from his terrible wounds, limped into the courtroom to give his testimony. Later he offered his services as counsel for the Modoc defendants but was persuaded by friends to withdraw the gesture. Only three witnesses were called for the defence: Scarface Charley and two Modocs whose words carried precious little weight. Jack's own speech was defeated and dismal. He was, however, scathing about the role played by his Modoc rival: 'Hooker Jim is the one that always wanted to fight, and commenced killing and murdering ... Life is mine only for a short term. You white people conquered me not; my own men did.'[43] Referring to the killing of the Modoc woman and baby at Lost River, Jack said: 'If the white men that killed our women and children had been tried and punished, I would not have thought so much of myself and companions. You people can shoot any Indian any time you want whether we are in war or in peace. I charge the white people with wholesale murder.'[44]

Some friendly whites quietly agreed with him, but the following day all six defendants were sentenced to death. The judge ruled that no others should be brought to trial, an instruction which greatly helped Hooker Jim and his confederates avoid civilian courts. An Oregon sheriff later arrived with warrants for their arrest but was turned away.

As six nooses dangled from a scaffold, the fort chaplain explained the sentences to the condemned men. Jack, without any obvious bitterness, said that he had believed his surrender would be rewarded with a pardon. The four renegades, he claimed, had beaten both himself and the US government. Asked who should be chief when he was gone he said that he could no longer trust any Modoc to do the job. Black Jim said he should be allowed to live to lead the tribe but Jack snorted in derision. The youngsters Barncho and Slolux simply denied that there was any blood on their hands, which was strictly true. Boston Charley confessed his involvement in the murders but declared he had believed that Canby and the commissioners were themselves plotting treachery. Schonchin John said: 'War is a terrible thing. All must suffer – the best horses, the best cattle and the best men.'

As dawn broke on 3 October 1873, the roads to Fort Klamath were packed with sightseers. There was a carnival atmosphere. At 9.30 a.m. a military detail drew up outside the guardhouse. Six figures stumbled into the sunshine. A wagon held just four coffins. The prisoners sat beside the boxes while a blacksmith cut their shackles. Then the wagon trundled to the scaffold where Barncho and Slolux were left on board – President Grant had commuted their sentences to life imprisonment due to their tender years.

Jack stood on the extreme right. Beside him in order were Schonchin Jim, Boston Charley and Black Jim. A corporal put a halter around Jack's neck while fellow infantrymen did the same for the rest. One stroke of an axe cut the rope securing the trap door beneath all four men.[44] From within a nearby stockade, Modoc prisoners screamed in anguish. When it was done, the bodies were cut down and placed in their rude coffins. Colonel Wheaton, in charge of the executions, was offered $10,000 for Jack's body by a showman. He indignantly refused the offer. Instead the heads of all four were hacked off and sent for examination to the Army Medical Museum in Washington.[45]

Jack left two widows. The survivors of the band were again split in two. The larger band, 155 strong, were sent to a malaria-ridden patch of earth in the south-west corner of Indian Territory. By 1905 they had declined to just fifty-six souls. The second group remained on the Klamath reservation. There they held their own and thirty years later numbered 223. The Modoc name did not vanish but never again did it pose a threat to the white man. In the 1940s, the executors of a dead army officer in Portland found three skulls in a box in a basement. One was labelled 'Captain Jack'.

The US forces lost at least seventy-three killed in the war – including two scouts and sixteen volunteers – and sixty-seven wounded. The cost was almost $500,000 compared to the $20,000 that would have been spent buying the land that the Modocs had asked for. The Modocs lost eleven men, including the four executed after hostilities ceased, at least eleven women and an unknown number of children. In terms of the numbers involved, the attrition rate was proportionally higher than most, and maybe all, of America's conflicts.

The war's two chief protagonists, more victims than heroes, both tried to avoid bloodshed. General Canby and Captain Jack were fine men by the standards of their respective tribes. Their words retain dignity across a century and a half. If matters had been left in their hands alone, the war may never have happened, but both lost control and allowed themselves to be swept along to a bloody finale. Both died by treachery, ill served by lesser men.

14

The Samoan Crisis
(1887–1889)

…their unwilling executioner.

Month after month the navies of the US, Imperial Germany and Britain faced each other, ready for battle over a war-torn Pacific archipelago. This was gunboat diplomacy of the most extreme kind. No side was prepared to blink first or sail away. One ill-judged shot could have sparked global conflict. Instead, nature stepped in, helped by 'an error of judgement that will forever remain a paradox in human psychology'.[1] The result was a forgotten disaster in which more than 200 sailors died and six warships sank.

* * *

The US, Britain and Imperial Germany all had greedy eyes on the Samoan Islands for reasons of trade, diplomacy and strategic influence. Although Britain remained the greatest sea power, America and Germany were keen to catch up in the naval arms race. All three were determined to exploit decades of turmoil and internal strife which had bloodied paradise.

By the late 1880s, rival Samoan factions fought in support of either Malietoa Laupepa or Mata'afa Iosefo as king of the island group. The latter was proclaimed king but then usurped and exiled. Germany gave limited military aid to another rival, Tamasese, but Mata'afa was more popular among the islanders. Tensions rose after German shelling of Mata'afa's rebel villages also resulted in the destruction of American-owned property in 1887. A battle at Vailele in September 1888 was followed by Mata'afa's warriors destroying an invading German contingent and plundering their plantations.[2] German landing parties from the corvette *Olga* lost two officers and thirteen men in the engagement.

Both the US and Imperial Germany had dispatched squadrons to the region to investigate and act according to their imperial interests. Their commanders had free rein. Germany sent the two gunboats,

Adler and *Eber*, to join *Olga*. America sent three warships – the sloop-of-war USS *Vandalia*, the screw steamer *Trenton* and the gunboat *Nipsic* – to monitor the island. Britain also sent a ship, the corvette HMS *Calliope*, to protect its interests.

Vandalia, commissioned in 1876, had seen service in the North Atlantic and Mediterranean squadrons, in the Gulf of Mexico and the Caribbean, along the Hawaiian Islands and along the Pacific coasts of north, central and South America. *Trenton*, commissioned in 1877, was the first US naval vessel to use electric lights, fitted in 1883. She had cruised the Mediterranean as well as visiting Ceylon, Singapore, China, Korea, Japan, Brazil, Panama and Tahiti.[3] *Nipsic* was an old Civil War blockade runner which later served in the South Atlantic and, after extensive rebuilding, off Africa. In January 1888 she had sailed for Cape Horn and Peru, leaving there in September for duty as station ship in Apia Harbour.

While the Samoan civil war spluttered and fizzled on land with no clear winner in sight, the three Western naval powers faced each other nervously across the cramped harbour at Apia for several months. All the captains and crews were experienced Pacific seamen and could not have failed to spot all the signs of impending disaster. It was cyclone season, and Apia had been hit by one just three years previously, which the captains of the ships heard about from local people. The weather began to change and the atmospheric pressure fell ominously. Apia was and is an exposed harbour, unprotected by high ground or an enclosing reef. The northern part is open to the Pacific, and wind and waves can sweep through and drive any shipping which remained in the bay on to the reefs at the southern end or toss them right up the beach. The naval men knew full well that the only chance they had of riding out the 100 mph winds was to take to the open sea. But no one would make the first move. There were undoubtedly elements of jingoism, national pride and masculine bravado involved. No one was willing to admit in front of the other nations' navies that they were afraid of the elements, and so all refused to take precautions. They also banned the merchant ships which accompanied them from moving, so thirteen ships remained at anchor close to one another in Apia harbour.[4] The anchorage was perhaps fit for four ships.[5]

A near-contemporary account recorded:

> The conditions during the early part of March 1889, seem to have been about normal up to the 4th, when British Meteorological Office reports from Suva, Fiji, and Nuku'alofa, Tonga, indicate that an anticyclone extended southward toward New Zealand ... It was on the 12th that the very earliest signs of the hurricane's approach were observed at Samoa ... On the 14th the weather grew still more threatening and the barometer continued its steady fall, now slowly, as the time of the daily maximum approached, and now more rapidly, as the fall due to the influence of the approaching storm combined with the daily ebb

of the barometric tide (always such a marked phenomenon in the tropics). Toward evening the ships got up steam in their boilers, that their engines might aid their anchors in keeping them off the reefs and preventing collisions with other vessels in the crowded harbor. It was doubtless an anxious moment for the commanders of the naval forces of the three great nations, responsible, as they were, not only for lives and ships but for the prompt execution of their instructions and the faithful guardianship of public interests committed to their care. To most of the others on board, both officers and men, free from at least some of the cares and responsibilities of their superiors, the actual danger of the situation was probably not fully evident till after the shift of wind to the northward Friday evening, when the long battle with the elements commenced in earnest.[6]

The account continued: 'The beautiful scene – for Apia, like all the islands of that sea, is a perfect paradise of loveliness – was somber with the hush and gloom of a coming storm.' When the cyclone hit, the result was catastrophic. The local populace, aware of the danger through bitter experience, took themselves to safety well before the storm struck, but the ships in the bay only began to evacuate at the very last minute, and thus were crowding towards the entrance to the bay when the hurricane arrived.

Rain fell in sheets, cutting visibility. Winds of 70–100 knots blew directly into the anchorage, trapping the ships in the V-shaped harbour. The harbour bottom was scoured by currents, and anchors lost their purchase. Operating their engines at full speed to resist the wind and waves, ships nevertheless dragged their anchors and were inexorably driven landward. Vessels collided.[7]

Chaos reigned as for thirty-six hours as the storm ravaged the harbour. Despite heroic efforts by the officers and crews of *Vandalia* and *Trenton*, the two vessels tore their bottoms out upon the reef. *Vandalia* struck at about noon and sank until her decks were completely awash, forcing her crew to scramble into the rigging. *Trenton*, having lost steam and rudder, was in imminent danger of foundering on the reef. An unusual manoeuvre suggested by navigator Lieutenant Robert M. G. Brown saved the flagship from complete destruction.[8] *Trenton*'s commander, Norman von Heidreich Farquar, ordered every man into the port rigging. With the wind striking against the compact mass of bodies, which acted as a sail, the vessel was steered away from the reef and into the bay. *Trenton* collided with *Olga* and then floated toward the sinking *Vandalia*. With her crew still in the rigging, the approach was slowed and another collision avoided, with *Trenton* safely manoeuvred alongside the *Vandalia*. After a miserable and terrifying night in the rigging, *Vandalia*'s crew escaped to deck of *Trenton*, but only after forty-three of her complement had drowned or been dashed to death on the rocks.[9] *Trenton* was tossed against the beach in the afternoon, dragged back into the sea and wrecked on a reef at 10 p.m., although the majority of her crew survived unhurt and were able to participate in the ensuing rescue operation. Out of *Trenton*'s 450 crew, only Landsman J. Hewlett was lost.

The correspondent quoted above wrote of *Vandalia*:

> Her rigging was thronged with men when the *Trenton* found herself in her worst difficulty. The fires were out, the sails gone, the pouring of oil on the waves had proved useless, and the danger was imminent of a collision between the *Trenton* and the *Vandalia,* which would destroy the last hopes of the survivors clinging to the rigging of the latter. At this juncture Lieutenant Brown, of the *Trenton*, ran up the ship's colors, the only flag that floated at Apia that day, ordered the ship's band to play 'The Star Spangled Banner' and sent half his company into the port rigging, rightly calculating that their weight on the side next to the storm, and their mass of resistance to the gale, might help the manoeuvring of the ship. As the *Trenton* and the *Vandalia* approached towards collision, the *Trenton* men cheered the *Vandalia* crew. The latter replied as well as they could, with their throats enfeebled by exposure, but with all goodwill, as recognising that the *Trenton* was their unwilling executioner. Yet, strangely enough, the *Trenton* never came alongside a dock more gently than her stem now touched the *Vandalia,* whose survivors swarmed upon the larger vessel's decks into comparative safety. Thus out of peril came sudden salvation, and the American corvette, which cheered our ship, not only lost no hands, but saved the survivors of the *Vandalia*, though she afterwards went to pieces.[10]

It continued:

> Here were three good vessels already gone, strewing the harbor waters with corpses and wreckage, and still the awful storm raged unabated. The American corvette *Vandalia*—a fine old-fashioned, wooden, bark-rigged ship of 2,100 tons, which carried General Grant in his tour round the world—was the next victim. The fury of the hurricane swept her loose, and dashed her on the reef, fifty yards from where the *Nipsic* lay, but, unlike that vessel, on hard rock, where the first wave washed her captain and many of the company to their death, and the next bilged the vessel in, so that she sank with part of her hull and her tall masts remaining above water, covered with clinging sailors.

Nipsic's captain, Cmdr D. W. Mullin, was able by superb seamanship to beach his ship. While severely damaged by the pounding she received on the beach, *Nipsic*'s hull was intact, although much of her topside structure was battered, all of her propeller blades damaged, two boilers spread and useless, and eight of her crew lost.

The German ships suffered much worse: SMS *Adler* and SMS *Eber* were caught at the harbour mouth by the initial blow and were bodily picked up and smashed together. Though *Eber* was the most modern of the seven warships present, damage to her propeller made it impossible for her to survive the violent wind and seas.[11] After a long struggle, *Eber* was forced against the edge of the harbour reef and sank quickly in deep water with the loss of seventy-three of her crewmen. *Adler* came to rest on her side, on the reef.

The contemporary account said:

Fearful was the strain upon every one of those seven warships off Apia when the light came on March 16, and hardly had it dawned before the *Eber*, a German gunboat, dragged helplessly, parted her cables, and, in spite of her hard-working engines, crashed on the rugged reef, slid back again with the reflex wave, and went down in the deep water under the coral shelf with all hands. A whole watch was below with hatches battened down, for the chain had very suddenly snapped. They were, of course, drowned with all their fellows, and hardly a cry heard; while shortly afterwards a huge wave wrenched the *Adler* from her anchors, hurled her upon the remorseless reef, and flung her broadside over its face. A few officers and men made their escape by favor of the waves...[12]

SMS *Olga* was thrown high on to the beach where she was wrecked but many of her crew survived, escaping onto higher ground. In total, ninety-six men from their crews drowned in the storm, and both ships were totally destroyed. All six of the merchant ships remaining in the harbour were wrecked, and the death toll was well over 200 sailors from several nationalities.[13]

American casualties totalled fifty-two killed. The survivors from *Vandalia*, *Trenton* and *Nipsic* soon sailed for Mare Island on board a chartered steamer, but *Vandalia* and *Trenton* themselves were so battered that they were soon dismantled and their scrap donated to the Samoans. One of *Vandalia*'s survivors was Naval Cadet John Lejeune, a future major general and thirteenth Commandant of the US Marine Corps.

Only HMS *Calliope* escaped. By 09.00 on the 16th, *Calliope*, although still riding at anchor, had been hit by one ship and narrowly missed by another, and Captain Henry Coey Kane decided to attempt to escape.[14] To relieve the strain on the five anchor cables, *Calliope*'s boilers were producing maximum pressure; the engines were worked 'red hot', and the propeller was making 74 revolutions, sufficient for 15 knots (28 km/h) in calmer waters. In spite of this titanic effort, the ship was barely able to make a 1-knot headway against the winds and the seas in the harbour, and anchor cables began to part. To port and only 20 feet away was the coral reef. Ahead were the *Vandalia* and *Trenton*, while to starboard were other warships. Hemmed in by these obstacles and with the rudder at times within 6 feet of the reef, *Calliope* seemed doomed.

Her bow and stern alternately rose and plunged into the incoming waves; the propeller at times spinning in air, requiring a careful hand on the throttle to keep the shaft from destruction. Green seas were boarding the vessel and running the length of the deck. There were ten men on the wheel and more below handling relieving tackle on the tiller to assist in maintaining control of the rudder. Captain Kane saw an opening, slipped the anchors and drove forward. Avoiding the helpless *Vandalia*, he approached the sinking *Trenton*, coming so close that *Calliope*'s fore yardarm passed over the American's deck. As *Calliope* rolled to port, the yard lifted over *Trenton*. The crew of the helpless and doomed American ship cheered *Calliope* as the corvette slipped past. The British ship's drive for the open sea was called by the American commander on the scene 'one of the grandest sights a seaman or anyone else ever saw; the lives of 250 souls depended on the hazardous adventure'.[15] *Calliope* had taken two desperate hours to travel four cables. Once out at sea she was easily able to ride out the ensuing winds. Her survival was attributed the skill of captain and crew, her size (2,227 tons) and her more powerful and modern engines, built only five years before, as compared to the ten to twenty years for many of the other ships.

The unnamed correspondent said of Kane's slow-motion dash to safety:

It was a momentous resolve, for the anchors and engines together had failed to save the other vessels in the harbour. When Captain Kane threw the head of the corvette into the teeth of the storm, and slipped his cables, the *Calliope* for an appreciable period of time, remained perfectly still. Then she gathered headway by inches, and finally moved at a snail's pace past the *Trenton*. As the *Calliope* steamed into safety the 450 men who formed the officers and crew of the *Trenton*, though momentarily expecting a fatal disaster to themselves, raised a ringing cheer as a tribute to the brave daring of the English commander. The crew of the *Calliope* returned the greeting as heartily.[16]

The storm kept *Calliope* at sea the next two days. Re-entering the harbour on 19 March to search for the missing anchors, the crew discovered that all of the other ships had been wrecked with loss of life. Unable to find the anchor amid the wreckage, and his ship having sustained significant damage, Kane decided to return to Australia. He turned over *Calliope*'s diving outfit to the US Navy to assist it in salvage in return for boats from the wrecked American ships to replace the boats which had been stripped from *Calliope* by the storm. In Sydney, Kane received a hero's welcome. According to one report: 'The narrowness of Calliope's escape; the excellence of the engines and the dedication of the crew, who kept the power plant in operation for many hours during the ordeal; the seamanship of Captain Kane and officers; their bravery in letting go of their anchor and facing the storm, trusting only in their ship and themselves; and the respect and encouragement given to them by the crew of *Trenton*; made *Calliope* famous.'[17] *Calliope*'s engineer Henry George Bourke was promoted to fleet engineer.[18] He attributed his success to the superior properties of the West Coast coal from New Zealand used to fire the ship's boilers.

Kane was showered with honours,[19] cited by the Admiralty for his 'nerve and decisions', given the command of HMS *Victory* in 1892, and in 1897 was promoted to rear admiral. He died in 1917. A young midshipman on the *Calliope*, Horace Lambert Alexander Hood, died a rear admiral on HMS *Invincible*, the first battle cruiser, at the Battle of Jutland in 1916 when she blew up with the loss of all but six of her crew of 1,032 officers and men. HMS *Calliope* survived as a moored training ship near Newcastle for Royal Navy Volunteer Reservists until 1951.

Nipsic was completely rebuilt in Hawaii to be longer and heavier, and from January 1890 cruised in the Hawaiian Islands guarding American interests. She was later turned into a prison ship in Puget Sound. She was sold in 1913 and scrapped for her estimated salvage value of $15,000.[20]

The contemporary account quoted above summed up:

> Greater and more majestic than any hurricane, than any death or disaster, is once more proved to be the spirit of man, which, in a scene of dreadful tumult of nature, where strong vessels were helpless as chips, and the stoutest skill was useless, could raise above the whirlwind that dauntless cheer to the *Calliope*, the expression of an immortal courage—a cry, all things considered, of such indomitable Anglo-Saxon pluck as to ring finer than any which has ever echoed under the flag of victory, or in the happiest hours of security and success.[21]

Worldwide it was pointed out that bull-headed pride was the cause of the disaster, and only the single captain – Kane of the *Calliope* – who was not obsessed with it came out of the affair with credit. German and American prestige suffered very badly while Kane's moral courage, leadership and superb seamanship ensured that the reputation of the Royal Navy was raised to new heights. Samoan resident Robert Louis Stevenson wrote: 'The behaviour of the American and German commanders has provided an illuminating case for psychologists studying aspects of pride, pragmatism and decision-making.'

The incident is often cited as a clear example of the dangers of putting national pride before necessity, especially in the face of natural disaster. But it did not blunt the Pacific ambitions of any of the imperial powers involved,[22] although from then on more care was taken to respect the weather phenomena of the Pacific.

After the disaster, the three powers decided that Laupepa would be the king. The great cyclone had, in the end, removed the immediate threat of outright colonial confrontation over Samoa, but the crisis would simmer on for many more years. Germany and the United States would not officially come to blows in the Pacific until the First World War.

* * *

Nine years later, in 1898, after the death of Malietoa Laupepa, hostilities broke out in a second Samoan civil war. Again, America had a vested interest in its outcome.

In January 1899, followers of Mata'afa Iosefo, the claimant supported by Germany, exiled Prince Tanu, who was supported by America and Britain. In March at Apia, those Samoan forces loyal to Prince Tanu were besieged by a larger force of rebel Mataafans. The US Navy and the Royal Navy were quick to respond, deploying three warships. Rear Admiral Albert Kautz of the cruiser USS *Philadelphia* arrived first on 13 March and held a meeting with the many different officials there. When no solution was agreed upon, a shore party was landed and Mata'afa's followers were ordered to leave Apia and go back to their villages. Instead of following this command, the Mataafans removed themselves from town but only to the outskirts, where they started evicting the European and American population from their homes. Refugees started fleeing to Apia where they were put up in houses along the coast, under the protection of naval guns. The British cruiser HMS *Porpoise* and corvette HMS *Royalist* were deployed to Apia; sailors and marines from these two vessels were also landed for the protection of the town.[23]

On 15 March, Rear Admiral Kautz demanded that the Mataafans leave the outskirts of the town. He was ignored and instead Mata'afa Iosefo increased the numbers of his men around Apia and attacked. The British and American commanders estimated that a total of over 4,000 rebel warriors armed with 2,500 rifles opposed them. Over the course of the siege there were about 260 British and American servicemen involved, fighting alongside about 2,000 Samoan warriors. The Americans held the Tivoli Hotel as their command post; sentries were also placed at various isolated consulates, which were mostly surrounded by dense jungle. At 12:30 a.m., the Mataafans rushed the British and American consulates guarded by sailors and marines under Lieutenant Guy Reginald Archer Gaunt of HMS *Porpoise* and Captain M. Perkins of the US Marines. The British and Americans held their fire, and the Samoans retreated after realising that Apia's garrison was on high alert and prepared for battle.

Just before 1 p.m., rebel boats were spotted off Vaiusu and were thought to be making an attack on the Samoan refugees in the village of Mulinuu. Kautz gave the order to open fire on the boats and on Mata'afa's front line. All three of the British and American warships began bombarding the boats and the rebel-held outskirts of Apia until 5 p.m., when HMS *Porpoise* was detached alone to shell the Vaiusu and Vaimoso villages. Several boats were sunk and hundreds of shells expended. The Mataafans decided to attack the American-held hotel the following night, 15 March. During this assault, the Samoan rebels advanced hastily and temporarily captured a 7-pounder artillery piece before being repulsed by fire from both the garrison and the warships. The casualties included 1 American sentry killed with 3 Britons; Samoan casualties are unknown. From then until the end of the siege, the fighting took the form of sniping and skirmishing. Mata'afa's army continued to occupy the outskirts of Apia and many of the surrounding villages. The Allied commanders concluded they had to combine their strength and attack the Mataafan front line, or wherever they were in large numbers. By engaging the rebels in a decisive action, they would be forced to abandon the siege.[24]

On 24 March, the cruiser HMS *Tauranga* under Captain Leslie Creery Stuart joined the Allied force at Apia, and Stuart took command of British naval operations in Samoa. The final engagement occurred on 30 March when the British, American and Samoan loyalists marched south to confront Mata'afa. Three miles south of Apia, the Allies under the command of Lieutenant Gault attacked and routed a large rebel force. There were 27 Mataafans dead with a loss of 3 more Britons, 1 American sailor and 1 Samoan warrior, and several others were wounded. After this, the rebels retreated to their main stronghold of Vailele. During the siege the German consulate was hit by shell fire and later its occupants protested the American and British use of force in Samoa.[25]

The Allies began operations against Vailele. On 1 April, an expedition of about 250 men proceeded to the settlement, supported by HMS *Royalist*. Two villages were burned along the way, and the Royalist bombarded Vailele's fortifications. But when the expedition approached the town, a superior force of Mataafans ambushed and forced it back. On 13 March, the rebels attacked the front line just outside Vailele, but this time it was they who were repulsed. On 17 March, the Allies attacked Vailele for the third and final time. British and Samoan loyalists, with aid from a small force of Americans, captured one of the stronghold's two forts but were forced to retreat soon after. During this action USS *Philadelphia* and the British warships bombarded the port.

But the Allies decided to make the best of a bad job. They declared that so long as the Mataafans stay out of Apia, they would not take action against them. One more skirmish occurred on 25 April when the Mataafans attacked an American marine patrol outside Apia but were driven off.[26] The conflict was quickly ended by the partitioning of the island chain at the Tripartite Convention of 1899. The final outcome was the annexation of East Samoa by the US and of West Samoa by the Germans – which they lost to British Empire forces in 1914.

American Samoa became host to US military bases and was a fertile recruiting ground for the army. It was one of only three places – the others being New Caledonia and Marajo Island, Brazil – to completely escape the flu pandemic that swept the globe at the end of the First World War as troops returned home. The American governor heard radio reports of the outbreak and immediately summoned quarantine ships from the US mainland.

15

The Spanish–American War (1898)

*There may be an explosion any day ... which would settle
a great many things.*

The newspaper magnate William Randolph Hearst, locked in a brutal
New York circulation war, sent the renowned illustrator Frederick
Remington to cover uprisings in Spanish Cuba. When the artist cabled
back that all was quiet on the island, Hearst is reported to have responded:
'Please remain. You furnish the pictures and I'll furnish the war.'[1] It is
almost certainly a self-promoting journalistic myth which played into his
own self-image, but the fact that it was widely believed illustrates the
febrile atmosphere of the time. Hearst's support of the Cuban rebels was
centred around his own political and business ambitions, in common
with much of America's ruling class, dressed up as 'heroic efforts to find
the truth on the island under unusually difficult circumstances'.[2] Hearst
got his war, which was rooted in a clash of interests between America,
fast becoming a world power, and the swiftly decaying Old World empire
of Spain.

* * *

Various American factions had long been casting a greedy eye on Spain's
territories, especially in the Caribbean. Under the 1823 Monroe Doctrine,
the US was committed to respecting newly independent states in its
hemisphere, but such fine sentiments could not compete with the dollar
signs associated with the sugar trade. By the mid-nineteenth century
Spain had lost most of its colonies in the Americas but was determined
to maintain its transatlantic presence, particularly in Cuba which had
been Spanish for almost 400 years and was viewed as an integral part
of the Spanish nation with its shared cultural and language.[3] Spaniards
regarded the spreading of Christian civilisation as their major objective

in the New World. Americans saw Spain's aims as a colonial hangover and its colonies as ripe for exploitation.

In 1854 Southern US interests tried to persuade Congress to buy Cuba and convert it into a new slave territory, but that was rejected by anti-slavery factions. After the Civil War and a decade of rebellion and suppression on Cuba, US businessmen began monopolising its devalued sugar markets. In 1894, 90 per cent of Cuba's total exports went to the US, which also provided 40 per cent of Cuba's imports. Cuba's US exports were almost times times larger than those to her mother country,[4] and while Spain still held political authority over Cuba, economic authority shifted to the US.

The US was also planning a trans-isthmus canal through either Nicaragua or Panama to drastically shorten the trade route between the Atlantic and the Pacific seaboards. In the last two decades of the nineteenth century America rapidly built a powerful fleet of steel warships. Heavily involved in that was Theodore Roosevelt, the Assistant Secretary of the Navy from 1897 to 1898 and an aggressive advocate of intervention in Cuba, which could provide strategic sites for naval bases.

Meanwhile, the *Cuba Libre* movement, led by intellectual Jose Marti until his death in 1895, established offices in Florida and the Cuban *Junta* under Tomas Estrada Palma spearheaded an effective propaganda campaign targeted at the American public. The *Junta* dealt with leading newspapers and Washington officials, held fund-raising events across the US, and smuggled weapons. Protestant churches and most Democrats were supportive.

The Cuban rebellion erupted in 1868 and took ten years to only partially subdue. Marti's revolutionaries would not give up the aims of wider autonomy from Spanish rule and, ultimately, full-blown independence. They stockpiled weapons, recruited many more to the cause and launched a three-pronged invasion of the island in early 1895.[5] One group sailed from Santo Domingo, another from Costa Rica, but the third from Florida was thwarted by US Customs officials. Although the first two forces landed successfully and made a *grito de Baire*, or call for revolution, there were not enough potential rebels to immediately topple the Spanish regime. The revolutionaries settled in to fight a protracted guerrilla campaign.

Spanish premier Antonio Cánovas del Castillo said that his nation 'is disposed to sacrifice to the last peseta of its treasure and to the last drop of blood of the last Spaniard before consenting that anyone snatch from it even one piece of its territory'.[6] Behind the scenes, however, he did much to stabilise Spanish politics and avoid warfare, but was assassinated in 1897 by an Italian anarchist, leaving Spain unable and unwilling to suffer any undermining of its prestige. There was to be no diplomatic solution.

Spanish counter-insurgency measures were initially lacklustre until veteran General Valeriano Weyler was sent from Spain. He deprived the insurgency of weaponry and supplies by forcing civilians in those Cuban districts sympathetic to the revolt to move to 'reconcentration' areas close to his military HQ. His tactics, not particularly brutal by the standards of colonial warfare, fanned the flames of anti-Spanish propaganda in the US. President William McKinley claimed that Weyler's approach 'was not civilized warfare' but 'extermination'.[7]

The sentiments whipped up provided ammunition for the newspaper industry in New York City. Hearst's *New York Journal* and his arch-rival Joseph Pulitzer's *New York Herald* both saw in the Cuban crisis massive potential for lurid headlines to boost circulation among an increasingly literate and sensation-hungry populace. Both papers unequivocally denounced Spain. Hearst has been stigmatised for cheap sensationalism, but his *Journal* was a sophisticated newspaper by contemporary standards. Although his journalism would be much maligned, biographer Kenneth Whyte wrote:

> All good yellow journalists ... sought the human in every story and edited without fear of emotion or drama. They wore their feelings on their pages, believing it was an honest and wholesome way to communicate with readers. This appeal to feelings is not an end in itself ... [they believed] our emotions tend to ignite our intellects: a story catering to a reader's feelings is more likely than a dry treatise to stimulate thought.[8]

The ongoing internal conflict was harming US commercial interests and initially US business leaders urged Congress and McKinley to do what they could to end the revolt and restore the damaged trade in sugar, shipping and other commodities. They wanted stability, not war, and any chance of that was now in the hands of diplomats. But as tension increased, the *Cuba Libre* movement again proved successful in pulling American sentiment towards armed intervention. It cannily drew parallels between the American Revolution and the Cuban revolt and painted the Spanish Government as the tyrannical colonial oppressor in the style of eighteenth-century Britain. Historian Louis Pérez wrote: 'The proposition of war in behalf of Cuban independence took hold immediately and held on thereafter. Such was the sense of the public mood.'[9] Many African American soldiers, rankling under growing racial discrimination at home and denied a vote by 'Jim Crow' laws, wanted an intervention as a way to advance the cause of equality, with service to country hopefully gaining political and public respect.[10] The most influential black leader, Booker T. Washington, argued that his race was ready to fight. War offered them a chance 'to render service to our country that no other race can' because, unlike Whites, they were 'accustomed' to the 'peculiar and dangerous climate' of Cuba. In March 1898, Washington promised the Secretary of the Navy that war would be answered by 'at least ten thousand loyal, brave, strong black men in the south who crave an opportunity to show their loyalty to our land, and would gladly take this method of showing their gratitude for the lives laid down, and the sacrifices made, that Blacks might have their freedom and rights'.[11]

President McKinley, genuine in his search for a peaceful solution, opened negotiations with the Spanish government, but in October 1897 it spurned his offer to act as a go-between with the rebels. When a more liberal government was elected in November, the Spanish eased their position, offering to drop its 'reconcentration' camp strategy on Cuba and recall that strategy's architect, the hard-line Spanish Governor General Valeriano Weyler, if there was a ceasefire. Now it was the rebel leaders who rejected any such compromise, hoping to drag America into the fight.[12]

Cubans loyal to Spain in general, and Weyler in particular, planned large demonstrations to take place when the next Governor General, Ramon Blanco, arrived in Cuba. US consul Fitzhugh Lee asked for a warship to protect American citizens in the inevitable disturbances.[13] President McKinley duly sent USS *Maine* to Havana. Built over nine years, *Maine* was commissioned in 1895 and was intended to counter the increase of naval forces in Latin America and match the latest European naval developments. But by the time she was launched, she lacked both the armour and firepower to serve as a ship of the line against enemy battleships and the speed to serve as a cruiser. Her officers, sailors and marines numbered 355. She carried four 10-inch turret guns capable of firing 510-pound shells 20,000 yards, six 6-inch guns with 105-pound shells, seven 6-pounders and four 18-inch torpedo tubes.[14] Those guns would not be fired.

US naval forces were moved into position to attack simultaneously on several fronts if the war was not avoided. *Maine* left Florida while a large part of the North Atlantic Squadron was moved to Key West and the Gulf of Mexico. Given Spain's remaining territories worldwide, other American vessels were also moved off Lisbon and Hong Kong.[15] America was ready for war, but few in Washington wanted it. Events were to change minds.

In a cryptic message which later fed conspiracy theories, Senator Lodge wrote: 'There may be an explosion any day in Cuba which would settle a great many things. We have got a battleship in the harbor of Havana, and our fleet, which overmatches anything the Spanish have, is masked at the Dry Tortugas.'[16] He was almost certainly advocating pre-emptive American action, but events gave his words new meaning.

At 9.40 p.m. on 15 February 1898, a massive explosion ripped apart *Maine* and she sank in Havana Harbour. More than 5 tons of powder charges for the vessel's guns detonated, obliterating the forward third of the ship. Most of *Maine*'s crew were sleeping or resting in the enlisted quarters, in the forward part of the ship, when the explosion occurred. In total,

260 men lost their lives in the explosion or shortly thereafter, and six more died later from injuries.[17] Captain Sigsbee and most of the officers survived, because their quarters were in the aft portion of the ship. Altogether there were eighty-nine survivors, eighteen of whom were officers. The remaining wreckage rapidly settled to the bottom of the harbour.

While McKinley urged patience and did not declare that Spain had caused the explosion, the deaths of so many Americans focused attention and fed into existing anti-Spanish prejudice.[18] There was a media firestorm. To appease such appalled public sentiment, McKinley asked Congress to appropriate $50 million to put the armed forces on a war footing, and Congress unanimously obliged. Spain appealed to the European powers, most of whom advised it to accept US conditions for Cuba's democratic and independent future in order to avoid war.[19] Throughout the negotiations, Britain, France and Russia generally supported the American position and urged Spain to give in. Spain repeatedly promised specific reforms that would pacify Cuba but failed to deliver.[20] Germany urged a united European stand against the US but took no action.[21]

The US Navy's investigation, made public on 28 March, concluded that the ship's powder magazines were ignited when an external explosion was set off under the ship's hull. This report poured fuel on popular indignation in the US, making war inevitable.[22] Spain's investigation came to the opposite conclusion: the explosion originated within the ship. Later inquiries vindicated that view, but at the time the competing parties had their own war-hungry agendas.[23]

Hearst and Pulitzer reported Spanish culpability in the sinking as cold, hard fact in their rival newspapers.[24] Both sensationalised often dubious accounts of 'atrocities' committed by the Spanish in Cuba. Headlines such as 'Spanish Murderers' and 'Remember the *Maine*' were commonplace. However, the actual influence of the new 'yellow journalism', confined almost exclusively to New York, remains hotly contested.[25] War fever was slow to start in a nation emerging from a series of economic slumps, and the uncertainties of warfare posed a serious threat to full economic recovery. 'War would impede the march of prosperity and put the country back many years,' warned the *New Jersey Trade Review*. The leading railroad magazine editorialised: 'From a commercial and mercenary standpoint it seems peculiarly bitter that this war should come when the country had already suffered so much and so needed rest and peace.' McKinley paid close attention to the strong anti-war consensus of the business community and strengthened his resolve to use diplomacy rather than brute force to end Spanish rule in Cuba. The *New York Journal's* crusade against Spanish rule in Cuba was not due to mere jingoism, although 'the democratic ideals and humanitarianism that inspired their coverage are largely lost to history,' as are their 'heroic efforts to find the truth on the island under unusually difficult circumstances.'[26]

The *Journal's* journalistic activism in support of the Cuban rebels, rather, was centred on Hearst's own political and business ambitions.

Hearst announced a reward of $50,000 'for the conviction of the criminals who sent 258 (*sic*) American sailors to their deaths.' The *New York World*, while overall not as lurid or as shrill in tone as the *Journal*, nevertheless indulged in similar theatrics, insisting continually that *Maine* had been bombed or mined. Privately, Pulitzer believed that 'nobody outside a lunatic asylum' really believed that Spain sanctioned *Maine's* destruction. Nevertheless, this did not stop the *World* from insisting that the only 'atonement' Spain could offer the US for the loss of ship and life was the granting of complete Cuban independence. Nor did it stop the paper from accusing Spain of 'treachery, willingness, or laxness' for failing to ensure the safety of Havana Harbour.[27]

While Hearst, Pulitzer and the yellow press did not directly cause America's war with Spain, they inflamed public opinion, especially the large working-class audience in New York City.[28] A powerful speech delivered by Republican senator Redfield Proctor of Vermont in March 1898 concluded that war was the only answer. Many in the business and religious communities, which had until then opposed war, switched sides, leaving McKinley almost alone in his reluctance to deploy military might.[29] The sinking of *Maine* served as a catalyst, accelerating the approach to a diplomatic impasse. On 11 April McKinley bowed to the inevitable and finally asked Congress for authority to send American troops to Cuba to end the civil war there. While Congress was deliberating, Republican senator Henry M. Teller of Colorado narrowly talked through an amendment to ensure that the US would not establish permanent control over Cuba after the war. The amended resolution demanded Spanish withdrawal and authorised the President to use as much military force as he thought necessary to help Cuba gain independence from Spain. McKinley signed the joint resolution on 20 April 1898, and the ultimatum was sent to Spain which severed diplomatic relations the next day as the US Navy began blockading Cuba. A state of war was declared by both sides on the 25th.[30]

US Undersecretary of War J. C. Breckenridge, in a memorandum to the Commander of the US Army, Lieutenant General Nelson A. Miles on 24 December 1897, stated that the Cuban people

> ... are indifferent to religion, and the majority are therefore immoral and simultaneously they have strong passions and are very sensual. Since they only possess a vague notion of what is right and wrong, the people tend to seek pleasure not through work, but through violence. As a logical consequence of this lack of morality, there is a great disregard for life. It is obvious that the immediate annexation of these disturbing elements into our own federation in such large numbers would be sheer madness, so before we do that we must clean up the country,

even if this means using the methods Divine Providence used on the cities of Sodom and Gomorrah. We must destroy everything within our cannons' range of fire. We must impose a harsh blockade so that hunger and its constant companion, disease, undermine the peaceful population and decimate the Cuban army. The allied army must be constantly engaged in reconnaissance and vanguard actions so that the Cuban army is irreparably caught between two fronts and is forced to undertake dangerous and desperate measures.

His memorandum added:

Once the Spanish regular troops are dominated and have withdrawn... we must create conflicts for the independent government. That government will be faced with these difficulties, in addition to the lack of means to meet our demands and the commitments made to us, war expenses and the need to organise a new country. These difficulties must coincide with the unrest and violence among the aforementioned elements, to whom we must give our backing. To sum up, our policy must always be to support the weaker against the stronger, until we have obtained the extermination of them both, in order to annex the Pearl of the Antilles.[31]

The navy was ready, but the under-supplied army was not. In the spring of 1898, the strength of the Regular Army was just 25,000 men. The army asked for 50,000 more but received over 220,000 through volunteers and the mobilisation of state National Guard units. New operational plans were hastily drawn up and new supply chains were established, much to the delight of avaricious suppliers who smelled a financial killing from the crisis.

Although freedom for Cuba was the stated target, the first shots of the war were fired half the world away in the Philippines. After 333 years of Spanish rule, the archipelago's educated classes had learnt the language of liberation from America and Europe. Filipino national hero Jose Rizal demanded larger reforms from the Spanish authorities. After a failed revolution, the exile of its leaders and an uneasy truce, there was at least the illusion of stability until April 1898 when it was reported that Spain expected Filipinos to join the coming war against the Americans.

Americans living on the Continental West Coast feared a Spanish attack at the outbreak of the war and became convinced that only a few US Navy warships, led Admiral George Dewey in the cruiser USS *Olympia*, stood between them and a powerful Spanish invasion fleet.[32] In fact, Admiral Montojo, a career Spanish naval officer who had been dispatched rapidly to the Philippines, was equipped with a variety of obsolete vessels. Spanish bureaucrats believed they could not win a war in the Pacific region and saw resistance as little more than a face-saving exercise. Administrative errors exacerbated Spanish war efforts – explosives meant for naval mines were sent instead to civilian construction companies while the Spanish fleet in Manila was seriously undermanned by inexperienced sailors who had not received any training for over a year. Reinforcements promised from Madrid resulted in only two poorly armoured scout cruisers being sent while at the same time the authorities transferred a squadron from the Manila fleet under Admiral Pascual Cervera to reinforce the Caribbean fleet. Admiral Montojo had originally wanted to confront the Americans at Subic Bay, northwest of Manila, but abandoned that idea when he learned the planned mines and coastal defensives were ineffective and the cruiser *Castilla* started to leak. Montojo placed his ships outside the range of Spanish coastal artillery, which might have evened the odds, and chose a relatively shallow anchorage, apparently intent on sparing Manila itself from bombardment and to allow any survivors of his fleet to swim to safety. The harbour was protected by six shore batteries and three forts whose fire during the battle proved to be almost useless. Only Fort San Antonio Abad had guns with enough range to reach the American fleet, but Dewey knew that and stayed away from the field of fire.[33]

The Spanish squadron consisted of seven ships of inferior quality to the American ships; the *Castilla* was unpowered and had to be towed by the transport ship *Manila*.[34] On 25 April, the squadron left Manila Bay and three days later heard reports that the Americans had left Hong Kong intent on the total destruction of their fleet.[35] At 7 p.m. on 30 April, Montojo was informed that Dewey's ships had been seen in Subic Bay that afternoon. As Manila Bay was considered unnavigable by foreigners at night, Montojo expected an attack the following morning. However, Oscar F. Williams, the US Consul in Manila, had provided Dewey with detailed information on the state of the Spanish defences and the lack of preparedness of the Spanish fleet. Based in part upon this intelligence, Dewey led his squadron into Manila Bay at midnight on 30 April.[36]

Larger ships normally used the north channel between Corregidor Island and the northern coast, and this was the only channel that was mined. Passing the entrance, two Spanish mines exploded but did little damage. Dewey then used the unmined south channel between El Fraile and Cabello Islands. The El Fraile battery fired a few rounds in the early hours of 1 May but the range was too great. The Cavite battery fired ranging shots, then the shore batteries and Spanish fleet opened fire but all the shells fell short. With the now famous phrase, 'You may fire when ready, Gridley', the *Olympia*'s captain was instructed by Dewey to begin the destruction of the Spanish flotilla. The US squadron swung in front of the Spanish ships and forts in line ahead, firing their port guns. They then turned and passed back, firing their starboard guns. This process was repeated five times, gradually closing the range from 5,000 yards to 2,000 yards. The Spanish forces were heavily outgunned. Eight Spanish ships, the land batteries, and the forts ineffectually returned fire for two and a half hours.

Montojo accepted that his cause was hopeless and ordered his ships to ram the enemy if possible. He then slipped the *Cristina's* cables and charged. His ship was shot to pieces. Of the crew of 400, more than 200, including Montojo, were either injured or killed and only two men were left to man her guns. The ship managed to return to shore and the injured Montojo ordered it to be scuttled. The *Castilla*, which only had guns on the port side, had her forward cable shot away, causing her to swing about, presenting her weaponless starboard side. The captain then ordered her sunk and abandoned. *Ulloa* was hit by a shell at the waterline that killed her captain and disabled half the crew. *Luzon* had three guns out of action. *Duero* lost an engine and had only one gun left in firing condition.

At 7.45 a.m., after Captain Gridley told Dewey that only fifteen rounds of 5-inch ammunition remained per gun, Dewey ordered an immediate withdrawal. He told his crew that it was to allow them to enjoy breakfast. A captains' conference on the Olympia revealed little damage and no men killed. It was discovered that the original ammunition message had been misread – instead of only fifteen rounds of ammunition per gun remaining, the message had meant to say only fifteen rounds of ammunition per gun had been expended. At 10.40 a.m. action was resumed but the Spanish offered little resistance, and Montojo issued orders for the remaining ships to be scuttled and the breechblocks of their guns taken ashore. *Olympia*, *Baltimore* and *Boston* then fired on the Sangley Point battery, putting it out of action, and followed up by sinking the heavily damaged *Ulloa* before she could be scuttled. *Concord* fired on the transport *Mindanao*, whose crew immediately abandoned ship. *Petrel* fired on the government offices next to the arsenal and a white flag was raised over the building after which all firing ceased. The Spanish colours were struck at 12:40 p.m.

Dewey won the battle with just nine men injured, and only a single fatality, Francis B. Randall, Chief Engineer on the McCulloch, from a heart attack. The Spanish later claimed that thirteen US crewmen were killed and thirty wounded, and that Dewey disguised the casualties by including their names among 155 who deserted during the short campaign.

A Spanish attempt to attack Dewey with the naval task force known as Cámara's Flying Relief Column failed and the naval war in the Philippines became a series of torpedo boat hit-and-run attacks. While the Spanish scored several hits, there were no American fatalities directly attributable to Spanish gunfire.

On 2 May, Dewey landed a force of marines at Cavite. They completed the destruction of the Spanish fleet and batteries and established a guard for the protection of the Spanish hospitals. The resistance of the forts was weak. *Olympia* turned a few guns on the Cavite arsenal, detonating its magazine, and ending the fire from the Spanish batteries. Dewey occupied Manila harbour,[37] which was filled with the warships of Britain,

Germany, France and Japan, but not the city. The German fleet of eight ships, ostensibly in Philippine waters to protect German interests, acted provocatively – cutting in front of American ships, refusing to salute the US flag, and landing supplies for the besieged Spanish harbour garrison. The Germans, with interests of their own, were eager to take advantage of whatever opportunities the conflict in the islands might afford[38] The Americans called the German bluff, threatening conflict if the aggression continued, and the Germans backed down.[39]

Elsewhere, on 20 June 1898, a US fleet under Captain Henry Glass, consisting of the cruiser USS *Charleston* and three transports carrying troops to the Philippines, entered Guam's Apra Harbour with previously sealed orders to capture it. *Charleston* fired a few rounds at Fort Santa Cruz without receiving return fire. Two local officials, not knowing that war had been declared and believing the firing had been a salute, came out to *Charleston* to apologise for their inability to return the salute as they were out of gunpowder.[40] The following day, Glass sent Lieutenant William Braunersruehter to meet the Spanish governor to arrange the surrender of the island and the Spanish garrison there. Some fifty-four Spanish infantry were captured and transported to the Philippines as prisoners of war.

Meanwhile, Commodore Dewey transported Emilio Aguinaldo, a Filipino leader who had led rebellion against Spanish rule in the Philippines in 1896, from exile in Hong Kong to rally more Filipinos against the Spanish colonial government. By 9 June, Aguinaldo's forces controlled most of the provinces and laid siege to Manila.[41] On 12 June, Aguinaldo proclaimed the independence of the Philippines. On 5 August, on instructions from Spain, Governor General Basilo Augustin turned over command of the Philippines to his deputy, Fermín Jáudenes.[42]

After his one-sided naval victory, Dewey mounted an effective blockade of Manila and waited for more land forces to arrive. The Eighth Army Corps, dubbed the Philippine Expeditionary Force, under the command of Major General Wesley Merritt, began sailing from San Francisco on 16 May, the vanguard under the command of Brigadier General Thomas Anderson.[43] That day the American consul in Hong Kong asking for advice on Spanish strength was told that the Spanish could field 21,000 men including 4,000 Filipinos.[44] Dewey, however, sent more accurate information: there were around 40,000 Spanish troops including around 16,000 Filipinos, about 15,000 of them in Manila itself, and nine artillery guns positioned around the city. By mid-June, some 40,000 Filipino revolutionaries under General Antonio Luna had dug 14 miles of trenches around Manila and seized control of its only pumping station, completely cutting off the water supply.[45]

The first contingent of American troops arrived in Cavite on 30 June, the second under General Francis Greene on 17 July, and the third under General Arthur MacArthur on 30 July, by which time 2,000 US troops had landed in the Philippines.[46]

Spanish Governor General Basilo Augustin initially refused American surrender terms, believing more Spanish troops would be sent to lift the siege,[47] but as the combined forces of Filipinos and Americans closed in, he realised that his position was hopeless. He opened negotiations and was promptly sacked by the Spanish Parliament. On 16 June, warships departed Spain to lift the siege, but they altered course for Cuba where the main Spanish fleet was under attack.[48] By August 1898, life in the walled centre of Manila had become intolerable. Refugees had swelled the normal population of 10,000 to around 70,000. Augustin's replacement as Governor General, Fermin Jáudenes, realised it was only a matter of time before the city fell, and feared vengeance and looting if the city fell to Filipino revolutionaries. Using the Belgian consul as a go-between, he suggested to Dewey that the city be surrendered to the Americans after a short 'mock' battle.

Military commanders were eager for action, but Dewey stalled while trying to work out a bloodless solution with Jáudenes.[49] Covert negotiations continued and it was agreed that Dewey would begin a bombardment at 9 p.m. on 13 August, shelling only the decrepit and unmanned Fort San Antonio Abad on the southern outskirts of Manila, and lobbing a few more shells at the impregnable citadel walls. Under the secret deal, Spanish forces would withdraw, and Filipino revolutionaries would be held back by US forces. Once a sufficient show of battle had been made, Dewey would hoist the signal 'D.W.H.B.' (meaning 'Do you surrender?),[50] whereupon the Spanish would hoist a white flag and Manila would formally surrender to the US alone.[51]

On 13 August 1898, with American commanders unaware that a peace protocol had been signed between Spain and the US the previous day, Dewey began his bombardment as scheduled. Dewey directed his ship captains to spare Manila any serious damage but gunners on one ship, unaware of the negotiated arrangements, scored several direct hits before their captain was able to cease firing and withdraw from the line.[52]

General Greene's brigade pushed rapidly through the Malate outskirts and over river bridges to occupy more districts, making good use of the new M1897 trench gun which was ideal for close combat. General MacArthur, advancing simultaneously on the Pasay road, encountered and overcame resistance at the blockhouses, trenches and woods to his front. Manila was in American hands apart from the citadel, which quickly raised the white flag.[53] Official surrender terms were swiftly agreed.

Although a bloodless mock battle had been planned, Spanish troops had opened fire in a skirmish which left six Americans and forty-nine Spaniards dead when Filipino revolutionaries, thinking that the attack was genuine, joined advancing US troops.[54] However, except for the unplanned casualties, the battle had gone according to plan; the Spanish had surrendered the city to the Americans, and it had not fallen to the Filipino revolutionaries.[55]

The fall of Manila brought about the end of the Spanish–American War in the Philippines, but also the end of Filipino–American collaboration, as the Americans' underhand tactics to deny them Manila was deeply resented.[56] This issue would in part lead to the far more deadly and costly war covered in the following chapter. The Filipinos felt betrayed by the Americans. They had looked on the Americans as aiding liberators against Spanish occupation. The Schurman Commission recommended that the US retain control of the Philippines, possibly granting independence in the future.[57]

In recognition of George Dewey's leadership during the Battle of Manila Bay, he was later promoted to the special rank of Admiral of the Navy – a rank that no one has held before or since. Building on his popularity, Dewey briefly ran for president in 1900, but withdrew and endorsed William McKinley, the incumbent, who won. The same year Dewey was appointed President of the General Board of the US Navy, where he would play a key role in the growth of the US Navy until his death in January 1917. His cynical betrayal of the Filipinos was airbrushed out of history.

* * *

The war's main action, inevitably, was in Cuba. As Assistant Secretary to the Navy, Theodore Roosevelt persuaded the US Army to raise an all-volunteer regiment, the 1st US Volunteer Cavalry, to be known as the 'Rough Riders', but US naval power would prove decisive, allowing expeditionary forces to disembark in Cuba against a Spanish garrison already facing nationwide Cuban insurgent attacks and further wasted by yellow fever.[58]

The largely volunteer army gathered in Florida ahead of embarkation, and the biggest transit camp was at the town of Lakeland, inland from Tampa. Private Charles Johnson Post, an artist-volunteer from New York, chronicled Lakeland camp life before embarking for Cuba, detailing the soldier's diet of coffee, hardtack and sowbelly, 'rancid and translucent in decay'; writing the practice drills in close order formation, 'much as in the days of Waterloo or Gettysburg'; puzzling over the area's alligators; and learning how to drive a mule team on the baggage carts. He went on: 'The sand made lovely beds, each shaped to the sleepers' figure before morning. There were six of us to a tent instead of four. Daytimes, the tent's side walls were rolled up after breakfast, so that each night the air in the tent was fresh, clean and fragrant with the incense of the pine grove.' He described cavalrymen, veterans of the frontier who had stepped out of a Frederick Remington painting:

> Lean, slit-eyed, hard-bitten men, who played Mexican monte or poker. Cards were no pastime here; they played for blood – and with blood sometimes. Once I saw a trooper reach for his knife, and a

half-dozen kibbutzers swarmed over him until he calmed down. They played in silence; with all the rigors of the game, eyes half-shut, cards close, and every sinew tense. But it was the teamsters, and the Ninth and Tenth Cavalry, the only Negro cavalry regiments, that taught us Northerners craps...[59]

Lakeland county had banned the sale of liquor on the principle of 'Plenty of bourbon for the white man, but no gin for the nigger', according to Post,[60] but there were plenty of ways to get around that. One was the establishment of 'ice cream parlours' selling 'General Robert E. Lee Milk Shake' and 'General Grant Ice Cream Soda' which gave a kick not dissimilar to bourbon.[61] A local sheriff complained that the townsfolk were disturbed by seeing black provost guards ordering white soldiers around. The sheriff told Post: 'It shore don't seem right for a niggra on a horse to be herdin' up white folk, even if they is in the army. Any you fellows ever punch the black bastard?'[62] Post also found that cans of bully beef had been filled with gristle and bone by Chicago meatpacking profiteers.

Drilling at Lakeland was old-school close formation – 'nice, formal, punctilios, and with every move to the singsong of a bugle'. Post noted wryly: 'It was half concert and half fight. Later at San Juan Hill, all of us, infantry and cavalry, went into action in close order. Columns of fours – a battle line in a clotted jungle of cowpaths ... We executed a "line-of-companies-on-left-front-into-line" in the unmapped, jungle meshed, unpatrolled, and unscouted no man's land. Fortunately, the Spaniards knew no more of what we were doing than we did ourselves.' Private Post, a pacifist at heart, wrote: 'This is war. Its payoff, its summation, is battle; and battle is bloody, cruel, merciless, and blind in its human destruction.' But he added: 'Together with Cromwell and Jefferson and Washington and Lincoln, I can believe in peace and yet realise that peace in this slow barbaric consciousness of our human era can only be preserved by battle. Peace can only be achieved through justice; and justice, so far, has to be fought for.'[63]

The Americans planned to capture the city of Santiago de Cuba to destroy the Spanish army's main division on the island and the anchored fleet. To reach Santiago they had to pass through concentrated Spanish defences in the San Juan Hills and in the small town of El Caney. The American forces were aided in Cuba by the pro-independence rebels led by General Calixto Garcia, who had considerable local support.[64]

On 25 June the American steamships *Fanita* and *Florida* accompanied by the gunboat USS *Peoria* left Key West carrying a cargo of troops, ammunition, supplies and arms to aid Cuban insurgents under Maximo Gomez. On board were 650 Cubans under General Emilio Gomez, 50 black US troopers of the Tenth Cavalry and twenty-five Rough Riders.[65] The first attempt to land took place on 29 June near the port of Cienfuegos, at the mouth of the

San Juan River, but the position was too heavily defended to risk a landing. The following day a landing party went ashore on a beachhead just west of Tunas de Zaza, near the mouth of the Tayacoba River.[66] Rowing onto the beach, the force crept into the jungle but was discovered by Spanish scouts and came under heavy fire. Unable to retaliate or even protect themselves, the Americans retreated onto the beach only to find that their boats had been sunk by Spanish cannon fire. Cuban insurgent Captain Núñez died of a gunshot wound to the head,[67] and two American officers and five Cuban soldiers were wounded. The party took cover in a mangrove swamp and one of them, a German surgeon named Dr Maximilian Lund, naked and armed only with a knife to fend off sharks, swam out to the *Peoria*, to report their predicament.[68] *Peoria* fired at Spanish troops hidden behind a grove of coconut palms. The first four rescue attempts from the *Florida* were repulsed by heavy enemy fire, but the fifth, operating in darkness and crewed by four cavalrymen under the command of Lieutenant Ahern, successfully located the landing party survivors and took them to safety. The body of Captain Núñez was left on the beach.

From 22 to 24 June, the Fifth Army Corps under General William R. Shafter landed at Daiquiri and Siboney, east of Santiago, and established an American base of operations. A contingent of Spanish troops, having fought a skirmish with the Americans near Siboney on 23 June, had retired to their lightly entrenched positions at Las Guasimas. An advance guard of US forces under former Confederate General Joseph Wheeler ignored Cuban scouting parties and orders to proceed with caution. They caught up with and engaged the Spanish rear guard of about 2,000 soldiers led by General Antero Rubin who effectively ambushed them on 24 June. In the heat of the battle, Wheeler apparently forgot for a moment which war he was fighting, calling out: 'Let's go, boys! We've got the damn Yankees on the run again!'

The US Army employed Civil War era skirmishers at the head of the four advancing columns, but the Spanish troops had learned the art of cover and concealment during their long campaigns against Cuban insurgents. The Americans advanced by rushes and stayed in the weeds so that they, too, were largely invisible to the Spaniards who used untargeted volley fire. While some troops were hit, this technique was mostly a waste of bullets as the Americans learned to duck as soon as they heard '*Fuego*', the Spanish word for 'Fire,' yelled by the Spanish officers. Spanish troops were equipped with smokeless powder-loaded Mauser rifles with high-speed rounds termed the 'Spanish Hornet' by the Americans because of the supersonic crack as they passed overhead. The battle ended indecisively, but slightly in favour of Spain. Three of the US volunteers walking point at the head of the American columns were killed, including Captain Allyn Capron, whom Theodore Roosevelt would describe as one of the finest natural leaders and soldiers he ever met. Only Oklahoma Territory Pawnee Indian Tom Isbell survived, albeit wounded seven times.[69]

Spanish General Arsenio Linares ordered up to 1,275 Spanish Army regular troops to hold the San Juan heights and ridge against an American offensive on 1 July. For unclear reasons, Linares failed to reinforce this position, choosing to hold nearly 10,000 Spanish reserves in the city of Santiago de Cuba. Spanish hilltop entrenchments, while typically well-concealed, were laid out along the geographic crest of the heights instead of the military crest. Most Spanish troops were recently arrived conscripts, but their officers were skilled in fighting Cuban insurgents. The Spanish were well equipped with supporting artillery, and all Spanish soldiers were armed with 7 mm Mauser M1893 rifles, a modern repeating bolt-action weapon with a high rate of fire that used high-velocity cartridges and smokeless powder. Spanish artillery units were armed mainly with modern rapid-fire breech-loading cannon, again using smokeless powder.[70]

The American regular forces and troopers were armed with bolt-action Krag rifles chambered in the smokeless .30 army calibre. However, US 3.2-inch artillery pieces were of an outmoded design, with a slow rate of fire due to bag powder charges and lack of a recoil mechanism. They also used less powerful black powder charges, which limited the effective range of support fire for troops. The Americans also had a four-gun Gatling Gun Detachment commanded by Lieutenant John Henry Parker. Although these guns were hand cranked, they were nevertheless capable of 700 rounds per minute or more in continuous fire and were equipped with swivel mounts to allow greater field of fire coverage.

General Shafter's Fifth Army Corps totalled about 15,000 troops in three divisions under Jacob Kent, Henry Lawton and Samuel Sumner. Shafter's plans of attack called for Lawton's division to move north and reduce the Spanish stronghold at El Caney, a task which was optimistically expected to take about two hours. Then they were to join with the rest of the troops for the attack on the San Juan Heights. The remaining two divisions would move directly against the heights, with Sumner in the centre and Kent to the south. Shafter, too ill to personally direct the operations, set up his headquarters 2 miles from the heights and communicated via mounted staff officers.

A company from the Signal Corps ascended in a hot air balloon to reconnoitre the hills but it merely made a good target for the Spaniards. A brigade under Colonel Charles Wikoff began heading down the trail at noon, and thirty minutes later Wikoff was struck by a Mauser bullet. He died as his staff officers carried him to the rear. Lieutenant Colonel William S. Worth, next in rank, assumed command, but within five minutes fell wounded. Lieutenant Colonel Emerson Liscom assumed command and within another five minutes received a disabling wound. Lieutenant Colonel Ezra P. Ewers, fourth in command of the brigade, assumed command. Kent and Sumner lined up for the attack and waited for Lawton's division to arrive from El Caney. Lawton did not arrive as scheduled, and no orders came from either Shafter or Wheeler. The troops waited at the base of the hill, plagued by constant Spanish Mauser gunfire in areas dubbed 'Hell's Pocket' or 'Bloody Ford'.

In the meantime, General Hamilton Hawkins' 1st Infantry Brigade was preparing to assault San Juan Hill, the higher of the two hilltops forming San Juan heights. The southernmost point was most recognisable for the Spanish blockhouse, a defensive fort that dominated the crest. In open view of the Spanish positions on the heights, the Americans suffered casualties while awaiting orders from General Shafter. As the volume of rifle and artillery fire increased, officers began to agitate for action.

The 2nd and 10th Infantry regiments were ordered by the brigade commander, Colonel E. P. Pearson, to advance towards the Spanish lines. Positioned on the far left of the American line, the two regiments moved forward in good order, advanced towards a small knoll on the Spanish right flank and drove groups of Spanish skirmishers back towards their trenches. A former brigade staff officer, First Lieutenant Jules Garesche Ord, the son of a general, appealed to General Hawkins: 'General, if you will order a charge, I will lead it.' Hawkins responded, 'I will not ask for volunteers, I will not give permission and I will not refuse it,' he said. 'God bless you and good luck!' Ord then asked the leaders to the right of the 10th Cavalry (members of the 3rd and 1st Volunteers) to 'support the regulars' when they charged the heights. With a sword in one hand and a pistol in the other, Ord stood up and ordered the advance of his unit. The Buffalo Soldiers of the dismounted 10th Cavalry moved out of the trenches and up the hill. Units to the right began moving forward in a ripple effect to support the regulars. To the left of the 10th, a cheer went out from members of the 24th all-black Infantry Regiment, and they too moved toward the top of the heights.[71]

The Gatling Gun Detachment, originally conceived to offer protection to the baggage train, was ordered to move forward in support of the assault, and Lieutenant John Parker received orders from his colonel to detach one gun to General Shafter's aide, Lieutenant John D. Miley, then to take the remaining three guns forward 'to the best point you can find'.[72] Parker set up his three Gatlings 600 yards from the San Juan Hill blockhouse and its surrounding trenches, occupied by Spanish regulars. Dangerously exposed, the Detachment soon came under attack and quickly lost five men to wounds and others to severe heat stroke. Ordinarily, four to six men were required to operate each Gatling gun, but the skeleton crews rose to the occasion.[73] Equipped with swivel mountings that enabled the gunners to rake Spanish positions, the three guns poured a continuous and demoralising hail of bullets into the Spanish defences. Many of the defenders fled.[74] The Gatlings continued to fire until an American infantry officer waved a white handkerchief as a signal for the battery to cease to avoid causing friendly fire casualties. The American assault then broke into a charge about 150 yards from the crest of the hill.[75]

Ord was among the first to reach the crest of San Juan heights. As the Spanish fled, Ord directed supporting fire into the remaining Spanish until he was mortally wounded by a shot to the throat. At 13.50, Private Arthur Agnew of the 13th Infantry pulled down the Spanish flag atop the San Juan blockhouse.[76] General Wood sent requests for General Kent to send up infantry to strengthen his vulnerable position. When General Wheeler reached the trenches, he ordered breastworks constructed.

The Rough Riders of the 1st US Volunteer Cavalry under Theodore Roosevelt, with the 3rd Cavalry Regiment, began a near simultaneous assault supporting the regulars of the 10th Cavalry up Kettle Hill, also supported by the fire from Parker's Gatlings. Trooper Jesse D. Langdon reported: 'We were exposed to the Spanish fire, but there was very little because just before we started, why, the Gatling guns opened up at the bottom of the hill... and away we went. The Gatlings just enfiladed the top of those trenches. We'd never have been able to take Kettle Hill if it hadn't been for Parker's Gatling guns.' During the battle, Parker's Gatlings expended approximately 18,000 rounds in eight and a half minutes (over 700 rounds per minute of continuous fire) into the Spanish defensive lines, disrupting the aim of any still alive who continued to resist. Roosevelt himself later gave much of the credit for the successful capture of the Spanish positions to Parker's inventive use of his Gatling Gun Detachment: 'I think Parker deserved rather more credit than any other one man in the entire campaign ... he had the rare good judgment and foresight to see the possibilities of the machine guns. He then, by his own exertions, got it to the front and proved that it could do invaluable work on the field of battle, as much in attack as in defense.' Roosevelt observed that the hammering sound of the guns raised the spirits of his men: 'While thus firing, there suddenly smote on our ears a peculiar drumming sound. One or two of the men cried out, "The Spanish machine guns!" but, after listening a moment, I leaped to my feet and called, "It's the Gatlings, men! Our Gatlings!" Immediately the troopers began to cheer lustily, for the sound was most inspiring.'[77]

Reporter Richard Harding Davis witnessed the charge:

Colonel Roosevelt, on horseback, broke from the woods behind the line of the Ninth, and finding its men lying in his way, shouted: 'If you don't wish to go forward, let my men pass, please.' The junior officers of the Ninth, with their Negroes, instantly sprang into line with the Rough Riders, and charged at the blue blockhouse on the right. Roosevelt, mounted high on horseback, and charging the rifle pits at a gallop and quite alone, made you feel that you would like to cheer. He wore on his sombrero a blue polka-dot handkerchief, a la Havelock, which, as he advanced, floated out straight behind his head, like a guidon. Afterward, the men of his regiment who followed this flag, adopted a polka-dot handkerchief as the badge of the Rough Riders.

I think the thing which impressed one the most, when our men started from cover, was that they were so few. It seemed as if someone had made an awful and terrible mistake. One's instinct was to call them to come back. You felt that someone had blundered and that these few men were blindly following out some madman's mad order. It was not heroic then, it seemed merely terribly pathetic. The pity of it, the folly of such a sacrifice was what held you.

They had no glittering bayonets, they were not massed in regular array. There were a few men in advance, bunched together, and creeping up a steep, sunny hill, the top of which roared and flashed with flame. The men held their guns pressed across their breasts and stepped heavily as they climbed. Behind these first few, spreading out like a fan, were single lines of men, slipping and scrambling in the smooth grass, moving forward with difficulty, as though they were wading waist high through water, moving slowly, carefully, with strenuous effort. It was much more wonderful than any swinging charge could have been. They walked to greet death at every step, many of them, as they advanced, sinking suddenly or pitching forward and disappearing in the high grass, but the others waded on, stubbornly, forming a thin blue line that kept creeping higher and higher up the hill. It was as inevitable as the rising tide. It was a miracle of self-sacrifice, a triumph of bulldog courage, which one watched breathless with wonder. The fire of the Spanish riflemen, who still stuck bravely to their posts, doubled and trebled in fierceness, the crests of the hills crackled and burst in amazed roars, and rippled with waves of tiny flame. But the blue line crept steadily up and on, and then, near the top, the broken fragments gathered together with a sudden burst of speed, the Spaniards appeared for a moment outlined against the sky and poised for instant flight, fired a last volley and fled before the swift-moving wave that leaped and sprang up after them.

The men of the Ninth and the Rough Riders rushed to the blockhouse together, the men of the Sixth, of the Third, of the Tenth Cavalry, of the Sixth and Sixteenth Infantry, fell on their faces along the crest of the hills beyond, and opened upon the vanishing enemy. They drove the yellow silk flags of the cavalry and the Stars and Stripes of their country into the soft earth of the trenches, and then sank down and looked back at the road they had climbed and swung their hats in the air. And from far overhead, from these few figures perched on the Spanish rifle pits, with their flags planted among the empty cartridges of the enemy, and overlooking the walls of Santiago, came, faintly, the sound of a tired, broken cheer.[78]

Under continuous fire, the advance slowed as troops dropped from heat exhaustion. Officers from the rest of Wood's brigade, along with Carroll's, bunched up under fire. When the regulars of the Buffalo Soldiers punched toward the top of the hill, the units became intermingled. One of the 10th's officers who took part in the attack, 1st Lieutenant John 'Black Jack' Pershing, would later reach the highest rank ever held by a living officer— General of the Armies of the United States. Pershing later recalled that

> ... the entire command moved forward as coolly as though the buzzing of bullets was the humming of bees. White regiments, black regiments, regulars and Rough Riders [i.e. volunteers], representing the young manhood of the North and the South, fought shoulder to shoulder, unmindful of race or color, unmindful of whether commanded by ex-Confederate or not, and mindful of only their common duty as Americans.

Although Roosevelt and the Rough Riders achieved considerable fame with the victory, Ord never received recognition for his actions; the army turned down] requests for a medal for his heroism from his commanding officer and his commanding general.

When the 10th, 3rd, and 1st Volunteers reached the summit of Kettle Hill, they briefly fought hand to hand within the defensive works before the Spanish retreated. The first American soldier to reach the crest of Kettle Hill was Sergeant George Berry of the 10th who carried the Cavalry battle flags to the summit.

After the Spanish positions on San Juan had been taken, two of Parker's Gatling guns were dragged by mules up the slope to the captured position on San Juan ridge, where both were hurriedly emplaced among a line of skirmishers. As the Americans were setting up the guns, the Spanish commenced a general counterattack on the heights. Though the attack on San Juan was quickly broken up, the men on Kettle Hill faced a more serious attack from some 120 Spanish regulars. Ignoring an order from Colonel Leonard Wood to reposition one or two of his Gatling guns to the top of Kettle Hill to support the 1st Volunteer and 3rd Cavalry, Parker instead ordered the closest Gatling, manned by Sergeant Green, to fire obliquely against 600 enemy soldiers attacking Kettle Hill. From a range of 600 yards, Green's Gatling responded, killing scores of the attackers.[79]

After the counterattack was driven off, Parker moved to Kettle Hill to view the American positions, where he was soon joined by Sergeant Weigle's Gatling and crew from San Juan who had been prevented by order from joining the previous action. Parker then ordered Weigle and his crew to emplace their gun on Kettle Hill. This Gatling was used to eliminate Spanish sniper fire against the American defensive positions.[80] Returning to the two Gatlings on San Juan Hill, Parker had the guns relocated near the road to avoid counter-battery fire. Despite this precaution, the guns were bombarded by a heavy Spanish 6.3-inch gun.

Parker located the enemy gun and trained the two Gatlings using a powerful set of field glasses. They opened fire, silencing the Spanish gun at a range of roughly 2,000 yards.

On 4 July, Parker ordered his three operational guns moved into the battle line around the city of Santiago. The wheels of the Gatling carriages were removed, and the Gatlings, along with two 7 mm Colt–Browning machine guns (a personal gift from Roosevelt) were placed in breastworks where they could command various sectors of fire. Lawton's division, which was supposed to have joined the fight early, did not arrive until noon the following day, having encountered unexpectedly heavy resistance in the Battle of El Caney.

At El Caney, 514 Spanish regular soldiers, with around 100 armed Spanish and Cubans loyal to Spain under the command of General Joaquin Vara del Rey y Rubio, were instructed to hold the northwest flank of Santiago. The Spanish regular infantry was armed with fast-firing Mauser rifles, while the loyalists were equipped with single shot, black powder Remingtons.[81] Denied promised reinforcements from Santiago, Vara de Rey and his forces held over 6,000 Americans from their position for nearly twelve hours before retreating, preventing General Lawton's men from reinforcing the US assault on San Juan Hill. Some of the American forces were hindered by their equipment; in the case of the 2nd Massachusetts, the men were equipped with antiquated single shot Springfield rifles. According to Frederick E. Pierce, a trooper of the 2nd Massachusetts, the Americans 'received such a shower of bullets that it seemed at one time as if the company must be wiped out of existence.'[80]

The American forces also lacked effective support fire, as the Gatling Gun Detachment was busy elsewhere, as we have seen. General Lawton's artillery support consisted of a single battery of four 3.2-inch field guns—light breech-loading rifled cannon using black-powder ammunition. The relatively short range of the American gun battery—with the signature cloud of black smoke generated with each volley—forced gun crews to endure a fusillade of Mauser rifle fire from the Spanish defenders. But during the fighting, General Vara del Rey was wounded in both legs. While being evacuated on a stretcher, he and several of his officers were killed by American fire. Despite Vara del Rey's death, Spanish resistance continued.

Lawton ordered his battery to concentrate fire on the El Viso blockhouse and they successfully breached the walls at a range of 1,000 yards. The 12th and the 25th infantry regiments attacked and after a bloody firefight, the blockhouse was captured. The US battery then reduced each Spanish strongpoint in turn.[83] About 185 Spanish escaped to the north, leaving the bodies of Vara del Rey, his two sons and his brother. Though eventually successful, the attack on the fortifications of El Caney had proved to be of little real value. The attack on strongly defended points resulted in delays and additional casualties.

Approximately 400–600 of the retreating Spanish defenders at El Caney later participated in the counterattack on Kettle Hill and were among those wiped out by Sergeant Green's Gatling.[84]

After the Battles of San Juan Hill and El Caney, the American advance halted. Spanish troops successfully defended Fort Canosa, allowing them to stabilise their line and bar the entry to Santiago. The Americans and Cubans began a bloody, strangling siege of the city. During the nights, Cuban troops dug successive series of raised parapets facing the Spanish positions. Once completed, these parapets were occupied by US soldiers and a new set of excavations went forward. American troops, while suffering daily losses from Spanish fire, suffered far more casualties from heat exhaustion, dysentery and mosquito-borne disease. At the western approaches to the city, Cuban general Calixto Garcia began to encroach on the city, causing much panic and fear of reprisals among the Spanish forces.

Lieutenant Carter P. Johnson of the 10th Cavalry, the former head of scouts during the Apache wars, chose fifty soldiers from the regiment to lead a deployment mission with at least 375 Cuban soldiers under Cuban Brigadier General Emilio Nunez and other supplies to the mouth of the San Juan River east of Cienfuegos. A reconnaissance team in landing boats from the transports *Florida* and *Fanita* attempted to land on the beach but were repelled by Spanish fire. A second attempt was made the following day, but a team of reconnaissance soldiers was trapped on the beach near the mouth of the Tallabacoa River. Four soldiers saved them and were awarded Medals of Honor. USS *Peoria* and the recently arrived USS *Helena* then shelled the beach to distract the Spanish while the Cuban deployment landed 40 miles east at Palo Alto, where they linked up with Cuban General Gomez.[85]

US artillery on the heights pounded Santiago, while the US and Cuban ground forces choked off all water and food supplies. However, a relief column was able to fight its way through Garcia's rebels and into the city, bringing the defence force to 13,500. On 4 July, a ceasefire was enacted to evacuate roughly 20,000 citizens from the city. The same day, the four Gatlings were moved to Fort Canosa in support of the siege, as was a dynamite gun and sixteen field guns. Over the next thirteen days, the Gatlings were used to fire 6,000 to 7,000 rounds, causing many casualties.[86]

A two-day truce and surrender negotiations came to nothing and Shafter was now pressed for time as yellow fever swept his ranks. Shafter and the US Navy continued to bomb the city with little effect militarily. General Miles arrived on 11 July with several regiments, eight field guns and eight light mortars. Everyone involved wanted a quick end to the campaign, and at 9 a.m. on 13 July the Americans proposed capitulation and the repatriation of the garrison to Spain. The Spanish commander agreed, allegedly after an American doctor and interpreter had plied him with a bottle of rye whiskey. On 16 July, the Spanish surrendered the garrison and all troops in the Division of Santiago, an additional 9,000 soldiers. The Spanish also ceded Guantanamo City and San Luis. By then a major offshore American victory had sealed the deal.

The port of Santiago de Cuba had throughout been the main target of US naval operations. The US fleet needed shelter from the summer hurricane season and Guantanamo Bay, with its excellent harbour, was chosen as the haven from which to attack Santiago. Between 6 and 10 June, a force of marines was landed with naval support.

Meanwhile, Admiral Pascual Cervera y Topete's squadron of four armoured cruisers and three torpedo boat destroyers were sent from Cape Verde to the war zone.[87] From the start Cervera believed his squadron lacked the strength necessary to engage the Americans, preferring instead to engage them near the Canary Islands or to mount an attack against the American coast, but he was overruled by his superiors in Madrid.[88] Cervera wrote: 'It is impossible for me to give you an idea of the surprise and consternation experienced by all on the receipt of the order to sail. Indeed, that surprise is well justified, for nothing can be expected of this expedition except the total destruction of the fleet or its hasty and demoralised return.'[89]

On 29 April, Cervera steamed from Cape Verde. He evaded the US fleet for several weeks before seeking refuge in the harbour of Santiago de Cuba. On 29 May, an American squadron sighted Cervera's newest ship, the cruiser *Cristóbal Colón*, and immediately established a blockade around the mouth of the harbour.[90] The Spanish cruisers were not heavily armoured and were out-gunned by the Americans.[91] The breech mechanisms in many of the Spanish guns were dangerously faulty, causing jams and other mishaps. Many of the ships' boilers were in need of repair; several ships desperately needed bottom cleaning as they were suffering from extra drag, while the *Cristóbal Colón* had not even had her main battery installed and carried wooden dummy guns instead. Cervera's crews were poorly trained, lacking experience in seamanship and practice in gunnery drills.

The primary elements of the American forces in Cuban waters were initially divided between two commands: Rear Admiral William T. Sampson of the North Atlantic Squadron and Commodore Winfield Schley, commanding the 'Flying Squadron'. The American fleet was composed of many different types of vessels. At the head of the fleet were Sampson's armoured cruiser USS *New York* and Schley's USS *Brooklyn*, both well-armed for their class. The primary firepower was in the battleships USS *Indiana*, USS *Massachusetts*, USS *Iowa* and USS *Texas*, all fast, modern, steam-powered and steel-hulled vessels built within the decade, armed with 13-inch guns. Off Santiago, Schley's 'Flying Squadron' was merged into the larger fleet under Sampson's overall command.

To bolster this force, the battleship USS *Oregon* sailed from California to join the fleet in the Caribbean. The 'West Coast's lone battleship' steamed from San Francisco around Cape Horn to Key West to join the rest of Sampson's fleet in early May, a 14,500-nautical-mile journey completed in sixty-six days.[92] Its combined speed and firepower gave *Oregon* the nickname 'bulldog of the Navy'. Other vessels included torpedo boats, light cruisers, and even a collier which was scuttled to help blockade the Spanish fleet.[93] Sampson structured the blockade as a semi-circle at the opening of the harbour. An auxiliary ship floated around the edges waiting to be used in case a forced entrance was necessary and a torpedo boat was stationed further off the front line.

For the Americans, blockade duty proved long, gut-wrenchingly tedious and unremitting.[94] During the day, the blockade stationed constant lookouts. During the night, a battleship shone a searchlight on the entrance of the harbour in case the Spanish fleet attempted an escape under the cover of darkness. This chore was repeated daily for nearly two months.

As long as Cervera remained within Santiago Harbour, his fleet was relatively safe. Cervera was content to wait, hoping for bad weather to scatter the Americans so that he could make a run to a position more favourable for engaging the enemy. However, when US land forces began to drive on to the city by the end of June, Captain General Ramon Blanco y Erenas, the top military commander in Cuba, ordered the squadron out along the coast westward to Cienfuegos, stating, 'it is better for the honor of our arms that the squadron perish in battle ...' Fatally, Cervera opted to sail by day to ensure the safe navigation of his ships through Santiago's narrow channel. On Sunday 3 July Cervera boarded his flagship *Infanta Maria Teresa* to lead the Spanish fleet out into hostile waters at seven-minute intervals.

Cervera told his fleet just before they set off:

The solemn moment has arrived to fight. This is what the sacred name of Spain and the honor of its glorious flag demands of us. I wanted you to attend this appointment with the enemy with me, wearing the dress uniform. I know that this order is strange, because it is improper in combat, but these are the clothes that the sailors of Spain dressed in in great solemnities, and I do not believe that there is more time in the life of a soldier than that in which he dies for the Homeland. The enemy codes our old and glorious hulks. For this he has sent against us all the might of his young squadron. But only the splinters of our ships will be able to take, and only snatch our weapons when, corpses, we float on these waters, which have been and are from Spain. My sons! The enemy surpasses us in the forces, but it does not equal us in value. Nail the flags and not a single prisoner! Endowment of my squad: Long live Spain! Battle stations, and may the Lord welcome our souls!

Just as his ships slipped their moorings at 8.45 a.m., Admiral Sampson and two ships of his command left their positions for a meeting with General Shafter, while the battleship *Massachusetts* and the cruisers *Newark* and *New Orleans* had already left to coal at Guantanamo Bay. This opened a gap in the western portion of the American blockade line, now in the immediate command of Schley in the *Brooklyn*. At 9.35 a.m., the navigator of *Brooklyn* sighted a plume of smoke coming from the mouth of the port and reported to Schley: 'The enemy's ships are coming out!' In the lead was Cervera's flagship *Infanta Maria Teresa*, followed by *Vizcaya*, *Cristóbal Colón*, *Almirante Oquendo*, travelling at around 8 knots, followed by the torpedo boat destroyers *Plutón* and *Furor.*

The battle swiftly began. At the mouth of the harbour, *Texas*, *Iowa*, *Oregon*, and *Indiana* engulfed the Spanish fleet in a 'hail of fire'.[95] The Spanish responded, supported by the batteries on Morro and Upper Socapa. After leaving the channel, the Spanish vessels took the initiative and turned westward in column towards the American fleet.[96] But their ships made slow progress due to the poor quality of their coal – an expected re-supply of high-quality anthracite had been captured a week earlier. After much confusion which almost saw American battleships collide, the two squadrons paralleled each other. *Oregon*, initially to the rear of the action but the fastest ship in the US fleet, soon raced past *Indiana*, which had an engine problem. *Iowa* had started from a disadvantaged position and was passed by *Infanta Maria Teresa* but hit her with two 12-inch rounds from 2,600 yards and swung into the chase.

Seaman W.J. Murphy, on *Iowa*, gave an account:

At 9:31 A.M., the Marie Tressa was sighted and at 9:34, she opened up with her forward 11 inch gun at the same instant the forts on either side chimed in with guns and mortars but they were a side issue now and were hardly thought of. Nearer our leading ships steamed towards each other and as the Spanish flag ship swung to the westward, the Oregon opened with a 13 inch shell from her forward tunnell. We were nearest to the enemy but held our fire for close quarters, 3000 yds. 2000 yds, and 1000 yds. was called out from the range finders in the upper top and then is when we headed for the center of the enemy's fleet turning at the same time with a starboard helm so as to bring our ship on a broadsides to and in the same direction our main battery opened fire and our shells could be seen tearing the flag ship to pieces while her projectiles fell harmlessly around us: the smoke had surrounded all the ships by this time and the leaders were lost sight of for an instant...[97]

As *Iowa* was passed in turn by *Cristóbal Colón*, the Spanish ship hit her with two shots from her secondary battery. One of these struck near the waterline and caused *Iowa* to slow and she therefore engaged

Almirante Oquendo, bringing up the rear of Cervera's four cruisers. With the Spanish fleet past the American blockade, the battle became a chase.

Cervera signalled his other ships to continue to the southwest while he attempted to cover their escape, directly engaging *Brooklyn*, his nearest enemy. Though *Brooklyn* was hit more than twenty times during the battle, she suffered only two casualties, while her return fire resulted in the deaths of most of Cervera's bridge crew and grave damage to the ship. *Infanta Maria Teresa* began to burn furiously.[98] Cervera ordered her aground in coastal shallows. He survived the beaching and was picked up near Punta Cabrera by the crew of *Gloucester*.

The rest of the Spanish fleet continued its race for the open sea. *Almirante Oquendo* was hit fifty-seven times and was driven out of the battle by the premature detonation of a shell stuck in a defective breech-block mechanism of an 11-inch turret, which killed the entire gun crew. A boiler explosion finished her, and she was ordered scuttled by her mortally wounded Captain Lazaga. *Almirante Oquendo* ran aground less than a mile away, *Plutón* and *Furor* made a dash in a direction opposite the rest of the Spanish squadron but were hit by close-range intensive fire from *Gloucester* and they were finished off by the battleships. By late morning Sampson turned his flagship *New York* around and raced to join the fight. *Furor* was sunk before making the beach while *Pluton* succeeded in grounding. The two Spanish destroyers lost two-thirds of their men.

Vizcaya was locked in a running gun duel for nearly an hour with *Brooklyn*. The Spanish ship fired nearly 300 shots, which caused almost no damage; later research suggested that nearly 85 per cent of the Spanish ammunition at Santiago was utterly useless, either defective or simply filled with sawdust as a cost-saving measure for practice.

Murphy continued:

> The *Vizcya* was seen next and the fire of our guns was directed on the pride of the Spanish Navy. The scene by this time became almost infernal for the ships were in close quarters and the roar of the big guns and the popping of the rapid fire and the shriek of the departing and arriving shells made conversation an impossibility. About this time, we were struck several times, one shell coming in through our forward berth deck smashing things up as it busted and riddled our starboard chain locker. Another imbedded itself in the cofferdam at the water line where it remains yet presumably unexploded. Our armor belt and quarter deck received several shells but the damage is hardly apparent. Soon the smoke was so dense that the fight went on in a Dony-brook Fair fashion where as soon as you see a head, hit it for it was impossible to see what ship you were firing at. The *Iowa* forging ahead out of the smoke saw the *Vizcya* and *Colon* ahead but as two other ships of our fleet were with them, Cap Bob turned his attention to the other two for it seemed the *Marie Tressa* being disable in the first part of the

battle had dropped to the rear with the *Oqunda* and now the cry from
the top was heard repel torpedo attack on the starboard quarters. It
seemed that the destroyers had lain back until the canopy of smoke
enclosed the ships and they had darted forward on the *Iowa* to lance
her while she was blind but luckily the smoke rose a little and then as
the rapid fire guns turned on them, they were literally torn to pieces
and to complete the work the *Gloucester* steamed straight for them and
the destroyers were now the destroyed, riddled with shell and shrapnel
with their boilers exploded and their crews shot, scalded or drowned.
They ran along side of the beach but greater events were happening
all this time for we now had the *Oqunda* and *Marie Tressa* on fire in
several places with their torn sides and stem exposed and the smoke
rising from a dozen places. The first cheer went up from the parched
throats of the crew. Being assured by this voluntary stranding of the
enemy's two ships that they could be counted out of the affair, we next
turned our attention to the *Vizcya* which was evidently trying to follow
in the wake of the *Colon* but seeing she could not resist the storm of
iron which fell around her, she imitated the *Oqunda* & *Tressa* and
turned for the land. But the rain of shell never ceased for we were in a
position now to rake her fore and aft and as the *Iowa* drew in close to
the shore line, the Flag of the *Vizcaya* could be seen coming down from
her main mast. The ships company when they witnessed the first ship
of the enemy strike her colors expended all their remaining energy in a
wild cheer which must have grated harshly on the ears of the defeated
survivors around the ill fated ship. Here ended the fight for the *Oregon*,
Brookline and *Texas* were chasing the *Colon* and it could be seen that
her capture was but a matter of time and distance. [99]

The *Brooklyn* had pounded *Vizcaya* with devastating fire. *Vizcaya*
continued the fight until overwhelmed, and by the end of the engagement
she had been struck as many as 200 times. The last round detonated a
torpedo being prepared for launch, sparking a huge explosion which in
turn set off reserves of ammunition on her deck. She hauled down her
flag and was grounded on the beach. The *Iowa*, *Ericsson*, and *Hist* aided
the crew of the burning *Vizcaya*, while other Americans braved their own
lives by rescuing surviving crew of *Infanta Maria Teresa* and *Almirante
Oquendo* in what later proved to be some of the most valiant American
actions performed that day.

Within a little more than an hour, five of the six ships of the Spanish
Caribbean Squadron had been destroyed or forced aground. Only one
vessel, the speedy new armoured cruiser *Cristóbal Colón*, still survived,
steaming for freedom. Though modern in every respect and possibly the
fastest ship in either fleet, *Cristóbal Colón* had one serious problem:
She had been only recently purchased from Italy, and her main 10-inch
armament was not yet installed because of a contractual issue with the

British firm of Armstrong. She therefore sailed with empty main turrets, albeit retaining her ten 6-inch secondary battery. This day, speed was her primary defence.

By the time *Vizcaya* was beached, *Cristóbal Colón* was nearly 6 miles beyond *Brooklyn* and *Oregon*. At her best rate of nearly 15 knots, she slowly distanced herself from the pursuing US fleet. As *Brooklyn* ineffectively fired 8-inch rounds at the rapidly disappearing vessel, there was only one ship in the US fleet with a chance of maintaining the pursuit, *Oregon*, which it did for sixty-five minutes. The Spaniard ran out of high-quality Cardiff coal and was forced to begin using an inferior grade obtained from Spanish reserves in Cuba, a coastal peninsula forced her to turn, and two shells fired at immense range from *Oregon* fell close by. Given the spectacular and highly visible fate of the *Vizcaya,* Captain Jose de Paredes decided that there was no point in seeing his crew needlessly killed, abruptly turned the undamaged *Cristóbal Colón* toward the mouth of the Turquino River and ordered the scuttle valves opened and the colours struck as she grounded.[100] Captain Cook of *Brooklyn* went on board to receive the surrender with orders to save her if possible. Despite all efforts, *Cristóbal Colón* sank in shoal water. As the ships of the US fleet pushed through the carnage, rescuing as many Spanish survivors as possible, one officer was fished out by sailors of *Iowa*. This man proved to be Captain Don Antonio Eulate of *Vizcaya*. He thanked his rescuers and presented his sword to Captain Robley Evans, who handed it back as an act of chivalry.

By the end of the battle, the Spanish fleet was completely destroyed. The Spanish lost more than 300 killed and 150 wounded out of 2,227 men. About 1,800 officers and men were taken prisoner and roughly 150 managed to escape to Santiago de Cuba. The American fleet lost only one killed and one wounded. The Spanish ships were devastated by the overwhelming barrage of firepower by the Americans. Yet, only 1–3 per cent of all rounds fired by the Americans found their mark.[101] Relative to the Americans' fleet, which consisted mainly of modern battleships, Cervera's force was lightly armed, a result of recent budget cuts and a naval policy that for many years favoured the construction of light, swift ships to patrol their far-flung oceanic empire.

The American victory bred controversy over the question of which commanding officer deserved credit for the victory. Should it be Sampson who was in operational command of the fleet, but absent when Cervera's force engaged the Americans, or Schley who remained in tactical command during Sampson's absence and who saw the fight to a successful close from the bridge of *Brooklyn*? That sordid controversy quickly became a public spectacle inflamed by journalistic sensationalism, popular interest and celebration of military heroism. It lasted for years and reflected no credit on either side. The *Springfield Republic* claimed the controversy was largely a product of writers determined 'to get a brilliant hero out of the Santiago battle at any cost.'[102]

Both the capitulation of Santiago and the American naval victory effectively ended the major fighting on Cuba, but the war was not yet over. Yellow fever had quickly spread among the American occupation force, crippling it. Mosquito bites led to nausea, incapacitating pains and liver and kidney problems. Dysentery, the scourge of armies across the ages, and malaria were also killers. A group of concerned officers of the American army chose Theodore Roosevelt to urge Washington that it withdraw the army, a request that paralleled a similar one from General Shafter, who described his force as an 'army of convalescents'. By the time of his letter, 75 per cent of the force in Cuba was unfit for service – around 4,000 US soldiers were ill with yellow fever, malaria and dysentery. The Fifth Army Corps was recalled and sent to Camp Wikoff, where of the 20,000 men sent there, only 257 died from yellow fever or malaria. On 7 August, the American invasion force started to leave Cuba. The evacuation was not total. The US Army kept the black Ninth US Cavalry Regiment in Cuba to support the occupation, reckoning that their race and the fact that many black volunteers came from southern states would protect them from disease; this logic led to these soldiers being nicknamed 'Immunes'. Still, when the Ninth left, seventy-three of its 984 soldiers had contracted the disease.

Hearst had sailed to Cuba with a small army of *Journal* reporters to cover the war; they took along portable printing equipment, which was used to print a single-edition newspaper in Cuba after the fighting had ended. Two of the *Journal's* correspondents, James Creelman and Edward Marshall, were wounded in the fighting. A leader of the Cuban rebels, General Calixto Garcia, gave Hearst a Cuban flag that had been riddled with bullets as a gift, in appreciation of Hearst's role in Cuba's liberation.[103]

Despite the staged withdrawal from Cuba, American forces were still engaged in Puerto Rico. In May 1898, Lieutenant Henry H. Whitney of the US Fourth Artillery was sent to Puerto Rico on a reconnaissance mission, sponsored by the Army's Bureau of Military Intelligence. He provided maps and information on the Spanish military forces to the US government. The American offensive had begun on 12 May 1898, when a squadron of twelve US ships commanded by Rear Admiral Sampson attacked the capital, San Juan. Although the damage inflicted on the city was minimal, the Americans blockaded the city's harbour. On 22 June, the cruiser *Isabel II* and the destroyer *Terror* counter-attacked but were unable to break the blockade and *Terror* was damaged.

The land offensive began on 25 July, when 1,300 infantry soldiers led by Nelson A. Miles disembarked off the coast of Guánica. The US seized control of Fajardo on 1 August but were forced to withdraw on 5 August after a group of 200 Puerto Rican-Spanish soldiers led by Pedro del Pino gained control of the city and most civilian inhabitants fled to a nearby lighthouse. The Americans encountered larger opposition as they advanced towards the main island's interior, but in a succession of skirmishes the Spanish and their local allies merely retreated in the face of overwhelming firepower. In one such encounter, Spanish forces were entrenched on the crest of two small hills, between which the road from Arroyo to Guayama ran. The Americans had crossed a stream in front of the hills when suddenly the Spanish opened fire. The Americans protected their position by the stream and increased their firepower as more reinforcements arrived. The outnumbered Spanish troops retreated to Guayama as the Americans made their advance on the hills. The firefight, which lasted half-an-hour, left three American wounded. When the 4th Ohio entered the town they discovered that the Spaniards had fled north and abandoned the city, ending the Battle of Guayama.[104]

On 6 August, two companies of the 4th Ohio were sent on a reconnaissance mission across and beyond a cast iron bridge that crossed the Río Guamaní as the road beyond the bridge was essential for the projected advance. The 4th Ohio requested reinforcements and on 9 August attacked the Spaniards and after a short firefight forced them to flee. Seven Americans were wounded, while the Spaniards suffered two dead and fifteen wounded. American troops met heavier resistance on the mountain *Cerro Gervasio del Asomante* and retreated after six of their soldiers were injured. Another action saw more non-fatal casualties until hostilities were suspended.

The Puerto Rico Campaign was short compared to the other theatres because the war came to an end before the military objectives of both sides were achieved. The Americans were also helped by widespread resentment felt by much of the populace to Spanish rule. Of those who participated on all sides, about 18,000 were Spanish, 10,000 were Puerto Rican and 15,472 were American military personnel. The Spanish and Puerto Ricans suffered 429 casualties which included seventeen dead, eighty-eight wounded and 324 captured. The American forces suffered forty-three casualties: three dead and forty wounded.

With defeats in Cuba, Puerto Rico and the Philippines, and both of its fleets destroyed, Spain sued for peace and negotiations were opened between the two parties. Dewey requested the Belgian consul to Manila, Édouard André, to act as intermediary with the Spanish Government.[105] Hostilities were halted on 12 August 1898, with the signing in Washington of a Protocol of Peace between the United States and Spain.[106] After over two months of tense talks, the formal peace treaty was signed in Paris on 10 December 1898, and was ratified by the US Senate on 6 February 1899. Under the treaty the US gained Spain's colonies of the Philippines, Guam and Puerto Rico, and Cuba became a US protectorate. The treaty came into force ion 11 April 1899, with Cubans participating only as observers.

What US Ambassador to the United Kingdom John Hay described in a letter to Roosevelt as 'a splendid little war' had lasted just ten weeks.[107]

* * *

The short and successful 1898 War greatly enforced the United States' vision of itself as a 'defender of democracy' and as a major world power. Historian Louis Pérez argued that it 'fixed permanently how Americans came to think of themselves: a righteous people given to the service of righteous purpose.'[108] Northerners and Southerners, black and white, had fought against a common foe and there were brief, over-optimistic hopes that Civil War scars could be eased if not entirely healed.[109] Four former Confederate generals had served in the war, although only one, Joseph Wheeler, had seen action. The war marked US entry into world affairs and entered a period of economic and population growth, and technological innovation.[110] The war redefined national identity, eased internal social divisions, and provided a model for all future news reporting. Critics, however, saw it as evidence of a new imperialism.

The Americans treated Spain's captured officers, soldiers, and sailors with respect, ultimately returning them with their 'honors of war' on American ships. The war greatly reduced the Spanish Empire which had in any case been in decline since the Napoleonic wars. And the loss of Cuba caused a national trauma because of the affinity of peninsular Spaniards with the island. A new wave called the Generation of '98 originated as a response to this trauma, marking a renaissance in Spanish culture. Economically, however, the war benefited Spain, because large sums of capital held by Spaniards in Cuba and the US were returned to the peninsula and invested in Spain. The cession of the war in Philippines alone involved payment of $20 million ($602,320,000 today) to Spain by the US to cover infrastructure owned by Spain. The massive flow of capital, equivalent to 25 per cent of the gross domestic product of one year, helped to develop large modern firms in the steel, chemical, financial, mechanical, textile, shipyard, and electrical power industries. But the political consequences were serious, defeat weakening of the fragile political stability that had been established earlier by the rule of Alfonso XII.

The Platt Amendment was a move by the US to shape Cuban affairs without violating the Teller Amendment. It forced a peace treaty on Cuba which prohibited it from signing treaties with other nations or contracting a public debt, and was pushed by imperialists who wanted to project US power abroad, in sharp contrast to the Teller Amendment which was pushed by anti-imperialists who called for a restraint on US rule. The new amendment granted the US the right to stabilise Cuba militarily, and deploy marines to Cuba if its freedom and independence was ever threatened or jeopardised by an external or internal force. Cuba may have technically gained its independence after the war ended, but America retained power and control over Cuban affairs. The US also established a perpetual lease of Guantanamo Bay.

The US annexed the former Spanish colonies of Puerto Rico, the Philippines and Guam. The notion of the US as an imperial power, with colonies, was hotly debated domestically. The American public largely supported the possession of colonies, but there were many outspoken critics such as Mark Twain. The defeat of the Spanish Navy gave the United States uncontested control of the seas surrounding Cuba. Much of the impetus for new territorial expansion was the need for foreign naval bases and the need for a larger navy in order to take and maintain control of such bases. The Philippines, Guam, Puerto Rico, and others provided overseas naval bases and coaling stations. Ultimately, the Spanish–American War brought to light deeply rooted conflicts between the principles of democracy and the urges of budding imperialism.

Roosevelt returned to the United States a war hero, and he was soon elected governor of New York and then became the vice president. At the age of forty-two he became the youngest man to become president after the assassination of President William McKinley.

The African American community which had strongly supported the rebels in Cuba and US entry into the war, gained prestige from their wartime performance in the army. It was also noted that thirty-three African American seamen had died in the *Maine* explosion.

The Spanish soldier Julio Cervera Baviera, who served in the Puerto Ricans campaign, published a pamphlet in which he blamed the natives of that colony for its occupation by the Americans, saying, 'I have never seen such a servile, ungrateful country … In 24 hours, the people of Puerto Rico went from being fervently Spanish to enthusiastically American … They humiliated themselves, giving in to the invader as the slave bows to the powerful lord.' The change in sovereignty of Puerto Rico, like the occupation of Cuba, brought about major changes in its economy. US monetary and legal policies made it both harder for local farmers to continue operations and easier for American businesses to accumulate land. This, with the large capital reserves of American businesses, led to a resurgence in the Puerto Rican nuts and sugar industries in the form of large American-owned agro-industrial complexes. In 1897 the United States purchased 19.6 per cent of Puerto Rico's exports while supplying 18.5 per cent of its imports; by 1905 the share jumped to 84 per cent and 85 per cent, respectively.[111] A tariff system also provided a protected market place for Puerto Rican tobacco exports. The tobacco industry went from nearly non-existent in Puerto Rico to a major part of the country's agricultural sector.

The moral justification or otherwise of the war has been hotly debated ever since. In his 1913 autobiography, Theodore Roosevelt wrote: 'Our own direct interests were great, because of the Cuban tobacco and sugar, and especially because of Cuba's relation to the projected Isthmian [Panama] Canal. But even greater were our interests from the standpoint of humanity. … It was our duty, even more from the standpoint of National honor than from the standpoint of National interest, to stop the devastation and destruction. Because of these considerations I favored war.' Historian Louis Perez wrote: 'Certainly the moralistic determinants of war in 1898 has been accorded preponderant explanatory weight in the historiography.'[112]

By the 1950s, however, American authors had widely discredited the idealism by suggesting the people were deliberately misled by propaganda and sensationalist yellow journalism. In 1953 political scientist Robert Osgood claimed that the drift to war came out of a confused mix of 'self-righteousness and genuine moral fervor', in the form of a 'crusade' and a combination of 'knight-errantry and national self-assertiveness'.[113] Osgood argued: 'A war to free Cuba from Spanish despotism, corruption, and cruelty, from the filth and disease and barbarity of General 'Butcher' Weyler's reconcentration camps, from the devastation of haciendas, the extermination of families, and the outraging of women; that would be a blow for humanity and democracy... No one could doubt it if he believed – and skepticism was not popular – the exaggerations of the Cuban Junta's propaganda and the lurid distortions and imaginative lies pervade by the "yellow sheets" of Hearst and Pulitzer at the combined rate of 2 million [newspaper copies] a day.'[114]

Paul Atwood of the University of Massachusetts wrote: 'The Spanish–American War was fomented on outright lies and trumped up accusations against the intended enemy. ... War fever in the general population never reached a critical temperature until the accidental sinking of the USS *Maine* was deliberately, and falsely, attributed to Spanish villainy.'[115]

The cause of *Maine*'s sinking remains a subject of speculation and controversy. The initial American investigation ruled it was from external onslaught; the Spanish minister of colonies, Segismundo, advised his officials 'to gather every fact you can, to prove the *Maine* catastrophe cannot be attributed to us.'[116] America rejected a joint board of inquiry and concluded that *Maine* had been blown up by a mine. The court was been unable to 'obtain evidence fixing the responsibility for the destruction of the *Maine* upon any person or persons.'[117]

The validity of this investigation has been repeatedly challenged since then. George W. Melville, a chief engineer in the navy, proposed that a more likely cause for the sinking was from a magazine explosion within the vessel. The navy's leading ordnance expert Philip R. Alger took this theory further by suggesting that the magazines were ignited by a spontaneous fire in a coal bunker. The coal used in *Maine* was bituminous, which is known for releasing firedamp, a gas that is prone to spontaneous explosions. There is stronger evidence that the explosion of *Maine* was caused by an internal coal fire which ignited the magazines.

In 1910 the US decided to mount a second Court of Inquiry, both to ensure a more thorough investigation and to facilitate the recovery of the bodies of the victims, so they could be buried at home. Such an inquiry could be held without the threat of war, which had been the case in 1898, and which lent it the potential for greater objectivity than had been possible previously.[118] Beginning in December 1910 a cofferdam was built around the wreck and water was pumped out, exposing the wreck by late 1911. The court of inquiry headed by Rear Admiral Charles E. Vreeland inspected the wreck and again concluded that an external explosion had triggered the explosion of the magazines. After the investigation, the newly located dead were buried in Arlington National Cemetery and the hollow, intact portion of the hull of *Maine* was refloated and ceremoniously scuttled at sea on 16 March 1912.

In 1974 Admiral Hyman Rickover began a private investigation, using information from the two official inquiries, newspapers, personal papers, and information on the construction and ammunition of *Maine*. He concluded that the explosion was not caused by a mine, and speculated that spontaneous combustion was the most likely cause, from coal in the bunker next to the magazine. Up to the time of the *Maine*'s building, he explained, common bulkheads separated coal bunkers from ammunition lockers, and American naval ships burned smokeless anthracite coal. With an increase in the number of steel ships, the navy switched to bituminous coal, which burned at a hotter temperature than anthracite coal and allowed ships to steam faster. A number of bunker fires of this type had been reported aboard warships before the *Maine*'s explosion, in several cases nearly sinking the ships.[119]

As many suspected at the time, almost certainly the spark for the 1898 war emanated from a coal bunker rather than Spanish perfidy.

The Philippines War (1899–1902)

We take no prisoners. At least the Twentieth Kansas do not.

A soldier from New York wrote:

> The town of Titatia was surrendered to us a few days ago, and two companies occupy the same. Last night one of our boys was found shot and his stomach cut open. Immediately orders were received from General Wheaton to burn the town and kill every native in sight; which was done to a finish. About 1,000 men, women and children were reported killed. I am probably growing hard-hearted, for I am in my glory when I can sight my gun on some dark skin and pull the trigger.[1]

Another, Corporal Sam Gillis, wrote home:

> We make everyone get into his house by seven p.m., and we only tell a man once. If he refuses we shoot him. We killed over 300 natives the first night. They tried to set the town on fire. If they fire a shot from the house, we burn the house down and every house near it, and shoot the natives, so they are pretty quiet in town now.[2]

The renowned writer Mark Twain wrote in a newspaper:

> I have tried hard, and yet I cannot for the life of me comprehend how we got into that mess. Perhaps we could not have avoided it — perhaps it was inevitable that we should come to be fighting the natives of those islands — but I cannot understand it … I thought we should act as their protector — not try to get them under our heel. We were to relieve them from Spanish tyranny to enable them to set up a government of their own, and we were to stand by and see that it got a fair trial. It was

not to be a government according to our ideas, but a government that represented the feeling of the majority of the Filipinos, a government according to Filipino ideas. That would have been a worthy mission for the United States. But now — why, we have got into a mess, a quagmire from which each fresh step renders the difficulty of extrication immensely greater. I'm sure I wish I could see what we were getting out of it, and all it means to us as a nation.[3]

All three correspondents were embroiled in a colonial war which, by the most conservative estimates, killed at least 200,000 people, most of them civilians, and possibly over a million. It ushered in what was meant to be a new century of modernity and enlightenment; instead it prefaced global conflicts of genocide. Although largely forgotten in mainstream America, it remains one of the biggest stains on the nation's history, along with slavery and the attempted extermination of the Native American peoples.

***

On 22 April 1898, the exiled Filipino revolutionary leader Emilio Aguinaldo, after a private meeting in Singapore with US Consul E. Spencer Pratt, decided to return to the Philippines during the Spanish–American War (*see* previous chapter). He later insisted, through Pratt, that Commodore George Dewey of the US Navy Asiatic Squadron had promised him America would recognise the independence of the Philippines. Both Dewey and Pratt later refuted that account.[4] But there is no doubt that Dewey and Aguinaldo had an informal alliance to fight a common enemy: the Spanish. Filipino historian Teodoro Agoncillo wrote of the Americans: 'They came to the Philippines not as a friend, but as an enemy masking as a friend.'[5]

Aguinaldo departed Hong Kong aboard the USRC *McCulloch* on 17 May, and less than three months after his return, his Philippine Revolutionary Army had conquered nearly all of the Philippines and surrounded Manila with a 12,000-strong force. Aguinaldo turned over 15,000 Spanish prisoners to the Americans. The secret agreement made by Commodore Dewey with the Spanish governor that the capital's garrison would surrender only to the Americans after a mock battle, excluding the revolutionary forces under the threat of fire, outraged the Filipinos. Relations continued to deteriorate as it became clear to Filipinos that the Americans were on the islands to stay.

The relentless search for trade and profit was an undoubted factor. Senator Henry Cabot Lodge said: 'We make no hypocritical pretense of being interested in the Philippines solely on account of others. While we regard the welfare of these people as a sacred trust, we regard the welfare of the American people first. We see our duty to ourselves as well as to others. We believe in trade expansion.'

Howard Zinn wrote:

The guns of Dewey in Manilla Bay were heard across Asia and Africa, they echoed through the palace at Peking and brought to the Oriental mind a new and potent force among western nations. We, in common with the countries of Europe, are striving to enter the limitless markets of the east ... These people respect nothing but power. I believe the Philippines will be enormous markets and sources of wealth. There was nothing wrong with the profit motive and gain should be the only reason for American expansion into the Pacific.

American naval power could not yet compete with the British and German navies who held sway in the Atlantic; in the Pacific region, however, it was another matter.

One newspaper editorial said: 'It is against the interests of the United States to have the fruits of Dewey's victory gathered by insurgents ... No native dictatorship or so-called republic is wanted until the United States fixes on its Philippine policy. When a flag replaces the blood-and-fear ensign of Spain, it should be our flag. Afterward there will be enough time to discuss native problems.'[6]

Senator Albert J. Beveridge said:

The Philippines are ours forever ... And just beyond the Philippines are China's illimitable markets. We will not retreat from either. We will not repudiate our duty in the archipelago. We will not abandon our opportunity in the Orient. We will not renounce our part in the mission of our race, trustee under God, of the civilization of the world. The Pacific is our ocean ... Where shall we turn for consumers of our surplus? Geography answers the question. China is our natural customer ... The Philippines give us a base at the door of all due East ... No land in America surpasses in fertility the plains and valleys of Luzon. Rice and coffee, sugar and cocoanuts, hemp and tobacco ... The wood of the Philippines can supply the furniture of the world for a century to come. At Cebu the best informed man on the island told me that 40 miles of Cebu's mountain chain are practically mountains of coal ... I have a nugget of pure gold picked up in its present form on the banks of a Philippine creek ... My own belief is that there are not 100 men among them who comprehend what Anglo-Saxon self-government even means, and there are over 5,000,000 people to be governed. It has been charged that our conduct of the war has been cruel. Senators, it has been the reverse ... Senators must remember that we are not dealing with Americans or Europeans. We are dealing with Orientals.[7]

After the Spanish defeat, the Philippines were indeed ceded to the US under the Treaty of Paris. Major General Elwell Stephen Otis was appointed Military Governor of the Philippines and issued a proclamation of American sovereignty. Aguinaldo on 5 January 1899 countered that he and his provisional government 'cannot remain indifferent in view of such a violent and aggressive seizure of a portion of its territory by a nation which arrogated to itself the title of champion of oppressed nations'. Otis regarded Aguinaldo's words as a statement of aggressive intent and put his forces on a war footing. The Filipinos were spurred to fight a former ally turned enemy.[8]

The first shots of the war were fired on the evening of 4 February by Private William W. Grayson, an English-born sentry of the 1st Nebraska Volunteer Infantry Regiment at the corner of Sociego and Silencio Streets in Santa Mesa.[9] He killed a Filipino lieutenant and another Filipino soldier who, it was claimed, were unarmed but who 'insolently' refused to respond to his challenge. Grayson reported that when the lieutenant refused to respond, 'Well, I thought the best thing to do was to shoot him. He dropped. If I didn't kill him, I guess he died of fright.'[10] Newspapers later reported that the US troops were 'expecting trouble and were glad to have an opportunity to square accounts with the natives, whose insolence of late was becoming intolerable'.[11]

The killings triggered the Battle of Manila, the biggest and bloodiest of the war. Filipino soldiers, occupying the former Spanish trench systems that surrounded Manila, overnight exchanged fire with the Americans. A Filipino battalion mounted a charge against the 3rd US Artillery, routed a company of American soldiers, and briefly captured two artillery pieces. But such minor victories were short-lived. The Filipino troops had been caught unprepared and leaderless, as their generals had gone home to their families for the weekend, while the American soldiers were ready and raring to go. Brigadier General Arthur MacArthur prepared an American advance.[12]

Aguinaldo was away but a Filipino captain in Manila wired him in Malolos, stating that the Americans had started the hostilities. Aguinaldo wanted to avoid open conflict while maintaining his position of leadership with his nationalist followers. The next day Aguinaldo sent an emissary to General Otis to mediate, saying 'the firing on our side the night before had been against my order'.[13] Otis, who was then confident that a military campaign against Aguinaldo would be swift, responded: 'Fighting having begun, must go on to the grim end.'[14] Aguinaldo then reassured his followers with a pledge to fight if forced by the Americans, whom he had come to fear as new oppressors come to replace the Spanish:

It is my duty to maintain the integrity of our national honor, and that of the army so unjustly attacked by those, who posing as our friends, attempt to dominate us in place of the Spaniards. Therefore, for the defense of the nation entrusted to me, I hereby order and command:

Peace and friendly relations between the Philippine Republic and the American army of occupation are broken — and the latter will be treated as enemies with the limits prescribed by the laws of War.[15]

When Filipino officers did arrive on the field, many tried to stop the fighting and Aguinaldo again sent emissaries to negotiate a ceasefire. But both Otis and MacArthur thought the crisis should be brought to a head and refused to negotiate. General MacArthur, in command of the North of Manila, had developed an aggressive-defensive plan which called for an all-out offensive along the Santa Mesa Ridge, the capture of the Filipino blockhouses, and the seizure of the Chinese hospital. General Thomas Anderson, along the southern lines, believed he faced imminent attack, so with permission from Otis he sent his entire division in a pre-emptive strike at first light. Brigadier General Pío del Pilar's forces fled into the Pasig River, where many drowned.[16] The Filipinos were shocked when the Americans attacked, having been used to Spanish tactics of retreating into fortified cities after a night-time raid. MacArthur's attack in the north captured the ridge overlooking Manila. After initial confusion, Brigadier General Anderson's attack in the south captured the village of Pasay and Filipino supplies stored there.

Physician-soldier F. A. Blake, in charge of the Red Cross, wrote:

I never saw such execution in my life, and hope never to see such sights as met me on all sides as our little corps passed over the field, dressing wounded. Legs and arms nearly demolished; total decapitation; horrible wounds in chests and abdomens, showing the determination of our soldiers to kill every native in sight. The Filipinos did stand their ground heroically, contesting every inch, but proved themselves unable to stand the deadly fire of our well-trained and eager boys in blue. I counted seventy-nine dead natives in one small field and learn that on the other side of the river their bodies were stacked up for breastworks.

Regular Army lieutenant Henry Page wrote:

The recent battle was somewhat of a revelation to Americans. They expected the motley horde to run at the firing of the first gun. It was my good fortune to be placed—about ten hours afterward—near the spot where this first gun was fired. I found the Americans still held in check. Our artillery then began to assail the enemy's position, and it was only by the stoutest kind of fighting that the Tennessee and Nebraska Regiments were able to drive him out. The Filipinos' retreat, however, was more creditable than their stand. Perfect order prevailed. One of their companies would hold our advance until the company in their rear could retire and reload, when in turn this company would stand until the former had retired and reloaded. A frequent exclamation along our lines was: 'Haven't these little fellows got grit?' They had more than grit—they had organization...[17]

The battle was fought along a 16-mile front and involved thirteen American regiments and thousands of Filipinos. American casualties totalled 238, of whom forty-four were killed in action or died from wounds.[18] The US Army's official report listed Filipino casualties as 4,000, of whom 700 were killed.[19] N. A. J. McDonnel, of the Utah Battery, wrote home:

The enemy numbered thousands and had courage, but could not shoot straight. People can never tell me anything about the Rough Riders charging San Juan. If these natives could shoot as accurately as the Spanish, they would have exterminated us. Fighting goes on all along the lines, many natives are killed, but we capture very few rifles, as they seem to have men to take them. Official reports say over four thousand two hundred natives have been buried by American troops. How many they have buried themselves and how many more are dead in the brush no one knows.[20]

Kansan Theodore Conly wrote:

Talk about dead Indians! Why, they are lying everywhere. The trenches are full of them ... More harrowing still: think of the brave men from this country, men who were willing to sacrifice their lives for the freedom of Cuba, dying in battle and from disease, in a war waged for the purpose of conquering people who are fighting as the Cubans fought against Spanish tyranny and misrule. There is not a feature of the whole miserable business that a patriotic American citizen, one who loves to read of the brave deeds of the American colonists in the splendid struggle for American independence, can look upon with complacency, much less with pride. This war is reversing history. It places the American people and the government of the United States in the position occupied by Great Britain in 1776. It is an utterly causeless and defenseless war, and it should be abandoned by this government without delay. The longer it is continued, the greater crime it becomes – a crime against human liberty as well as against Christianity and civilization ... Those not killed in the trenches were killed when they tried to come out ... No wonder they can't shoot, with that light thrown on them; shells bursting and infantry pouring in lead all the time. Honest to God, I feel sorry for them.[21]

The Filipinos were counting on an uprising by the citizens of Manila to divide American forces and interrupt American supply lines. Although some fires were set inside the city, no general uprising occurred, since Brigadier General Robert P. Hughes' Provost Guard quickly suppressed any disturbances. However, some small units of Philippine soldiers who had not been part of the force that was routed skirmished with the Americans for several days on the outskirts of Manila before being driven out.

To many, the war had begun by accident, but powerful American voices argued that it was both necessary and inevitable. The annexation of the Philippines had to be imposed by brute force as peaceful alternatives had clearly failed. Stuart Creighton Miller wrote: 'Americans altruistically went to war with Spain to liberate Cubans, Puerto Ricans, and Filipinos from their tyrannical yoke. If they lingered on too long in the Philippines, it was to protect the Filipinos from European predators waiting in the wings for an American withdrawal and to tutor them in American-style democracy.'[22] The *New York Herald* argued: 'The slaughter at Manila was necessary, but not glorious. The entire American population justifies the conduct of its army at Manila because only by a crushing repulse of the Filipinos could our position be made secure ... We are ... the trustees of civilization and peace throughout the islands.' The 'white man's burden' had been thrust on the United States by 'the impotent oppression of Spain and the semi-barbarous conduct of the Philippines'.

A week after the first shots were fired, the USS *Petrel* and the USS *Baltimore* bombarded the city of Iloilo before it was captured by ground forces led by Brigadier General Marcus Miller, with no loss of American lives. Over the following months American forces moved northward, engaging in combat at brigade and battalion level in pursuit of the fleeing insurgents.[23] Frank M. Erb, of the Pennsylvania Regiment, wrote:

> We have been in this nigger-fighting business now for twenty-three days, and have been under fire for the greater part of that time. The niggers shoot over one another's heads or any old way. Even while I am writing this the black boys are banging away at our outposts, but they very seldom hit anybody. The morning of the 6th a burying detail from our regiment buried forty-nine nigger enlisted men and two nigger officers, and when we stopped chasing them the night before, we could see 'em carrying a great many with them. We are supposed to have killed about three hundred. Take my advice, and don't enlist in the regulars, for you are good for three years. I am not sorry I enlisted, but you see we have had some excitement and we only have about fourteen months' time to serve, if they keep us our full time, which is not likely. We will, no doubt, start home as soon as we get these niggers rounded up.

And Anthony Michea, of the Third Artillery, wrote: 'We bombarded a place called Malabon, and then we went in and killed every native we met, men, women, and children. It was a dreadful sight, the killing of the poor creatures. The natives captured some of the Americans and literally hacked them to pieces, so we got orders to spare no one.'[24] Private Fred B. Hinchman, Company A. United States Engineers, wrote from Manila:

The general gave me a memorandum with regard to sending out a Tennessee battalion to the line. He tersely put it that 'they were looking for a fight.' At the Puente Colgante [suspension bridge] I met one of our company, who told me that the Fourteenth and Washingtons were driving all before them and taking no prisoners. This is now our rule of procedure for cause. After delivering my message I had not walked a block when I heard shots down the street. Hurrying forward, I found a group of our men taking pot-shots across the river, into a bamboo thicket, at about 1,200 yards. I longed to join them, but had my reply to take back, and that, of course, was the first thing to attend to. I reached the office at 3 P.M., just in time to see a platoon of the Washingtons, with about fifty prisoners, who had been taken before they learned how not to take them.[25]

Kansas trooper Arthur Minkler wrote:

We advanced four miles and we fought every inch of the way; ... saw twenty-five dead insurgents in one place and twenty-seven in another, besides a whole lot of them scattered along that I did not count ... It was like hunting rabbits; an insurgent would jump out of a hole or the brush and run; he would not get very far ... I suppose you are not interested in the way we do the job. We do not take prisoners. At least the Twentieth Kansas do not.

Californian Burr Ellis wrote:

They did not commence fighting over here (Cavite) for several days after the war commenced. Dewey gave them till nine o'clock one day to surrender, and that night they all left but a few out to their trenches, and those that they left burned up the town, and when the town commenced burning the troops were ordered in as far as possible and said, Kill all we could find. I ran off from the hospital and went ahead with the scouts. I did not cross the ocean for the fun there was in it, so the first one I found, he was in a house, down on his knees fanning a fire, trying to burn the house, and I pulled my old Long Tom to my shoulder and left him to burn with the fire, which he did. I got his knife, and another jumped out of the window and ran, and I brought him to the ground like a jack-rabbit. I killed seven that I know of, and one more I am almost sure of: I shot ten shots at him running and knocked him down, and that evening the boys out in front of our trenches now found one with his arm shot off at shoulder and dead as h___; I had lots of fun that morning. There were five jumped out of the brush and cut one of the Iowa band boys, and we killed every one of them, and I was sent back to quarters in the hurry. Came very near getting a court-martial, but the colonel said he had heard that I had done excellent work and he laughed and said: 'There's good stuff in that man,' and told me not to leave any more without orders. Well, John, there will always be trouble here with the natives unless they annihilate all of them as fast as they come to them.[26]

Tom Crandall of the Nebraska Regiment wrote:

The boys are getting sick of fighting these heathens, and all say we volunteered to fight Spain, not heathens. Their patriotism is wearing off. We all want to come home very bad. If I ever get out of this army I will never get into another. They will be fighting four hundred years, and then never whip these people, for there are not enough of us to follow them up ... The people of the United States ought to raise a howl and have us sent home.

Captain Elliott of the Kansas Regiment wrote:

Talk about war being 'hell,' this war beats the hottest estimate ever made of that locality. Caloocan was supposed to contain seventeen thousand inhabitants. The Twentieth Kansas swept through it, and now Caloocan contains not one living native. Of the buildings, the battered walls of the great church and dismal prison alone remain. The village of Maypaja, where our first fight occurred on the night of the fourth, had five thousand people in it at that day,—now not one stone remains upon top of another. You can only faintly imagine this terrible scene of desolation. War is worse than hell.

Looting was combined with slaughter. Ozark soldier Leonard F. Adams of the Washington Regiment wrote: 'I don't know how many men, women, and children the Tennessee boys did kill. They would not take any prisoners. One company of the Tennessee boys was sent into headquarters with thirty prisoners and got there with about a hundred chickens and no prisoners.'[27] D. M. Mickle of the Tennessee Regiment described an incident at Iloilo:

The building had been taken possession of by a United States officer, and he looted it to a finish. I suspected something and followed one of his men to the place. I expected to be jumped on by the officer as soon as I found him there, as I was away from my post, but it seems he was afraid I would give him away; in fact, we were both afraid of each other. He was half drunk, and every time he saw me look at anything he would say, 'Tennessee, do you like that? Well, put it in your pocket...'

The house was a fine one, and richly furnished, but had been looted to a finish. The contents of every drawer had been emptied on the floor. You have no idea what a mania for destruction the average man has when the fear of the law is removed. I have seen them — old sober business men too — knock chandeliers and plate-glass mirrors to pieces just because they couldn't carry them off. It is such a pity.

E. D. Furnam, of the Washington Regiment, wrote: 'We burned hundreds of houses and looted hundreds more. Some of the boys made good hauls of jewelry and clothing. Nearly every man has at least two suits of clothing, and our quarters are furnished in style; fine beds with silken drapery, mirrors, chairs, rockers, cushions, pianos, hanging-lamps, rugs, pictures, etc. We have horses and carriages, and bull-carts galore, and enough furniture and other plunder to load a steamer.'[28]

The Filipinos swiftly learnt the lesson that pitched battles against better-armed American forces were doomed. Given the rigid caste system that existed in the Philippines during the Spanish colonial era and beyond, Aguinaldo's main challenge was to unify opposition to American rule as the peasants, who represented the majority of the fighting forces, had interests markedly different from their *ilustrado* leaders and the *principales* of their villages. Faced with the logistics of maintaining irregulars while balancing competing local priorities, the Filipino commanders had to be pragmatic. General Francisco Macabulos described the Filipinos' war aim as 'not to vanquish the US Army but to inflict on them constant losses'. They hoped that sufficient attrition would ensure McKinley's defeat by the anti-imperialist William Jennings Bryan in the upcoming presidential elections, believing that Bryan would withdraw the American forces from the Philippines.[29] That was not to be. For most of 1899, the revolutionary leadership viewed guerrilla warfare only as a tactical option of final recourse, not as a means of operation which better suited their disadvantaged situation. But on 13 November Emilio Aguinaldo decreed that guerrilla war would be waged.[30]

Estimates of the Filipino forces vary between 80,000 and 100,000, with tens of thousands of auxiliaries. Most of the latter were armed only with *bolo* knives, bows and arrows, spears and other primitive weapons.[31] However, during the first four months of the guerrilla war, the Americans suffered nearly 500 casualties[32] in bloody ambushes and raids. For a while it seemed that the Filipinos might be able to fight the Americans to a stalemate and force them to withdraw; President McKinley certainly considered withdrawal when the guerrilla raids began. But in response to such hit-and-run tactics, American military strategy shifted to hard-nosed suppression, aiming to control key areas with internment and segregation of the civilian population in 'zones of protection' from the guerrillas.[33] It foreshadowed by more than half a century the 'Strategic Hamlet Program' unsuccessfully deployed during the Vietnam War. Due to disruption of war and unsanitary conditions, many of the interned civilians died from dysentery.[34]

General MacArthur explained why, in American eyes, the switch to guerrilla war justified pretty much anything: 'Since guerrilla warfare was contrary to the customs and usages of war, those engaged in it divest themselves of the character of soldiers, and if captured are not entitled to the privileges of prisoners of war.' That was certainly the dictum of General Otis who, despite contrary orders from Washington, refused to accept anything but unconditional surrender from the Philippine Army. After the one-sided Battle of Manila, he assumed Filipino resistance would collapse quickly; even after this proved false he insisted that the insurgency had been defeated and that the ongoing casualties were caused by 'isolated bands of outlaws'.[35]

Like all weak men carrying a big stick, he was sensitive to any criticism. When letters describing American atrocities reached the American media, the War Department demanded that Otis investigate. Otis had each press clipping forwarded to the original writer's commanding officer, who would 'convince' the soldier to write a retraction of the original statements. When a soldier refused to do so, as was the case with Private Charles Brenner of the Kansas regiment, he was court-martialled 'for writing and conniving at the publication of an article which ... contains wilful falsehoods'.[36]

Otis claimed that Filipino insurgents tortured American prisoners in 'fiendish fashion', saying many were buried alive or were placed up to their necks in ant hills. He claimed others had their genitals removed and stuffed into their mouths and were then executed by suffocation or bleeding to death. It was also reported that Spanish priests were horribly mutilated before their congregations, and natives who refused to support Emilio Aguinaldo were slaughtered by the thousands. General 'Fighting Joe' Wheeler insisted that it was the Filipinos who had mutilated their own dead, murdered women and children, and burned down villages, solely to discredit American soldiers.

In January 1899, the *New York World* published a story by an anonymous writer about an American soldier, Private William Lapeer, who had allegedly been deliberately infected with leprosy. No such person existed[37] but other newspapers described deliberate attacks by Filipino sharpshooters upon American surgeons, chaplains, ambulances, hospitals and wounded soldiers.[38] An unsubstantiated incident was described where several crewmen of a landing party were fired upon and later cut into pieces by Filipinos while the insurgents were flying a flag of truce.[39]

During the closing months of 1899, Aguinaldo attempted to counter Otis' account by suggesting that neutral parties – foreign journalists or representatives of the International Committee of the Red Cross (ICRC) – inspect his military operations. Otis refused, but Aguinaldo smuggled four reporters – two English, one Canadian, and one Japanese – into the Philippines. The correspondents returned to Manila to report that American captives were 'treated more like guests than prisoners', were 'fed the best that the country affords, and everything is done to gain their favor'. The story said that American prisoners were offered commissions in the Filipino army and that three had accepted. The four reporters were expelled from the Philippines as soon as their stories were printed.[40] It was claimed that the journalists had fallen for stage-managed propaganda, but US Navy Lieutenant J. C. Gilmore, whose release was forced by American cavalry pursuing Aguinaldo into the mountains, insisted that he had received 'considerable treatment' and that he was no more starved than were his captors.[41] When F. A. Blake of the ICRC arrived at Aguinaldo's request, Otis kept him confined to Manila. Blake slipped away and, while never crossing American forward lines, saw burned-out villages and 'horribly mutilated bodies, with stomachs slit open and occasionally decapitated'. Blake did not report what he saw until his return to the safety of San Francisco, where he said that 'American soldiers are determined to kill every Filipino in sight'.[42]

That was largely borne out by the letters home that continued to filter into American newspapers and the publications of anti-war societies. Guy Williams, of the Iowa Regiment, wrote: 'The soldiers made short work of the whole thing. They looted every house, and found almost everything, from a pair of wooden shoes up to a piano, and they carried everything off or destroyed it.'[43] And Charles Bremer, of Minneapolis, describing a fight at Caloocan, wrote:

> Company 1 had taken a few prisoners, and stopped. The colonel ordered them up in to line time after time, and finally sent Captain Bishop back to start them. There occurred the hardest sight I ever saw. They had four prisoners and didn't know what to do with them. They asked Captain Bishop what to do, and he said: 'You know the orders,' and four natives fell dead.[44]

Corporal Robert D. Maxwell of Company A, 20th Kansas, reported:

> Sometimes we stopped to make sure a native was dead and not lying down to escape injury. Some of them would fall as though dead and, after we had passed, would climb a tree and shoot every soldier that passed that way. Even the wounded would rise up and shoot after we passed. This led to an order to take no prisoners, but to shoot all.[45]

McKinley's election victory in 1900 was demoralising for the insurgents, but equally American troops were growing increasingly disenchanted with the sneaking feeling that their cause was not as just as they had been told. Their letters again appear to be forerunners of those sent from Vietnam. General Reeve, lately Colonel of the Thirteenth Minnesota Regiment, wrote: 'I deprecate this war, this slaughter of our own boys and of the Filipinos, because it seems to me that we are doing something that is contrary to our principles in the past. Certainly we are doing something that we should have shrunk from not so very long ago.' Arthur H. Vickers, Sergeant in the First Nebraska Regiment, wrote: 'I am not afraid, and am always ready to do my duty, but I would like someone to tell me what we are fighting for.' Sergeant Elliott, of Company G, Kansas Regiment, wrote:

> Most of the general officers think it will take years, and a large force of soldiers, to thoroughly subjugate the natives. And the unpleasant feature of this is that unless the conditions change radically there will be few soldiers who will care to stay there. There's no use trying to conceal the fact that many of the men over there now, especially the volunteers, are homesick, and tired of fighting way off there, with nothing in particular to gain. There is not one man in the whole army now in the Philippines who would not willingly give up his life for the flag if it was necessary, but it isn't pleasant to think about dying at the hands of a foe little better than a savage, and so far away from home. And the thought of its not ending for several years is not an especially pleasant one, either.[46]

The gruelling, life-sapping war continued, and, like all such conflicts, continued to demoralise. Martin P. Olson, of the 14th Regulars, wrote:

> We can lick them, but it will take us a long time, because there are about 150,000 of the dagos back in the hills, and as soon as one of them gets killed or wounded there is a man to take his place at once; and we have but a few men in the first place, but we are expecting about 8,000 more soldiers every day, and I hope they will soon get here, or we will all be tired out and sick … This is an awful bad climate and there have been from two to four funerals every day. The boys have chronic diarrhoea and dysentery, and it just knocks the poor boys out. You mustn't feel uneasy about me, because I don't think there is a Spanish bullet made to kill me; it is disease that I am most afraid of.[47]

Sylvester Walker, of the 23rd Regulars, wrote: 'There has not been a night for the last ten days we have not had fighting. Our force is too weak, and we cannot spare any more men, and will have to wait for more troops. Then we will have hard fighting, for there are so many that, no matter how many we kill or capture, it doesn't seem to lessen their number.'

Otis was dismissed in May 1900 and replaced by General Arthur MacArthur Junior, who in December placed the Philippines under martial law. Under US General Order 100, guerrillas who wore no uniform but peasant dress and those civilians who accepted and then abused US protection would be treated as 'war rebels or war traitors' and shot.[48]

It was an open invitation to commit further atrocities. In November 1901, the Manila correspondent of the *Philadelphia Ledger* wrote: 'The present war is no bloodless, opera bouffe engagement; our men have been relentless, have killed to exterminate men, women, children, prisoners and captives, active insurgents and suspected people from lads of ten up, the idea prevailing that the Filipino as such was little better than a dog.'[49] Reports were received from soldiers returning from the Philippines that, upon entering a village, American soldiers would ransack every house and church and rob the inhabitants of everything of value, while those who approached the battle line waving a flag of truce were fired upon.[50]

On 23 March 1901, General Frederick Funston and his troops captured Aguinaldo in Palanan, Isabela, with the help of American-supporting Filipinos known as the Macabebe Scouts. The Americans pretended to be captives of the Scouts, who were dressed in Philippine Army uniforms. Once Funston and his 'captors' entered Aguinaldo's camp, they immediately fell upon the guards and quickly overwhelmed them and the weary, ailing Aguinaldo.[51] On 1 April in Manila, Aguinaldo swore an oath accepting the authority of the US over the Philippines and pledging his allegiance to the American government. On 19 April, he issued a Proclamation of Formal Surrender, telling his followers to lay down their weapons and give up the fight. 'Let the stream of blood cease to flow; let there be an end to tears and desolation,' Aguinaldo said. 'The lesson which the war holds out and the significance of which I realized only recently, leads me to the firm conviction that the complete termination of hostilities and a lasting peace are not only desirable but also absolutely essential for the well-being of the Philippines.'[52]

The capture of Aguinaldo dealt a severe blow to the Filipino cause, but not as much as the Americans had hoped. General Miguel Malvar took over the leadership of what remained of the Filipino government[53] and launched all-out offensive against the American-held towns in the Batangas region, as did General Vicente Lukbán in Samar.

Despite Aguinaldo's earlier orders that American prisoners should be treated humanely, the Filipino guerrillas committed documented atrocities, particularly after his confinement. The Filipino historian Teodoro Agoncillo conceded that, albeit for understandable reasons, they could match and even exceed American brutality towards some prisoners of war. In some cases, ears and noses were cut off and salt applied to the wounds. In others, captives were buried alive.[54] Another account recorded:

A detachment, marching through Leyte, found an American who had disappeared a short time before crucified, head down. His abdominal wall had been carefully opened so that his intestines might hang down in his face. Another American prisoner, found on the same trip, had been buried in the ground with only his head projecting. His mouth had been propped open with a stick, a trail of sugar laid to it through the forest, and a handful thrown into it. Millions of ants had done the rest.[55]

The worst and deadliest incident triggered a ferocious American backlash.

In the summer of 1901, Brigadier General Robert P. Hughes, who commanded the Department of the Visayas and was responsible for Samar, instigated a scorched earth plan, burning crops and food stocks, and destroying property and livestock in a bid to starve the island's insurgents into surrender.[56] His strategy included the closure of three key ports on the southern coast – Basey, Balangiga and Guiuan – to prevent food supplies reaching guerrillas under the command of General Vicente Lukbán, who had been sent there in December 1898 to govern the island on behalf of the First Philippine Republic.[57] Samar was a major centre for the production of Manila hemp, a trade believed to be financing the guerrillas; US interests were also keen to secure control of the trade so that vital materials could supply the US Navy and American agro-industries.

On 11 August, Company C of the 9th Infantry Regiment arrived in Balangiga. Earlier in the year, town mayor Pedro Abayan had written to Lukbán pledging to 'observe a deceptive policy with [Americans] doing whatever they may like, and when a favorable opportunity arises, the people will strategically rise against them'. However, relations between the soldiers and the townspeople were generally friendly, with extensive fraternisation by way of palm wine drinking and baseball games. But tensions rose when commanding officer Captain Thomas W. Connell ordered the town cleaned up in preparation for a visit by the US Army's Inspector General. To comply, the townspeople inadvertently cut down vegetation with food value, in violation of Lukbán's order to maintain supplies. Around 400 guerrillas appeared in the vicinity to impose sanctions on the town for that and for fraternising with the Americans. The threat was defused by the parish priest. Connell, unaware that the situation was on a knife-edge, had the town's male residents rounded up and detained for tardiness in the clean-up operations. Around eighty men were kept in two Sibley tents unfed overnight and abandoned by the guerrillas. They formed their own plan of action.

Town police chief Valeriano Abanador and Captain Eugenio Daza, a member of Lukbán's staff, fearful of the lack of manpower to face the well-armed Americans, called in outsiders disguised as workmen preparing the town for a local fiesta. Much palm wine was brought in to ensure that the American soldiers would be drunk the day after the fiesta.

Hours before the attack, women and children were sent away to safety. To mask the disappearance of the women from the dawn service in the church, thirty-four men cross-dressed as women worshippers. These 'women', carrying two small coffins, were challenged by Sergeant Scharer of the sentry post about the town plaza. Opening one of the coffins with his bayonet, he saw the body of a dead child who, he was told, was a victim of a cholera epidemic. Abashed, he let them pass, unaware that the other coffins hid *bolos* and other weapons.[58]

Early on the morning of 28 September, the townspeople struck. Mayor Abanador, who had been supervising the prisoners' communal labour in the town plaza, grabbed the rifle of Private Adolph Gamlin, one of the American sentries, and stunned him with a blow to the head. This served as the signal for the rest of the communal labourers in the plaza to rush the other sentries and soldiers of Company C, who were mostly having breakfast in their mess. Abanador fired Gamlin's rifle at the mess tent, hitting one of the soldiers. The church bells and the blowing of conch shells summoned the rest of the attackers. Some of the Company C troopers were hacked to death before they could grab their rifles; those few who survived the initial onslaught fought almost barehanded, using kitchen utensils, steak knives, and chairs. One private used a baseball bat before being overwhelmed.

The men detained in the Sibley tents broke out and made their way to the municipal hall. Simultaneously, attackers hidden in the church broke into the parish house and killed the three American officers there. An unarmed Company C soldier was ignored, as was Captain Connell's Filipino houseboy. The attackers initially occupied the parish house and the municipal hall; however, the attack at the mess tents and the barracks failed, with Private Gamlin recovering consciousness and managing to secure another rifle, causing considerable casualties among the Filipinos. With the initial surprise wearing off, Abanador called a retreat. The surviving Company C soldiers escaped by sea. The townspeople buried their dead and abandoned their town.

Of the seventy-four men in Company C, thirty-six were killed outright in action, including all three commissioned officers; twenty-two were wounded; four were missing, presumed dead; eight died later of their wounds; only four escaped unscathed. The villagers captured about 100 rifles and 25,000 rounds of ammunition and suffered twenty-eight dead and twenty-two wounded.[59] Basey commander Captain Edwin Victor Bookmiller sailed immediately with Company G, 9th Infantry Regiment for Balangiga aboard a commandeered coastal steamer. When they found the town abandoned, they buried the American dead and set fire to the town.

The Balangiga attack, at a time when they believed that Filipino resistance was almost over, shocked Americans living in Manila. Men started to openly wear sidearms and some women were evacuated to Hong Kong. The shock was even greater among the US public, with newspapers equating the massacre to Custer's Last Stand in 1876. Major General Adna R. Chaffee, military governor of the Philippines, received orders from President Roosevelt to pacify Samar. He appointed Brigadier General Jacob Hurd Smith to carry out a brutal task. General Smith in turn instructed Major Littleton Waller, commanding officer of a battalion of 315 US marines: 'I want no prisoners. I wish you to kill and burn, the more you kill and burn the better it will please me. I want all persons killed who are capable of bearing arms in actual hostilities against the United States.' Waller asked: 'I would like to know the limit of age to respect, sir?' Smith replied: 'Ten years.' Waller: 'Persons of ten years and older are those designated as being capable of bearing arms?' Smith: 'Yes.' To his credit, Waller countermanded it in orders to his own men.[60]

But others enthusiastically followed Smith's initial orders. Colonel Frederick Funston told a Chicago banquet:

I personally strung up thirty-five Filipinos without trial, so what was all the fuss over despatching a few treacherous savages? If there had been more Smiths … the war would have been over long ago. Impromptu domestic hanging might also hasten the end of the war. For starters, all Americans who had recently petitioned Congress to sue for peace in the Philippines should be dragged out of their homes and lynched.[61]

Smith's medical officer said: 'It makes me sick to see what has been said about him. If people knew what a thieving, treacherous, worthless bunch of scoundrels those Filipinos are, they would think differently than they do now. You can't treat them the way you do civilized folks. I do not believe that there are half a dozen men in the US Army that don't think Smith is all right.'[62] Major Edwin Glenn did not deny that he made forty-seven prisoners kneel and 'repent of their sins' before ordering them bayoneted and clubbed to death.[63] And General William Shafter recorded: 'It may be necessary to kill half the Filipinos in order that the remaining half of the population may be advanced to a higher plane of life than their present semi-barbarous state affords.'

All food and trade to Samar were cut off, in a renewed bid to force the inhabitants to stop supporting the guerrillas and turn to the Americans from fear and starvation. Troops swept the interior in search for guerrilla bands and in attempts to capture Lukbán. American columns destroyed homes and indiscriminately shot people and draft animals. Waller, in a report, stated that over an eleven-day period his men burned 255 dwellings. The Judge Advocate General of the Army observed that only the good sense and restraint of the majority of Smith's subordinates prevented a complete reign of terror in Samar. The abuses outraged anti-Imperialist groups in the US when they were reported in March 1902.

The exact number of Filipinos killed by US troops in Samar will never be known. A population shortfall of about 15,000 is apparent between the Spanish census of 1887 and the American census of 1903, but how much of the shortfall is due to disease and known natural disasters and how many due to combat and massacre is difficult to determine. Population growth in nineteenth-century Samar was amplified by an influx of workers for the booming hemp industry, an influx which certainly ceased during the Samar campaign. Research in the 1990s tentatively put the figure at about 2,500. Some American and Filipino historians believe it to be around 5,000. American military historians' opinions on the Samar campaign are echoed in the February 2011 edition of the US Army's official historical magazine, *Army History Bulletin*: '... the indiscriminate violence and punishment that US Army and Marine forces under Brig. Gen. Jacob Smith are alleged to have unleashed on Samar have long stained the memory of the United States' pacification of the Philippine Islands.'

Events in Samar resulted in prompt investigations. On 15 April 1902, Secretary of War Elihu Root sent orders to relieve officers of duty and to court-martial General Smith.

> The President (Theodore Roosevelt) desires to know and in the most circumstantial manner all facts, nothing being concealed, and no man being for any reason favored or shielded. For the very reason that the President intends to back up the Army in the heartiest fashion in every lawful and legitimate method of doing its work, he also intends to see that the most rigorous care is exercised to detect and prevent any cruelty or brutality, and that men who are guilty thereof are punished.[64]

Jacob H. Smith and Littleton Waller faced courts-martial as a result of their heavy-handed treatment of Filipinos; Waller specifically for the execution of twelve Filipino bearers and guides. Waller was found not guilty, a finding that senior military officials did not accept. Smith was found guilty, admonished and forced to retire. A third officer, Captain Edwin Glenn, was court-martialled for torturing Filipinos.[65]

In late 1901, Brigadier General James Franklin Bell took command of American operations in Batangas and Laguna provinces.[66] Bell also embarked on a scorched earth policy to defeat the guerrillas. 'Zones of protection' were established, and civilians were given identification papers and forced into *reconcentrados,* concentration camps, which were surrounded by free-fire zones. Colonel Arthur Wagner, the US Army's chief public relations officer, insisted that the camps were to 'protect friendly natives from the insurgents, and assure them an adequate food supply' while teaching them 'proper sanitary standards'. That assertion was undermined by a letter from a commander of one of the camps, who described them as 'suburbs of Hell'.[67] Between January and April 1902, 8,350 out of approximately 298,000 prisoners died, and some camps experienced mortality rates as high as 20 per cent. Bell explained the high death toll: 'One-sixth of the natives of Luzon have either been killed or have died of the dengue fever in the last few years. The loss of life by killing alone has been very great, but I think not one man has been slain except where his death has served the legitimate purposes of war. It has been necessary to adopt what in other countries would probably be thought harsh measures.'

Civilians were put under curfew, after which all persons found outside of camps without identification could be shot on sight. Men were rounded up for questioning, tortured, and summarily executed. Torture was routinely employed during interrogation, and entire villages were burned or otherwise destroyed.[68]

What is now called 'waterboarding' was rife. Lieutenant Grover Flint told one inquiry:

> A man is thrown down on his back and three or four men sit or stand on his arms and legs and hold him down; and either a gun barrel or a rifle barrel or a carbine barrel or a stick as big as a belaying pin, – that is, with an inch circumference, – is simply thrust into his jaws and his jaws are thrust back, and, if possible, a wooden log or stone is put under his head or neck, so he can be held more firmly. In the case of very old men I have seen their teeth fall out, – I mean when it was done a little roughly. He is simply held down and then water is poured onto his face down his throat and nose from a jar; and that is kept up until the man gives some sign or becomes unconscious. And, when he becomes unconscious, he is simply rolled aside and he is allowed to come to. In almost every case the men have been a little roughly handled. They were rolled aside rudely, so that water was expelled. A man suffers tremendously, there is no doubt about it. His sufferings must be that of a man who is drowning, but cannot drown ... I did not stop it, because I had no right to...[69]

An unnamed officer reported:

> We have a company of Macabebe scouts who go out with white troops, and, if they cannot get any guns voluntarily, they proceed to give the fellows the water cure; that is, they throw them on their backs, stick a gag in their months to keep it open, then proceed to fill them with water till they cannot hold more. Then they get on them, and a sudden pressure on the stomach and chest forces the water out again. I guess it must cause excruciating agony.[70]

George Kennan wrote:

> A company of Macabebes enter a town or barrio, catch some man, – it matters not whom, – ask him if he knows where there are any guns, and,

upon receiving a negative answer, five or six of them throw him down, one holds his head, while others have hold of an arm or a leg. They then proceed to give him the 'water torture,' which is the distension of the internal organs with water. After they are distended, a cord is sometimes placed around the body and the water expelled. From what I have heard, it appears to be generally applied; and its use is not confined to our section. Although it results in the finding of a number of guns, it does us an infinite amount of harm. Nor are the Macabebes the only ones who use this method of obtaining information. Personally, I have never seen this torture inflicted, nor have I ever knowingly allowed it; but I have seen a victim a few minutes afterward, with his mouth bleeding where it had been cut by a bayonet used to hold the mouth open, and his face bruised where he had been struck by the Macabebes. Add to this the expression of his face and his evident weakness from the torture, and you have a picture which once seen will not be forgotten. I am not chickenhearted, but this policy hurts us. Summary executions are, and will be, necessary in a troubled country, and I have no objection to seeing that they are carried out; but I am not used to torture. The Spaniards used the torture of water, throughout the islands, as a means of obtaining information; but they used it sparingly, and only when it appeared evident that the victim was culpable. Americans seldom do things by halves. We come here and announce our intention of freeing the people from three or four hundred years of oppression, and say, 'We are strong, and powerful, and grand.' Then to resort to inquisitorial methods, and use them without discrimination, is unworthy of us, and will recoil on us as a nation.[71]

There was indeed a backlash at home. Utah Senator Joseph Lafayette Rawlins told the Senate: 'Until recently, I had thought that these things (torture) were sporadic and isolated, but I have been forced to the belief that they are but a part of the general plan of campaign.'[72] He was right, but by the brutal standards of this most brutal war, Bell's strategy was successful. A Republican congressman who visited the Philippines reported:

You never hear of any disturbances in Northern Luzon; and the secret of its pacification is, in my opinion, the secret of the pacification of the archipelago. They never rebel in Northern Luzon because there isn't anybody there to rebel. The country was marched over and cleaned out in a most resolute manner. The good Lord in heaven only knows the number of Filipinos that were put under ground. Our soldiers took no prisoners, they kept no records; they simply swept the country, and, wherever or whenever they could get hold of a Filipino, they killed him. The women and children were spared, and may now be noticed in disproportionate numbers in that part of the island.[73]

General Bell relentlessly pursued Malvar and his men, forcing the surrender of many of the Filipino soldiers. Finally, Malvar surrendered, along with his sick wife and children and some of his officers, on 16 April 1902.[74] By the end of the month nearly 3,000 of Malvar's men had also laid down their weapons. The Filipino war effort dwindled until a fragile peace could be declared.[75]

The Philippine Organic Act approved on 1 July 1902 stipulated that a legislature would be established composed of a popularly elected lower house, the Philippine Assembly, and an upper house consisting of the Philippine Commission. On 4 July, Theodore Roosevelt, who had succeeded the murdered McKinley as president, proclaimed an amnesty for those who had participated in the conflict.[76]

The total number of Filipino who died remains a matter of debate. Some modern sources cite a figure of 200,000 Filipino civilians dead, with most losses attributable to famine and disease. Some estimates reach 1 million dead.[77] Manuel Arellano Remondo wrote: 'The population decreased due to the wars, in the five-year period from 1895 to 1900, since, at the start of the first insurrection, the population was estimated at 9,000,000, and at present (1908), the inhabitants of the Archipelago do not exceed 8,000,000 in number.' Between 16,000 and 20,000 Filipino soldiers and active insurgents were killed.[78] The US Department of State reckoned that the war resulted in the death of over 4,200 American combatants, and many more injuries from combat and debilitating disease, out of around 126,000 troops who took part.

During and after most of the events described above, American troops were engaged elsewhere in the Philippines to suppress another insurgency.

* * *

The Moro, a people of the southern Philippines including Mindanao, Jolo and the Sulu Archipelago, had been fighting the Spanish for 300 years and did not lay down their arms for the American occupation. A culture of jihad and resistance was in their DNA. Before their territory was ceded to the US, the Spanish garrisons were restricted to forts and the coast as it was so dangerous to advance into the vast rural hinterland. American forces took control in May 1899 and at Zamboanga in December 1899. The Kiram-Bates Treaty with the Moro Sulu Sultanate guaranteed the Sultanate's autonomy and internal self-governance and included Article X that guaranteed the preservation of slavery. But once the Northern Filipinos were largely subdued and their leader Aguinaldo captured, the Americans removed Article X and, ahead of the expected uprising, invaded Moroland.[79]

Moro forces were commanded by General Nicolas Capistrano, and American forces pursued him during the winter of 1900/1901, capturing him in late March. At the end of August new American commander

Brigadier General George Whitefield Davis adopted a conciliatory policy towards the Moros. American forces under his command had standing orders to buy Moro produce when possible and to have 'heralds of amity' precede all scouting expeditions. Peaceful Moros would not be disarmed; polite reminders of America's anti-slavery policy were allowed. Captain John J. Pershing, one of Davis' subordinates assigned to the American garrison at Iligan, successfully established friendly relations with Amai-Manabilang, the retired Sultan of Madaya, and the Maranao tribes on the northern shore of Lake Lanao. Manabilang was the area's most influential leader and the alliance did much to secure American standing. Not all of Davis' subordinates were as diplomatic as Pershing, however, including veterans of the Indian wars whose catchphrase was 'civilize 'em with a Krag'.[80]

Three ambushes of American troops by Moros to the south of Lake Lanao, outside of Manabilang's sphere of influence, prompted the military governor of the Philippines, Major General Adna R. Chaffee, to demand that the offenders be handed over. There was no response, so an expedition under Colonel Frank Baldwin set out to punish the south-shore Moros. A worried Davis joined the expedition as an observer. On 2 May 1902, Baldwin's expedition attacked a Moro *cotta* (fortress) at Pandapatan, but the defences proved unexpectedly strong, leading to eighteen American casualties. On the second day, the Americans used ladders and moat-bridging tools to break through the Moro fortifications, and a general slaughter of the Moro defenders followed.

Pershing reported that the vanguard 'crossed to the berm and sprang upon the parapet, encountering Moros in hand-to-hand combat ... Three men were wounded almost instantly, but short work was made of the remaining Moros, who in all parts of the fort continued to fight desperately to the death.' James Arnold wrote:

Pershing's terse account fails to capture the full horrors of Bacolod. When the storming party entered the fort they were met by hordes of desperate Moro warriors who emerged from bombproofs and tunnels. It was a kill-or-be-killed melee pitting Kris and kampilan against bayonet and rifle butt. Chaplain George Rice was among the first to enter the fort. He wanted to record the scene with his Brownie camera – a simple, boxy, handheld device introduced by Eastman Kodak only three years earlier – and almost died in the attempt when the Panandungan appeared from a covered passage and charged with his Kris. Rice managed to dodge the attack. The Panandungan turned to attack surgeon Lieutenant R. Patterson, who was kneeling to attend the mutilated Sergeant Hafer (one of the first over the parapet). Patterson, a big, strong man, lashed out with his fist and struck the Panandungan on the chest, thereby buying time for nearby comrades to kill the Moro leader.[81]

The fort was torched.

When on 4 July President Roosevelt declared an end to hostilities in the Philippines he added, 'except in the country inhabited by the Moro tribes, to which this proclamation does not apply'. Later that month, Davis was promoted and replaced Chaffee as the supreme commander of American forces in the Philippines. Command of the Mindanao-Jolo Department went to Brigadier General Samuel S. Sumner. Meanwhile, Pershing settled down to conduct diplomacy with the surrounding Moros, and one celebration had 700 guests from neighbouring *rancherios*. In February 1903, Pershing was declared a *datu* by the formerly hostile Bayan Moros who had been defeated at Pandapatan, the only American to be so honoured. Pershing led a march around Lake Lanao which was largely peaceful apart from a few skirmishes. It became a symbol of American control of the region among Moros of the Maranao clans.

On 1 June 1903, the Moro Province was created, which included 'all of the territory of the Philippines lying south of the eighth parallel of latitude, excepting the island of Palawan and the eastern portion of the northwest peninsula of Mindanao'. The province was divided into five districts, with American officers serving as district governors and deputy governors. The districts were sub-divided into tribal wards, with major *datus* serving as ward chiefs and minor *datus* serving as deputies, judges, and sheriffs.

In August 1903, Major General Leonard Wood became governor of Moro Province and commander of the Department of Mindanao-Jolo. Wood officially abolished slavery and imposed the cedula, a registration poll tax which outraged the Moro who saw it as a form of tribute. Wood took a heavy-handed and uncompromising line, being 'personally offended by the Moro propensity for blood feuds, polygamy, and human trafficking'[80] and with his 'ethnocentrism sometimes [leading] him to impose American concepts too quickly in Moroland'. Wood also faced an uphill Senate battle over his appointment to the rank of major general, which drove him to seek military laurels in order to shore up his lack of field experience. Although Wood had served as an administrator in Cuba, he had seen only 100 days of field service during the Spanish–American War [83] Furthermore, Wood had been promoted over the heads of many officers of greater seniority, bringing charges of favouritism against president and fellow Rough Rider Teddy Roosevelt. Even though his promotion had been confirmed, Wood's reputation had suffered. As a result, he led the army on punitive expeditions over minor incidents that would have been better handled diplomatically by the district governors. Wood's governorship saw the hardest and bloodiest fighting of America's occupation of Moroland.

The Moros used arrows, bayonets, a few outdated guns, and *kris* swords against repeating rifles, waterboarding and artillery, and suicide attacks became a popular tactic due to the overwhelming firepower of the Americans in conventional battles. Moro women dressed identically to men took part in the resistance, leading to the song sung by American troops called 'If a Lady's Wearin' Pantaloons'. Barbed wire proved no impediment since *juramentado* warriors (swordsmen who sought martyrdom) surged through even as it ripped at their flesh and even as they were shot repeatedly with bullets.[84] One *juramentado*, Panglima Hassan, was shot dozens of times before he went down. As a result, the Americans phased out .38 revolvers favour of Colt .45s. Pershing wrote that *juramentado* attacks 'were materially reduced in number by a practice the army had already adopted, one that the Mohammadans held in abhorrence. The bodies were publicly buried in the same grave with a dead pig. It was not pleasant to have to take such measures but the prospect of going to hell instead of heaven sometimes deterred the would-be assassins.'[85] There is no evidence that Pershing himself gave such orders. Nor is the claim made twice in 2016 and 2017 by Donald Trump that Pershing executed forty-nine 'Muslim terrorists' with bullets dipped in pig's blood, then let the fiftieth go free to spread the word about the religious atrocity, given any credence by responsible historians.

At the beginning of February 1906, Major General Tasker H. Bliss replaced General Wood as the commander of the Department of Mindanao-Jolo, but Wood remained governor of Moro Province. Although Moro hostilities had died down during the latter days of Wood's governorship, the tenure of General Bliss was a period of relative peace. But tensions rose among the Moros living on the island of Jolo, who objected to the curtailing of slave-trading, cattle-raiding and women-stealing privileges.

A Moro named Pala ran amok in British-held Borneo and then fled to Jolo. Colonel Hugh Scott, the governor of the District of Sulu, attempted to arrest Pala, but his *datu* gave him sanctuary. During the resulting fight, Pala escaped. He avoided capture for several months, setting up his own *cotta* and becoming a *datu* in his own right. Wood led an expedition against Pala but was ambushed by Moros. Wood beat off the ambushers, and many of them found refuge in the volcanic crater of Bud Dajo.

Bud Dajo is 2,100 feet above sea level. It is steep, conical and has thickly forested slopes. Only three major paths lead up the mountain, and the thick growth kept the Americans from cutting new paths. However, there were many minor paths, known only to the Moros, which would allow them to resupply even if the main paths were blocked. The crater at the summit is 1,800 yards in circumference and easily defended. The mountain itself is 11 miles in circumference, making a prolonged siege nearly impossible.

Over the months that followed, the occupants of Bud Dajo were swelled by more Moro locals. Water was plentiful, their families joined them, and they began farming rice and potatoes. Major Scott described them as harmless villagers seeking refuge from the upheaval on Jolo caused by the actions of American forces. Wood ordered an attack in February 1906, but Scott convinced him to rescind the order, arguing that the opposition of the surrounding *datus* would keep Bud Dajo isolated.[86] Unfortunately, occupants of Bud Dajo began raiding nearby Moro settlements for women and cattle. Although the *datus* of Jolo continued to condemn the occupants of Bud Dajo, there began to develop popular support of a general uprising among the Moro commoners of Jolo. They included the survivors of two or three previous revolts, poll tax rebels, die-hards against the American occupation, and some outlaws who recognised no rulers. It was decided that action had to be taken against them.

On 2 March, Wood ordered Colonel J. W. Duncan of the 6th Infantry Regiment stationed at, the provincial capital of Zamboanga to lead an expedition against Bud Dajo. Duncan and Companies K and M took the transport right to Jolo. Governor Scott sent three friendly *datus* up the mountain to ask the Bud Dajo Moros to disarm and disband, or at least send their women and children to the valley. They refused and Scott ordered Duncan to begin the assault.

The assault force was more than 700 strong – 272 men of the 6th Infantry, 211(dismounted) men of the 4th Cavalry, sixty-eight men of the 28th Artillery Battery, fifty-one Philippine Constabulary, 110 men of the 19th Infantry and six sailors from the gunboat Pampanga. The battle began on 5 March, as mountain guns fired forty rounds of shrapnel into the crater. The following day, Wood arrived, but left Duncan in direct command. One last attempt to negotiate with the occupants was rejected and the Americans drew up into three columns and proceeded up the three main mountain paths with the troops ascending a 60 per cent slope, using machetes to clear the path.

Early on the morning of 7 March, Major Bundy's detachment met a barricade 500 feet below the summit. American snipers picked off some of the defenders, barricade was shelled with rifle and then assaulted in a bayonet charge. The Moros counter-charged with *kris* and spear. About 200 Moros died in the engagement, and Major Bundy's detachment suffered heavy casualties. Captain Rivers' detachment also encountered a barricade and took it after several hours of fighting during which Rivers suffered a severe spear wound. Captain Lawton's detachment advanced up the third path which was so steep in places that the Americans proceeded on hands and knees, continuously harassed by Moros hurling boulders; Lawton finally took the defensive trenches on the crater rim by storm.

The remaining Moro defenders retreated into the crater and fighting continued until nightfall. During the night, the Americans used block and tackle to haul mountain guns to the crater's edge. At daybreak, the mountain guns and the guns of the Pampanga opened up while a well-placed machine gun swept the position relentlessly without any regards to the non-combatants, women and children, in their gunsights. A natural fortification became a death trap. The Americans charged the surviving adult Moros with fixed bayonets, and the Moros fought back with improvised grenades made with black powder and seashells. Out of the estimated 800–1,000 Moros at Bud Dajo, only six survived. Corpses were piled 5 feet deep, and many of the bodies were wounded multiple times. Those of all the children and most of the women were blown apart. With a death rate of 99 per cent, higher, for example, than every other 'massacre' of the era, including Wounded Knee. By any estimate, Bud Dajo was the bloodiest engagement of the Moro Rebellion. American casualties were up to twenty-one killed and seventy-five wounded, although many subsequent calculations have put it much lower.

President Roosevelt sent Wood a congratulatory cablegram, but reporters stationed at Manila cabled their own accounts. The description of the engagement as a 'battle' was swiftly disputed because of the overwhelming firepower of the attackers and the lopsided casualties. Mark Twain wrote: 'In what way was it a battle? It has no resemblance to a battle ... We cleaned up our four days' work and made it complete by butchering these helpless people.' The engagement proved a pyrrhic victory for the Americans; it was an unmitigated public-relations disaster. The *New York Times* headlines read,

WOMEN AND CHILDREN KILLED IN MORO BATTLE
Mingled with Warriors and Fell in Hail of Shot
FOUR DAYS OF FIGHTING
Nine Hundred Persons Killed or Wounded —
President Wires Congratulations to the Troops.[87]

Such coverage resonated with an American public which already had deep misgivings about the behaviour of their troops elsewhere in the Philippines and who had also been largely unaware of the continuing violence in Moro Province. The propaganda effort was not helped when Major Scott pointed out that the crater had previously been used as a place of refuge during Spanish assaults. He claimed that those who fled to the crater 'declared they had no intention of fighting, – ran up there only in fright...'

Under pressure from Congress, Secretary of War Taft cabled Wood for explanation of the 'wanton slaughter' of women and children. The explanations included claims that the Moros had used their families as human shields, claims rejected by post-conflict reports that indiscriminate shelling and machine-gun fire was wholly responsible for the civilian carnage. Despite not being in command of the assault (although he was the senior officer present), Wood accepted full responsibility, a move which gained him respect in the army. By the time the scandal died down, Wood had assumed his post as Commander of the Philippine Division.

Aware of the potential for another public relations backlash, General Bliss launched no punitive expeditions during his term in office, but his peace was superficial as it tolerated high levels of lawlessness. Heavily outnumbered Constabulary forces in pursuit of Moro fugitives often found themselves forced to abandon their chase after the fugitives took refuge at their home *cottas*.[88]

On 11 November 1909, the now Brigadier General John Pershing assumed his duties as the third and final military governor of Moro Province. In order to extend rule of law into the interior, Pershing stationed the Philippine Scouts in small detachments throughout the interior. This reduced crime and promoted agriculture and trade, at the cost of reduced military efficiency and troop training. The benefits of this reform outweighed the costs. The legal system was streamlined in a way which pleased the Moros, since it was quick, simple, and resembled their traditional unification of executive and judicial powers. Pershing promised to donate government land for purposes of building Muslim houses of worship. He recognised the practice of *sacopy* – indentured servitude in exchange for support and protection – as legitimate but reaffirmed the government's opposition to involuntary slavery. The economy of Moro Province continued to expand under Pershing. The three most important exports – hemp, copra, and lumber – increased 163 per cent during his first three years, and Moros began to make bank deposits for the first time in their history. The Moro Exchange system bought and sold goods to and from the Moros at fair prices.

But Moro diehards refused to go away, and many went to ground at their home *cottas*, requiring an entire troop of police or soldiers to arrest them. There was always the danger of a full-fledged battle breaking out during such an arrest, and this led to many known outlaws going unpunished. In 1911, Pershing resolved to disarm the Moros. Leonard Wood, now Army Chief of Staff, disagreed with this plan, stating that the Moros would hide their best arms, turning in only their worst. Pershing waited until roads into the interior had been completed, so that government troops could protect disarmed Moros from holdouts. Pershing's deadline for disarmament was 1 December 1911.

The attempted enforcement of this order was fiercely resisted in Jolo and led to the 'Second Battle of Bud Dajo'. An estimated 800 Moros fortified the top of the dormant volcano. Pershing, realising the Moros had no time to provision their fortress, used two infantry battalions, a machine gun platoon, six troops of the 2nd Cavalry, a field artillery battery, five companies of the Philippines Scouts, and a company of Constabulary. By cutting a lateral trail which encircled the mountain, 300 yards downhill from the crater rim, Pershing cut off the Moros from the hidden mountainside paths and then persuaded the majority of the assembled Moros to return home. While involving roughly equivalent forces as the first engagement, it was far less bloody, causing only 12 Moro casualties. By 1913, Pershing agreed that the Moro Province needed to transition to civil government and in December he was replaced as governor of Moro Province by a civilian.

During the Moro Rebellion, the Americans suffered 130 killed and 323 wounded. Another 500 or so died of disease. The Philippine Scouts who augmented American forces during the campaign suffered 116 killed and 189 wounded; the Philippine Constabulary suffered more than 1,500 losses, of which half were fatalities. Moro casualties have proved impossible to estimate but must have been high, as few surrendered in combat.

* * *

Before, during and in the decades after, American domestic opinion was polarised about the morality of the war, a debate which from the start was fed by the tsunami of letters home from the front, many of which were reprinted by anti-war and anti-imperialist societies and extensively quoted above. One newspaper editorial said:

> In many letters there is an eerie contrast between the writers' disregard for the slaughter of Filipino goo-goos and their concern for the health of their parents and friends. William Eggenberger described with boyish glee an incident in which he and a fellow private had terrorized the inhabitants of a nipa hut by sticking their bayonets through the side of the house. He then concluded his letter with the request: 'Don't you and the old man work so hard all the time ... hoping these lines will find you all in the best of health, a kiss for you all.'[89]

The political debate between the pro- and anti-war factions were, of course, coloured by hypocrisy. The industrialist Andrew Carnegie offered to buy the Philippines from the US in order give the islands their independence, saying: 'I would gladly pay twenty million today to restore our republic to its first principles.' In another speech he said: 'To be popular is easy; to be right when right is unpopular, is noble ... I repudiate with scorn the immoral doctrine, "Our country, right or wrong."'[90] But in reference to Carnegie's attempted suppression of steelworkers on the domestic front, Secretary of State John Hay observed: 'He does not seem to reflect that the government is in a somewhat robust condition even after shooting down several American workers in his interest at Homestead.'

Christian zealotry was, again of course, a factor in the arguments of both sides. Baptist minister Revd H. P. Faunce declared: 'The Kingdom of Heaven is to come as a grain of mustard seed, not as a thirteen-inch shell.'[91] But, as Mark Twain, faced by pro-war Christian fundamentalists, pointed out:

> Extending the Blessings of Civilization to our Brother who Sits in Darkness has been a good trade and has paid well, on the whole; and there is money in it yet, if carefully worked – but not enough, in my judgment, to make any considerable risk advisable. The People that Sit in Darkness are getting to be too scarce – too scarce and too shy. And such darkness as is now left is really of but an indifferent quality, and not dark enough for the game. The most of those People that Sit in Darkness have been furnished with more light than was good for them or profitable for us. We have been injudicious ... Is it, perhaps, possible that there are two kinds of Civilization – one for home consumption and one for the heathen market?

At the heart of the ongoing controversy was, and is, how American behaviour in the Philippines can be squared with its founding principles and its own war of independence from the British. William James raged: 'God damn the U.S. for its vile conduct ... We can destroy their [Filipino] ideals but we can't give them ours.' Senator Carl Schurz, a reforming journalist, wrote early on: 'If we turn this war, which was heralded to the world as a war of humanity, in any sense into a war of conquest, we shall forever forfeit the confidence of mankind.' And Charles Elliot Norton declared: 'The United States has lost her unique position as a leader in the progress of civilization and has taken up her place simply as one of the grasping and selfish nations of the present day.'[92]

After Cuba, the burgeoning press also saw commercial opportunities in stirring up passions. The editor of *The Nation*, E. L Godkin, said of his yellow journalism competitors: 'They rely mostly on large sales, and for large sales on sensational news. Now nothing does so much to keep sensational news coming in over the considerable period of time as war ... Next to war they welcome the Promise of war.'[93]

Another dominating domestic issue, pertinent today, was over whether America was pursuing colonial policies designed to create its own global empire. Pamphlets sent out by the Anti-Imperialist League to American troops in the field in the Philippines, as a test of free speech, were decreed 'seditious' by Postmaster Charles Smith.[94] At the onset of war, League President Moorfield Stanley forecast that

> if our success is a rapid and bloodless one as the most sanguine can hope, such a victory is more dangerous than defeat. In the intoxication of such a success, we would reach out for fresh territory, and to our present difficulties would be added an agitation for the annexation of new regions which, unfit to govern themselves, would govern us.

We would be fairly launched upon a policy of military aggression, of territorial expansion, of standing armies and growing navies, which is inconsistent with the continuance of our institutions. God grant that such calamities are not in store for us.

History proved him right, but the war's defenders were also honest in their aims. *The Nation* editorialised:

The struggle must continue until the misguided creatures there shall have eyes bathed in enough blood to cause their vision to be cleared, but that those whom they are now holding as enemies have no purpose toward them expect to consecrate to liberty and to open for them a way to happiness.[95]

The *Literary Digest* said: 'Whether we like it or not, we must go on slaughtering the natives in English fashion, and taking what muddy glory lies in wholesale killing til they have learned to respect our arms. The more difficult task of getting them to respect our intentions will follow.'[96]

A staunch imperialist, journalist George Kennan, nevertheless wrote:

That we have inspired a considerable part of the Philippine population with a feeling of intense hostility toward us, and given them reason for deep-seated and implacable resentment, there can be no doubt. We have offered them many verbal assurances of benevolent intention; but, at the same time, we have killed their unresisting wounded, we hold fifteen hundred or two thousand of them in prison, we have established at Guam a penal colony for their leaders, and we are now resorting directly or indirectly to the old Spanish inquisitorial methods such as the 'water torture' in order to compel silent prisoners to speak or reluctant witnesses to testify ... that the present generations of Filipinos will forget these things is hardly to be expected.[97]

Underlying everything was the deep-seated racism of the time among imperial powers. Worthington C. Ford wrote:

Questions of conscience need not trouble us ... Here are rich lands, held by those who do not or cannot get the best out of them, and awaiting the fructifying application of capital and organization in commerce. Under this beneficent view the natives, an inferior race, must get out or become laborers. The Filipino is an incumbrance to be got rid of, unless he accepts the mandates of a purchasing and a conquering power.[98]

It also goes a long way to explaining the almost unbelievable cruelty inflicted on 'savages' by 'decent' Midwest farm boys, city clerks and Harvard-educated officers. H. L. Wells wrote:

> There is no question that our men do 'shoot niggers' somewhat in the sporting spirit, but that is because war and their environments have rubbed off the thin veneer of civilization ... Undoubtedly, they do not regard the shooting of Filipinos just as they would the shooting of white troops. This is partly because they are 'only niggers', and partly because they despise them for their treacherous servility ... The soldiers feel they are fighting with savages, not with soldiers.

A *Boston Herald* correspondent reported: 'Our troops in the Philippines ... look upon all Filipinos as of one race and condition, and being dark men, they are therefore "niggers", and entitled to all the contempt and harsh treatment administered by white overlords to the most inferior races.' Imperial and colonial arrogance, and the ingrained assumption of superiority, was not the sole domain of the old European powers. The most benevolent Americans regarded Filipinos as 'big children, who must be treated as little ones'.[99] Another newspaper editorialised: 'Today the torrid zone is a belt of semi-barbarism. Its inhabitants resist the civilization of the temperate zones instinctively, because they know they have not the mental and moral fiber to uphold it ... Climate and costless sustenance have made these people what they are, and no great intellectual and industrial advance can be expected until the conditions are changed.'[100] And a widely quoted but anonymous American trader mused: 'How "strange" it was that such an easy, slumbering, happy-go-lucky race ... should have such turbulent politics.' No one in the Philippines except the Japanese had 'the least idea of how to make machinery do the work of man.' Many other articles, even in the liberal, anti-imperialist press, described Filipinos as 'treacherous, arrogant, stupid and vindictive, impervious to gratitude, incapable of recognizing obligations.' It was argued that 'centuries of barbarism' had made them cunning and dishonest, which meant that Americans could not 'safely' be treated as equals.

The trouble is that no one could explain how such a 'backward' people could fight a modern, well-armed and industrialised America almost to a standstill for three long, bloody years. The millennia-old racist inclination of those who underestimate a foe offers one explanation. Lafayette College professor Richard E. Welch wrote:

> The American soldier viewed his Filipino enemies with contempt because of their short stature and color. Contempt was also occasioned by the refusal of the Filipino 'to fight fair' – to stand his ground and be shot down like a man. When the Filipino adopted guerrilla tactics,

it was because he was by his very nature half-savage and half-bandit. His practice of fighting with a bolo on one day and assuming the guise of a peaceful villager on the next proved his depravity.

From the first few weeks there was considerable sympathy for the Filipinos among the US rank and file, mixed with growing questioning – common to most wars – of what they were really doing there. Ellis G. Davis, of Company A, 20th Kansas, wrote:

They will never surrender until their whole race is exterminated. They are fighting for a good cause, and the Americans should be the last of all nations to transgress upon such rights. Their independence is dearer to them than life, as ours was in years gone by, and is today. They should have their independence, and would have had it if those who make the laws in America had not been so slow in deciding the Philippine question. Of course, we have to fight now to protect the honor of our country but there is not a man who enlisted to fight these people, and should the United States annex these islands, none but the most bloodthirsty will claim himself a hero. This is not a lack of patriotism, but my honest belief.[101]

Nebraskan soldier J. E. Fetterly wrote towards the end of the campaign: 'Some think the insurgents are disheartened, but I think they will make a desperate struggle for what they consider their rights. I do not approve of the course our government is pursuing with these people. If all men are created equal, they have some rights which ought to be respected.'

Over the following decades, various US legislation would pave the way for belated independence after the Japanese occupation of the Philippines during the Second World War. Despite such progress, the American occupation was, despite the bravery of some combatants, never a matter for national pride. Former US Governor-general William Howard Taft admitted during the insurgency: 'The severity with which the inhabitants have been dealt would not look well if a complete history of it were written out.'[102] It was not written out of the history books, but today remains largely forgotten.

General Elwell Stephen Otis was appointed major general in the regular army in 1906. Some regarded him as a skilled general and able administrator, others saw him as pompous and fuzzy and incapable of exuding any authority. His troops called him 'Granny'. He died in Rochester, New York, in 1909 after a painful bout of angina.

Leonard Wood retired from the army in 1921 and was appointed Governor General of the Philippines. Given his role in the massacre at Batu Dajo, and ongoing Filipino resentment, it was not an inspired choice. His tenure was characterised by marked tension between him and key Filipino officials, which came to a head after two years when he vetoed the dismissal of a Manila police detective accused of rape and 'of immorality and misconduct in office'. Wood died in 1927 in Boston after undergoing surgery for a brain tumour that had first been diagnosed seventeen years earlier.

Emilio Aguinaldo y Famy lived to become a national hero. He was seventy-seven years old when the US government recognised Philippine independence on 4 July 1946. After 469 days in hospital, he died of coronary thrombosis aged ninety-four in 1964.

Mark Twain wrote: 'I am opposed to having the [American] eagle put its talons on any other land.'[103] That aim went unfulfilled.

Afterword

And so, by these providences of god ... we are a world power.

The United States of America was born out of a revolution which rejected the rampant colonialism of the fast-growing British Empire. Quite right, too, even though the spark was a revolt by rich businessmen who did not like paying taxes and the rebellion which ensued was more a civil war than a clear-cut fight for independence. Ever since, successive presidents through periods of alleged isolationism or world policing or global warfare have maintained a pretence of anti-imperialism. Barack Obama, for example, trod a broadly justifiable line in having no truck with the British legacy in Africa. But, as we have seen in previous chapters, America's claim to have shunned an imperial role has always been a sham. At the very least, the US has maintained an empire of influence designed to advance America interests in all aspects of global affairs.

George Washington's farewell address may have promised good faith and justice towards all nations and cultivating peace and harmony with all, excluding both 'inveterate antipathies against particular nations, and passionate attachments for others', and advocating trade with all nations, but such high ideals were rarely put into practice.

Right from the start, before independence, English and European colonists moved westwards into the lands of Native Americans, driven by a continental expansionism. By any definition, from birth the US was an imperial nation bent on conquest. Washington himself described the new nation as an 'infant empire', and that was held as an obvious truth by other Founding Fathers – Benjamin Franklin wrote that 'the Prince that acquires new Territory [and] removes the Natives to give his own People Room ... may be properly called [Father] of [his] Nation', while Thomas Jefferson bluntly stated that the US 'must be viewed as the nest from which all America, North & South is to be peopled'. Modern-day philosopher Noam Chomsky, a renowned linguist who chooses his words carefully, said that 'the United States is the one country that exists, as far as I know, and ever has, that was founded as an empire explicitly'.[1]

Quite understandably, the interests of a new nation entering a new area of industrial and military might put its own interests top of its agenda. 'America first', if you like. The 1823 Doctrine issued by President James Monroe during a State of the Nation address proved a defining moment in US foreign policy; in return for America staying out of European conflicts, the Old Powers should not interfere with the affairs of sovereign nations located in the Americas. The Doctrine's authors, notably John Quincy Adams, publicly defined it as a proclamation by the US of moral opposition to colonialism. It never quite worked that way, but it was used by power-hungry subsequent presidents as a smokescreen to disguise American pursuit of its own form of colonialism. Crucially, the Doctrine placed no limitations on the US's own actions. Academic Jay Sexton notes that the tactics used to implement the Doctrine were 'modeled after those employed by British imperialists' in their territorial competition with Spain and France. It has been called 'imperial anti-colonialism'.[2]

Despite several wars with European Powers – the Quasi War with France, the War of 1812 with Britain and the 1898 Spanish–American War – the nineteenth century was mainly marked, from the American perspective, by the epic task of turning half a continent into a nation. That involved domestic wars with Native Americans, Mexican neighbours and, of course, a tragic civil war that resulted in the nation's biggest butcher's bill. The drive for expansion was also facilitated with the 1803 Louisiana Purchase from France (which at a stroke doubled the nation's size), the 1819 ceding of Florida from Spain, the annexation in 1845 that brought in the independent Texas Republic; the war with Mexico that added California, Arizona, Utah, Nevada and New Mexico in 1848, providing a total of 525,000 square miles of previously Mexican territory in the latter case.[3] Most, if not all, were deals which emerged from brutal conflict.

Before the trauma of the Civil War, vested American interests aimed to expand into Central America, notably William Walker's foray into Nicaragua. Senator Sam Houston of Texas even proposed a resolution in the Senate for the 'United States to declare and maintain an efficient protectorate over the States of Mexico, Nicaragua, Costa Rica, Guatemala, Honduras, and San Salvador'. Such fantasies were supported by the slave states as they offered a new supply of human livestock and by tycoons behind the Nicaraguan Transit, the main trade route connecting the Atlantic and Pacific Oceans before the Panama Canal was built. Later, President Ulysses S. Grant in 1870 tried and failed to annex the Dominican Republic because of a lack of Senate support.

The Indian Wars were spread across most of the nineteenth century as natives were squeezed into ever-shrinking territories and eventually demeaning reservations by military invasions, civilian encroachments and unfair treaties – that is, those treaties that weren't simply torn up when it suited white interests. This was an explicitly colonial process, as the Native American nations were usually recognised as sovereign entities prior to annexation.[4]

More peaceably, the US bought Alaska from the Russian Empire in 1867, and it annexed the independent Republic of Hawaii in 1898. Victory over Spain in 1898 brought the Philippines and Puerto Rico, as well as oversight of Cuba. At the same time, punitive expeditions in response to slights real and imagined strengthened a US stranglehold on trade across much of the globe, particularly when Washington looked so far to the west that it became the east.

America, along with the older Great Powers, clearly and deliberately followed the diktats of a 'New Imperialism' in the late nineteenth century by rapidly expanding overseas territories. Factors in that eruption of land grabs by both stealth and gunboat diplomacy included overt racism, missionary zeal to convert 'lesser' races to the glories of Christianity, the practice of social Darwinism, and simple greed.[5] Roosevelt claimed that he rejected imperialism but embraced expansionism, insisting that there was a difference. Early in his career, as Assistant Secretary of the Navy, he was an enthusiastic proponent of testing the US military in battle, stating: 'I should welcome almost any war, for I think this country needs one.'[6] He looked to both the crumbling Spanish Empire and the Pacific. In numerous small-scale Oriental adventures he adopted the tactics and strategies of the British.

Apart from presidential vainglory, trade and industry were the two main drivers of military incursions overseas. The lucrative popularity of Dole bananas, to use a profitably mundane example, grew from US intervention in Latin America and Hawaii. Annexed territories generated millions of dollars for those ready to exploit local assets, to bring new commodities to the home markets and boost US exports to the newly 'civilized' regions. In 1898, Senator Albert Beveridge proclaimed: 'American factories are making more than the American people can use; American soil is producing more than they can consume. Fate has written our policy for us; the trade of the world must and shall be ours.'[7]

But the scramble for overseas fortunes left a bitter taste among those at home who still clung to the belief that American imperialism, no matter how apparently benign, should have no place in the land of the Founding Fathers. Early in June 1898 retired Massachusetts banker Gamaliel Bradford had published a letter in a Boston newspaper proposing a public meeting to organise opponents of American colonial expansion.[8] A fervent opponent of the Spanish–American War, Bradford decried what he saw as an 'insane and wicked' colonial ambition among some American decision-makers which was 'driving the country to moral ruin'.[9] After a few weeks the meeting was held against 'the adoption of an imperial policy by the United States'. Bradford and an organising committee contacted religious, business, labour and humanitarian leaders to stop what they saw as a growing menace of American colonial expansion into Hawaii and the former colonial possessions of the Spanish Empire.[10] After a successful letter-writing campaign involving newspaper editors, the Anti-Imperialist League was born. Its president, until his death in 1905, was former Massachusetts governor, congressman, and senator George S. Boutwell. It quickly attracted the great and the good, the famous and the infamous, including former President Grover Cleveland, industrialist Andrew Carnegie and the latter's arch-enemy on the industrial front line, labour leader Samuel Gompers.

The group's largest and most influential local affiliates were located in New York City, Philadelphia, Chicago, Minneapolis, Cincinnati, Portland, Oregon, Los Angeles and Washington, DC, with over 25,000 activists.[11] The League swiftly pumped out political leaflets and pamphlets against American imperialist activities, including a series of 'broadsides' which made use of extensive quotations from George Washington, Thomas Jefferson and James Monroe pointing to fundamental contradictions between the ideas upon which the republic was founded and designs for colonial expansion being advanced by the nation's contemporary political leaders.

The best known of all its supporters and propagandists was the best-selling author Mark Twain who seemed to represent all the good things that Americans felt about themselves.[12] He wrote an essay, 'To the Person Sitting in Darkness', which appeared in the *North American Review* in February 1901 and had a major impact. Twain satirically portrayed the moral and cultural superiority of Americans compared to Filipinos to comment on what he believed to be the great irony of the Philippines' annexation – that America's international role was not to subjugate other nations for material gain, but to see 'a nation of long harassed and persecuted slaves set free'. Twain had already thundered: 'I have seen that we do not intend to free, but to subjugate the people of the Philippines. We have gone to conquer, not to redeem ... And so I am an anti-imperialist. I am opposed to having the [American] eagle put its talons on any other land.'[13] And during the mopping-up operations, Twain wrote:

> We have pacified some thousands of the islanders and buried them; destroyed their fields; burned their villages, and turned their widows and orphans out-of-doors; furnished heartbreak by exile to some dozens of disagreeable patriots; subjugated the remaining ten millions by Benevolent Assimilation, which is the pious new name of the musket; we have acquired property in the three hundred concubines and other

slaves of our business partner, the Sultan of Sulu, and hoisted our protecting flag over that swag. And so, by these providences of god — and the phrase is the government's, not mine — we are a World Power.

He was being ironic, but also prophetic. In 1904, President Roosevelt amended the Monroe Doctrine to treat Latin America as a marketplace for expanding US commercial interests. Roosevelt's amendment was designed to wield economic and military clout to make the US the dominant power in the Western Hemisphere. More interference in the affairs of other nations, no matter whether democracies or dictatorships, was thus made inevitable. Roosevelt watched the naval arms race between the British and German Empires, the clash of seagoing titans in the 1905 Russo–Japanese War and the launch of the state-of-the-art HMS *Dreadnought* the following year and was determined that the US should catch up in terms of maritime power. He launched a new construction programme and by 1907 had sixteen new battleships, sending his 'Great White Fleet' on a world cruise, a nominally peaceful training exercise. Its real purpose, however, was as a naked exhibition of American power. At every port, politicians and naval officers of both allies and potential enemies were welcomed on board and given tours which focused on the firepower and range of the new vessels. The cruise had the desired effect, and American sea power was never again under-estimated.[14]

The US Navy learnt from the voyage that more fuelling stations were needed around the world as the Great White Fleet required almost fifty coaling ships, and during the cruise most of the fleet's coal was purchased from the British, who could deny access to fuel during a military crisis, as they did with Russia during the Russo–Japanese War. The voyage similarly demonstrated that the Panama Canal, which was to be completed in 1914, was of huge strategic importance in extending America's military reach. Overall, Roosevelt's policy was that of 'speaking softly but carrying a big stick' and was enthusiastically followed by successive administrations while causing more controversy at home. The Anti-Imperialist League never fully recovered from Roosevelt's election as president and the internal squabbles it sparked over the gold standard and the best way to maintain civil rights. Despite its anti-war record, the League did not object to US entry into the tail-end of the First World War. It disbanded on 27 November 1920.[15]

Pretty much every American president who went to war used democracy to justify military intervention abroad, with wildly mixed results. International relations professor Abraham Lowenthal judged that US attempts to export democracy have been 'negligible, often counterproductive, and only occasionally positive'.[16] The US has since been repeatedly charged with aiding coups which overthrew democratically elected governments, in Iran, Guatemala, Chile and elsewhere. Historian Walter LaFeber claimed: 'The world's leading revolutionary nation (the US) in the eighteenth century became the leading protector of the status quo in the twentieth century.'

After the First World War broke out in Europe, President Woodrow Wilson promised American neutrality throughout the war, fearing that the 'great white nations' would destroy themselves in endless conflict, but eventually broke that pledge after evidence that the German Empire had designs on American territories. Feelings at home were mixed – there had been outrage over the sinking of the liner *Lusitania* by a German U-boat, but many states had been colonised by German immigrants. Civil rights leader W. E. B. Du Bois claimed it was 'a war for empire' to control vast raw materials in Africa and other British-colonised areas but that the German and Austro-Hungarian empires had a worse record of colonial exploitation and abuse. What is clear is that trade had a major influence on Wilson's about-turn. America's belated entry into the war opened up more international markets to surplus US production. In a memo to Secretary of State Bryan, the president described his aim as 'an open door to the world'. Wilson also declared that 'concessions obtained by financiers must be safeguarded by ministers of state, even if the sovereignty of unwilling nations be outraged in the process ... the doors of the nations which are closed must be battered down'.

Wilson had also promised to 'make the world safe for democracy', yet his actions often belied his official doctrine of moral diplomacy. In 1915 he ordered the invasion of Haiti after free elections because he did not believe its people were ready for self-government but did believe that US overlordship would bring stability to the region.[17] The leader of the Haiti expedition, General Smedley Darlington, spoke ruefully in a speech almost twenty years later:

> I was a racketeer, a gangster for capitalism. I suspected I was just part of a racket at the time. Now I am sure of it ... I helped make Mexico, especially Tampico, safe for American oil interests in 1914. I helped make Haiti and Cuba a decent place for the National City Bank boys to collect revenues in. I helped in the raping of half a dozen Central American republics for the benefits of Wall Street ... Looking back on it, I feel that I could have given Al Capone a few hints. The best he could do was to operate his racket in three districts. I operated on three continents.[18]

A vision of empire based on economic interest assumed the necessity of the US to 'police the world' in the aftermath of the war.

In an October 1940 report to Franklin Roosevelt, key State Department liaison officer Isaiah Bowman wrote that 'the US government is interested in any solution anywhere in the world that affects American trade. In a wide sense, commerce is the mother of all wars.' In 1942, by which time Pearl Harbour had finally propelled America into a world war on fascism, the idea of economic globalism was enshrined as the 'Grand Area' concept. Secret documents now unlocked show that under that plan, which indeed came to fruition, the US would have covert control over the 'Western Hemisphere, Continental Europe and Mediterranean Basin (excluding Russia), the Pacific Area and the Far East, and the British Empire (excluding Canada).' That encompassed all known major oil-bearing areas outside the Soviet Union, largely at the behest of corporate partners such as the Foreign Oil Committee and the Petroleum Industry War Council. The US thus avoided overt territorial acquisition, like that of the British and French empires, as being too costly, choosing the cheaper option of forcing countries to open their doors to American capitalism.[19]

Fear and loathing of communism in the early 1950s saw America drop all pretence of anti-colonialism in its support for France's doomed control of Vietnam. As with its backing of anti-Red Chinese forces, it became in the words of Raymond Fosdick 'allied with reaction'. In 1951 the young Massachusetts congressman John F. Kennedy wrote during a trip to Saigon: 'We are more and more becoming colonialists in the minds of the people.'[20] Such warnings went unheeded, not least by JFK himself when he became president, and the outcome was the long tragedy of the Vietnam War.

Kennedy, by the time he was assassinated, had committed 16,000 military personnel to South Vietnam and his successor Lyndon Johnson well knew the dangers inherent in escalation, especially while heading towards the 1964 presidential elections. LBJ showed, when opting for an escalation, the problems a democracy faces when the focus is entirely on the ballot box at home. He later said:

> I knew from the start that I was bound to be crucified either way I moved. If I left the woman I really loved – the great Society – in order to get involved with that bitch of a war on the other side of the world, then I would lose everything at home ... But if I left that war and let the Communists take over South Vietnam, then I would be seen as a coward and my nation would be seen as an appeaser and we would both find it impossible to accomplish anything for anybody anywhere on the entire globe.[21]

That speaks volumes about the American mindset at the time and, it can be argued, since.

Americans profess surprise that their efforts to promote democracy are misunderstood and that their self-appointed role as global police too often sparks hatred rather than appreciation. The view that, as America is the greatest nation on earth, it is always on the right side has throughout history been shared by empire-building countries such as Britain, France and Germany. But American intervention has more than most been marked by failure. Of thirty-five US interventions from 1945 to 2004, only in the case of Colombia did a fully fledged, stable democracy emerge in the following decade. Nation-building in other countries, notably Iraq and Afghanistan, quickly unravelled in the aftermath.

The CIA and other US departments and agencies have almost routinely assisted in the overthrow of foreign governments, including Iran (1953), Guatemala (1954) Congo (1960), the Dominican Republic (1961), South Vietnam (1963), Brazil (1964) and Chile (1973). The tools used ranged from outright bribery to downright assassination. The case of Guatemala proved particularly disastrous for the people of that unfortunate country, another legacy that is too often overshadowed by other, bigger conflicts. The United Fruit Company lobbied hard for the overthrow of the democratically elected left-wing government of Jacobo Árbenz and his replacement with a business-friendly military dictator, Carlos Castillo Armas. In Operation PBSUCCESS, the CIA aided the local military in achieving just that, painting the toppled government's much-needed land reforms as a communist threat. The coup triggered a decades-long civil war which claimed the lives of an estimated 200,000 people, mainly in massacres of the Maya population. An independent Historical Clarification Commission found that US corporations and government officials 'exercised pressure to maintain the country's archaic and unjust socio-economic structure', and that US military assistance had a 'significant bearing on human rights violations during the armed confrontation'.

During the massacre of at least 500,000 alleged communists in 1960s Indonesia, US government officials encouraged and applauded the mass killings while providing covert assistance to the Indonesian military perpetrators.[22] This included the US Embassy in Jakarta supplying Indonesian forces with lists of up to 5,000 names of suspected members of the Communist Party of Indonesia (PKI), who were subsequently killed.[23] In July 2016, an international panel of judges ruled the killings constitute crimes against humanity, and that the US, along with other Western governments, were complicit in these crimes. According to one study, the US intervened in eighty-one foreign elections between 1946 and 2000, while the Soviet Union or Russia intervened in thirty-six.[24]

America's gradual entanglement in Vietnam, propping up successive corrupt and hopeless regimes in the South, showed that neither Kennedy, nor Johnson, nor hawkish military commanders, nor gung-ho politicians, had learnt any lessons from even recent history. British military historian Max Hastings, a journalistic veteran of Vietnam, wrote: 'The Americans, so proud of their own anti-colonialist heritage and mindset, were bent upon conducting a war in exactly the style of colonial governments across the ages.' Hastings also quoted a US advisor's summing up of the average American's 'callous disregard' of those who would eventually defeat them: 'Americans of all grades joked about Vietnamese technology being defined by picking up one thing with two sticks or carrying two things with one stick.'[25] But then the Philippines and other prior conflicts outlined above demonstrated the casual racism that was so marked in the Vietnam tragedy.

The escalation of US involvement in Vietnam followed LBJ's 1964 election win as he regarded victory at any cost a matter of personal reputation. His bullish machismo in a foreign enterprise was in sharp contrast to his impressive reforms on civil rights and poverty – far greater than those achieved by the Kennedys – on the domestic front. Much has been written about the anti-war movement which developed as the 1960s progressed, and far less on the American public's passive acceptance earlier in the decade. But the latter is a good example of the closet imperialistic mindset of the time. Wars far away did not win or lose elections, provided the home front was unsullied. Middle America was inclined to trust the nation's leadership across parties in a way that never applied again after Vietnam and Watergate. Hastings wrote:

> Patriotism helped to stifle debate when American boys were already dying ... The foremost reason for public passivity was surely that no gunfire was being heard, no shells or bombs were falling on their own continent ... If the rubble on the streets of Saigon, the tears of the peasants in the paddies of the Mekong delta, had lain instead on Pennsylvania Avenue or fallen on North Carolina tobacco fields, Americans might have already been demonstrating as vigorously as were Vietnam's Buddhists.[26]

There was, of course, nothing new in American *realpolitik* disguising its acceptance of brutal regimes routinely using torture, human rights abuses, violations of international law and state murder to prop up the indefensible. Declassified records indicate that the CIA under Allen Dulles and the FBI under J. Edgar Hoover aggressively recruited more than 1,000 Nazis, including those responsible for war crimes, to use as spies and informants against the Soviet Union in the Cold War.[27]

US-led airstrikes and targeted killings by drones, designed to reduce the number of body-bags returning to America, have in recent years proved a blunt weapon which provides a handy recruitment tool for international terrorists. In 2016 the US dropped 26,171 bombs on seven different countries: Syria, Iraq, Afghanistan, Libya, Yemen, Somalia and Pakistan. The US has been accused of complicity in war crimes for backing the Saudi-led intervention in the Yemeni Civil War that triggered a humanitarian catastrophe.

During the Cold War, America's leaders excused support for anti-communists as a necessary evil, better than an outcome which resulted in Red or fundamentalist dictatorships. That was perhaps an understandable viewpoint, but not borne out in the 'post-war' era.

Friendly tyrants assured of US support resisted necessary reforms, while sucking up to dictators sparked a backlash among foreign populations with long memories. The post-9/11 view that such attacks on America justify anything which helps the 'war on terror' has proved both false and counter-productive.

Times change, but America and the Great Powers, old and new, have always been slow to understand that. Max Hastings, reviewing Sean McFate's 2019 analysis *Goliath – Why the West Doesn't Win Wars and What We Need to Do About It*, warned that Russian troll factories 'influence western elections and referenda, pour forth disinformation that explodes mines beneath traditional western bastions'. Subversion is critical and, according to McFate, 'War is going underground and will be fought in the complicated shadows. Militaries can no longer kill their way out of problems.' Bloated defence budgets in which billions are spent on aircraft carriers and nuclear weaponry belong to another era and go hand-in-hand with massive failures in intelligence gathering and a wider failure to understand enemies who don't stand still or fight conventional campaigns.[28]

The debate over America's role and its covert sense of imperial destiny continues. According to the US State Department, 'Democracy is the one national interest that helps to secure all the others. Democratically governed nations are more likely to secure the peace, deter aggression, expand open markets, promote economic development, protect American citizens, combat international terrorism and crime, uphold human and worker rights, avoid humanitarian crises and refugee flows, improve the global environment, and protect human health.' According to former US President Bill Clinton: 'Ultimately, the best strategy to ensure our security and to build a durable peace is to support the advance of democracy elsewhere. Democracies don't attack each other.'[29]

There are obvious parallels between the British Empire and the imperial role of the US, and all empires past and present have had both positive and negative aspects. America's positive aspects concerning democracy, free speech and optimism could, if it learns from history and its mistakes, greatly outweigh its negative aspects. But in the current climate it might be best not to hold your breath.

During the era of Donald Trump, isolationism, protectionism, colonialism and the gifts and dangers of superpower status in a powder-keg world of political uncertainties – contradictory concepts in most circumstances – are subsumed in the 'art of the deal'. America's foremost colonists, regardless of who holds ultimate office, are now not just to be found in the White House and Congress but also in the boardrooms of multinational companies, as smugglers of arms, drugs and people, and among the children of Silicon Valley. Imperialism, American-style.

Notes

Introduction

1. Army Center of Military History, July 31 2003
2. Wiltse, 142–145
3. Belko, 170–179
4. Cunliffe, 112
5. London *Times* review, May 11 2019
6. Nevin, 121
7. Nichols, 240–249
8. Cunliffe, 29
9. Dunkelman, 24–34
10. Satin, 84–89
11. Cunliffe, 8
12. Jacoby, 632
13. Tucker, 140
14. Cunliffe, 425
15. Hook and Pegler, 36
16. Miller, 15
17. Miller, 17–19
18. Miller, 59
19. *Encyclopedia of the War of 1812*, Naval Institute Press, 218
20. Miller, 84
21. Miller, 94
22. Burg, 53–78
23. Sweetman, 37
24. Sweetman, 44
25. Sweetman, 48–51
26. Howarth, 182–185
27. Howarth, 191
28. Howarth, 203–205
29. *Naval Encyclopedia* 2010, 462

30. Miller, 146–147
31. Sondaus, 126–128, 173–179
32. Sweetman, 87
33. Miller, 152
34. Laffin, 49

1. Lord Dunmore's War and Native Americans in The Revolutionary War

1. *Southern Literary Messenger*, Volume 16, September 1850, 533–540
2. HistoryofMassachusetts.org: Rebecca Beatrice Brook
3. Sterner, *Journal of the American Revolution*, July 2017
4. Gage to Haldimand, June 3 1773, Library of Congress
5. Dowd, 42–43
6. Faragher, 69–96
7. *Connolly Journal*, May 28 1774, George Washington papers, Library of Congress
8. *American Archives*, Fourth Series, Volume 1, 479
9. Carlyle Henshaw, Cornstalk et al blog, December 2007
10. Beverly Two Feathers-Owens, Native American Totems website, February 2014
11. *Southern Literary Messenger*, September 1850, 540–545
12. Swisher, 5
13. Roosevelt, chapters VIII and XI
14. Hinraker and Mancall, 139
15. Sterner, *Journal of the American Revolution*, July 2017
16. Swisher, 11
17. Sterner, 201
18. Swisher, 17
19. Swisher, 9
20. *Virginia Magazine of History and Biography*, Volume 77, No 3
21. Foote, chapter 12
22. Swisher, 8
23. Bicentennial register of members, Virginia State Library, 105–197
24. Armstrong, 27
25. Randall and Ryan, 96
26. Hurt, 211
27. O'Donnell, 710
28. *Red Hill Archived*, November 2012
29. Lanning, 59
30. Royal Society of Edinburgh, July 2006
31. Zaremba, 95
32. Foote, 533–542
33. Beverly Two Feathers-Owens, Native American Icons website, February 2014
34. Calloway, 49
35. Calloway, 33–34

36. Downes, 195
37. Downes, 211
38. Nelson, 101–107
39. Calloway, 39
40. Calloway, 36
41. Calloway, 65
42. Rindfleisch, *Journal of the American Revolution* website
43. Pope, 17
44. Calloway, 103
45. Colonel J.T. Holmes family papers, Columbus, Ohio 1915
46. Quaife, 515
47. Sipe, 404
48. Frost, 147–153
49. Keiber, 298–299
50. Pipkin, 45–47
51. Calloway, 44
52. Ramsey, 261–265
53. Tennesseans in the Revolutionary War website, Battle of Boyd's Creek
54. Calloway, 50

2. Little Turtle's War

1. Cayton, 147–148
2. Gugin and St Clair, 238
3. Carter, 45–47
4. Sword, 175
5. Carter, 48
6. Gaff, 247–248
7. Perry, 36
8. Barnhard, 284–285
9. Poinsatte, 23
10. Winkler, 15
11. Carter, 94
12. Barnhart, 284
13. Allison, 73
14. Carter, 92–93
15. Barnhart, 285
16. Allison, 74–76
17. Winkler, 15
18. Lemonds, 47
19. Zimmer, 97–101
20. Butts, 297
21. *The American Museum* or *Universal Magazine*, Volume III, 19
22. Stewart, 29
23. Johnson, October 2004
24. Allison, 81
25. Allison, 82

26. Army History Center 1784–1860 website
27. Allison, 83–85
28. Sword, 196
29. Sword, 199
30. Gaff, 11
31. Hogeland, 151
32. Sword, 218
33. Gaff, 13
34. Sword, 223–227
35. Sword, 240–246
36. Gaff, 149–150
37. Sword, 220
38. Gaff, 86
39. Sword, 221
40. Nelson, 52–60
41. Gaff, 109–110
42. The Army Historical Foundation, Arlington, 'Arthur Wayne and the Battle of Fallen Timbers'
43. Gaff, 234
44. Sword, 270
45. Winkler, 53
46. Gaff, 250–252
47. Carter, 137
48. Army Historical Foundation, Arlington
49. Gaff, 366–367
50. Sugden, 180
51. Gaff, 366–367
52. Madison, 36
53. Rafert, 74
54. Gugin and St Clair, 234–235

3. Shays' Rebellion and The Whiskey Rebellion

1. Trumball, 491
2. Elmer S. Smail, Descendants of Daniel Shays, November 1934, worldcat.org
3. Zinn, 71–72
4. Gross, 1
5. Szatmary, 25–31
6. Richards, 85
7. Hotten, 65–73
8. Szatmary, 29–34
9. Szatmary, 38–45
10. Zinn, 91
11. Hahn, 33
12. Zinn, 93
13. Richards, 87–88

14. Szatmary, 38
15. Morse, 28
16. Szatmary, 56
17. McClintock, 409–411
18. Belknap, 395–404
19. Richards, 84–85
20. Holland, 245–247
21. Starkey, footnote, 13
22. Manuel, 219
23. Szatmary, 92–99; Richards, 27–29
24. Richards, 28
25. Szatmary, 102–105
26. Richards, 31
27. Richards, 34–38
28. Freer, 402
29. Starkey, 164–168
30. Szatmary, 120–122
31. Szatmary, 127
32. Freer, 395
33. Chernow, 327–330
34. Hogeland, 67
35. Hogeland, 63
36. Slaughter, 105
37. Slaughter, 147–149
38. Slaughter, 108
39. Hogeland, 103–104
40. Slaughter, 119–127
41. Slaughter, 170
42. Slaughter, 177
43. Hogeland, 146–148
44. Hogeland, 153–154
45. Slaughter, 181–185
46. Elkins and McKitrick, 479
47. Slaughter, 196–200
48. Annals of the Third Congress, 1413
49. Slaughter, 208
50. Higginbottom, 189–198
51. Slaughter, 290–291
52. Hogeland, 238
53. Hogeland, 242

4. The Quasi War

1. Kohn, 225–242
2. Maier, 247–249
3. Office of the Historian, Milestones 1784–1800, Department of State
4. Miller, 9

5. Williams, 25
6. Harris, 25–32
7. Toll, 135
8. Toll, 134
9. *Dictionary of American Fighting Ships*, Defense Department, Naval Division, 84
10. Toll, 120
11. McBride, 27
12. Seawell, 143
13. Toll, 114–119
14. Mackenzie, 40
15. Lewis, 191–192
16. Lewis, 28–30
17. Jennings, 70
18. Allen, 184–185
19. Fehlings, volume 53
20. Hall, 210
21. Maclay, 207–298
22. *Pennsylvania Magazine of History and Biography* death notice, November 29 1800
23. Lyons, 305–333

5. The Barbary Wars

1. *Western Morning News*, April 11 2013
2. Colley, 70
3. Masselman, 205
4. Rojas, 160–186
5. Battistini, 246–447
6. Parker, 11
7. Founders Online, 7:571
8. Founders Online, 10:86
9. Roberts and Roberts, 163–170
10. Roberts and Roberts, 155–156
11. Parker, 66–86
12. Rojas, 168–169
13. Rojas, 165
14. *Naval Documents*, 1:405–409
15. *Thomas Jefferson Encyclopedia* website, August 2 2011
16. American State Papers, *Foreign Relations*, 352
17. Tucker, 297
18. Toll, 171,
19. Allen, 169
20. Toll, 122
21. Tucker, 78
22. Mackenzie, 76
23. Mackenzie 331–335

24. Mackenzie, 79
25. Mackenzie, 80
26. Tucker, 57
27. Mackenzie, 64–80
28. Mackenzie, 122
29. *Naval Documents Relating to the US Wars with the Barbary Powers*, Volume 1, 553–557
30. Tucker, 167
31. Herring, 100
32. Toll, 180
33. Tucker, 464
34. Leiner, 39–41
35. Allen, 281
36. Harris, 198–199
37. Waldo, 248
38. Maclay, 90–91
39. Allen, 281–282
40. Panzac, 352
41. London, 237–239
42. *Lloyd's List*, number 49876
43. Waldo, 250
44. Tucker, 168
45. Taylor, 289
46. Taylor, 10
47. Taylor, 292
48. Leiner, 39–50
49. Mackenzie, 291
50. Tucker, 175
51. Lewis, 94
52. Tucker, 180
53. Mackennzie, 316
54. Tucker, 179
55. Mackenzie, 440
56. Gutteridge, 257–260
57. Gutteridge, 262
58. Mackenzie, 331–335
59. Library of Congress, *Decatur*, 90

6. The German Coast Rebellion

1. Rasmussen, 142
2. *PSB Newshour*, January 27 2007
3. Lorraine Diehl, *New York Magazine*, October 1992
4. Pencak, 161
5. Aptheeker, 187–189
6. McCulla, *Colonial North America*, Harvard University website
7. Slave database, Whitney Plantation Historic District

8. Midlo Hall, 344
9. Rasmussen, 40
10. Rasmussen, 111
11. Hatfield, 156–180
12. Robert D. Taber, *History Compass 2015* online, 235–250
13. Rasmussen, 89–90
14. Rasmussen, 135
15. *Inventory of the community property of Jacques Deslondes and his wife Marguerite Picou,* Civil records of St John Parish, 1795, No. 60
16. Thompson, 311
17. Robert L. Paquette, 64 Parishes Project 2018, Louisiana Endowment for the Humanities
18. Kitchin, 31
19. Genovese, 592
20. Robert L. Paquette, 64 Parishes Project 2018, Louisiana Endowment for the Humanities
21. Rasmussen, 151
22. Rasmussen, 156
23. Rothman, 115–116
24. *Journal of the Abraham Lincoln Association,* Number 27, 1–27

7. Aegean Sea Anti-Piracy Operations

1. Field, 124
2. Wombwell, 84–85
3. *Naval History and Heritage Command,* November 2017
4. Roosevelt, 34
5. Cooper, 245
6. Love, 146–147
7. Swartz, 4
8. Field, 128
9. Swartz, 5
10. Love, 147
11. Detorakis, 401
12. Wombwell, 80–82
13. Swartz, 5

8. Sumatra Expeditions

1. Meacham, 213
2. Warriner, 104
3. Leatherneck Association 1980, 51
4. Corn, 295
5. Warriner, 94
6. Johnson, 44
7. Long, 207
8. New England Historic Genealogical Society 1863, 147
9. Earl, 119

10. New England Historic Genealogical Society 1863, 147
11. Murrell, 70

9. The Pork and Beans War and The Pig War

1. Keenlyside, 144–152
2. Aroostook Ewar: Historical Sketch and Roster of Commissioned Officers and Enlisted Men, *Kennebec Journal*, 1904
3. Keenlyside, 153
4. Remini, 535–564
5. Garraty, 336
6. Hayes, 171–178
7. Schofield, 303–306
8. White, 2
9. Chuck Woodbury, *Out West 15*, 2000
10. White, 4
11. Bell, 789–808

10. More Pirates and 'Savages'

1. Philbrick, 78
2. Stanton, 224–237
3. Ellsworth, 177–176
4. Macdonald, 38
5. Wilkes, 56–61
6. Ellsworth, 72–74
7. Stanton, 219–220
8. Smithsonian Institute Archives
9. Hening, 181–182
10. Hening, 183–184
11. Sewall, xxxvi
12. Griffis, 155
13. Ellsworth, 3–7
14. Ellsworth, 6
15. Ellsworth, 7
16. Morison, 431
17. *Memorandum on Fiji Land Claims*, US Department of State 1902, 55–56
18. Wallis, 16
19. Thornley, 176
20. *Irregular Warfare and the Vandalia expedition in Fiji, 1859*, Naval History Blog
21. *Irregular Warfare and the Vandalia expedition in Fiji, 1859*, Naval History blog
22. Mennell, Thakombau entry

11. The Cortina Wars

1. Elman, 189
2. Robenalt, 3
3. Elman, 189–190
4. McClary, 5
5. McClary, 6
6. Ford, 54
7. Ford, 236
8. Robenalt, 4
9. Robenalt, 5
10. Ford, 271
11. Robenalt, 6
12. Ford, 274
13. Ford, 289
14. Ford, 305–306
15. Thompson, 51
16. Texas State Archives
17. Ford, 434

12. The Shinmiyangyo Korean Expedition

1. Niderost, 1
2. *New York Herald*, June 17 1871
3. Lee Wha Rang, 2
4. Lee Wha Rang, 3
5. Letter published in *Missionary Magazine*, 1866
6. Kajong government archives relating to SHINMIYANGYO
7. Oh Moon Whan, *Christian News*, December 8 1926
8. Gyu Mu, 4–7
9. Kajong government archives relating to SHINMIYANGYO
10. US Diplomatic correspondence, 1870
11. Cable, 62 12, Tyson, 6 13 Chang, 10
14. Personal papers of Captain McLane Tilton, USMC, Archives and Library, Historical Branch, Headquarters Marine Corps, May 16 1871, *Annual Report of the Secretary of the Navy on the Operations of the Department for the year 1871*
15. Tilton, May 20 1871
16. Report of Rear Admiral John Rodgers, June 3 1871, Government Printing Office, Washington
17. Tilton, May 26 1871
18. Report of the Secretary of the Navy and of the Postmaster General, Government Printing Office, Washington 1871, 277
19. Tilton, June 4 1871
20. Tyson, 7
21. Asian Station Reports, Volume 2, July–November 1871
22. Niderost, 3–4
23. Rodgers, July 5 1871

24. Tilton, June 21 1871
25. Tilton, June 16 1871
26. Tilton, June 16 1871
27. *Lexington Morning Herald*, November 26 1897
28. Reports of Commander L.A. Kimberly USN to the Secretary of the Navy, July 5 1871
29. Tilton, June 20 1871
30. *Lexington Morning Herald*, November 26 1897
31. Rodgers to the Secretary of the Navy, June 23 1871
32. *New York Times*, August 22 1871
33. Nahm, 149
34. Tilton, June 21 1871
35. Tilton, June 16 1871
36. Deck logs for the USS *Colorado*, USS *Alaska*, USS *Benecia*, USS *Monocacy* and USS *Palos* from June 10, 1871 to July 3, 1871
37. Nahm, 149–150
38. Tilton, June 21 1871
39. Personnel Department, HQMC Records, Washington
40. US Marine Corps Historical Division

13. The Modoc War

1. Dunlay, 117
2. Sides, 87
3. Riddle, 28–30
4. Harvey V. Sproull, *Modoc Indian War*, Lava Beds Natural History Association, 1975
5. Sides, 87
6. Riddle, 28–30
7. Brown, 222
8. Murray, 71
9. Riddle, 252
10. Fisher and Doerr report
11. Riddle, 45
12. Cozzens, 144
13. Murray, 97–99
14. Cozzens, 143
15. Thompson, 28–29
16. Cozzens, 145
17. *New York Herald*, February
16. 1873
18. Cozzens, 146
19. United States War Department, *A Compilation of the Official Records of the Union and Confederate Armies*, US Government Printing Office, 875
20. Cozzens, 142

21. Reports to the Otis Conference, April 3 1873, and Otis to Odenal correspondence, April 11 1873, Library of Congress
22. Cozzens, 147
23. Meacham, 440–443
24. Brown, 231
25. Riddle, 71–72
26. Riddle, 72–76
27. Cozzens, 149
28. Riddle, 70–71
29. Meacham, 430–432
30. Heyman, 370–374
31. Heyman, 379
32. Cozzens, 150
33. Brown, 238
34. Thompson, 83–86
35. Cozzens, 151
36. Cozzens, 152
37. Riddle, 124–125
38. Cozzens, 152
39. Meacham, 441
40. US Congress, 43rd, 1st Session, House Executive Document 122, 111
41. Thompson, 115
42. Cozzens, 152 43 US Congress, 43rd, 1st Session, House Executive Document 122, 111
43. Riddle, 188–189
44. Cozzens, 154
45. *Army and Navy Journal*, October 25 1873, 16

14. The Samoan Crisis

1. Regan, 28
2. Kohn, 479–480
3. *New York Times*, March 10 1889
4. Regan, 30–31
5. Wilson, 53
6. *Proceedings* 1927, quoted by Hoppe, 2
7. Rousmeniere, 93–94
8. *Washington Herald*, December 15 1906
9. Hocking, 713
10. Hoppe, 45
11. Naval Historical Center, March 23 2002
12. Hoppe, 3
13. *New York Times*, March 30 1889
14. Wilson, 53
15. Rousmeniere, 87
16. Hoppe, 3
17. Wilson, 54

18. *The London Gazette*, January 7 1889
19. *The London Gazette*, May 30 1889
20. *The Marine Review*, November 1915, 411
21. Hoppe, 4–5
22. *New York Times*, August 14 1892
23. Mains, 249
24. Clowes, 257–259
25. Mains, 250
26. Clowes, 260

15. The Spanish–American War

1. Campbell, 72
2. Whyte, 260
3. Baycroft and Hewison, 225–226
4. Perez, 149
5. Trask, 2–3
6. Trask, 6
7. Rhodes, 44
8. Whyte, 314
9. Perez, 24
10. Russell, 8
11. Gatewood, 23–29
12. Faulkner, 231
13. Tone, 28
14. Reilly and Scheina, 28, 30
15. Offner, 56
16. Atwood, 98–109
17. Naval History and Heritage Command paper
18. Thomas, 48
19. Keenan, 372
20. Offner, 86–110
21. Tucker, 614
22. Offner, 57
23. Perez, 58
24. Thomas, 4–5, 209
25. Smythe, 192
26. Whyte, 260
27. Musicant, 152
28. Nasar, 133
29. Offner, 173–174
30. Trask, 57
31. Hansen, 86–88
32. *Historic Ships on a Lee Shore*, National Maritime Historical Society (144), August 2013, 12–13
33. *Battle of Manila*, Navy Historical Center website
34. Saravia and Garcia, 12–13

35. Saravia and Garcia, 27–29
36. Hendrickson, 44
37. Field, 659
38. Trask, 284
39. *Manila Times*, September 21 2006
40. Rogers, 110–112
41. Saravia and Garcia, 62
42. Saravia and Garcia, 109
43. Wolff, 94–95
44. Agoncillo, 169–170
45. Karnow, 115
46. Wolff, 100
47. Agoncillo, 194
48. Agoncillo, 110
49. Karnow, 123
50. Trask, 419
51. Karnow, 123–124
52. Agoncillo, 124
53. Halstead, 107
54. Karnow, 124
55. Wolff, 129
56. Lacsamana, 126
57. Brune and Burns, 290
58. Perez, 89
59. Post, 50–51
60. Post, 53
61. Post, 58
62. Post, 55
63. Post, 63–65
64. Norton, 582
65. Schubert, 135–139
66. *The Spokane Review*, July 14 1898
67. *The Day*, New London, July 15 1898
68. *Minneapolis Journal*, July 15 1898
69. Roosevelt, 572
70. Roosevelt, 423
71. *New York Times*, July 22 1898
72. Armstrong, 101
73. *American Heritage Magazine*, August 1969
74. Armstrong, 104
75. *American Heritage Magazine*, August 1969
76. *New York Times*, July 22 22 1898
77. Roosevelt, 568
78. *The Rough Riders Storm San Juan Hill, 1898*, eyewitnesstohistory. com 2004
79. Roosevelt, 568

80. Parker, 68
81. Roosevelt, 572; Tucker, 840
82. Dierks, 103
83. Tucker, 200
84. Parker, 59–60
85. Schubert, 135–139
86. Parker, 68
87. *War Notes*, Issue 1–8 (1898), Office of Naval Intelligence, 60–64
88. Trask, 60–71
89. Leeke, 84–86
90. Trask, 105
91. Carter, 101
92. Gannon, 83
93. Leeke, 115
94. Leeke, 121–122
95. Trask, 268
96. Goode, 298
97. Murphy, W.J., *Battle of Santiago, Eyewitness Account*, Naval History and Heritage Command
98. Goode, 299
99. Murphy, W.J., *Battle of Santiago, Eyewitness Account*, Naval History and Heritage Command
100. Trask, 264
101. Trask 265–266
102. West, 290
103. Whyte, 427
104. *The American Army Moves on Puerto Rico*, Spanish American War Centennial Website
105. Wolff, 175
106. *Protocol of Peace*, Washington DC, August 12 1898
107. Millis, 340
108. Perez, 11
109. Montoya, 78
110. Bailey, 657
111. Bergad, 74–75
112. Perez, 23, 56
113. Perez, 46–47
114. Osgood, 53
115. Atwood, 98–102
116. O'Toole, 125
117. Musicant, 164
118. Wegner, 11–13
119. Wegner, 8–11

16. The Philippines War

1. Miller, 83
2. Miller, 89
3. *New York World*, October 6 1900
4. *New York Times*, August 26 1899
5. Agoncillo, 213–214
6. *San Francisco Chronicle*, June 5 1898
7. *Harper's New Monthly Magazine* 98, May 1899
8. Agoncillo, 214–215
9. Chaputt, 255–266
10. Miller, 20
11. *New York Sun*, Winter 1994
12. Constantino, 225
13. Agoncillo, 218
14. Miller, 63; *The Nation*, May 4 1899
15. Feuer, 89–90
16. Linn, 48–52
17. Foner and Winchester, 323
18. Linn, 52
19. US Congressional series issue 3902, 372
20. Foner and Winchester, 322
21. Foner and Winchester, 322
22. Miller, 2
23. Lone, 56
24. Foner and Winchester, 323
25. Foner and Winchester, 316
26. Foner and Winchester, 320
27. Foner and Winchester, 321
28. Foner and Winchester, 322
29. Deady, 57–58
30. Linn, 186–187
31. Deady, 55, 67
32. Sexton, 237
33. Worcester, 290–292
34. Lone, 58
35. Miller, 63–68
36. Miller, 89
37. Brody, 69–71
38. *San Francisco Call*, February 21 1899
39. *San Francisco Call*, May 29, 1899
40. Miller, 93; *San Francisco Call*, March 30 1899
41. Miller, 93–96; *Literary Digest*, Volume 18, 1899
42. Miller, 94; *Boston Globe*, July 27 1900
43. Foner and Winchester, 317
44. Foner and Winchester, 319
45. Foner and Winchester, 323

46. Foner and Winchester, 319
47. Foner and Winchester, 320
48. Linn, 23–24
49. Zinn, 236
50. *San Francisco Call*, August 1 1899
51. Linn, 175
52. Brands, 59
53. *Manila Times*, June 2 2008
54. Agoncillo, 227–231
55. Worcester, 384
56. Bruno, 34
57. *Philippine Newslink*, December 15 2004
58. Couttie, 146
59. Annual Reports of the War Department, Volume 9, 629
60. Miller, 230
61. Literary Digest, No 19, 1899
62. Miller, 235
63. Miller, 220
64. US Senate Committee Hearings, *Affairs in the Philippine Islands*, February 3, 1902, Volume 3, 2341
65. *New York Times*, July 17 1902
66. Schirmer, 17
67. Miller, 244
68. Storey and Codman, 10,38, 48, 61, 95
69. Congressional 1 Session (1903), 1767–1768
70. *Munsey Magazine* No 21, 1899
71. *Literary Digest* No 18, 1899
72. *New York Times*, May 7 1902
73. *Boston Transcript*, March 4 1902
74. Tucker, 217
75. Tucker, 477
76. *New York Times*, July 4 1902
77. Tucker, 478
78. Rummel, 201
79. *New York Times*
80. Hunt, 198; Simmons, 68
81. Arnold, 69–70
82. *Boston Globe*, March 12 2006
83. Lane, 125–126
84. *The Field Artillery Journal,* volume 32
85. Pershing, 284–287
86. Lane, 127–128
87. *New York Times,* March 11 1906
88. Mannix, 164
89. *New York Tribune*, editorial, 1899

90. Zinn, 314
91. Miller, 147
92. Miller, 119
93. Miller, 154
94. Miller, 153
95. *The Nation*, June 23 1898
96. Literary Digest No 17, 1898
97. Miller, 155
98. Miller, 107
99. *San Francisco Call*, September 26 1900
100. *New York Sun*, September 24 1900
101. Foner and Winchester, 321
102. *Springfield Republican*, April 25 1900
103. *New York Herald*, October 15 1900

Afterword

1. Noam Chomsky lecture, April 7 2010
2. Sexton, 2–9
3. Field, 644–668
4. Williams, 810–831
5. Friedman, 381
6. *Crucible of Empire Timeline*, PBS online
7. Jones, 160–170
8. Tompkins, 122–123
9. *Boston Evening Transcript*, June 2 1898
10. Tompkins, 126
11. Report of the executive committee of the Anti-Imperialist League, February 10 1898
12. Tompkins, 128
13. *New York Herald*, October 15 1900
14. Miller, 166–171
15. Ryan and Schlup, 19
16. Lowenthal, 1, 4–5
17. Steigerwald, 30–40
18. Federation of American Scientists, 1933 archive online
19. Gonzalez, 69–89
20. Hastings, 29
21. Kearns, 263
22. Simpson, 193
23. Bellamy, 210
24. Renouard, 324
25. Hastings, 181
26. Hastings, 197–198
27. *Democracy Now!*, October 31 2014
28. *Sunday Times*, May 26 2019
29. *New York Times*, November 28 2010

Bibliography

Introduction

Belko, William S., *John C. Calhoun and the Creation of the Bureau* of Indian Affairs: An Essay on Political Rivalry, Ideology, and Policymaking in the Early Republic (South Carolina Historical Magazine 2004)

Burg, B.R., *Sodomy, Masturbation, and Courts-Martial in the Antebellum American Navy* (Journal of the History of Sexuality, 23, January 2014)

Cunliffe, Marcus, *Soldiers and Civilians – The Martial Spirit in America 1775–1865* (Eyre & Spottiswoode, London 1969)

Dunkelman, Mark H., *A just right to select our own officers': Reactions in a Union regiment to officers commissioned* (Civil War History 44, March 1998)

Hook, Jason, and Pegler, Martin, *To Live and Die in the West: The American Indian Wars, 1860–90* (Taylor & Francis, 2001)

Howarth, Stephen, *To Shining Sea: A History of the United States Navy, 1775–1998* (University of Oklahoma Press, 1999)

Jacoby, Jr., Alvin M., *The Nez Perce and the Opening of the Northwest* (Yale University Press, 1965)

Laffin, John, *Americans in Battle* (J.M. Dent and Sons, London 1973)

Langley, Harold, *Social Reform in the United States Navy, 1798–1862* (University of Illinois Press, 1967)

Miller, Nathan, *The U.S. Navy: A History (3rd ed.)* (Naval Institute Press, Annapolis, 1997)

Nevin, David, *The Old West – The Soldiers* (Time-Life Books, 1973–74)

Nichols, Roger L., *Army Contributions to River Transportation, 1818–1825* (Military Affairs magazine 33, 1969)

Satin, Allan, *The Development of the Army Corps System in the Union Army* (Ohio Civil War Genealogy Journal 14, June 2010)

Sondhaus, Lawrence, *Naval Warfare 1815–1914* (Routledge, London 2001)

Sweetman, Jack, *American Naval History: An Illustrated Chronology of the U.S. Navy and Marine Corps, 1775–present* (Naval Institute Press, Annapolis 2002)

Tucker, Spencer C., *The Encyclopedia of North American Indian Wars, 1607–1890: A Political, Social and Military History* (ABC–CLIO, 2011)

Wiltse, Charles M., *John C. Calhoun, Nationalist, 1782–1828* (Bobbs-Merrill Company, 1944)

1. Lord Dunmore's War and Native Americans in the Revolutionary War

Armstrong, Virginia Irving, *I Have Spoken : American History through the voices of the Indians* (Sage Books, University of Michigan 1971)

Butterfield, Consul Willshire, *An Historical Account of the Expedition against Sandusky under Col. William Crawford in 1782* (Clarke, Cincinnati 1873)

Calloway, Colin G., *The American Revolution in Indian Country: Crisis and Diversity in Native American Communities* (Cambridge University Press, 1995)

Crumrine, Boyd, *History of Washington County, Pennsylvania With Biographical Sketches of Many of Its Pioneers and Prominent Men* (L. H. Everts & Co., Philadelphia 1882)

David, James Corbett, *Dunmore's New World: The Extraordinary Life of a Royal Governor in Revolutionary America – with Jacobites, Counterfeiters, Land Schemes, Shipwrecks, Scalping, Indian Politics, Runaway Slaves, and Two Illegal Royal Weddings* (University of Virginia Press, 2013)

Dowd, Gregory Evans, *A Spirited Resistance: The North American Indian Struggle for Unity, 1745–1815* (Johns Hopkins University Press, Baltimore 1992)

Downes, Randolph C., *Council Fires on the Upper Ohio: A Narrative of Indian Affairs in the Upper Ohio Valley until 1795* (University of Pittsburgh Press, 1940)

Faragher, John Mack, *Daniel Boone: The Life and Legend of an American Pioneer* (Holt, New York 1992)

Foote, the Reverend William Henry, *Sketches of Virginia: Historical and Biographical* (1856)

Frost, John, *Heroes and Hunters of the West* (H.C. Peck & Theo Bliss, Philadelphia 1858)

Hindraker, Eric, and Peter C. Mancall, *At the Edge of Empire: The Backcountry in British North America* (John Hopkins University Press, Baltimore and London 2003)

Hintzen, William, *The Border Wars of the Upper Ohio Valley (1769–1794)* (Precision Shooting Inc., Connecticut 2001)

Hurt, R D., *The Indian Frontier, 1763–1846* (University of New Mexico Press, Albuquerque 2002)

Kellogg, Louise Phelps, Cornstalk entry in the *Dictionary of American Biography, Volume II* (Scribner, New York 1928)

Kleber, John E., *The Kentucky Encyclopedia* (University Press of Kentucky, Louisville 1992)

Lanning, Michael Lee. *African Americans in the Revolutionary War* (Citadel Press, 2005)

Lewis, Virgil A., *History of the Battle of Point Pleasant* (Charleston Tribune, West Virginia 1909)

Lofaro, Michael. *Daniel Boone: An American Life* (University Press of Kentucky, 2003)

Nelson, Larry L., *A Man of Distinction among Them: Alexander McKee and the Ohio Country Frontier, 1754–1799*. (Kent State University Press, Ohio)

Nester, William, *The Frontier War for American Independence* (Stackpole Books, Mechanicsburg, PA 2004)

O'Donnell, James H., *William Crawford, American National Biography* (Oxford University Press, New York 1999)

Pipkin, J.J., *The Story of a Rising Race: The Negro in Revelation, in History, and in Citizenship* (N.D. Thompson Publishing, St Louis 1902)

Pope, Franklin Leonard, *The Western Boundary of Massachusetts: A Study of Indians and Colonial History* (Privately printed, 1886)

Quaife, Milo Milton, *The Ohio Campaigns of 1782* (Mississippi Valley Historical Review 17, no. 4, March 1931)

Ramsay, J.G.M., *The Annals of Tennessee to the End of the Eighteenth Century* (Grambo & Co., Philadelphia 1853)

Randall, E. O. *The Dunmore War* (Heer Publishing, Columbus, Ohio 1902)

Randall, Emilius Oviatt and Daniel Joseph Ryan, *History of Ohio: the rise and progress of an American state, Volume 2* (The Century History Company, 1912)

Rindfleisch, Bryan, *The Stockbridge-Mohican Community, 1775–1783* (Journal of the American Revolution, February 2016)

Roosevelt, Theodore. *The winning of the West, Volume 1* (Putnam's Sons, 1889)

Sipe, C. Hale, *The Indian wars of Pennsylvania : an account of the Indian events, in Pennsylvania, of the French and Indian war, Pontiac's war, Lord Dunmore's war, the revolutionary war, and the Indian uprising from 1789 to 1795 ; tragedies of the Pennsylvania frontier* (Telegraph Press, Harrisburg 1929)

Skidmore, Warren and Donna Kaminsky, *Lord Dunmore's Little War of 1774: His Captains and their Men who Opened Up Kentucky & the West to American Settlement* (Heritage Books, Bowie, Maryland 2002)

Smith, Thomas H., ed. *Ohio in the American Revolution: A Conference to Commemorate the 200th Anniversary of the Ft. Gower Resolves* (Ohio Historical Society, Columbus 1976)

Smith, Zachariah, *The History of Kentucky* (Courier-Journal Job Printing Company, Louisville, Kentucky 1885)

Sugden, John. *Blue Jacket: Warrior of the Shawnees* (University of Nebraska Press 2000)

Swisher, James K., *Lord Dunmore's War: The Battle of Point Pleasant* (Warfare History Newtwork 2018)

Sword, Wiley, *President Washington's Indian Wagr: The Struggle for the Old Northwest, 1790–1795* (University of Oklahoma Press 1985)

Thwaites, Reuben Gold and Louise Phelps Kellogg, eds. *Documentary History of Dunmore's War, 1774* (Wisconsin Historical Society, 1905)

Williams, Glenn F., *Dunmore's War: The Last Conflict of America's Colonial Era* (2017)

Winkler, John F., Fallen Timbers 1794: The US Army's First Victory (Osprey Publishing, Oxford 2013)

Zaremba, Robert E. and Danielle R. Jeanloz, *Around Middlebury* (Arcadia Publishing, 2000)

2. Little Turtle's War

Alderman, Pat, *Dragging Canoe: Cherokee-Chickamauga War Chief* (Overmountain Press, Johnson City 1978)

Allison, Harold, *The Tragic Saga of the Indiana Indians* (Turner Publishing Company, Paducah 1986).

Bakeless, John, *Background to Glory: The Life of George Rogers Clark* (University of Nebraska Press, 1957)

Barnhart, John D. and Riker, Dorothy L., *Indiana to 1816: The Colonial Period* (Indiana Historical Society, 1971)

Brackenridge, Henry M., *Recollections of persons and places in the West* (James Kay Jun. and Brother, Philadelphia 1834)

Butts, Edward, *Simon Girty: Wilderness Warrior* (Vol 29, Quest Biography, Dundurn 2011)

Calloway, Colin G., *The American Revolution in Indian Country: Crisis and Diversity in Native American Communities* (Cambridge University Press, 1995)

Carter, Harvey Lewis, *The Life and Times of Little Turtle: First Sagamore of the Wabash* (University of Illinois Press, Urbana 1987)

Cayton, Andrew R. L., *Frontier Indiana* (Indiana: Indiana University Press, Bloomington 1996)

Clifton, James A., *Dunquat- American National Biography, Vol 7* (Oxford University Press, New York 1999)

Dowd, Gregory Evans, *A Spirited Resistance: The North American Indian Struggle for Unity, 1745–1815* (Johns Hopkins University, Baltimore and London 1992)

Downes, Randolph C., *Council Fires on the Upper Ohio: A Narrative of Indian Affairs in the Upper Ohio Valley until 1795* (University of Pittsburgh Press, 1940)

Drake, Samuel Adams, *The Making of the Ohio Valley States: 1660–1837* (1899)

Edel, Wilbur, Kekionga! The Worst Defeat in the History of the U.S. Army (Praeger Publishers, Westport 1997)

Eid, Leroy V., *Little Turtle, American National Biography* (Oxford University Press, New York 1999)

Fernandes, Melanie L., *Under the auspices of peace – The Northwest Indian War and its Impact on the Early American Republic* (The Gettysburg Historical Journal: Vol. 15, Article 8, 2016)

Gaff, Alan D., *Bayonets in the Wilderness* (University of Oklahoma Press, 2004)

Grenier, John., *The First Way of War: American War Making on the Frontier, 1607–1814* (Cambridge University Press, 2005)

Greve, Charles Theodore, *Centennial History of Cincinnati and Representative* Citizens (Biographical Publishing Company, 1904)

Gugin, Linda C., and James E. St Clair, eds., *Indiana's 200: The People Who Shaped the Hoosier State* (Indiana Historical Society Press, Indianapolis 2015)

Hurt, R. Douglas, *The Ohio Frontier: Crucible of the Old Northwest, 1720–1830* (Indiana University Press, Bloomington 1996)

Jennings, Francis, *The Founders of America* (Norton, New York 1993)

Johnson, Jeffery L., *Saving Private Boone: Joseph Boone at Harmar's Defeat* (Compass, The Boon Society October 2004)

Kellogg, Louise P., ed., *Frontier Advance on the Upper Ohio, 1778–1779* (State Society of Wisconsin, Madison 1916)

Kenton, Edna, *Simon Kenton: His Life and Period, 1755–1836* (Originally published 1930; reprinted by Ayer, Salem 1993)

Klink, Karl, and James Talman, ed., *The Journal of Major John Norton* (Champlain Society, Toronto 1970)

Lemonds, Leo L., *Colonel William Stacy – Revolutionary War Hero* (Cornhusker Press, Hastings, Nebraska 1993)

Lossing, Benson, *The Pictorial Field-Book of the War of 1812* (Harper & Brothers, 1868)

Madison, James H., *Hoosiers: A New History of Indiana* (Indiana University Press and the Indiana Historical Society Press, Bloomington and Indianapolis 2014)

Nelson, Larry L., *A Man of Distinction among Them: Alexander McKee and the Ohio Country Frontier, 1754–1799* (Kent State University Press, Ohio 1999)

Nelson, Paul David, *Anthony Wayne. Soldier of the Early Republic.* (Bloomington, Indiana: Indiana University Press, Bloomington 1985)

Nester, William., *The Frontier War for American Independence* (Stackpole Books, Mechanicsburg, PA, 2004)

Nogay, Michael Edward, *Every Home a Fort, Every Man a Warrior* (Tri-State Publishing Co. 2009)

Odo, William O., *Destined for Defeat: an Analysis of the St Clair Expedition of 1791* (Northwest Ohio Quarterly, 1993)

Perry, James, Arrogant Armies (Castle Books, Edison 2005)

Poinsatte, Charles, *Outpost in the Wilderness: Fort Wayne, 1706–1828* (Fort Wayne Historical Society, 1967)

Pratt, G. Michael, *The Battle of Fallen Timbers: An Eyewitness Perspective* (Northwest Ohio Quarterly. No 67, 1995)

Quaife, Milo Milton, *The Ohio Campaigns of 1782* (Mississippi Valley Historical Review 17, no. 4, March 1931)

Rafert, Stewart, *The Miami Indians of Indiana: A Persistent People. 1654–1994* (Indiana Historical Society, Indianapolis 1996)

Skaggs, David Curtis, ed., *The Old Northwest in the American Revolution* (The State Historical Society of Wisconsin, Madison 1977)

Sosin, Jack M., *The Revolutionary Frontier, 1763–1783* (Holt, New York 1967)

Sugden, John (2000), *Blue Jacket: Warrior of the Shawnees* (University of Nebraska Press, Lincoln and London 2000)

Stewart, David O., American Emporer (Simon and Schuster, New York 2011)

Sword, Wiley, *President Washington's Indian War: The Struggle for the Old Northwest, 1790–1795* (University of Oklahoma Press 1985)

Taylor Jr., Robert M.; Errol Wayne Stevens; Mary Ann Ponder; and Paul Brockman, *Indiana: A New Historical Guide* (Indiana Historical Society, Indianapolis 1989)

Thwaites, Reuben G. and Louise P. Kellogg, eds., *Frontier Defense on the Upper Ohio 1777–1778* (Originally pub 1912, Kraus reprint, Millwood, NY 1977)

Van Every, Dale, *A Company of Heroes: The American Frontier, 1775–1783* (Morrow, New York 1962)

White, Richard, *The Middle Ground: Indians, Empires, and Republics in the Great Lakes Region, 1650–1815.* (Cambridge University Press 1991)

Winkler, John F., *Fallen Timbers 1794: The US Army's First Victory* (Osprey Publishing, Oxford 2013); *Wabash 1791: St Clair's Defeat*; Osprey Campaign Series, Oxford 2011)

Zimmer, Louise, *More True Stories from Pioneer Valley* (Sugden Book Store, Marietta, Ohio 1993

3. Shay's Rebellion and the Whiskey Rebellion

Baldwin, Leland D., *Whiskey Rebels: The Story of a Frontier Uprising* (University of Pittsburgh Press, 1968)

Belknap, Jeremy, *The History of New Hampshire* (Stevens and Ela & Wadleigh, Dover 1831)

Bell, Charles Henry, *History of the Town of Exeter, New Hampshire* (J.E. Farwell & Co., Boston 1888)

Boyd, Steven R., ed., *The Whiskey Rebellion: Past and Present Perspectives* (Greenwood Press, Westport, Connecticut: Greenwood Press 1985); *The Whiskey Rebellion, Popular Rights, and the Meaning of the First Amendment In The Whiskey Rebellion and the Trans-Appalachian Frontier*, edited by W. Thomas Mainwaring (Washington and Jefferson College, 1994)

Chernow, Ron, *Alexander Hamilton* (Penguin Press, New York 2004)

Cooke, Jacob E., *The Whiskey Insurrection: A Re-Evaluation* (Pennsylvania History 30, July 1963)

Elkins, Stanley M. and Eric L. McKitrick, *The Age of Federalism* (Oxford University Press, 1995)

Feer, Robert, *Shays's Rebellion and the Constitution: A Study in Causation* (The New England Quarterly, Volume 42, No. 3, September 1969)

Foner, Eric, *Give Me Liberty! An American History* (W.W Norton, New York 2006)

Griffin, Simon Goodell, *A History of the Town of Keene* (Sentinel Printing Company, Keene 1904)

Gross, Robert A., *The Uninvited Guest: Daniel Shays and the Constitution* (University Press of Virginia, 1993)

Hahn, John Willard, *The background of Shay's rebellion: a study of Massachusetts history 1780–1787* (University of Wisconsin-Madison, 1946)

Heffernan, Nancy Coffey, and Stecker, Ann Page, *New Hampshire: Crosscurrents in Its Development* (University Press of New England, Lebanon 1986)

Hogeland, William, *The Whiskey Rebellion: George Washington, Alexander Hamilton, and the Frontier Rebels Who Challenged America's Newfound Sovereignty* (Scriber. New York 2006)

Holland, Josiah Gilbert, *History of Western Massachusetts* (S. Bowles, Springfield 1855)

Holt, Wythe, *The Whiskey Rebellion of 1794: A Democratic Working Class Insurrection* (The Georgia Workshop in Early American History and Culture, 2004)

Holton, Woody, *Unruly Americans and the Origins of the Constitution* (Farrar, Straus, and Giroux, 2007)

Manuel, Frank Edward, and Manuel, Fritzie Prigohzy, *James Bowdoin and the Patriot Philosophers* (American Philosophical Society, Philadelphia 2004)

McClintock, John Norris, *History of New Hampshire* (B.B. Russell, Boston 1888)

Minot, George Richards, *History of the Insurrection in Massachusetts* (Isaiah Thomas, Worcester 1788)

Morse, Anson, *The Federalist Party in Massachusetts to the Year 1800* (Princeton University Press, New Jersey 1909)

Richards, Leonard L., *Shays's Rebellion: The American Revolution's Final Battle* (University of Pennsylvania Press, Philadelphia 2002)

Sanborn, Franklin Benjamin, *New Hampshire: An Epitome of Popular Government* (The Riverside Press, Cambridge 1904)

Slaughter, Thomas P., *The Whiskey Rebellion: Frontier Epilogue to the American Revolution* (Oxford University Press, 1986)

Starkey, Marion L., *A Little Rebellion* (Knopf, New York 1955)

Szatmary, David P., *Shays' Rebellion: The Making of an Agrarian Insurrection* (University of Massachusetts Press, 1980)

Trumbull, James Russell, *History of Northampton, Massachusetts from its settlement in 1654* (Gazette Printing Company, Vol. II, Northampton 1898–1902)

Zinn, Howard, *A People's History of the United States* (HarperCollins, New York 2005)

4. The Quasi War

Abbot, Willis J., *American Merchant Ships and Sailors* (Dodd, Mead & Company, New York 1902)

Allen, Gardner Weld, *Our Naval War With France* (Houghton Mifflin, Boston and New York 1909)

DeConde, Alexander, *The Quasi-War: The Politics and Diplomacy of the Undeclared War with France, 1797–1801* (Charles Scribner's Sons, 1966)

Fehlings, Lt-Col Gregory E., *America's First Limited War* (Naval War College Review, Volume 53, Number 3, Summer 2018)

Hall, John E. (editor), *Recollections of a Voyage to Italy in the year 1800* (The Port Folio and New York Monthly Magazine, Philadelphia September 1822)

Harris, Thomas, *The Life and Services of Commodore William Bainbridge, United States Navy* (Carey Lea & Blanchard, Philadelphia 1837)

Hickey, Donald R., *The Quasi-War: America's First Limited War, 1798–1801* (The Northern Mariner XVIII, Nos. 3–4, July–October 2008)

Kohn, Richard H., *Eagle and Sword: The Federalists and the Creation of the Military Establishment in America* (Free Press, 1975)

Lewis, Charles Lee, *Famous American Naval Officers* (L.C.Page & Company, Inc., 1924); *The Romantic Decatur* (Ayer Publishing, 1937)

Love, Robert, *History of the U.S. Navy Volume One 1775–1941* (Stackpole, Harrisburg 1992)

Lyon, E. Wilson, *The Franco-American Convention of 1800* (Journal of Modern History, Vol 12, The University of Chicago Press, September 1940)

Jennings, John, *Tattered Ensign - The Story of America's Most Famous Fighting Frigate, U.S.S. Constitution* (Thomas Y. Crowell, 1966)

Mackenzie, Alexander Slidell, *The Life of Stephen Decatur: A Commodore in the Navy of the United States* (C. C. Little and J. Brown, 1846)

Maclay, Edgar Stantan, *A History of the United States Navy, from 1775 to 1894* (D. Appleton and Company, New York 1895)

Maier, Pauline, *Ratification: The People Debate the Constitution 1787–1788* (Simon and Schuster, New York 2010)

McBride, James, *Naval biography consisting of memoirs of the most distinguished officers of the American navy* (Morgan, Williams & Co., Cincinnati 1815)

Nash, Howard Pervear, *The forgotten wars: the role of the US Navy in the quasi war with France and the Barbary Wars 1798–1805* (AS Barnes, 1968)

Palmer, Michael A., *Stoddert's war: Naval operations during the quasi-war with France, 1798–1801* (Naval Institute Press, 1999)

Seawell, Molly Elliot, *Twelve naval captains: being a record of certain Americans who made themselves immortal* (Kegan, Paul, Trench, Trubner, & Co. Ltd., London 1898)

Toll, Ian W., *Six Frigates: The Epic History of the Founding of The U.S. Navy* (W.W. Norton, New York 2006)

Waldo, Samuel Putnam, *The Life and Character of Stephen Decateur* (P. B. Goodsell, Hartford 1821)

Williams, Greg H., *The French Assault on American Shipping, 1793–1813: A History and Comprehensive Record of Merchant Marine Losses* (McFarland Publishers, 2009)

5. The Barbary Wars

Adams, Henry, *History of the United States of America During the Administrations of Thomas Jefferson.* (Originally published 1891; Library of America edition 1986)

Allen, Gardner Weld, *Our Navy and the Barbary Corsairs* (Houghton Mifflin & Co., Boston, New York and Chicago 1905)

Allison, Robert J., *Stephen Decatur American Naval Hero, 1779–1820* (University of Massachusetts Press, 2005)

Appelbaum, Yoni, The Third Barbary War (The Atlantic., March 2011)

Battistini, Robert, *Glimpses of the Other before Orientalism: The Muslim World in Early American* Colley, Linda, *Captives – Britain, Empire and the World* (Pimlico, London 2003)

Gruppe, Henry, *The Frigates* (Time-Life Books, 1979)

McKee, Christopher, *Edward Preble: A Naval Biography 1761–1807* (Naval Institute Press, Annapolis 1972)

Guttridge, Leonard F., *Our Country, Right Or Wrong: The Life of Stephen Decatur* (Tom Doherty Associates, New York 2005)

Hagan, Kenneth J., *This People's Navy: The Making of American Sea Power* (The Free Press, New York 1992)

Hernon, Ian, *Fortress Britain: All the Invasions and Incursions Since 1066* (The History Press, Stroud 2013)

Herring, George C., *From Colony to Superpower: U.S. Foreign Relations since 1776* (Oxford University Press, New York 2008)

Hickman, John, *Early American Wars* (Kurose Ross, 1982)

Keynes, Edward, *Undeclared War* (Penn State Press, 2004)

Lambert, Frank, *The Barbary Wars: American Independence in the Atlantic World* (Hill and Wang, New York 2005)

Leiner, Frederick C., *The End of Barbary Terror: America's 1815 War Against the Pirates of North Africa* (Oxford University Press, New York 2006)

Lewis, Charles Lee, *Famous American Naval Officers* (L.C.Page & Company, Inc., 1924)

London, Joshua E., *Victory in Tripoli: How America's War with the Barbary Pirates Established the U.S. Navy and Shaped a Nation* (John Wiley & Sons, Inc., New Jersey 2005)

Mackenzie, Alexander Slidell, *Life of Stephen Decatur: A Commodore in the Navy of the United States* (C. C. Little and J. Brown, 1846)

Maclay, Edgar Stanton, *A History of the United States Navy, from 1775 to 1893* (D. Appleton & Company, New York 1894)

Masselman, George, *The Cradle of Colonialism* (Yale University Press, New Haven 1963)

Oren, Michael B., *Power, Faith, and Fantasy: The United States in the Middle East, 1776 to 2006* (W.W. Norton & Co, New York 2007)

McKee, Christopher, *Edward Preble: A Naval Biography 1761-1807* (Naval Institute Press, Annapolis 1972)

Panzac, Daniel, *The Barbary Corsairs: The End of a Legend, 1800–1820* (K. Brill, Netherlands 2005)

Parker, Richard B., *Uncle Sam in Barbary* (University Press of Florida, Gainesville 2004)

Pratt, Fletcher, Preble's Boys: Commodore Preble and the Birth of American Sea Power (New York: William Sloane, New York 1950)

Roberts, Priscilla H. and Richard S., *Thomas Barclay 1728–1793: Consul in France, Diplomat in Barbary* (Lehigh University Press, Bethlehem 2008)

Rojas, Martha Elena, *Insults Unpunished' Barbary Captives, American Slaves, and the Negotiation of Liberty* (Early American Studies: An Interdisciplinary Journal. 1.2, 2003)

Smethurst, David, *Tripoli: The United States' First War on Terror* (Presidio Press, New York 2006)

Taylor, Stephen, *Commander: The Life and Exploits of Britain's Greatest Frigate Captain* (Faber and Faber, London 2012)

Toll, Ian W., *Six Frigates: The Epic History of the Founding of the U.S. Navy* (W. W. Norton, 2006)

Tucker, Glenn, *Dawn Like Thunder: The Barbary Wars and the Birth of the U.S. Navy* (Bobbs-Merrill, Indianapolis 1963)

Waldo, Samuel Putnam, *The Life and Character of Stephen Decatur* (P. B. Goodsell, Hartford 1821)

Wheelan, Joseph, *Jefferson's War: America's First War on Terror, 1801–1805* (Carroll & Graf, New York 2003)

Whipple, A. B. C., *To the Shores of Tripoli: The Birth of the U.S. Navy and Marines* (Bluejacket Books, 1991)

Zacks, Richard, *The Pirate Coast: Thomas Jefferson, the First Marines, and the Secret Mission of 1805* (Hyperion, New York 2005)

6. The German Coast Rebellion

Aptheker, Herbert, *American Negro Slave Revolts* (Columbia University Press, New York 1943)

Berlin, Leslie, *Slavery in New York* (New Press, New York 2005)

Carter, Clarence Edwin, editor, *The Territorial Papers of the United States, V. 9: The Territory of Orleans – 1803–1812* (U.S. Government Printing Office, 1940)

Conrad, Glenn R., editor, *The German Coast: Abstracts of the Civil Records of St Charles and St John the Baptist Parishes, 1804–1812* (Center for Louisiana Studies, Lafayette 1981)

Dormon, James H., *The Persistent Specter: Slave Rebellion in Territorial Louisiana* (Louisiana History 28, Autumn 1977)

Engerman, Stanley, Seymour Drescher, and Robert Paquette, editors, *Slavery* (Oxford University Press, New York 2001)

Genovese, Eugene D., *Roll, Jordan, Roll: The World the Slaves Made* (Vintage Books, New York 1976)

Hatfield, Joseph Tennis, *William C. C. Claiborne, Congress, and Republicanism, 1797–1804* (Tennessee Historical Quarterly, 24(2), 1965)

Horton, Lois, *Slavery and the Making of America* (Oxford University Press, New York 2005)

Katz, William Loren, *Black Legacy, A History of New York's African Americans* (Atheneum, New York 1997)

Kolchin, Peter, *American Slavery, 1619–1877* (Hill and Wang, New York 1994)

Midlo Hall, Gwendolyn, *Africans in Colonial Louisiana* (Louisiana State University Press, 19921)

Paquette, Robert L., *Revolutionary St Domingue in the Making of Territorial Louisiana, in A Turbulent Time: The French Revolution in the Greater Caribbean* (Indiana University Press, Bloomington 1997); *Slave Insurrection of 1811* (Encyclopedia of Louisiana, Louisiana Endowment for the Humanities, January 2011)

Pencak, William, *Historical Dictionary of Colonial America* (Scarecrow Press, July 2011)

Rasmussen, Daniel, American Uprising: The Untold Story of America's Largest Slave Revolt (Harper/HarperCollins Publishers, 2011).

Rodriguez, Junius P., *Always En Garde: The Effects of Slave Insurrection upon the Louisiana Mentality* (Louisiana History 33, Autumn 1992)

Rothman, Adam, *Slave Country: American Expansion and the Origins of the Deep South* (Harvard University Press, Cambridge, Massachusetts 2005)

Sitterson, J. Carlyle, *Sugar Country; the Cane Sugar Industry in the South, 1753–1950* (University Press of Kentucky, Lexington 1953)

Thompson, Thomas Marshall Thompson, *National Newspaper and Legislative Reactions to Louisiana's Deslondes Slave Revolt of 1811* (The Louisiana Purchase Bicentennial Series in Louisiana History, Vol 3: The Louisiana Purchase and its Aftermath, 1800–1830, University of Louisiana, Lafayette, 1998)

Thrasher, Albert, editor, *On to New Orleans! Louisiana's Heroic 1811 Slave Revolt* (second edition, Cypress Press, New Orleans 1996)

7. Aegean Sea Anti-Piracy Operations

Abbot, Willis J., *The Naval History of the United States* (Peter Fenelon Collier, New York 1890)

Allen, Gardner Weld, *Our Navy and the Barbary Corsairs* (Houghton Mifflin & Co., Boston, New York and Chicago 1905)

Cooper, James Fenimore, *Lives of distinguished American naval officers* (Carey and Hart, Philadelphia 1846); *History of the Navy of the United States of America* (Stringer & Townsend, New York 1856)

Detorakis, Theocharis, *Turkish rule in Crete* (Panagiotakis, History and Civilization 1988)

Field, James A., *America and the Mediterranean World: 1776–1882* (Princeton University Press, 1969)

Hanks, Robert J., *Commodore Lawrence Kearny, the Diplomatic Seaman* (US Naval Institute Proceedings November 1970)

Paullin, Charles Oscar, *Commodore John Rodgers* (The Arthur H. Clark Company, Cleveland, Ohio 1910)

Roosevelt, Theodore, *The Naval War of 1812* (G.P. Putnam's sons, New York 1883)

Schroeder, John H., *Commodore John Rodgers: Paragon of the Early American Navy* (University Press of Florida, 2006)

Swartz, Peter M., *US–Greek Naval Relations Begin: Antipiracy Operations in the Aegean Sea* (Center for Naval Analyses, Center for Strategic Studies, Alexandria, Virginia 2003)

Toll, Ian W., *Six Frigates: the Epic History of the Founding of the U.S. Navy* (W. W. Norton & Company, New York 2008)

Wombwell, A. James, *The Long War Against Piracy: Historical Trends* (Combat Studies Institute Press, Fort Leavenworth, Kansas 2010)

8. Sumatra Operations

Corn, Charles, *The Scents of Eden: A History of the Spice Trade* (Kodansha America, New York 1999)

Earl, George S. W., *On The Leading Characteristics of the Papuan, Australian and Malay-Polynesian Nations* (Journal of the Indian Archipelago and Eastern Asia, 1850)

Johnson, Robert Erwin, *Thence Round Cape Horn* (Ayer Publishing, New York 1980)

Long, David Foster, *Gold Braid and Foreign Relations: Diplomatic Activities of U.S. Naval Officers 1798-1883* (Naval Institute Press, Annapolis 1988)

Meacham, Jon, Andrew Jackson in the White House (Random House, New York 2008)

Murrell, William Meacham, *Cruise Of The Frigate Columbia Around The World Under The Command Of Commodore George C. Read* (Benjamin B. Mussey, Boston1840)

Warriner, Francis, Cruise of the United States frigate *Potomac* round the world during the years 1831-34 (Leavitt, Lord & Co., New York 1835)

9. The Pork and Beans War and The Pig War

Baker, Betty, *The Pig War* (HarperCollins Canada, 1969)

Bell, Christopher M., *Thinking the Unthinkable: British and American Naval Strategies for an Anglo-American War, 1918–1931* (The International History Review, No. 19, November 1997)

Carroll, Francis M., *The Passionate Canadians: The Historical Debate about the Eastern Canadian-American Boundary* (New England Quarterly, Vol. 70, No. 1. March 1997)

Coleman, E.C., *The Pig War: The Most Perfect War in History* (The History Press, Stroud 2009)

Garraty, John A., *The American Nation* (Houghton Mifflin, 1997)

Hayes, Derek, *Historical Atlas of the Pacific Northwest: Maps of exploration and Discovery* (Sasquatch Books, 1999)

Jones, Howard, *Anglophobia and the Aroostook War* (New England Quarterly, Vol. 48, No. 4 December 1975)

Kaufman, Scott, *The Pig War* (Lexington Books, 2003)

Keenlyside, Hugh; Brown, Gerald S., *Canada and the United States: Some Aspects of their Historical Relations* (Alfred A. Knopf, 1952)

Neering, Rosemary, *The Pig War: The Last Canada–US Border Conflict* (Heritage House Publishing Co. Ltd., 2011)

Remini, Robert V., *Daniel Webster – The Man and His Time* (W.W. Norton, 1997)

Scholefield, Ethelbert Olaf Stuart; Howay, Frederick William, *British Columbia from the earliest times to the present, Volume 2* (The S.J. Clarke Publishing Company, 1914)

White, Francis, *The Pig War: The Real Story of 1859's Strangest Conflict* (History of War magazine, June 2015)

10. More Pirates and 'Savages'

Exploring Expedition

Ellsworth, H. A., *One Hundred Eighty Landings of United States Marines 1800 to 1934* (US Marines History and Museums Division, Washington DC 1934)

Macdonald, B., *Cinderellas of the Empire: Towards a history of Kiribati and Tuvalu* (London 2002)

Philbrick, N., *Sea of Glory: America's Voyage of Discovery – the U.S. Exploring Expedition, 1838–42* (Viking Adult, 2003)

Stanton, W. R., *The Great United States Exploring Expedition of 1838–1842* (University of California Press, Berkeley 1975)

Tyler, D. B., *The Wilkes Expedition: The First United States Exploring Expedition 1838–1842* (American Philosophical Society, 1968)

Wilkes, Charles, *Narrative of the United States exploring expedition – During the years 1838, 1839, 1840, 1841, 1842* (Philadelphia: Lea and Blanchard, Philadelphia 1845)

Ivory Coast

Copes, Jan M., *The Perry Family: A Newport Naval Dynasty of the Early Republic* (Newport Historical Society 66, Part 2, 1994)

Ellsworth, Harry A., *One Hundred Eight Landings of United States Marines 1800–1934* (US Marines History and Museums Division, Washington DC 1974)

Griffis, William Elliot, *Matthew Calbraith Perry: a typical American naval officer* (Cupples and Hurd, Boston 1887)

Hening, E. F., *History of the African mission of the Protestant Episcopal Church in the United States: with memoirs of deceased missionaries, and notices of native customs* (Stanford and Swords, 1850)

Morison, Samuel Eliot, '*Old Bruin' Commodore Matthew Calbraith Perry* (Little, Brown and Company, Boston 1967)

Sewall, John S., *The Logbook of the Captain's Clerk: Adventures in the China Seas* (Chas H. Glass & Co., Bangor, Maine 1905)

Skaggs, David Curtis, *Oliver Hazard Perry: Honor, Courage, and Patriotism in the Early U.S. Navy* (US Naval Institute Press, 2006)

Fijii Expeditions

Cooney, David M., *A Chronology of the U.S. Navy 1775–1965* (F. Watts, 1965)

Long, F. David, *Gold braid and foreign relations: diplomatic activities of U.S. naval officers, 1798–1883* (Naval Institute Press, Annapolis, Maryland 1988)

Mennell, Philip, *Thakombau; Calvert, Rev. James* (The Dictionary of Australasian Biography. London: Hutchinson & Co., London 1892)

Thornley, Andrew, *Exodus of the I Taukei: The Wesleyian Church in Fiji 1848–74* (Institute of Pacific Studies, University of the South Pacific, Suva 2002)

Wallis, Mary, *Life in Feejee : five years among the cannibals, a woman's account of voyaging the Fiji Islands aboard the 'Zotoff' 1844–49* (Narrative Press, Santa Barbara, California 2002)

11. Cortina Wars

Acuna, Rodolfo, *Occupied America: A History of Chicanos* (2 ed., New York: Harper and Row, New York 1981)

Angell, Robert H., *Texas Politics & the Legends of the Fall* (McGraw Custom Publishing, 2003)

Canales, J.T., *Cortina: Bandit or Patriot?* (Address to the Lower Rio Grande Valley Historical Association, October 22 1951)

Chance, Joseph E., *Jose Maria de Jesus Carvajal: The Life and Times of a Mexican Revolutionary* (Trinity University Press, 2006)

Cox, Mike., *The Texas Rangers: Men of Action and Valor* (Eakin Press, Austin 1991)

De Leon, Arnoldo, *They Called Them Greasers: Anglo Attitudes Toward Mexicans in Texas 1821–1900* (University of Texas Press, Austoin 1983)

Elman, Robert, *Badmen of the West* (Ridge Press, 1974)

Fehrenbach, T.R., *Lone Star: A History of Texas and the Texans* (New York: Macmillan Publishing Company, New York 1968)

Ford, J.S., *Rip Ford's Texas* (Edited by Stephen B. Oates. University of Texas Press. Austin 1987)

Goldfinch, Charles W. and Canales, Jose T., *Juan N. Cortina: Two Interpretations* (Arno Press, New York 1974)

Larralde, Carlos, and Jacobo, José R., *Juan Cortina and the Struggle for Justice in Texas* (Kendall Hunt, 2000)

Perry, Laurens Ballard, *Juárez and Díaz: Machine Politics in Mexico* (Northern Illinois University Press, DeKalb 1978)

Robenalt, Jeffrey, *Trouble Along the Rio Grande: The First Cortina War* (jeffrobenalt@yahoo.com, January 2013)

Rippy, J. Fred, *Border Troubles along the Rio Grande, 1848–1880* (Southwestern Historical Quarterly 23, October 1919)

Thompson, Jerry, *Cortina: Defending the Mexican Name in Texas* (Texas A&M Press, 2007); Juan Cortina and the Texas–Mexico Frontier 1859–1877 (Southwestern Studies, 1994)

12. The Shinmiyangyo Korean Expedition

Cable, E.M, *United States Korean Relations, 1866–1871* (Y.M.C.A. Press, Seoul 1939)

Chang, Gordon H., *Whose Barbarism? Whose Treachery? Race and Civilization in the Unknown United States–Korea War of 1871* (Journal of American History, Vol. 89, No. 4, March 2003)

Field, James A. Jr., *History of United States Naval Operations: Korea* (Department of the Navy – Naval Historical Center)

Grimmett, Richard F., *Instances of the Use of United States Armed Forces Abroad 1798–2004* (Congressional Research Service report RL30172, Naval Historical Center, 2004)

Gyu Mu, Professor Han, *The General Sherman Incident of 1866 and Rev. Thomas' Martyrdom* (Kwang-ju University, Korea 2001)

Lee, Ki-baek, *A New History of Korea* (Ilchogak, Seoul 1984)

Lee Wha Rang, *Sinking of the General Sherman, A US Marine Merchant Ship* (website posts March 19 2000)

Nahm, Andrew C., *Korea: A History of the Korean people (2nd ed.)* (Hollym, Seoul 1996)

Tyson, Caroline A., *Marine Amphibious Landing in Korea, 1871* (Naval Historical Foundation website, G-3 Division, Marine Corps)

Utz, Curtis A., *Assault from the Sea – The Amphibious Landing at Inchon* (The U.S. Navy in the Modern World Series No. 2)

Niderost, Eric, *The General Sherman Incident & the Shinmiyangyo Korean Expedition* (Warfare History Network, September 2018)

Yŏng-ho Ch'oe; William Theodore De Bary; Martina Deuchler and Peter Hacksoo Lee, *Sources of Korean Tradition: From the Sixteenth to the Twentieth Centuries* (Columbia University Press, New York 2000)

13. The Modoc War

Beeson, John., A Plea for the Indians: With Facts and Features of the Late War in Oregon (published by author, New York 1858)

Brown, Dee, *Bury My Heart At Wounded Knee* (Holt, Rinehart & Winston Inc, New York 1970)

Cothran, Boyd, *Remembering the Modoc War: Redemptive Violence and the Making of American Innocence* (University of North Carolina Press, Chapel Hill 2014)

Cozzens, Peter, *The Earth Is Weeping – The Epic Story of the Indian Wars for the American West* (Atlantic Books, London 2016)

Drannan, William F, Thirty One Years on the Plains and in the Mountains (Rhodes & M'Clure Publishing Co., Chicago 1899)

Dunlay, Tom, *Kit Carson and the Indians* (University of Nebraska Press, 2000)

Fisher, Don C., and Doerr, John E. Jnr, *Outline of Events in the History of the Modoc War, Nature Notes From Crater Lake*, Volume 10, No. 2, July 1937, Crater Lake Institute

Heyman, Max L. Jr., *Prudent Soldier; A Biography of Major General E. R. S. Canby 1817–1873* (Arthur H. Clark Co., Glendale, California1959)

Meacham, Alfred B., *Wigwam and Warpath; or, The Royal Chief in Chains, a history of the War* (J. P. Dale & Co., Boston 1875)

Murray, Keith A., *The Modocs and Their War* (University of Oklahoma Press, 1984)

Quinn, Arthur, *Hell With the Fire Out: A History of the Modoc War* (Faber and Faber, New York 1998)

Riddle, Jeff C. Davis, *The Indian History of the Modoc War and the Causes that Led to It* (Marnell and C., 1914)

Sabin, Edwin L., *Kit Carson Days, Volumes 1 & 2* (University of Nebraska Press, 1995)

Sides, Hampton, *Blood and Thunder* (Doubleday, 2006)

Thompson, William A., *Scouting with Mackenzie* (Journal of the US Cavalry Association 10, 1897)

Utley, Robert Marshall, *Frontier Regulars: the United States Army and the Indian, 1866–1891* (University of Nebraska Press, 1984)

Fisher, Don C., and Doerr, John E. Jnr, *Outline of Events in the History of the Modoc War, Nature Notes From Crater Lake*, Volume 10, No. 2, July 1937, Crater Lake Institute

14. The Samoan Crisis

Clowes, William Laird, *The Royal Navy: A History from the Earliest Times to the Present, Volume 7* (Sampson Low, Marston Company, London 1903)

Grant, Ulysses Simpson Grant, *The Papers of Ulysses S. Grant: November 1, 1876-September 30, 1878* (SIU Press, 2005)

Gray, J.A.C., *Amerika Samoa: A History of American Samoa and Its United States Naval Administration* (U. S. Naval Institute, Annapolis 1960)

Hildebrand, Hans H., Röhr, Albert, and Steinmetz, Hans-Otto, *Die Deutschen Kriegsschiffe (Band 6) [The German Warships (Volume 6)]* (Mundus Verlag. Ratingen 1993)

Hocking, Charles, *Dictionary of Disasters at Sea During The Age of Steam* (The London Stamp Exchange, London 1990)

Hoppe, John, *The Apia Cyclone of 1889* (Naval History Blog, 2016)

Kohn, George C., *Dictionary of Wars, Third Edition* (Facts on File Inc.)

Regan, Geoffrey, *Naval Blunders* (Andre Deutsch, 2001)

Rousmaniere, John, *After the Storm: True Stories of Disaster and Recovery at Sea* (International Marine/McGraw-Hill, Camden 2002)

Ryden, George Herbert, *The Foreign Policy of the United States in Relation to Samoa* (Yale University Press, New York 1928)

Sisung, Kelle S., *The Benjamin Harrison Administration, Presidential Administration Profiles* (Detroit: Gale Group, Detroit 2002)

Stevenson, Robert Louis, *A Footnote to History, Eight Years of Trouble in Samoa* (Cassell/University of Adelaide Library 1892)

Wilson, Graham, *Glory for the Squadron: HMS Calliope in the Great Hurricane at Samoa 1889* (Journal of the Australian Naval Institute No 22, May–July 1996)

15. The Spanish–American War

Armstrong, David A., *Bullets and Bureaucrats: The Machine Gun and the United States Army 1861–1916* (Greenwood Publishing, 1982)

Atwood, Paul, *War and Empire* (Pluto Press, New York 2010)

Bailey, Thomas Andrew, *The American Pageant: A History of the Republic* (Heath Publishing, 1961) Baycroft, Timothy; and Hewitson, Mark, *What is a Nation? Europe 1789–1914* (Oxford University Press, 2006)

Bergad, Laird W., *Agrarian History of Puerto Rico, 1870–1930* (Latin American Research Review 13, 1978)

Brune, Lester H.; and Burns, Richard Dean, *Chronological History of US Foreign Relations: 1607–1932, Volume 1* (Routledge, 2003)

Campbell, W. Joseph, *You Furnish the Legend, I'll Furnish the Quote; Yellow Journalism: Puncturing the Myths, Defining the Legacies* (American Journalism Review, 2001 and 2003)

Carter, Alden R., *The Spanish–American War* (Franklin Watts, Inc, New York 1992)

Clodfelter, M., *Warfare and Armed Conflicts: A Statistical Encyclopedia of Casualty and Other Figures, 1492–2015 (4th ed.)* (McFarland, 2017)

Dierks, Jack, *A Leap to Arms: The Cuban Campaign of 1898* (J.B. Lippincott Company, Philadelphia 1970)

Dinwiddie, William, *Puerto Rico: Its Conditions and Possibilities* (Harper & Brothers, New York 1899)

Dyal, Donald H; Carpenter, Brian B.; Thomas, Mark A., *Historical Dictionary of the Spanish American War* (Greenwood Press, 1996)

Faulkner, Harold, *Politics, reform, and expansion, 1890–1900* (Harper, New York 1963)

Field, James A., *American Imperialism* (American Historical Review 83, June 1978)

Gannon, Joseph, *The USS Oregon and the Battle of Santiago* (Comet Press Book, New York 1958)

Gatewood, Willard B., *Black Americans and the White Man's Burden, 1898–1903* (University of Illinois Press, 1975)

Goode, W.A.M., *With Sampson through the War* (Doubleday & McClure CO., New York 1899)

Hakim, Joy, *History of US: Book Eight, An Age of Extremes* (Oxford University Press, New York 1994)

Hansen, Jonathan M., *Guantanamo: An American History* (Farrar, Straus and Giroux, 2011)

Hendrickson, Kenneth E., Jr., *The Spanish–American War* (Greenwood, 2003)

Karnow, Stanley, *In Our Image* (Century, 1990)

Keenan, Jerry, *Encyclopedia of the Spanish–American & Philippine–American Wars* (ABC–CLIO, 2001)

Lacsamana, Leodivico Cruz, *Philippine History and Government* (Phoenix Publishing House, 2006)

Langley, Harold D., and Bradford, James C., ed., *Winfield Scott Schley and Santiago: A New Look at an Old Controversy* (Naval Institute Press, Annapolis 1993)

Leeke, Jim, *Manila and Santiago: The New Steel Navy In The Spanish–American War* (Naval Institute Press, Annapolis 2009)

Millis, Walter, *The Martial Spirit* (Ayer Publishing, 1979)

Montoya, Arthur, *America's Original Sin: Absolution and Penance* (Xlibris Corporation, 2011)

Musicant, Ivan, *Empire by Default: The Spanish–American War and the Dawn of the American Century* (Henry Holt and Company, New York 1998)

Nasaw, David, *The Chief: The Life of William Randolph Hearst* (Gibson Square, 2013)

Nofi, Albert A, *The Spanish–American War 1898* (Combined Books/Da Capo Press, Conshohocken, Pennsylvania 1996)

Norton, Mary Beth Norton; et al., *A People and a Nation, Volume II: Since 1865* (Cengage Learning, 2014)

Offner, John L., *McKinley and the Spanish–American War* (Presidential Studies Quarterly 34, 2004) Osgood, Robert Endicott, *Ideals and Self-interest in America's Foreign Relations: The Great Transformation of the Twentieth Century* (1953)

O'Toole, G.J.A., *The Spanish War: An American Epic 1898* (W.W. Norton, New York 1984)

Parker, Lieutenant John H., *History of the Gatling Gun Detachment, Kansas City* (Hudson-Kimberly Publishing Co., Kansas City 1898)

Pérez, Louis A., *The War of 1898: The United States and Cuba in History and Historiography* (UNC Press Books, 1998)

Post, Charles Johnson, *The Little War of Private Post* (Little, Brown, Boston and Toronto reissue 1960)

Pratts, Edgardo, *De Coamo a la Trinchera del Asomante (1st ed.)* (Fundación Educativa Idelfonso Pratts, Puerto Rico 2006)

Reilly, John C.; and Scheina, Robert L., *American Battleships 1886–1923: Predreadnought Design and Construction* (Naval Institute Press, Annapolis 1980)

Rhodes, James Ford, *The McKinley and Roosevelt Administrations 1897–1909* (READ BOOKS, 2007)

Rickover, Hyman George, *How the Battleship Maine was Destroyed (Second Revised ed.)* (Naval Institute Press, Annapolis 1995)

Rogers, Robert F., *Destiny's Landfall: A History of Guam (illustrated ed.)* (University of Hawaii Press, 1995)

Roosevelt, Theodore, *The Rough Riders* (Charles Scribner's Sons, New York 1899)

Russell, Timothy Dale, *African Americans and the Spanish–American War and Philippine Insurrection* (University of California, Riverside 2013)

Saravia, José Roca de Togores y; and Garcia, Remigio, *Blockade and Siege of Manila in 1898* (National Saravia Historical Institute, 2003)

Schubert, Frank N, *Black Valor: Buffalo Soldiers and the Medal of Honor, 1870–1898* (Scholarly Resources Inc, 1997)

Seekins, Donald M., *Historical Setting – Outbreak of War, 1898* (Library of Congress, Washington 1991)

Smythe, Ted Curtis, The Gilded Age Press, 1865–1900 (Praeger, 2003)

Thomas, Evan, *The War Lovers: Roosevelt, Lodge, Hearst, and the Rush to Empire, 1898* (Little, Brown and Co., 2010)

Trask, David F., *The War with Spain in 1898* (University of Nebraska Press, 1996)

Tone, John, *War and Genocide in Cuba, 1895–1898* (University of North Carolina Press, Chapel Hill 2006)

Tucker, Spencer, *The Encyclopedia of the Spanish–American and Philippine–American Wars: A Political, Social and Military History* (ABC–CLIO, 2009)

West, Richard S., Jr., *Admirals of American Empire; the Combined Story of George Dewey, Alfred Thayer Mahan, Winfield Scott Schley and William Thomas Sampson* (Bobbs-Merrill, Indianapolis 1948)

Whyte, Kenneth, *The Uncrowned King: The Sensational Rise of William Randolph Hearst (*Counterpoint, Berkeley 2009)

Wolff, Leon, *Little Brown Brother: How the United States Purchased and Pacified the Philippine Islands at the Century's Turn* (Wolff Productions, 1961)

16. The Philippines War

Agoncillo, Teodoro A., *History of the Filipino People (Eighth ed.)* (Garotech Publishing, Quezon City 1990)

Arnold, James R., *The Moro War: How America Battled a Muslim Insurgency in the Philippine Jungle, 1902–1913* (Bloomsbury Publishing, New York 2011)

Akyol, Mustafa, *Islam without Extremes: A Muslim Case for Liberty* (W. W. Norton, 2011)

Borrinaga, Rolando O., *The Balangiga Conflict Revisited* (New Day Publishers, 2003)

Bayor, Ronald H., The Columbia Documentary History of Race and Ethnicity in America (Columbia University Press, 2004)

Beede, Benjamin, *The War of 1998 and U.S. Interventions, 1898–1934: An Encyclopedia* (Routledge, 2013)

Birtle, Andrew J., *U.S. Army Counterinsurgency and Contingency Operations Doctrine 1860–1941* (United States Government Publishing Office, Washington DC 1998)

Brands, Henry William, *Bound to Empire: The United States and the Philippines* (Oxford University Press, 1992)

Brody, David, *Visualizing American Empire: Orientalism and Imperialism in the Philippines* (University of Chicago Press, 2010)

Bibliography

Bruno, Thomas A., *The Violent End of Insurgency on Samar 1901–1902* (Army Center of Military History, February 2011)

Chaput, Donald, *Private William W. Grayson's War in the Philippines 1899* (Nebraska History No 61, 1980)

Constantino, Renato, *The Philippines: A Past Revisited* (Constantino, 1975)

Couttie, Bob, *Hang the Dogs, The True and Tragic History of the Balangiga Massacre* (New Day Publishers, 2004)

Deady, Timothy K., *Lessons from a Successful Counterinsurgency Philippines 1899–1902* (Parameters, United States Army War College, Carlisle, Pennsylvania 2005)

Dolan, Ronald E., ed., *United States Rule, Philippines: A Country Study* (United States Library of Congress, Washington DC 1991)

Escalante, Rene R., *The Bearer of Pax Americana: The Philippine Career of William H. Taft 1900–1903* (New Day Publishers, Quezon City 2007)

Foner, Philip S., and Winchester, Richard, *The Anti-Imperialist Reader: A Documentary History of Anti-Imperialism in the United States, Vol. 1* (Holmes and Meier, New York 1984)

Golay, Frank Hindman, *Face of Empire: United States-Philippine Relations, 1898–1946* (Ateneo de Manila University Press, Quezon City 2004)

Guevara, Sulpico, ed., *The Laws of the First Philippine Republic (the Laws of Malolos) 1898–1899* (University of Michigan Library, Ann Arbor 1972)

Hagedorn, Hermann, *Leonard Wood: A Biography* (Harper & Brothers, New York 1931)

Halstead, Murat, *The Story of the Philippines and Our New Possessions, including the Ladrones, Hawaii, Cuba and Porto Rico* (Our Possessions Publishing Company, Chicago 1898)

Hunt, Geoffrey, *Civilize 'Em with a Krag, Colorado's Volunteer Infantry in the Philippines War, 1898–9* (University of New Mexico Press, Albuquerque 2006)

Ileto, Reynaldo Clemeña, *Pasyon and Revolution: Popular Movements in the Philippines, 1840–1910* (Ateneo de Manila University Press, Quezon City 1997)

Jones, Gregg, *Honor and Dust – Theodore Roosevelt, War in the Philippines and the Ruse and Fall of the American Dream* (New American Library, New York 2012)

Kalaw, Maximo Manguiat, *The Development of Philippines Politics (1872–1920)* (Oriental Commercial Company, Inc., Manila 1927)

Legarda, Benito Justo, *The Hills of Sampaloc: The Opening Actions of the Philippine–American War, February 4–5 1899* (Bookmark, 2001)

Lane, Jack C, *Armed Progressive: General Leonard Wood* (Presidio Press, 1978)

Linn, Brian McAllister, *The U.S. Army and Counterinsurgency in the Philippine war, 1899–1902* (University of North Carolina Press, Chapel Hill 2000)

Lone, Stewart, *Daily Lives of Civilians in Wartime Asia: From the Taiping Rebellion to the Vietnam War* (Greenwood Publishing Group, Santa Barbara 2007)

Mannix, Daniel P., IV, *The Old Navy* (Macmillan Publishing Company, 1983)

May, Glenn Anthony, *Battle for Batangas: A Philippine Province at War* (Yale University Press, New Haven 1991)

Miller, Stuart Creighton, *Benevolent Assimilation: The American Conquest of the Philippines, 1899–1903* (Yale University Press, New Haven 1982)

Rummel, Rudolph J., *Statistics of Democide: Genocide and Mass Murder Since 1900* (Verlag Münster, 1998)

Schirmer, Daniel B., and Shalom, Stephen Rosskamm, *The Philippines Reader: A History of Colonialism, Neocolonialism, Dictatorship and Resistance* (South End Press, 1987)

Sexton, William Thaddeus, *Soldiers in the Sun* (Nabu Press, Charleston, South Carolina 1939)

Smallman-Raynor, Matthew, and Cliff, Andrew D., *The Philippines Insurrection and the 19902–4 Cholera Epidemic* (Journal of Historical Geography, No 24[1], 1998)

Smythe, Donald, *Guerrilla Warrior: The Early Life of John J. Pershing.* (Charles Scribener's Sons, New York 1973)

Storey, Moorfield, and Codman, Julian,

Secretary Root's Record – 'Marked Severities' in Philippine Warfare (George H. Ellis Company, Boston 1902)

Taft, Helen Herron, Recollections of Full Years (Butterick Publishing, New York 1914)

Vandiver, Frank E., *Black Jack: The Life and Times of John J. Pershing* (Texas A&M University Press, 1977)

Wolff, Leon, *Little Brown Brother* (Wolff Productions, 2006)

Worcester, Dean Conant, *The Philippines: Past and Present, Volume II* (Macmillan Publishers, New York 1914)

Yegar, Simmons, Edwin H., *Civilize 'Em with a Krag, The United States Marines: A History* (Naval Institute Press, Annapolis, 2003)

Young, Kenneth Ray, *The General's General: The Life and Times of Arthur Macarthur* (Westview Press, Boulder 1994)

Zinn, Howard, *A People's History of the United States* (The New Press, New York 2003)

Zwick, Jim, *Mark Twain's Weapons of Satire: Anti-Imperialist Writings on the Philippine–American War* (Syracuse University Press, 1992)

Afterword

Bailey, Thomas, *A Diplomatic History of the American People* (Prentice Hall, 1980)

Beisner, Robert L., *Twelve Against Empire: The Anti-Imperialists, 1898–1900* (McGraw-Hill, New York 1968)

Bellamy, Alex J., *Massacres and Morality: Mass Atrocities in an Age of Civilian Immunity* (Oxford University Press, 2012)

Chomsky, Noah, *Hegemony or Survival: America's Quest for Global Dominance* (Metropolitan Books, 2003); *Lectures on Modern-Day American Imperialism: Middle East and Beyond* (Boston University, April 7 2010)

Field, James A., Jr., *American Imperialism: The Worst Chapter in Almost Any Book* (*The American Historical Review 83*, June 1978)

Friedman, Thomas, *The Lexus and the Olive Tree* (Farmer, Strauss and Giroux, 1999)

Gonzalez, George A., *Urban Sprawl, Global Warming, and the Empire of Capital* (SUNY Press, 2009) Hastings, Max, *Vietnam – An Epic History of a Tragic War* (William Collins, London 2018)

Herring, George C., *From Colony to Superpower: U.S. Foreign Relations Since 1776* (Oxford History of the United States, 2008)

Hixson, Walter L., *The Myth of American Diplomacy: National Identity and U.S. Foreign Policy* (Yale University Press, 2009)

Jones, Gregg, *Honor in the Dust: Theodore Roosevelt, War in the Philippines, and the Rise and Fall of America's Imperial Dream* (Penguin, 2013)

Kearns, Doris, *Lyndon Johnson and the American Dream* (Simon and Schuster, 1976)

Lowenthal, Abraham F., *Exporting Democracy : The United States and Latin America*. (The Johns Hopkins University Press, 1991)

Peceny, Mark, *Democracy at the Point of Bayonets* (Pennsylvania State University Press, 1999)

Renouard, Joe, *Human Rights in American Foreign Policy: From the 1960s to the Soviet Collapse* (University of Pennsylvania Press, 2016)

Perkins, Bradford, *The Cambridge History of American Foreign Relations: Volume 1, The Creation of a Republican Empire, 1776–1865* (Cambridge University Press, 1995)

Ryan, James Gilbert; and Schlup, Leonard C., *Historical Dictionary of the Gilded Age* (M.E. Sharpe, 2003)

Sexton, Jay, *The Monroe Doctrine: Empire and Nation in Nineteenth-Century America* (Farrar, Straus and Giroux, 2011)

Seymour, Richard, *American Insurgents: A Brief History of American Anti-Imperialism* (Haymarket Books, Chicago 2012)

Simpson, Bradley, *Economists with Guns: Authoritarian Development and U.S.–Indonesian Relations, 1960–1968* (Stanford University Press)

Smith, Neil, American Empire: Roosevelt's Geographer and the Prelude to Globalization (University of California Press, 2004)

Steigerwald, David, *Wilsonian Idealism in America* (Cornell University Press, 1994)

Tompkins, E. Berkeley, *Anti-Imperialism in the United States: The Great Debate, 1890–1920* (University of Pennsylvania Press, 1970)

Welch, Richard E. Jr., *Response to Imperialism: The United States and the Philippine–American War, 1899–1902* (University of North Carolina Press, Chapel Hill 1979)

Williams, Walter L., *United States Indian Policy and the Debate over Philippine Annexation: Implications for the Origins of American Imperialism* (*The Journal of American History 66*, 1980) Zwick, Jim (editor), *Mark Twain's Weapons of Satire: Anti-Imperialist Writings on the Philippine–American War* (Syracuse University Press, New York 1992)

Index